Praise for
The Flying Tigers

"A brisk and personable narrative." —*The Wall Street Journal*

"A brisk history . . . Challenges wistful backward glances to the seemingly straightforward American intervention in World War II. . . . Kleiner ensures that we never look back uncritically. . . . *The Flying Tigers* reads like an adventure story, as Kleiner deftly takes his reader from cramped cockpits to quiet Washington corridors. . . . A sobering reminder of the costs of American military intervention. . . . Ripe for cinematic adaptation."
—*Los Angeles Review of Books*

"The story of the Flying Tigers is extraordinary, and Kleiner does an excellent job describing their creation and exploits." —*Military Review*

"A terrific book about the courageous and daring American pilots who helped China resist the Japanese onslaught and helped the United States and its allies win the Second World War in East Asia. . . . Kleiner tells the story better than it has been told before . . . [and] brings the real Claire Chennault to life again, and relates the equally compelling stories of other individual pilots—their heroism, fears, loves, hates, friendships, and tragedies; all against the dramatic and horrific backdrop of World War II in East Asia."
—*Asian Review of Books*

"The air fights in the book are right out of Hollywood, only more immediate with all of the wonderful first-hand accounts in the pilots' own words."
—*China Daily*

"A well-told story by a gifted debut author whose talent has been to weave the disparate parts of . . . [a] complex history into a cohesive, fast-paced whole. . . . [A] thoroughly researched and finely modulated account of courageous young men at war. Highly recommended."
—*Aviation History Magazine*

"A well-told amalgamation of the best stories about the American Volunteer Group . . . Informative, action-packed, and easy to read."
—*Publishers Weekly*

"Kleiner illuminates the battles, personalities, and personal lives of the Flying Tigers, a band of rag-tag pilots sure to enthrall general readers and military history buffs."   —*Library Journal*

"An exciting story of bravery in the skies—and a picture of America at its best at a time of peril. A five-star read."   —*The Washington Times*

"In the dark days after Pearl Harbor, a swashbuckling band of volunteer pilots gave America something to cheer about with their exploits against the Japanese in far-off China. Through long-lost letters and diaries, Sam Kleiner has brought these gallant warriors to life. *The Flying Tigers* is a rousing tale that will keep you turning the page."

—Evan Thomas, *New York Times* bestselling author of *Sea of Thunder*

"This is a movie waiting to be made—a great adventure story that is all the more gripping because it really happened. These pilots remind us of why we're proud to be American, ordinary young men who became heroes at a time when American victories were scarce. Some were killed, leaving their hometowns grieving. Some spent years as prisoners of the Japanese, uncertain whether they'd ever make it home again. All should be remembered. Kleiner is a gifted researcher and storyteller. He does the story of these men justice, and that is saying something."

—Michael Punke, #1 *New York Times* bestselling author of *The Revenant*

"*The Flying Tigers* is a meticulously researched work of history that reads like a thriller. Packed with characters that come off the pages, it draws the reader into a world of daredevil flying and covert operations in China in the opening days of World War II. *The Flying Tigers* marks the debut of an incredibly talented new historian and is a must-read not only for World War II aficionados but for anyone who likes a good story. It is full of them."

—Amy Chua, Yale Law professor and *New York Times* bestselling author of *Battle Hymn of the Tiger Mother* and *Political Tribes*

"As the United States navigates a complex and challenging relationship with China today, *The Flying Tigers* offers a vivid reminder that our two countries have pulled together in the past to meet shared threats. Sam Kleiner artfully tells the story of the forgotten World War II alliance and the role of dynamic individuals in shaping it—and anyone interested in understanding America's relationship with China should delve into this gripping history."
—Jake Sullivan, former national security adviser to the vice president and director of policy planning at the U.S. Department of State

"*The Flying Tigers* has it all: aerial guerilla warfare, foreign intrigue, inspiring heroism, and a Hollywood-worthy cast of colorful misfits, rebels, and patriotic adventurers, all woven into an electrifying narrative."
—Thurston Clarke, author of *Pearl Harbor Ghosts* and *The Last Campaign*

"Sam Kleiner has bridged a critical gap in American military history with a gripping account of how the Roosevelt administration was secretly leading us into World War II a half a year before Pearl Harbor. This is a story with mercenaries, aerial dogfights, love affairs, burning cities, and shadow diplomacy, but more than that, this tells us how the United States got an early jump on its war against Imperial Japan at the beginning of the Pacific Century." —Tom Zoellner, author of *Uranium*

"Kleiner's meticulous research provides crucial, unexplored background on Claire Chennault and the formation of the American Volunteer Group and lends important context to Roosevelt's decision to help China before Pearl Harbor pulled the United States into the war. He covers the topic from the operational perspective without becoming mired in tactical details or irrelevant controversies. His is thus the clearest narrative of the group we've been given yet and will doubtlessly capture the imagination of a new generation of readers who have not heard this incredible story."
—Dan Jackson, author of *Famine, Sword, and Fire: The Liberation of Southwest China in World War II*

"Sam Kleiner's book brings back memories of China and Burma. I'm glad he is continuing the legacy of the Tigers."
—Frank Losonsky, last surviving Flying Tiger

ABOUT THE AUTHOR

Sam Kleiner is a historian and attorney. He received a BA from Northwestern University and a doctorate from the University of Oxford, where he was a Marshall Scholar. He has a JD from Yale Law school and now practices law in New York City. His writing has appeared in the *Los Angeles Times*, *Foreign Policy*, and *The Atlantic*.

THE
FLYING TIGERS

The Untold Story of the
American Pilots Who Waged a
Secret War Against Japan

SAM KLEINER

PENGUIN BOOKS

PENGUIN BOOKS
An imprint of Penguin Random House LLC
penguinrandomhouse.com

First published in the United States of America by Viking Penguin,
an imprint of Penguin Random House LLC, 2018
Published in Penguin Books 2019

Map illustration by Jeffrey L. Ward

ISBN 9780399564154 (paperback)

THE LIBRARY OF CONGRESS HAS CATALOGED THE HARDCOVER EDITION AS FOLLOWS:
Names: Kleiner, Samuel M. (Samuel Miller), 1987– author.
Title: The Flying Tigers : the untold story of the American pilots
who waged a secret war against Japan / Sam Kleiner.
Description: New York : Viking, 2018. | Includes bibliographical references and index. |
Identifiers: LCCN 2018013214 (print) | LCCN 2018013636 (ebook) |
ISBN 9780399564130 (hardcover) | ISBN 9780399564147 (ebook) |
Subjects: LCSH: China. Kong jun. American Volunteer Group—History. |
Sino-Japanese War, 1937-1945—Aerial operations. | Sino-Japanese War,
1937-1945—Participation, American. | Chennault, Claire Lee, 1893-1958.
Classification: LCC DS777.533.A35 (ebook) | LCC DS777.533.A35 K54 2018 (print) |
DDC 951.04/2—dc23
LC record available at https://lccn.loc.gov/2018013214

Printed in the United States of America
1 3 5 7 9 10 8 6 4 2

Set in Sabon LT Pro

Contents

Map   ix

Introduction   1

CHAPTER 1: **Dancing in the Sky**   5

CHAPTER 2: **Meeting the Princess**   22

CHAPTER 3: **The Rape of Nanking**   31

CHAPTER 4: **The International Squadron**   43

CHAPTER 5: **Exile in the Chinese Hinterland**   52

CHAPTER 6: **An Air Unit for China**   61

CHAPTER 7: **Training in Toungoo**   88

CHAPTER 8: **Wartime**   100

CHAPTER 9: **Legends in Their Own Time**   112

CHAPTER 10: **Christmas in Rangoon**   122

CHAPTER 11: **Burmese Days**   131

CHAPTER 12: **Aerial Guerrilla Warfare**   157

CHAPTER 13: **Last Stand**   185

CHAPTER 14: **Black Sheep Down**   214

Epilogue   228

Acknowledgments   237

Notes   241

Index   285

INTRODUCTION

The freezing temperatures in New York City on December 7, 1941, didn't stop more than fifty-five thousand football fans from packing the stands at the Polo Grounds in upper Manhattan. This was the highly anticipated crosstown rivalry game between the New York Giants and the Brooklyn Dodgers. After the underdog Dodgers took a 7–0 lead, they kicked the ball down the field, and listeners at home heard the announcer on WOR radio call the play. "It's a long one, down to around the three-yard line," he said, and the Giants' Ward Cuff made the catch and started to run it down the field. Over the cheers of the crowd, the announcer continued: "Cuff's still going, he's up to the twenty-five and now he's hit, and hit hard about the twenty-seven yard line. Bruiser Kinard made the tack—"

Suddenly the reporting of the game was cut off as another voice broke in: "We interrupt this broadcast to bring you this important bulletin from the United Press. Flash Washington. The White House announces Japanese attack on Pearl Harbor. Stay tuned to WOR for further developments, which will be broadcast immediately as received."

Inside the stadium, the game went on without any kind of announcement. The crowd watched as the Brooklyn Dodgers clinched an upset 21–7 victory. The sun was setting as the fans headed for the exits. Then the public address system came on: "All navy men in the audience are ordered to report to their posts immediately. All army men are to report to their posts tomorrow morning. This is important."

"There was a sudden, startled buzz in the crowd," the sportswriter for the *Brooklyn Eagle* reported. "What had happened? No one knew, not until he got close to the nearest radio or within hearing range of newsboys yelling in the streets."

The Navy Department's censors delayed releasing photographs of the destruction in Hawaii, but on December 29 *Time* magazine featured them in its coverage of the HAVOC IN HONOLULU. One image showed large clouds of black smoke rising from the wreckage of the U.S.S. *Arizona,* and another, a P-40 fighter plane that had been wrecked on the field and "never fought." A hangar at the army's Hickam Field had also been destroyed. This was the carnage from "Japan's sneak attack." *Time* carried a dire headline in that December 29 issue: INVASION OF THE U.S.? It reported that antiaircraft guns were deployed in New York City to defend "power plants, aircraft factories, docks and shipyards" against the threat of a Luftwaffe attack. The fear was more pronounced in the West: "At forest-fire lookout towers, in little tarpaper-covered shacks scattered on the hills along the coast, spotters watched the grey skies, 24 hours a day, in three-hour shifts." San Francisco was blacked out, and reporter Ernie Pyle said that its darkened streets looked like "the dusty remnants of a city dead and uninhabited for a hundred years."

But that edition of *Time* included another story, one that would capture the imaginations and raise the hopes of Americans in the dark days after Pearl Harbor. In China, a unit of U.S. volunteers was battling the Imperial Japanese air force, whose planes had been bombing Chinese cities and killing thousands of civilians for the past four years. They were known as the Flying Tigers, and *Time* reported their exploits in stirring fashion:

> Last week ten Japanese bombers came winging their carefree way up into [China], heading directly for Kunming . . . the Flying Tigers swooped, let the Japanese have it. Of the ten bombers, said [Chinese] reports, four plummeted to earth in flames. The rest turned tail and fled. Tiger casualties: none.

Members of the Tigers would soon become familiar figures: their leader, Colonel Claire L. Chennault, and pilots like David "Tex" Hill and "Scarsdale Jack" Newkirk. Years before American soldiers stormed the beaches of Normandy or raised the flag on Iwo Jima, it was Chennault's Flying Tigers who rallied the country with victories when the Axis forces appeared unstoppable.

"A hundred American volunteers had taken the measure of the enemy," Clare Boothe wrote in *Life*. "Who, in the face of that measure, dared doubt that America could—if it would—defeat Japan?"

The Flying Tigers' shark-nosed P-40s—also known as Tomahawks—would go down in history as one of the iconic images from World War II. Hollywood executives knew a heroic story when they saw one, and in 1942 Republic Pictures rushed out *Flying Tigers,* starring John Wayne as the swashbuckling commander of the unit. Hollywood produced its own version of their adventures, but the truth was that the pilots were "doing deeds that a movie director would reject, in a script, as too fantastic," as *Time* described them in April 1942.

Despite the hyperbole, the Flying Tigers were indeed undertaking an important mission: they helped to keep China in the war. If China fell, Japan would be able to focus its forces against an unprepared and under-armed United States.

It would take five decades for the Pentagon to acknowledge the truth about the Flying Tigers: namely, that the mission was a covert operation authorized at the highest levels of the Roosevelt White House—in violation of America's neutrality, and out of view of an isolationist Congress—months before Pearl Harbor. Its pilots and ground crew resigned from the U.S. military, bade their loved ones farewell, and crossed the Pacific on ocean liners, carrying passports listing false professions to disguise the truth about their mission. Over one hundred pilots arrived at a makeshift camp in the jungles of Burma to discover planes many didn't know how to fly. Determined and desperate, they drilled in new techniques to fight the Japanese air force's more agile planes, and were just about to enter into battle when the Japanese struck Pearl Harbor. When President Roosevelt declared war, they were practically behind enemy lines, outnumbered and with no reinforcements coming. Yet between December 20, 1941, and July 4, 1942, they shot down scores of Japanese planes in Burma and southern China.

For over seventy-five years, the most detailed accounts of the Flying

Tigers lay buried in pilots' diaries and letters that were hidden away in closets and at the backs of drawers after the war and in combat reports that lay moldering in the basement of an unremarkable brick building in Georgetown. Their achievements are even more remarkable and stirring than the myth created by Hollywood.

The story of the Flying Tigers begins with a boy growing up in rural Louisiana with dreams of seeing the world.

CHAPTER 1

DANCING IN THE SKY

o understand Claire Chennault you have to trace his roots to the backwoods of northeast Louisiana. The Chennault house was a few miles south of Gilbert, a town of just a few hundred people. Raised up several feet to protect it from the floods that plagued the flatlands, the house was a small, single-story cottage with gingerbread trim and an inviting porch in the back. It was a modest abode, but it was the pride of John Chennault, Claire's father, a cotton farmer who had built the house with his own hands in 1905 when Claire was a boy. Claire Chennault would fondly recall "roaming the oak woods and moss-draped cypress swamps of the Mississippi flood plains in northeast Louisiana." The Tensas River basin was Chennault's childhood playground—he spent time hunting and fishing by himself in the swamps. As he grew older, his father would let him go on treks for days at a time. Claire would take a fishing rod and survive on whatever he could catch, frying catfish and bream with a slab of bacon. He would live in a lean-to he built out of tree branches and sleep on a pile of leaves, and when he wanted to bathe would jump in a watering hole. He shot his first gun, a Winchester rifle, at the age of eight and soon graduated to shooting squirrels. He learned how to build a pyramid trap, a box that was held up by a twig with some oat or corn flakes as bait. He became self-reliant during this idyllic childhood, which resembled that of the hero of *The Adventures of Huckleberry Finn,* one of his favorite books. His solitary adventures in the woods, however, may have masked a darker side of his childhood. His mother died when he was only five, and a stepmother he loved passed away a few years later. The woods were always there for him.

Chennault also had a vivid imagination that drew him to distant lands, and he dreamt of someday seeing more of the world. Although he didn't excel at school—he didn't like following instructions or sitting still—he found a collection of books at his grandfather's house about the ancient Greek and Roman wars and would spend hours transfixed by reading them. He recalled, "Although I had no idea where Greece, Carthage and Rome were, I was enthralled by the charging elephants, armored warriors and burning ships in the colored engravings of the battles of Thermopylae, Zama, Cannae and Salamis." He wanted to escape from his seemingly inevitable fate as a cotton farmer like his father, and instead become a soldier. In fact, he came from a long line of fighting men. He could trace his paternal lineage to a soldier who had fought in the American Revolution; his mother was a direct descendant of General Robert E. Lee.

In 1909 Chennault enrolled at Louisiana State University to study agriculture, the only course that was open to him based on his primary education, but quickly signed up for ROTC training. He was determined to live up to what was expected of him as a soldier. When he was ordered to stand guard over a stairway, marching back and forth with a bayoneted rifle in hand, upperclassmen poured buckets of water on him from the floor above, but as he later recalled, "I continued to walk my post, drenched to the skin." Whatever merit he may have had as a soldier, he quickly found that he couldn't keep up academically due to his limited primary education. He also found that despite his efforts, he struggled with attending to the minute details that characterized life as a cadet. He racked up forty demerits in just one month. During a dress inspection, he was caught with his trouser legs rolled up, which was against regulations. An officer yanked him front and center and yelled in his face: "Chennault, you will never make a soldier." The experience scarred Chennault, who came to feel that perhaps his lot in life was to be a cotton farmer after all. Over a break he returned home to fish, a source of comfort since his youth, and never returned to Louisiana State.

He dreaded what the future might hold. He knew cotton farming

would mean "trying to eke a living . . . in a losing battle against pal-
metto root, bad weather, fluctuating prices, and the passing years."
He'd seen the toll that life had taken on his father. The low price of
cotton during the financial panic of 1907 had nearly wiped out the
family's small farm, and an infestation of boll weevils could destroy an
entire year's crop. "The future seemed very dull indeed," Chennault
recalled, and though he was "looking for bright new worlds to con-
quer," he couldn't seem to find in what direction they lay. That all
would change on one Sunday afternoon at the state fair.

The Fifth Annual Louisiana State Fair was held in Shreveport in November 1910. It was primarily a celebration of the state's agricultural
traditions, with prizes awarded for the best crops and livestock, but it
also featured horse races, tightrope walkers, and concerts by a military
band. At eight o'clock each night a thousand dollars' worth of fireworks lit up the skies, a spectacular performance set to the music of the
"Last Days of Pompeii."

The fair was a place where Louisianans could gather to take pride
in the state's history, but it also offered them a glimpse of the future
with a display of some new technology. The big attraction in 1910 was
a biplane. Less than seven years after the Wright Brothers' achievement
at Kitty Hawk, few Americans had actually seen a plane in flight.

The local papers promoted the event, promising that the pilots would
"astonish the people who visit the Fair by their daring skill in the air."
The main pilot, Stanley Vaughn of Ohio, had designed his plane himself, modeling it after one constructed by Curtiss. On November 3, the
second day of the fair, his biplane ascended but as it rose fifty feet above
the field it suddenly plummeted to the earth, just "like a duck suddenly
shot," as the *Shreveport Times* described it. After the plane hit the
ground, the stunned crowd ran toward it, but Vaughn "stepped out of
the [plane] without a scratch, though he had received quite a jar from
the fall." He vowed that he would fly again and his machine would be
ready. His next performance would be on Sunday, November 6.

"Sunday was a big day at the Shreveport State Fair," the New Orleans
Times-Democrat reported. There were thousands in attendance, coming
from all over Louisiana, as well as neighboring Texas and Arkansas.

Claire Chennault had traveled a hundred and fifty miles from Gilbert. The *Shreveport Times* reported that "the sky was perfectly clear and it was just cool enough to make the exertion of sightseeing a pleasure."

As the sun began to set, Chennault and the other spectators crowded into the stands. From the tent at the edge of the field, "the whir of the engine on the aeroplane was heard, and the people soon saw the slim lines of the heavier-than-air machine roll out of the tent, and make for the center of the race course." As the craft began to roll, "eyes were strained through the dusk to see the machine, and soon outlined against the sky lighted by the setting sun, the machine arose like a mighty bird," and started to climb. After flying for a quarter mile, however, Vaughn experienced engine trouble and brought the plane down, crashing through the race-course fence. Once again he walked away unharmed.

Still, the crowd considered the flight a success—the plane had gotten off the ground. For Claire Chennault, witnessing the plane gliding overhead, even for just a few moments, was a revelation. He now saw "a new frontier" that "sowed the seed of my desire to fly," one that would shape the rest of his life. His urge was intense and immediate, but years would pass before he got his first chance to take to the sky.

Chennault was studying at Louisiana State Normal and, when he finished, set out on a new course: he was going to become a teacher. He got a lucky break when his uncle, a respected teacher in the area, helped him get a job teaching at the one-room country schoolhouse in Athens, Louisiana. Chennault was warned that he might have to raise a fist to keep discipline among the older students in his classroom. Legend has it that on his first day of teaching he was writing on the blackboard when he felt something hit him in the back. He turned around and demanded to know which of the students had thrown an eraser at him. A boy the size of a man stood up. Chennault dismissed the class and invited the perpetrator out back, where he beat the daylights out of him. That was the end of the disciplinary problem at the Athens School. Teaching was rewarding, but Chennault couldn't envision himself spending years tending to the "annual crop of oversize farm boys [who] made the life of a teacher miserable and had cut the average tenure to less than a term."

At the conclusion of the 1910 school year, Chennault's uncle, a principal at another school, invited him to come watch the graduation ceremony. It "was just like any other graduation, with the girls and boys in their best clothes, with the decorated rostrum, the school choir singing hymns, and the address of welcome by the best scholar." That address was delivered by a graduating senior, Nell Thompson, and Chennault was captivated by the stunning brunette. That one glimpse of beauty seared him, and he began to court her. A biographer noted that Chennault was "impressed by her independence, her lively curiosity, her quiet strength, and her cheerful spunk."

Even though they were both only eighteen, he and Nell were wed on Christmas Eve in 1911 and settled into married life. The routine didn't cure his desire to do bigger things with his life, but that desire was superseded by the need to support a family; he and Nell had their first son, John Stephen, in 1913, and their second, Max, the next year.

His growing family convinced Chennault that he had to leave Gilbert and finally take his chance to make his mark on the world. The Chennaults moved to New Orleans, the largest city in the South, where Claire Chennault earned a diploma in typing, the sort of degree that could set him up for an office job. On the side, he was working as the athletic director at the local YMCA. The physical culture movement, a fairly novel belief that men needed to be concerned with fitness and to go to the gymnasium to exercise, was sweeping the nation. That was the work that seemed to excite Chennault and he would take jobs in a series of YMCAs in Ohio and Kentucky and eventually would become the director of the YMCA in Louisville. He embraced the virtues of physical rigor and was proud of his own strength. But working at the Y didn't pay well, even as a director. He knew he'd need something more to support his loved ones.

In 1916, he took the train to Akron, Ohio. He showed up with a few suitcases and a trunk, one of thousands of men who poured into America's fastest-growing city looking for work. He rented the attic of a house for five dollars a week, then his family followed. It wasn't much, but Chennault finally found a rewarding line of work. Every morning he'd get up and ride the trolley to the Goodyear Tire & Rubber Co. factory. Goodyear was known for their tires, helping to put Henry

Ford's Model Ts on the road, but in 1917 the company was hired by the U.S. Navy to make blimplike balloons that could be used to spot U-boats along the coast. Chennault signed on as an inspector on the balloon-production line, a small step closer to his dream of flying. With his salary, the family was able to upgrade to a full house, paying fifteen dollars a week rent. It was a comfortable life. He liked the work, and Nell could stay at home with their kids.

Chennault might have followed that path for years. Except that in April 1917, America entered the Great War. Even though it would mean leaving his family, Chennault felt that he had to prove to himself that he could make it as a soldier. The army had sent out a request for pilots, particularly men who could operate the observation balloons that Chennault was making at Goodyear. Applicants had to be between nineteen and twenty-five years old, and the twenty-three-year-old Chennault was confident that he'd finally get his chance to fly.

But the army was looking for a certain type of man to become a pilot, one who was "energetic and forceful and of good moral character and clean habits," as a newspaper described the ideal candidate; it said, too, that he must "have a good education." Hiram Bingham, a Yale professor and an explorer who had rediscovered Machu Picchu, was in charge of recruitment. In his view a pilot should be "'an officer and a gentleman.' He must be the kind of man whose honor is never left out of consideration. . . . He must be resourceful, keen, quick, and determined." Unsurprisingly, the army believed that Ivy Leaguers made the best pilots, especially polo players and quarterbacks. Few Americans in 1917 had flown in a plane, and the army concentrated on finding the best and the brightest from the flying clubs on Ivy League campuses to serve as America's pilots in the Great War. A factory worker like Chennault didn't stand a chance. He received a cruelly blunt rejection letter that he'd remember for the rest of his life: "Applicant does not possess necessary qualifications for a successful aviator." The army believed men like Chennault, common men, were needed for the infantry, and he accepted the job he was offered. He reported for basic training at Fort Benjamin Harrison in Indiana, one of the newly established bases where the army was turning civilians into newly commissioned officers.

He spent three months there, making him one of the "90-day wonders" that filled the army's burgeoning ranks.

Though he was an infantry officer, fate showed its hand when he was ordered to a base in Texas connected to Kelly Field, where the army was training its new pilots. Chennault spent his days drilling new infantry soldiers, but would visit the field where the planes were taking off, drawn by "the roar of their motors, the harsh thrashing of their propellers and the strange rattle they made as they flew," as biographer Keith Ayling wrote. He desperately wanted to fly.

He eventually finagled from one of the flight officers an unauthorized lesson in the "Jenny," a two-seater with a place in front for the instructor and one behind for the student. As the Jenny jolted into the air, shaking like a kite in the wind, Chennault could see the white tents in neat rows at Kelly Field and the open Texas landscape that spread to the horizon. Seven years from when he'd first seen that plane take off at the state fair, he was finally flying. Soon he was even trying his hand at soloing. The instructors, impressed with Chennault's drive to learn, or maybe just worn down by his persistence, would taxi to the flight line, then climb out as Chennault "jumped in and took off." In total, he estimated that he accrued eighty hours of "bootleg" flying time. But in the army's books, he was still an infantryman.

Chennault's unit was getting ready to deploy to France in the fall of 1918, but they only made it as far as Mitchel Field in New York before they were told that there would be no trip overseas. The German surrender was expected imminently; Chennault had missed his chance to fight in the Great War. His unit was ordered to Langley Field in Virginia to work on a ditch-digging project. While he was on a troop transport, he caught the Spanish flu, a deadly disease that was spreading rapidly, brought by troops returning from Europe.

Chennault was quarantined in an aircraft hangar. The flu "hit me hard. I was hauled away one afternoon to a small outbuilding where the dying spent their last hours. The officer next to me died early in the evening." Barely conscious, he could hear a doctor and nurse discussing his prognosis. He "isn't dead yet," the nurse said. "He will be before morning," the doctor replied. Someone slipped him a quart of bourbon, hoping to ease his final hours. But by morning he was still breathing and clutching the bottle in his hand. Chennault would have lasting respiratory problems that he traced back to this episode, but he always believed he had been spared for some reason. He came to believe that God had something planned for him and that there was some great mission that would guide his life. When the Armistice was declared on November 11, 1918, he was on a train going back to Kelly Field, determined to become a pilot.

After his recovery, he applied again and his perseverance paid off. His orders for flight training came through. With his hours of flight experience, Chennault was impatient with the slow pace of the formal training. His instructor didn't appreciate his attitude and recommended that Chennault be washed out. He had one last chance to stay flying, and that was to sufficiently impress a senior instructor in what might be his final flight. Not only did Chennault redeem himself, but the instructor, Ernest Allison, recognized something special in him. Allison took him in hand and taught him acrobatic flying, daredevil stunts that pushed the limit of the airplane. Chennault learned how to flip the craft upside down, hanging tight against the safety belt. He loved the "kaleidoscope of sky and earth" as the plane turned upside down. This unrestrained brand of flight hooked him, he said, "like a Tensas River bass on a minnow-covered barb." From then on, "I had the taste of flying in my craw and could not get it out." Chennault finally obtained a permanent commission in the Air Service in 1920 and was assigned to the Twelfth Observation Squadron in El Paso, Texas, in 1921. He flew unarmed planes over the deep canyons of the Big Bend district, a sort of aerial border patrol. The work wasn't exciting, but he was accruing valuable hours in the cockpit and gaining greater confidence in his skills as a pilot. He brought his family with him to El Paso and Nell gave birth to their sixth child, David. It was a happy time for them. "We were a very close family in the early years," Chennault's daughter Peggy recalled. "He made time to be with us. We had bridge sessions every night."

As he grew into a more mature pilot, Chennault came to see the potential for using his aerial stunts as a type of entertainment. He hadn't grown up with much exposure to theater, but he intuitively understood how to create a good performance. On Washington's Birthday in 1923, Chennault's squadron put on a public display in El Paso. During the first part of the show Chennault remained in the stands, wearing a long wig and Nell's coat and shoes. At one point in the program, the announcer called for the oldest woman in the crowd to come down and ride in the airplane. "Grandma Morris" walked onto the field. This woman, the announcer told the crowd, was so old that she remembered traveling in a covered wagon. Now she would get to experience flight. As Grandma made her way into the cockpit, the pilot climbed out to check on the engine. Suddenly, the plane darted forward with the helpless old woman holding the stick. "Spectators gasped as the runaway plane rose into the air, narrowly missing trees, hangars," a witness recalled. For the next fifteen minutes, Grandma kept the crowd mesmerized as she circled overhead "performing impossible loops, banks, dives." And then, to the shock of the crowd, the plane landed perfectly, and jumping from the plane, Chennault removed his wig and revealed the ruse.

Chennault was undergoing a transformation. He had been born a Southerner but was now acquiring a more global perspective. After the stint at Fort Bliss, he transferred to Hawaii, where he was stationed at Luke Field on Ford Island, right next to Pearl Harbor. He was like "a boy with his first love," he'd later write, as he took his biplane out over the Pacific Ocean. He was put in command of the 19th Fighter Squadron, the "Fighting Cocks," and taught his squadron how to fly their MB-3 biplanes in a coordinated attack when they took on the enemy.

Under the Pacific sun his body was "growing lean, tanned and hard," he recalled in his memoir. With his wing-tipped mustache and his white dress uniform, he was "in the best fighter-pilot tradition."

By 1932, now one of the army's more experienced pilots, he was assigned to Maxwell Field in Alabama. He was to serve as an instructor in the Air Corps Tactical School, a job that reflected Chennault's growing reputation. But the commander had another idea: Would Chennault help start the army's first flying acrobatic team? The plan was to establish a performing troupe that would travel to the country's air shows, serving as a sort of public relations team for army fliers. Chennault eagerly took on the task, assembling a three-person team that became known as the Three Men on the Flying Trapeze, after the popular song. Chennault went through a number of wingmen, but would eventually settle on two, William "Billy" McDonald and John "Luke" Williamson, whom he would learn to trust with his life.

"Our team was picked by the simple process of inviting all candidates to try to stick on my wing for thirty minutes of violent acrobatics." McDonald and Williamson made the grade. The three men flew their Boeing P-12 biplanes in unison, only a few feet separating their wingtips, dipping and twirling as if they were one. Their ease in the air took a lot of practice. But all the practice in the world couldn't change a basic fact. Stunt flying was dangerous. Fatalities were not uncommon.

By 1934, the Flying Trapeze had started to travel the country and the act was a hit. Future major general Haywood Hansell served with them for a time. They were greeted by newspapers like the *Miami News* as "the outstanding thrill producers of all time in the aviation world." Girls would rush out from the crowd to have their pictures taken with the smiling pilots. Newsmen from Fox, Universal, Hearst, and Paramount filmed them in action. They even got a sponsor, and Chennault became a pitchman: "You will find that all fliers use gum, and I consider Wrigley's the best."

At the time, air races were major sporting spectacles. Mired in the depths of the Great Depression, Americans were turning their eyes heavenward, looking to these soaring planes to imagine a better future for their country. Perhaps someday everyone could fly. "It is true that aviation hasn't reached the stage where the farmer going to town with a basket of eggs can get a lift from a passing airplane, but possibly this will come in the future," was a typical take in *Popular Aviation*.

There were so many shows for Chennault that the extraordinary became routine. But an appearance the Three Men on the Flying Trapeze made in Miami would shape the contours of Chennault's life for years to come.

The Seventh Annual Miami Air Races in January 1935 marked one of the largest gatherings of airplanes in American history up to that time, with five hundred planes expected to converge on Miami from across the nation. Thousands of Miamians paid sixty cents for a chance to see the nation's best pilots push the limits of what could be done in a plane. This was advertised as "the thrills of a lifetime crowded into three short afternoons." Crowds at the municipal airport reached over 7,500 people. The British and Nazi air force attachés made the trip from Washington, D.C., to see the latest developments in aviation, and a contingent of Chinese officers scouting out new planes were in the stands as well. There would be parachutists, demonstrations of bomb dropping (using sacks of flour), and races featuring an array of different styles of planes. But no attraction was more anticipated by the crowd than the Three Men on the Flying Trapeze.

As they'd practiced countless times before, the three pilots began to twist and turn together. "They were in so tight a formation during the performance that from the ground the wing tips seemed to overlap," the *New York Times* reported. The planes did wing-overs and spins with "a perfection that seemed as if the three planes were controlled by one mind."

Chennault felt he was finally being recognized for the talents in the cockpit he'd spent years perfecting. When businessman William Pawley extended an invitation to his yacht to the three men, Chennault accepted, as Pawley was nothing short of the godfather of aviation in Miami. He'd established the city's routes to Central America and Cuba, and had developed a lucrative trade selling Curtiss-Wright planes to the Chinese. An adventurer who liked to make deals, Pawley would be described by his biographer as a "cross between Indiana Jones and Donald Trump." He'd recently opened a factory in Hangchow (modern-day Hangzhou) to assemble the planes from American-made parts. Now he was back from China with a small entourage from the Chinese Air Force, whom he wanted Chennault to meet.

When they gathered on the yacht, the leader of the group, Colonel P. T. Mow, must have impressed the Americans with his nearly perfect English. Mow had been traveling with his team to Russia, France, Germany, England, and Italy seeking to buy more planes for China and hire more pilots to train its air force. He believed that China, "a young country, in aviation," had much to learn from expert pilots in the West. He already had a number of former army pilots working as instructors at one of China's aviation academies, led by West Point graduate John Jouett, but he wanted more. When he met the Three Men on the Flying Trapeze, Mow quickly got to the point, telling Chennault and his team that they should come to China. Such an invitation wasn't unusual at the time. Lured by adventure and money, dozens of American pilots were flying under foreign flags. Pilots in the Lafayette Escadrille had fought for France in the Great War before America's entry. After the Armistice, the Army Air Corps had been reduced in size but many of its members were eager to take part in combat abroad. Some formed the Kościuszko Squadron to help Poland in its struggle against the Soviet Union, while others joined the Cuban Air Force and the small air forces of South American republics. In 1928 Chennault himself had received a tempting proposal to take his skills abroad, when, after viewing some drills, a visiting Soviet general had given Chennault some vodka, chocolate, and caviar as preliminary gifts to open a conversation about coming to advise the Red Army's new air force. Chennault got them to agree to $1,000 a month, which was a steep raise over the $225 he was earning in the army, but he ultimately turned them down. However tempting Mow's offer might have been, Chennault, McDonald, and Williamson declined. Chennault had his job in the army and a large family to look after—he and Nell now had eight children. But Mow was not a man easily discouraged. The pilots remembered him saying, "You will hear from me again."

Back at Maxwell, Chennault focused on his teaching. He was one of the small cadre of instructors at the base charged with developing the army's air strategy. What kind of planes should they use in combat? What were the most successful tactics? It was an academic task, involving debates among the faculty and the drafting of long articles. Since 1911, when an Italian reconnaissance pilot decided to drop grenades on Turkish forces in Libya, aerial bombing had excited the imagination of military planners. By the 1930s, the prevailing view in the Army Air Corps was that bombers were the future of air power. As British prime minister Stanley Baldwin famously put it, "the bomber will always get through." Fighter planes, like the one Chennault flew in the Flying Trapeze, were judged to be useless against the overwhelming force of the bombers. Chennault dissented vehemently with this position, arguing that the fighter could control the skies. He didn't see his work with the Flying Trapeze as just a stunt—he thought of his aerial finesse as "convincing proof . . . that fighters could battle together through the most violent maneuvers of combat" and take down the bombers. This debate, waged in academic journals and in classrooms, wasn't just theoretical. It would determine how the Army Air Corps invested its budget and what tactics it would teach its pilots.

Chennault's colleagues dismissed his ideas and came to resent him. It didn't help his cause that he was brash and arrogant about his opinions. He wrote strident articles and fired them off to senior army officers, who greeted them with stony indifference. "Who is this damned fellow Chennault?" General Hap Arnold wrote after reading one of Chennault's papers. "The personal battles within the tactical school began to wear on Chennault," one historian noted.

In addition to the emotional anguish of having his ideas rejected, his physical health was in decline. He smoked cigarettes by the pack, and crisscrossing the country to put on air shows had begun to take a toll on him. Flying in the open cockpit of his plane irritated his lungs. He was put on a diet of raw liver, which was supposed to help give him strength, but it didn't do much more than make mealtimes unpleasant. He was coughing uncontrollably, and when doctors diagnosed bronchitis he was sent to the Army Navy Hospital in Hot Springs, Arkansas, to recuperate. "Lying on a hospital bed in Hot Springs," Chennault wrote, "there was ample time to look back over my forty-seven years and think about the future." Chennault was struggling with more than poor health. He felt stymied and belittled. "When you're thwarted in every respect, you're just depressed," his oldest daughter, Peggy, would later recount.

During his recovery he received news that only confirmed his disillusionment with the army: his wingmen, McDonald and Williamson, had been passed over for promotion. Chennault had by then worked with the two men for years, and he took the army's decision as a personal rebuke. He wrote and urged them to take up the offer to go to China. Recognizing that their army careers were limited, they decided to take his advice.

William McDonald, who had grown up in Birmingham, Alabama, was then thirty years old and about to embark on an adventure unlike anything he'd contemplated before. Luke Williamson was from South Carolina and was the kind of pilot who would earn his way into the South Carolina Aviation Association's Hall of Fame for taking an army plane and flying to his hometown. He would perform acrobatic stunts for the residents before landing the plane and going to see his family. This would be an adventure on a much grander scale. The Flying Trapeze pilots were joined on their journey east by a handful of other Americans who would be going to China to work with the air force, including Sebie Smith, an airplane mechanic who had helped the Flying Trapeze team. On July 11, 1936, this band of former army men boarded the *Empress of Russia,* a large steamer ship in Seattle, almost giddy with excitement about what lay ahead. On July 27, they arrived in Shanghai, which was overwhelming, beyond what they had imagined. It was, as Smith recalled, "the busiest place any of us had ever seen. Throngs of Chinese and some foreigners bustled about the docks and embankment mostly on foot, bicycle or rickshaw." Chinese officers escorted them to a tailor to have their Chinese uniforms fitted. They then headed southeast to the Central Aviation School at Hangchow and were housed at a luxurious hotel. From their new home, they could look out at the West Lake, and on the weekends would have picnics by the water and hire boatmen to take them out for pleasure cruises. They would go into town to see somewhat out-of-date American movies at a small theater that had a Chinese interpreter who stood next to the projector and explained the plots in Chinese. They bought bicycles to explore the area and found a Buddhist temple deep in a bamboo forest that they liked to visit.

The work itself was rewarding for the pilots. They woke at 6:15 each morning and with the help of interpreters taught tactics to the Chinese recruits until 6:30 P.M. They were pleased with the progress the new pilots were making. After a few months, they were ready to graduate a class, and the ceremony was as festive as a Fourth of July celebration. The Americans were guests of honor, invited to sit on the reviewing stand with Chinese leader Chiang Kai-shek and his wife, Madame Chiang.

The Curtiss biplanes roared overhead in formations of three, and "the successive flybys of so many new aircraft were an inspiring sight for everyone." As if to underscore that the men had been trained for a potential war, targets had been placed on the ground, and "the ships came roaring down past us with their machine guns blazing away." The graduation festivities lasted all day and culminated with a spectacular fireworks display.

In December 1936, one of the senior American aviation instructors died of a heart attack just before he was to conduct a comprehensive survey of the Chinese Air Force. Madame Chiang, who spoke fluent English with a Southern drawl acquired during her years studying at schools in Georgia, was at the funeral. She asked the American pilots whether there was a suitable pilot back in the United States who could come to China to replace him. They told her they knew the perfect candidate—Claire Chennault. At her instruction, they wrote him a letter with an invitation to come to China.

This time Chennault would not refuse.

Chennault's career in the army had stalled. He likely faced a future that would involve no flying, and he didn't want to just sit behind a desk. The letter asking him to go to China couldn't have come at a better time. This wasn't just an offer to teach at the aviation school. He was being asked to do a survey of the Chinese Air Force and offer ideas about how to develop it in the years ahead. This was the recognition he wanted—not just as one of America's best pursuit pilots, but as a strategic thinker. The pay wasn't bad either at a thousand dollars a month for the three-month assignment. He would also be provided with a car, chauffeur, and interpreter, and he could fly any plane in the Chinese Air Force that he wished.

Chennault explained his decision to accept in a letter to his brother: "When an old, well-plowed road is blocked, a new path must be opened." His work in China, he speculated, "may amount to very little except a good paying position or it may amount to a great deal. . . ." He felt destiny calling in no small way: "It is even possible that my 'feeble' efforts may influence history for some few hundreds of years."

China was not actively at war, but in 1931 Japan had invaded China and annexed Manchuria, and the status quo in the Far East was far from stable. Chennault understood his job with the Chinese would be "to prepare them to whip h[ell] out of Japan."

For some time, Chennault had managed to balance his two great loves, flying and family, but this time Nell and the children, who had accompanied him from base to base, would remain in America. Despite the demands of his career, the Chennaults had a happy marriage, and Nell supported his flying. She would sit on the front porch and watch the pilots fly down the Selma Road in front of her house, taking notes on improvements that were needed. After years of seminomadic existence, the family had finally settled in a large antebellum home a few miles outside of Birmingham, Alabama. The family played bridge together, and Chennault taught his younger sons how to hunt and fish. He loved his children and his wife, but he felt that he was stuck in an eddy and being "sucked under." China looked to him like a life raft.

Nell opposed the whole idea and worried about the impact on the children. But she couldn't control her husband and, besides, they had always been short of money, and there were still young children they needed to feed, and someday send to college. If he took on this mission in China, their financial problems could be addressed, and Claire assured Nell that he wouldn't be gone long. Still, his family never believed this had been about the money. His daughter Peggy would later say that her father left "because he wanted to prove his theories." While Chennault explained the job as a three-month assignment, one historian suggests that he already knew he was signing up for a longer two-year contract.

Before he left, Chennault helped the family move to a farm in rural Louisiana. Nell had been born on a farm and he hoped that she'd feel at home there. The house was in a town called Waterproof, on the banks of Lake St. John. There was a porch out front and plenty of space in the back for Nell to grow a garden and raise chickens, as well as orchards of fruit and pecan trees nearby.

Chennault handed in his army resignation in April 1937. The *Shreveport Times* took note, saying that the officer had been "ill several months," and that this was the reason for his retirement. In reality, Chennault felt invigorated by the mission that lay ahead. He had no second thoughts as he boarded a train on May 1 for San Francisco. "I felt a compulsion to go," he would recall, "that I couldn't resist." He began a diary to chronicle the "great adventure."

CHAPTER 2

MEETING THE PRINCESS

laire Chennault was aboard the S.S. *President Garfield* as it set out from San Francisco on May 8, 1937. The weather was rough, "showers, wind and considerable sea." He had crossed these waters when he was stationed in Hawaii over a decade ago, but on this trip he no longer wore an army uniform. His new passport listed his occupation as "farmer," a cover for his actual mission. In his stateroom he spent his time "working on my plans and studies." He had a survey to conduct, but beyond the brief conversation he'd had with Colonel P. T. Mow two years earlier and the letters that he'd received from his friends in China, he knew little about what awaited him. The "voyage continues uneventfully" and time seemed to pass slowly. He found the passengers "uniformly uninteresting," but he still joined them for games of bridge and table tennis. "Tried to dance in the evening but ship rolled too much," he wrote. When the ship docked in Honolulu, he stopped for a cocktail at the Alexander Young Hotel. His posting in Hawaii with his family had been one of the happier periods in his career, as he'd enjoyed the carefree pleasures of island living, but now he was just passing through.

Before reaching China, the *President Garfield* would stop in Japan. Chennault knew he would have to maintain the fiction of being a farmer in the event of a police interrogation, as Japanese authorities had already lodged protests with the U.S. government about American pilots volunteering to serve with the Chinese. When the ship docked, the plan was for him to meet up with Billy McDonald. The two men would tour the country, gathering whatever intelligence they could on the Japanese military. McDonald, like Chennault, was understandably wary about entering Japan—essentially as a spy—and needed a cover story. He had been drinking at a bar in Shanghai that was popular with expats when he'd run into an old fraternity brother. It turned out that this man was the manager of a circuslike troupe, a group that McDonald described as a mix of Russian singers, Chinese jugglers, and a trio from the Philippines called the Dixie Girls. The group was on the way to Japan for a few shows, and McDonald's friend said he could come along, posing as their manager. The con worked and he passed through customs without an issue. After hanging backstage at the troupe's performance, McDonald slipped away to meet Chennault.

Chennault arrived in Kobe at 10:00 P.M. on May 27. The following day he and McDonald rented an open-air car, and with cameras hidden beneath their topcoats, drove around industrial districts booming with new factories. Chennault filled a notebook with observations and they took photographs. The duo then boarded the *President Garfield* and cruised down the Seto Inland Sea, where Japan's rapid industrialization was on impressive display. Chennault made note of the bustling shipping lanes and islands with new factories. "Industry seemed to be expanding," he recalled, "with the suspicious speed of a military enterprise." Though China had hired him to prepare them for another war with Japan, he couldn't help but find the country "very attractive" and was captivated by its "beautiful scenery."

When the *President Garfield* pulled into the Port of Shanghai on May 31, 1937, Chennault felt as if he were entering another world. Rickshaws darted along the docks, and though the humid heat was oppressive, this new land fascinated him. Because Shanghai was an international port city, the great powers shared control with the Chinese, and warships of many nationalities stood in the harbor, including British, French, and even American. Luke Williamson was waiting for them at the dock. To celebrate Chennault's arrival, the Americans gathered for a welcome dinner at the Metropole Hotel in the heart of Shanghai's International Settlement. They went up to the roof, where "the weather was perfect that night for the affair," Sebie Smith wrote, "and the dinner was grand. All guests seemed to have been able to satisfy their curiosity about the famous Claire Lee Chennault." "At last

I am in China," Chennault wrote in his diary, where he confided that he hoped to "be of service to a people who are struggling to attain national unity and new life."

On the afternoon of June 3, Chennault was picked up in a car by Roy Holbrook. Holbrook was an American ex-army pilot who had worked on procuring new planes for the Chinese government. As they made their way through the city, Chennault saw the potholes in the street, remnants of the Japanese bombing of Shanghai in 1932. The car turned onto a wide tree-lined avenue in the French Concession, a neighborhood designed to mimic Paris, and stopped outside an imposing gate. The home with the grand garden was the residence of China's premier couple, Chiang Kai-shek and Madame Chiang.

Chennault had come to meet with Madame Chiang to receive the details of his assignment. He took a seat in a dimly lit waiting area, following Holbrook's lead. Then "suddenly a young girl clad in a modish Paris frock tipped into the room, bubbling with energy and enthusiasm." Chennault assumed she was one of Holbrook's friends and didn't greet her until Holbrook nudged him and said, "Madame Chiang, may I present Colonel Chennault?"

Chennault had been expecting an older woman, and Madame Chiang looked younger even than her thirty-nine years. She introduced herself in flawless English. Soong Mei-ling had spent almost a decade living in the United States. Her father, Charlie Soong, was a wealthy businessman who wanted his children to be educated in America. In 1908, ten-year-old Soong Mei-ling was sent to Macon, Georgia, to live with her older sister, who was attending Wesleyan College. She came to consider herself a native. When a teacher asked her to explain Sherman's march across Georgia during the Civil War, she replied, "Pardon me, I am a southerner, and that subject is very painful to me." She also attended Wesleyan, but then transferred to Wellesley College in Massachusetts to be close to her brother, T. V. Soong, who was at Harvard. She majored in English and had a fairly routine life as a student, playing tennis and joining the art society, Tau Zeta Epsilon. After graduation and a tearful farewell to friends at Grand Central Station, she took a train to Vancouver and boarded a steamship back to China, a land she had known only as a young child. But she was determined from a young age to play a role in shaping China's future, and after she returned she met and fell in love with Chiang Kai-shek. He was a rising star in the nation's military—though many would claim that she "loved power" more than any man, and that her interest in him was due to the fact that he worked directly for Sun Yat-sen, the founder of modern China.

It was an unlikely match. Chiang was more than a decade older than her and divorced with two sons. He was a Buddhist and she was a Christian. But they shared a love for China and a concern for their country's destiny. After he converted to Christianity, they were married on December 1, 1927. By then Chiang had succeeded Sun to become Nationalist China's leader, and Madame Chiang (as she came to be known) intended to play a major role in running the country. Though the Chiangs led Nationalist China, the reality was that China remained quite fractured. There were warlords leading other factions that remained quasi-independent of the Nationalist government. The Communist Party was led by Mao Zedong. Though Chiang and Mao had been able to forge a "United Front" in 1936, their alliance was an uneasy one. The tensions would be submerged to face a common foe, but were bound to resurface eventually.

Madame Chiang worked side by side with her husband in managing China's future, and was considered the most powerful woman in the world. She wanted to unite China's factions and make it into a great power, viewing the United States as not only a model for China's development, but as an important ally. During one trip to the United States, she said, "When we need a friend we can always look toward our sister republic."

She was all business in that first meeting with Chennault. As secretary general of the Chinese Aeronautical Affairs Commission, she focused on building up China's air force. She was a fervent believer in air power, and she felt that the airplane could help stitch together the feuding fiefdoms that made up China. If the powerful Japanese military machine attacked again, she believed that it would be the air force rather than the army that would be crucial to the nation's defense. But with so many of the Chinese air bases located far from Shanghai, she had little idea of what condition the air force was actually in. That's why she needed Chennault to travel to these remote outposts to gather information about the condition of the pilots and planes.

This was the sort of assignment that Chennault had been eager to undertake, a high-level mission for which his opinion would be valued. He told her he'd have the survey completed within a few months. "I reckon you and I will get along all right in building up your air force," Chennault reportedly said. "I reckon so," Madame Chiang replied. Chennault, like so many others before and after, was smitten. That night he noted in his diary that Madame Chiang would "always be a princess to me." He later wrote that the meeting was "an encounter from which I never recovered."

Chennault faced a tough task, for there was little reliable information about the status of the Chinese Air Force. By 1937 it had grown, on paper, to include over six hundred aircraft that could be used in a war. In their rush to build their arsenal, the Chinese had imported a range of American and European planes. There were a number of different training schools, some run by American pilots and others by Italians, but the air force was primarily under the command of the latter after the Americans on the Jouett mission withdrew in 1935. There were Fiat planes on the runways, and near one air base, there was even a "Little Italy," complete with cafés like those in Rome.

Despite the bravado of the Italian officers, Madame Chiang was concerned about their work, as they were apparently graduating every cadet, whatever their skill level. There were also rumors that many of the planes weren't airworthy. Chennault would spend several weeks flying a zigzag route across China inspecting bases. Accompanying him in his Douglas BT-2, a two-seater biplane widely used as a trainer, was Sebie Smith, and in a second plane were Billy McDonald and their interpreter, Colonel P. Y. Shu.

"I had my hand on a throttle again for the first time since the Air Corps grounded me the previous autumn," Chennault wrote, and it "felt good to be in the air again with Billy on my wing and a broad muddy river below that could easily have been the Mississippi instead of the Yangtze." But the great distance he had traveled from home became clear as he observed the countryside and realized that the "brilliant green carpet below could come only from growing rice, and the web of canals and black slate-roofed villages reminded us that it was really China below."

As they made their first stops at Nanking and Nanchang, Chennault began to see the extent to which the Italians had been exaggerating the strength of the air force in their reports to the Chinese. In Nanking, General Silvio Scaroni, one of Italy's leading aces from the Great War, "roared through the streets in a big black limousine, his uniform dripping medals and gold braid." Chennault was put off by the bombastic demeanor of the Italian pilots and was so unimpressed by the flying he saw that he was moved to write: "The Italians did all they could to sabotage China."

His most important stop was in Loyang (modern-day Luoyang), a base in central China that the Italians had taken over from the Americans in 1935 and where they had established a major flight school. Getting there involved flying over vast empty stretches of land, and McDonald wrote that he was "glad we did not have motor trouble in that region." Chennault quickly discovered that the roster of planes there had been wildly inflated by counting hulks of metal that would be worthless in battle. It was becoming clear that it would take years to build a truly modern air force for China. "Am appalled by situation here and would go home if I did not want to serve China," he wrote in his diary on June 25, 1937. He had come to appreciate China's rich history, and he wanted to be part of shaping its future. While in Loyang he hiked through the mountains to see one of China's great wonders, the Longmen Grottoes, where intricate images of Buddha had been carved into the cliffs, some reaching over fifty feet tall. "It is nothing to see something 2000 years old here," McDonald wrote to his parents.

While Chennault was in Loyang, five hundred miles to the northeast a new round of conflict was taking shape between China and Japan. Ever since the Japanese had helped suppress the Boxer Rebellion—a native uprising against Western influence at the beginning of the twentieth century—Japanese forces had been stationed in a garrison outside Peking (modern-day Beijing). On the evening of July 7, the Japanese held an unannounced training mission, and in the darkness they traded fire with Chinese troops at the Marco Polo Bridge. It took a couple of days for the news to reach Chennault, and it still was vague, but the "Marco Polo Bridge Incident" marked the renewal of war between Japan and China.

Chennault saw the fighting as a call to action. He believed that one should "never run from a fight." For almost twenty years he had developed tactics for aerial combat, and now that war had been thrust upon him, he "wanted a chance to give [my ideas] an acid test in combat." His opportunity to shape history was in the offing. He sent a telegram offering his assistance to the Chinese. The reply came from Chiang Kai-shek himself: "Your voluntary offer of services gratefully accepted."

Before reporting the dire condition of their air force to the Chiangs, Chennault returned to Nanchang to work with Colonel Mow. Nanchang's summer heat was, according to Chennault, like "a Turkish bath," and the clouds of dust on the airfield left his challenged lungs gasping for air. He accompanied Mow to the airfield, but he was discouraged by what he saw. The "air force," Chennault wrote in his diary, "is terribly unprepared for war." In the evenings he and Mow drank cold beer and ate watermelon as they discussed the long war ahead of them.

The two men then traveled to Kuling (modern-day Guling), in the central part of the country, where the Chiangs spent the summer at a sprawling villa with a courtyard full of trees and flowers. The city was nestled at the top of Mount Lushan and was considered one of China's great resort towns. Chiang greeted them "Western style," shaking their hands, Chennault recalled, and "preliminaries dispensed with, the Generalissimo turned to Mow and in sharp staccato Chinese began to quiz him on the condition of the air force." Madame Chiang translated for Chennault.

"How many first-line planes are ready to fight?" Chiang asked.

Mow could only respond with the pathetic truth: "Ninety-one, Your Excellency."

Chiang turned red, went outside to the porch, and began to walk up and down the steps, shouting something Chennault could only guess the meaning of, his words seeming to "coil and strike like a snake." Colonel Mow stood at attention, the terror visible in his eyes as he stared straight ahead while the "color drained from [his] face." "The Generalissimo has threatened to execute him," Madame Chiang whispered to Chennault. "We should have five hundred first-line planes ready to fight."

Chiang, as one journalist wrote, had a "shortness of temper that exhibited itself in bizarre ways." It wasn't out of the question that Chennault would bear the brunt of Chiang's fit of anger. As historian Hannah Pakula wrote, "Chiang's temper was not always used against the deserving. Watching a movie in his home one evening and vastly annoyed by a particular scene, he stalked out of the room and ordered that the projectionist be thrashed."

Chiang returned from his pacing and asked Chennault directly in Chinese: "What does your survey show?" Madame Chiang translated the question.

With Madame Chiang translating, Chennault explained that those "figures are correct." He went on to describe the sorry state of the air force. He waited for another tirade, but Chiang must have felt some degree of respect for his honesty. Chennault would later write that this was a pivotal moment in his relationship with the Chinese leader, because it "laid the foundation of a reputation for absolute frankness."

Chennault was invited to accompany the Chiangs to a war council in Nanking, where warlords from across the nation would gather. Many of these men had been feuding for years, but Chiang was intent on rallying them together for the common defense. Chennault was just an observer on the sidelines, but he saw history in the making.

On August 13, during a meeting, a messenger entered the hall and passed a note to Chiang. He read it and handed it to his wife, who began to sob as she read it, and then explained to Chennault: "They are shelling the Shanghai Civic Center. They are killing our people. They are killing our people."

"What will you do now?" Chennault asked. Regaining her composure, she answered, "We will fight."

The *Izumo,* a Japanese cruiser, was anchored just a quarter mile from Shanghai and used its eight-inch and six-inch guns to attack the city. Madame Chiang wanted to strike back. When Chennault proposed the idea of launching a dive-bombing mission against the ship, she told him to organize it. Chennault wouldn't fly in the attack himself, but he would be responsible for organizing it. He stayed up until 4:00 A.M. "poring over maps and planning the missions." He would use a few Curtiss Hawk dive-bombers along with some Northrop light bombers to strike the *Izumo* with 1,100-pound bombs.

Chennault felt the pressure of the moment: "After twenty years of practicing for war I was finally playing for keeps." The attack would require precision, but if it was successful it would be a stunning victory that could shift the tide of the nascent war.

There were already warning signs, however, that things weren't going to proceed according to plan. In his diary McDonald had complained of the Chinese pilots. One review: "Technique poor, Dive shallow—Aim Bad." The next day, August 14, 1937, the sky over Shanghai was dark with rain clouds, conditions that would make flying more challenging, but Chennault gave the go-ahead for the mission.

Three Chinese planes made their way toward the harbor. They had intended to fly at an altitude of 7,500 feet, but were forced by the storm as low as 1,500 feet to stay below the clouds and see where they were going. "The [Chinese] attackers appeared over the cruiser with lightning suddenness," an Associated Press reporter wrote. They dove down and released their bombs, but "missed their mark by the narrowest of margins." The bombs fell straight into the International Settlement. The explosion was deafening, and the results were horrifying.

"I saw the streets littered with dead and dying," United Press correspondent John Morris wrote. The wounded were carried into the hotel, and the tile floors soon became slippery with blood. "Acrid fumes from burning buildings and automobiles filled the air" and he could see fires "shooting high into the air as tinder-dry buildings and houses burned." He described it as "one of the most frightful holocausts ever inflicted on civilized people." The dead numbered over eight hundred, with some estimates as high as five thousand. The Chinese would remember that terrible day as "Bloody Saturday."

If Chennault needed any evidence of the cost of a poorly trained air force, he now had it in blood.

CHAPTER 3

THE RAPE OF NANKING

The following day Chennault had lunch at the Metropolitan Hotel in Nanking with a few other Americans who had been involved with the flight school. They were all staying on the northern edge of town in a hotel that one account said, "might have been a boarding-house in a second-rate American country resort." The rooms didn't have windows and were filled with mosquitoes that flew in from the pond. It was a hot summer day, the kind of weather that earned Nanking its reputation as one of the "furnaces of China." As they were finishing their meal, they heard air-raid sirens.

Chennault rushed out into the garden and watched as a large formation of planes closed in. "It was still inconceivable to me that people would be trying to wage war by dropping bombs on cities," Sebie Smith would recall. "Sharp machine-gun reports were coming from everywhere. Bright shell bursts could be seen dotting the skies, and bombs started exploding." Chennault ran toward a dugout and jumped in, not daring to lift his head but hearing the cacophony of car horns, shouting, and barking dogs as the bombs rained down across the city. He survived but this was the beginning of a new phase in his relationship to aerial warfare: for years he had studied it, but now he was actually seeing the carnage up close.

Nanking was undergoing a transformation to prepare for the war. But along with the sense of urgency came a dark foreboding. One man said he felt the city was making itself ready for a "funeral on a large scale."

The city had always had natural advantages when it came to defense.

"Water and mountain provided not only beauty for Nanking but military protection," historian Iris Chang observed of its geography, and a fifty-foot wall with a moat stretched around it. The hills were covered with "a bristling ring of anti-aircraft guns," noted a newspaper account, and guns also dotted the rooftops of government buildings, the roofs themselves painted gray to make them harder to see from the sky. Gas masks had been distributed to the city's residents, who had dug holes in which they could take shelter during air raids.

The Japanese planes came back day after day, their raids announced by wailing sirens and the angry crack of antiaircraft guns in the distance. During each raid, the men could hear the engines of the incoming aircraft "get louder and louder," as Sebie Smith recalled. "The sound of whining and droning airplanes, the pop-pop-pop of machine guns and the thunder from the flashing bombs and anti-aircraft guns will make most anyone shudder and tremble." Nanking's residents sought shelter in the dugouts, plugging cotton in their ears to block out the pounding explosions of the bombs, but they had an inescapable feeling that they might be taking cover in their own graves. "The clock ticks off the time which is often the last few precious minutes of many people's lives," Smith put it, as they all wondered, "Who will it be this time?" They waited dark eternities for the blast of the all-clear siren to signal that they could emerge from their hiding places.

As the air raids continued, Chennault got to work setting up a defense for Nanking. The air force was "terribly handicapped by a lack of equipment," he wrote in a letter, but he was determined to fight. He helped organize a "warning net" that consisted of a series of outposts in the hills around Nanking that were linked by radio and could provide an early warning of an impending attack. The Chinese Air Force in Nanking had only a few dozen Hawk III biplanes, an American-made craft that was bulky and designed along the lines of the planes from the Great War, and a handful of P-26 Peashooters, a sleeker monoplane made by Boeing.

It wasn't much of an arsenal. But Chennault had identified what he believed was a vulnerability in the Japanese attack plan. Japanese bombers were flying in from air bases in Japan and Formosa (present-day Taiwan), which meant they had traveled across vast expanses of water and land to reach their targets. Many of the planes flew an incredible 1,250 miles round trip. Chennault knew that the Japanese were dispatching their bombers without fighter escorts, and though Japan's double-engine G3M bombers were fast, they were vulnerable. If a few Chinese fighters could manage to surround one of the bombers and aim for its fuel tank, they could successfully bring it down.

Chennault had argued for years that fighter planes could defeat bombers. Now was his chance to prove it. He gave instructions to the Chinese pilots, hoping to teach them "all the tricks I've learned in all the years I've flown." He suggested one particularly aggressive tactic: "Don't be afraid to ram them," Sebie Smith recalled him saying. "The Japanese can't survive a collision of that kind. You might tear off a wing tip, but that would be [the] extent of your damage."

When the Japanese bombers appeared, Chennault and McDonald would stand outside and watch the skirmish with binoculars. McDonald wrote about one battle in a letter he sent home: "The Jap has the upper hand, suddenly a swift maneuver and the Jap has the Chinese on his tail, round and round then—We see the Chinese plane draw close to the Jap and then a little burst of smoke and straight down into the city: the Jap plane hits the ground and bursts into flames, piling smoke almost as high as the Chinese plane that is victoriously circling his fallen foe. We cheer until we are hoarse." Another observer, Royal Leonard, a Texan pilot who flew for the Chiangs, recorded that during one attack "the Chinese pilots swarmed over [the Japanese bombers] like bees. They got under the bellies of the bombers, behind their tails, and let go bursts of machine-gun fire."

Among the Chinese pilots was a group of Chinese-Americans from Portland, Oregon, whose training the Chinese government had sponsored in a stateside aeronautical school. One of them, Arthur Chin, had also been sent to Germany for advanced training with the Luftwaffe. Chin scored his first kill in the opening days of the air battle over Nanking, but his real challenge came in a later contest when he found himself facing a Japanese squadron after he had run out of bullets. Chennault recalled how he observed Chin "deliberately ram the Jap leader as he came in for the kill. Both planes burst into flame but Art hit the silk safely." When they found him, he was "directing the salvage of the precious machine guns from his wrecked plane." Chin handed one of the weapons to Chennault and asked, "Sir, can I have another airplane for my machine gun?"

The Japanese had clearly intended the steady bombardment to break Nanking's spirit, but when Chennault walked its streets he saw its people striding with purpose, determined to go on with their lives. He heard music playing on phonographs in people's homes and savored the aromas wafting out of the "wine-shops, steaming noodle vendors, and sticky sweetshops." "China will not be cowed, no matter how much the air arm of the Japanese militarists may do," wrote the *China Press*. Life went on. Chennault and McDonald met for golf on the course behind the Nanking Country Club, played cribbage, and frequented the shops downtown. They learned to live with the air-raid sirens.

During a rainy period in the fall of 1937, Nanking was shielded by clouds that kept the bombers at bay. "Bad weather," McDonald wrote in his diary, "if only we could control this we could certainly arrange for at least two weeks of this kind of weather." There were rumors that the Japanese would return after the weather cleared with an attack that "may be the most terrible air raid the world has ever known," as one newspaper put it. This could "blow Nanking, with its 1,000,000 in-habitants, off the map." On the morning of September 25, 1937, the sun appeared, and by 9:00 A.M. the sound of approaching planes was heard. A squadron of Chinese pilots took off to defend the city, but they were too late. It soon became clear that the attackers weren't aim-ing at military targets but rather at civilians downtown. A pair of thousand-pound bombs just missed the hospital, leaving 30-foot-wide holes on the tennis courts where they landed. Many more strikes were successful, and "gallons of civilian blood flowed," a radio broadcaster reported. McDonald wrote in his diary that China would "fight to the last man."

As the attacks continued, Chennault and McDonald started each day with the same question: "What time do you think the Japs will come today?" One morning one of the Americans showed up to break-fast wrapped in a towel, as he had soiled the only pair of pants he owned during a raid, and the servants were trying to clean them. Once Billy McDonald was in the middle of getting a haircut when the alarm was sounded. "Our visit to the shop was cut short, so was our hair." The Chinese Air Force could do little to halt the assaults. The American pilots talked about growing their own ranks: "How wonderful it would be if we had a group of American-trained pilots to help fight in defense of China. At the time the idea was so far-fetched that none of us thought it might ever come about," Smith recalled.

The valiant efforts of Chennault's small force were Pyrrhic victories at best. But the dream of American reinforcements became more fervent as fighter planes fell and casualties mounted. "Only a few planes left to defend the city," McDonald wrote in his diary. The "lack of equipment" and "lack of experienced pilots" made victory seem elusive, if not impossible. Chennault despaired that the Chinese Air Force was at "the end of its rope."

Madame Chiang spent most of her days in her office writing orders on her typewriter, but there was little she could do to affect the dire situation. She kept two machine guns from downed Japanese planes next to her desk as war prizes, and like Chennault would watch the battle unfold whenever there was an air raid. She was eager to see her beloved pilots and would regularly come down to the airfield. On one such occasion, she brewed tea for the airmen while she awaited their return from a raid, and joined Chennault on the runway as the planes appeared. "The first pilot overshot and cracked up in a rice paddy. The next ground-looped and burst into flame," Chennault wrote, and in total "five out of eleven planes were wrecked and four pilots killed." Watching the chaos unfold, Madame Chiang shouted out, "What can we do, what can we do?" However much she prized her air force, she was well aware that it was incapable of defending Nanking.

As Japanese troops neared the city, Chennault prepared to get into the cockpit himself. The American mechanics readied a special plane, the Hawk 75, especially for him. Unlike the older Hawk III biplanes, this was a sleek monoplane that could achieve incredible speeds. Chennault supplied some of his own personal touches. He stripped the plane of everything inessential, to make it lighter and faster. He pulled out the radio, making a little cubby in which he could keep a bedroll, which could be useful if he was ever shot down over the wilderness. He took the Hawk 75 on long reconnaissance missions on which he "spotted troop movements and checked enemy airdromes," which revealed that it wouldn't be long before the Japanese army would reach Nanking. At one point, Chennault ordered his mechanic to "get some guns on this ship and get 'em on in a hurry."

Chennault denied up until his dying days that he ever took part in combat missions during the defense of Nanking, which would seem to violate American law. Whether Chennault's story was true, or a judicious lie, only he could confirm. The mere possibility of an American pilot fighting for China had begun to cause problems. The Associated Press had run an article about Chennault's trip to China, which had "aroused speculation" about its purpose, and now "mystery surrounded his activities there." The U.S. consul in Shanghai, Clarence Gauss, sent a cable to the State Department saying that "Colonel Chennault, retired officer United States Army Air Corps, is implicated" in combat operations. Gauss was a foreign service officer who had spent his career in China and he was carefully trying to maintain American neutrality. He was "round-shouldered from a life spent bending over a desk, with an underexposed complexion," as one of his colleagues described him. For years the Japanese had been warning that the presence of American pilots in China could spark a war, and in August 1937 things seemed to boil over as reports circulated that some thousand mercenary pilots were heading to China from the United States. Foreign Minister Koki Hirota gave a speech pushing for the United States to crack down on these renegade pilots. Of course, the men in question were former military pilots, but that distinction didn't matter to the Japanese. Secretary of State Cordell Hull, also trying to keep the United States out of this war, had the State Department issue a memo titled "American Citizens Engaging in Military Activities in China: Prohibition of," warning that Americans fighting for China could be prosecuted. To control the scale of the problem, the State Department limited the number of passports for travel to China. When a passport was issued it came with a new restriction: "This passport is not valid for travel to or in any foreign state in connection with entrance into or service in foreign military or naval forces." The mercenary pilots the press had been talking about never showed up. Chennault received direct warnings from Gauss, who threatened to have him arrested and "also intimated a court-martial and loss of citizenship were in store for me."

What Chennault and his men had believed would be a relatively brief Asian sojourn now looked as if it could land them behind bars. Fifteen of the civilian pilots with the China National Aviation Corporation (CNAC) decided to leave. An official with the airline explained that they wanted to avoid any action that could compromise U.S. neutrality. Luke Williamson left to become a pilot for Delta Air Lines.

Chennault still felt the pull of duty to remain in China and fight, but was it worth the risk? What if he wasn't able to return to his home and family? In quiet moments, when he was alone at night, he was filled with a longing for home. He wrote to a friend, "Though so far away, I felt again the soft, cool night air of Louisiana and its stillness and serenity." Whenever he received a letter from Nell he would eagerly read the updates and then brag about his sons' accomplishments: "baseball progress, motorcycle maintenance." But nostalgia was no match for his sense of destiny.

As he wrote in his diary: "All Am[ericans] Ordered to evacuate. Guess I am Chinese."

Chennault had undergone a remarkable transformation in these few months in China, for he now felt empowered as a leader and trusted as an airman. Even though he was working for a foreign country, this was his battle. "All my life I had been fighting every fight to the finish," he later wrote, "and I knew I would have to see this one through." Aware that questions would be raised in the United States about his being in China, he wrote a letter that would be published in the *Montgomery Advertiser,* offering no indication of regret for his actions, and explaining that China was "fighting the war of all the Pacific nations."

By the late fall of 1937, Nanking's air defense had all but vanished. The Imperial Japanese Army took Shanghai and moved toward Nanking, overrunning Chinese outposts along the way. Soldiers who tried to surrender were executed—a prelude to what was to come.

The Nationalist Chinese Army braced for the assault. Troops dug in behind the city's wall, behind minefields, walls of sandbags, and rows of barbed wire. "You're being watched by the entire nation, indeed by the entire world," Chiang Kai-shek told his generals. "We cannot abandon Nanking!"

But that was precisely what the city's civilian population was doing. "Rickshaws and automobiles were piled high with packing crates, bundles, furniture and humanity," a European journalist wrote. "It was impossible to find packing crates or brown paper anywhere—the shops were all sold out." Eventually Chiang determined that he, too, would have to evacuate, and told Chennault to do the same before the city fell. The Chiangs fled the doomed city on December 7.

A few weeks earlier, just before Thanksgiving, American diplomats had reached out to Chennault and his crew, inviting them to a dinner hosted by Clarence Gauss at the American embassy in Nanking. The officials "apologized, more or less, for their earlier actions in ordering Americans to depart China," Sebie Smith wrote, and assured Chennault that they wanted to help him. An American navy ship, the U.S.S. *Panay,* was docked in the Yangtze River, and would offer Chennault and his men safe passage out of the city.

On December 2, the embassy issued a "final warning to all Americans that they should withdraw from Nanking as soon as possible," and told them that if they didn't seek refuge on the *Panay* their escape might be "impossible." As the city descended into chaos, a handful of American journalists packed their bags, piled into a Chevy truck, and made their way down to the *Panay.* The evacuation felt like a defeat to men like Norm Alley, a cameraman whose creed was "go to hell if you must—*but bring back pictures of it.*"

Before dawn on December 4, Chennault drove out to the airfield with a few remaining Americans, including Sebie Smith. The burning oil depots illuminated the dark sky, and machine-gun fire was too close for comfort. Smith was able to hitch a ride in one of the last Boeing transports to leave Nanking, but Chennault wanted to depart in his own plane, the Hawk 75.

"I taxied out to the end of the runway in the dark and waited with engine idling and hand on throttle for the first faint streaks of dawn to break over the city wall and light my take-off," he later wrote. As the sun began to rise, he could see enough of the runway, littered with bomb craters, to take off. He rose over the city one final time, and as he looked back, the rising sun cast "a pink glow over the stricken city, which gradually changed to a prophetic bloody red."

When Nanking fell into the hands of the Japanese, the occupying forces dispatched "barbaric cruelties" on the city's residents, as Tillman Durdin, the *New York Times* correspondent who stayed behind, described the ensuing bloodshed. Japanese soldiers went house to house taking whatever they pleased—including the bodies of the Chinese women. Minnie Vautrin, an American missionary teacher at Ginling College, a small Christian school for women, opened the gates of the school and allowed an estimated ten thousand women to fill its small campus. She was hoping to shield them from the horror that was unfolding in the streets. When the Japanese soldiers demanded that she unlock a door to a building where women were hiding, she refused. A soldier slapped her in the face but she didn't back down. She wrote in her diary: "I have heard scores of heartbreaking stories of girls who were taken from their homes." The night was filled with horrible screams: "Tonight a truck passed in which there were eight or ten girls, and as it passed they called out '*Jiu Ming! Jiu Ming!*' (save our lives) . . . Oh, God, control the cruel beastliness of the soldiers in Nanking tonight. . . ."

The Japanese soldiers soon broke through the locked doors into the college. She chased after them but when she got to room 538 of the Faculty House she was too late—there was already a Japanese soldier "raping a poor girl."

The most appalling horrors of what would become known as the Rape of Nanking involved what Iris Chang called "sexual torture." Japanese soldiers raped untold numbers of women, some soldiers even using a beer bottle, golf stick, or, in one case, a firecracker, whose explosion killed its victim. "The Japanese drew sadistic pleasure in forcing Chinese men to commit incest—fathers to rape their own daughters, brothers their sisters, sons their mothers," Chang wrote. After being raped, the women were usually killed. Women weren't the only victims. Japanese soldiers stripped a Chinese man naked and then unleashed German shepherds on him.

John Rabe, a German industrialist with the Siemens Corporation and member of the Nazi Party, was horrified by what he witnessed. Germany was not yet formally allied with Japan, and in fact had been trying to maintain some balance in its relations with Japan and China. During the aerial bombardments, Rabe had put out a massive Nazi flag on his property to warn the Japanese bombers to stay away, and he allowed Chinese civilians to seek refuge on his land. As the Japanese rampaged through the city, Rabe put on his Nazi armband and tried to patrol the streets, shouting at a Japanese soldier he saw assaulting a young woman. He wrote a scathing report to Hitler, denouncing the atrocities committed by the Japanese soldiers, saying "I saw the victims with my own eyes."

A few days after the occupation began, the remaining American journalists acknowledged that the time had come to flee. Tillman Durdin was boarding a boat to Shanghai when he saw some two hundred Chinese men being held by Japanese soldiers. As he would write in the *New York Times,* he looked on in horror as "the men were lined against a wall and shot. Then a number of Japanese, armed with pistols, trod nonchalantly around the crumpled bodies, pumping bullets into any that were still kicking." It turned out that Chennault was fortunate to not seek refuge aboard the *Panay.* On December 12, Japanese warplanes attacked the ship, killing three Americans and wounding more than forty. For a moment, it seemed like the type of international incident that could lead to a conflict. Americans, including President Roosevelt himself, were outraged about the attack, but Japanese officials issued an apology and paid an indemnity. They claimed their pilots hadn't seen the ship's American flags.

After the loss of Nanking, Chiang Kai-shek struck a defiant tone: "We may have suffered defeats on the battlefield, but that doesn't mean that the war is over." A new capital was established in Hankow (modern-day Hankou), four hundred miles up the Yangtze River. A port town that had hosted foreign military ships, its foreign concessions gave the city a European flair. To foreigners, Hankow was known as the "Chicago of China" because of its incredible industrial production. Arriving in the dead of winter, Chennault had to contend with worsening bronchitis—a seemingly annual malady he suffered, for which he drank cod liver oil to help soothe the inflammation.

Hankow was preparing to become the next battleground, and the mission to defend it was an international effort. It included a group of German advisers who had been helping Chiang for years, led by Alexander von Falkenhausen, a lanky sixty-year-old general who could often be seen wearing a suit and fedora as he walked his dachshunds. Falkenhausen wasn't an ideological Nazi, but a longtime German soldier who had spent years deployed to China and had become devoted to its cause. Using his experience in trench warfare during the Great War, he was instructing China's soldiers on earthworks. To supplement the Chinese Air Force, planes and pilots had been dispatched by the Soviet Union. "Olive-drab Russian planes bearing the blue and white Chinese sunflower insignia began arriving in Hankow by the dozens," historian Edward Leiser wrote. Chennault found the Russians to be an impressive group: "On duty the Russians enforced iron discipline. In contrast to the American custom of standing alert duty lounging or playing poker in an alert shack, the Russians sat stiffly all day long in their cramped cockpits."

Chennault had a group of fewer than a dozen expat American pilots who had refused to evacuate China. He was grateful to have this handful of Americans, and soon more were coming. Chinese diplomats had been engaging in a quiet effort to enlist Western pilots, some of whom were expats already in the Far East. These were true "mercenary pilots," as Sebie Smith called them. Most were American, but there was a smattering of French and German pilots, too. Some claimed that they had been fighting with the Republicans in Spain, but there was no way for Chennault to authenticate any of their backstories.

Together they became known as the International Squadron. They commandeered a group of five rooms in a hostel, the Anlee House, that quickly became their de facto headquarters. As these new recruits trickled into Hankow, Chennault was faced with the daunting challenge of determining which of these vagabonds could actually fly. He was suspicious, for example, of a "young lad who exhibited a stack of logbooks in which he had listed a total of twelve thousand hours flying time." He asked Billy McDonald to take him out for a test flight, and as they reached the flying line, the young man became pale. "I guess I better not," he blurted out. "I've never flown a plane before."

Word of this operation didn't stay secret for long. Leaks about the

debacle soon started reaching the press. "Hired abroad at fabulous salaries," the *Washington Post* reported, "many of these men were found,
on their arrival, to be adventurers out for a free trip across the Pacific."
Even the men who were legitimate airmen weren't particularly good.
"He has no military training and so should not have come to China,"
read the report on one. "Can fly, but not very well," said another.

But as Chennault assessed his candidates, he did find some excellent
fliers, including Elwyn Gibbon, a former army pilot. His reviews described him as "excellent" and a "valuable man." Chennault liked
what he saw in the twenty-six-year-old with the dimpled chin and the
tattoo of a sailing ship on his arm. He gave Gibbon the honor of piloting his beloved Hawk 75.

Gibbon grew up in Seattle, and he was only thirteen when four
Douglas World Cruisers took off from a nearby lake in the first successful attempt to circumnavigate the globe by air. Aviation was in the air
and he had his eyes set on flying. When he was old enough, he joined
the army and became a pilot. His career dead-ended when he wound up
in an army hospital with stomach ulcers. After the army released him
he found a job in the Philippines as a pilot transporting parts and supplies to remote mines. When a Chinese consulate officer approached
him with an offer to fly for China he accepted on one condition—he
could bring his wife, Toni, with him. It was a deal. Gibbon could tell
that he was in for a remarkable journey under Chennault's command in
Hankow. "I imagine that we are the oddest part of this odd war. We've
come from a half-dozen corners of the globe," he wrote, but still "have
as much *esprit de corps* as squadrons in most regular forces."

Another standout in this new crop was Vincent Schmidt, a six-
footer who seemed to live in his dark leather jacket. Details about his
background were never certain, but he claimed that he'd been a professional soldier of fortune for twenty years, and that this would be his
sixth war. After serving as an artillery adviser in the Great War, he'd
left America, and according to a profile in the *South China Morning
Post,* he fought in the "Mexican revolutionary war, the Shanghai fighting of 1932. He fought in Spain with the Loyalists, in Ethiopia with the
Negus." This mercenary lived by one rule: "I fight with the underdog."

CHAPTER 4

THE INTERNATIONAL SQUADRON

At 1:00 P.M. on January 4, 1938, an air-raid siren rang out across Hankow for the first time. A wild scramble ensued as thousands fought their way to the dugouts, cellars, and warehouses they hoped would keep them safe during the bombardment. A Reuters reporter described how the crowds cleared out, leaving Hankow a ghost city where "not a sound was heard." The silence was short-lived. As the drone of enemy aircraft in the distance grew louder, Chinese antiaircraft guns thundered. Smoke littered the sky where their shells exploded, but still the Japanese bombers emerged from the clouds unscathed.

As civilians were hiding, a car raced through the streets. Elwyn Gibbon had one hand firmly on the horn as he barreled toward the airfield. A rickshaw darted out in front of him and he tugged at the wheel, narrowly missing it. "I keep my foot on the gas—keep the car moving," he wrote. The crowds cleared out and he shifted the car into high gear. The clock was ticking.

Elwyn Gibbon climbed into the cockpit of the Hawk 75 as the bombers neared their targets, desperate to get off the ground before the bombs fell. It was very cold out. One of the Frenchmen tried to crank the propeller, cursing as the cold motor refused to let out more than a whine. The man cranked it once more. "This time," Gibbon wrote, "the motor catches, barks, and roars with the propeller vanishing in a shiny arc."

The Frenchman ducked out of the way. Gibbon shoved the throttle forward and the plane gained speed down the runway, finally lifting off into a steep ascent. He climbed to twelve thousand feet, the snow-covered rice paddies of the Yangtze plain receding below. The bombers released their payloads in line, leaving columns of orange flame and black smoke lifting skyward from their targets.

Gibbon spotted them as they were turning back and turned in pursuit. As he closed in at 280 miles per hour he could make out the "red rising suns on their wings." Time seemed to slow. He would later recall: "I looked through my ring sight, and the first Japanese airplane settles into the center." He felt calm and detached, as if he were watching the enemy planes in a motion picture. He felt a surge of adrenaline as his forefinger tightened on the trigger and then he pulled. Four bursts of flame rushed from his machine guns. He pulled again. The bullets flashed from his wings as the Japanese bomber started to tumble off to one side. He sped past, narrowly missing the plane, and glanced back over his shoulder. He couldn't see whether it had fallen, but he did see two enemy fighters now tailing him. He knew that if he kept his course he would be easy prey. His only choice was to plummet below the clouds, hoping to lose the Japanese planes in a power dive.

It was a risky maneuver that could prove fatal if he lost consciousness as the g-forces drained the blood from his head during the pullout, but Gibbon took that chance as he pushed his stick forward. The nose of the plane lurched down and the altimeter began to spin violently. The gravity tore at his stomach and jerked his jaw open like a broken hinge. "It squeezed me down in the seat," he would write, "as though some giant had shoved me into it with all his weight in one, great lunging push." He fought against the g-forces and the plane's momentum to bring it back to level. When he regained his bearings, he looked behind him. The Japanese planes were nowhere to be seen.

Gibbon headed for the runway and landed the plane. "I climb out of the ship and stand on the firm ground and begin to realize how much the last hour has taken out of me," Gibbon recalled. "I hold one hand up and look at it curiously. It is steady as a rock. But the furious sense of need for concentration will not leave me. I am tightened up inside by a taut, twanging exhaustion. . . . It is an effort to move my feet."

A crowd had gathered to meet him on the runway.

"Well, I think I got one of them. I had my guns right on him," he said.

Other forays bore mixed results. A Chinese aviator had managed to engage some of the Japanese planes in a dogfight but the Chinese plane was hit and crash-landed in a cabbage field. Soon there was more speculation about these American airmen. The *New York Times* reported that another American pilot, identified as Frederick Kreuzberg, had in fact been killed in combat during that opening battle. "It is believed he was shot down by the Japanese during Tuesday's air raid here. If this is true, Kreuzberg is the first American aviator reported killed while engaged in actual air combat for the Chinese in the Chino-Japanese hostilities."

The screech of the air siren would become a familiar part of the daily routine for the citizens of Hankow. As the air raids continued, the airmen under Chennault's command tried to defend the city as best they could. "Foreign pilots have become the backbone of the Chinese Air Force," the *China Weekly Review* reported.

Despite the knowledge of the extreme dangers the pilots faced, Elwyn Gibbon felt invulnerable. "I can't really believe I will be killed," he wrote. He noted a "crazy kind of fear" overtook him when he flew into combat—crazy because instead of paralyzing him it propelled him into battle. "I've been scared green. But that is routine, too, now, a familiar part of the existence that has come to seem orderly and usual. If you ever played football you got used to getting scared every Saturday before a game. Fear can give you a clairvoyant insight into things that happen in split seconds, and sometimes a kind of crazy strength."

While Gibbon was flying, his wife, Toni, waited nervously in the apartment they'd been given close to the river. She could see the bomb impacts and smoke from the landing field in the distance through the big double windows in her bedroom, she wrote a friend, "each burst of noise tearing at my nerves and making my heart jump and pound." When Elwyn returned, relief would pour over her in waves. Amid all the upheaval of Elwyn's combat missions, the couple tried to maintain some sense of normalcy. They found a favorite restaurant for dinners out. She would get the crispy fish and he would order chicken dumplings. They drank tea with flower blossoms at the bottom and small cups of rice wine. Like any young couple back home, they went out on the town. There was a line of bars and cabarets on Dump Street in Hankow where they drank with some of the other pilots, trying to let loose because, as Gibbon put it, "unpleasant things might happen to me tomorrow."

One night, Toni and Elwyn were dancing at a nightclub to the rhythm of a swing band when an air-raid siren screamed over the music and the lights went out. The full moon outside had provided just enough light for Japanese bombers to strike in the dark, but the band didn't stop playing and the bartenders just kept mixing more drinks in the pitch-black club. Gibbon went outside and his eyes followed the searchlight beams into the sky. He couldn't see the bombers but he could hear the faint, metallic drone of planes high above. Then the night exploded with a flurry of antiaircraft shells. Gibbon could see fire where the enemy bombs were landing, and though the party went on that night, he had seen enough of "modern war being waged," he wrote. "Swing music is an anticlimax after a show like a raid."

The brutality of the war, the endless bombings, and the futility of their mission, so mightily overmatched by the enemy, began to wear on members of the International Squadron. The spark that had brought these young pilots to fight in Hankow began to fade. It didn't help that the bonus they'd been promised for shooting down Japanese planes failed to materialize. As Vincent Schmidt said, the Chinese government, "under one pretext or another, refused to pay the prize." There was even a dispute about their travel expenses, and a Chinese general told them that their request for more money was denied.

The reality was that they had never been a particularly functional unit. Chennault would write that these pilots "subsisted entirely on high-octane beverages" found at the bars of Dump Street. Neither employers nor employees were happy, and the decision was made to disband the unit.

Most of the men decided that they'd head back to the United States. Sebie Smith decided that his time had come. He had a fiancée waiting for him back home and he hoped that she was still there when he got back. Even Chennault seemed to waver. In a letter home to his father he wrote, "farming and country life has its compensations."

Ultimately Chennault made the same choice he always made: to stay in China. But Toni and Elwyn Gibbon decided to join the migration homeward. The Gibbons took a train to Shanghai and in April 1938 boarded a Canadian passenger liner. After months of air raids in Hankow, the peaceful voyage promised to be a reprieve.

On the way home, the ship made a scheduled stop in Yokohama. The Japanese police were known to search foreign ships for spies and criminals, and they boarded the ship to conduct an inspection. As the police searched cabin by cabin, Toni stashed away Elwyn's packet of papers that included his battle maps from China, but he had a problem. Almost a month before the ship docked in Japan, Elwyn's name had been published in the *New York Times* as a member of the "foreign legion of the air" that was being disbanded in China. The Japanese police seemed to know what—or whom—they were looking for. When they found Elwyn, they took him to the Grand Hotel for questioning. His papers identified him as a mining engineer and he stuck to that story during a three-hour interrogation. The bluff seemed to work and the police let him go back to the ship. A foreign correspondent saw him during his detention at the Grand Hotel and yelled out questions at him. "You heard what I said," Elwyn responded. "I am a mining operator who flies sometimes."

It seemed his story would hold up, but the next morning, just half an hour before the ship was set to weigh anchor, the police returned to arrest him. All Toni could do was watch as her husband was led off the ship. The *New York Times* ran the story: AMERICAN IS HELD IN JAPANESE JAIL.

The cell, which already held five Japanese prisoners, was tiny. Gibbon paced, measuring it out to be eight by twelve feet. His fate was out of his hands.

For years the Japanese had been protesting that American pilots were fighting in China and now they had caught one red-handed. Gibbon eventually dropped his cover and admitted to his interrogators that, yes, he had served as an instructor in the Chinese Air Force, but that he had done so only as a contractor and was heading home, never to return. The Japanese officials said that Gibbon was being held in violation of a criminal law because he'd fought for an enemy power. An interpreter read the Japanese law to him and explained that he could be executed for fighting for a foreign power. "I thought my number was up."

After Elwyn had been taken captive, Toni sent a telegram to Gibbon's brother, a lawyer in Seattle: "ELWYN TAKEN BY JAPS AT YOKOHAMA STOP DO SOMETHING. . . ." That message set off an effort to get her husband out of jail that began with the two senators from the state of Washington, then worked its way to the State Department. This was exactly the kind of scenario that the State Department had been afraid the freelance pilots fighting in China would provoke. If Gibbon died in Japanese custody, it could set off a chain reaction that led to war. In Tokyo, Ambassador Joseph Grew demanded Gibbon's release. There were reports that he was suffering from ill treatment and meager prison rations. But there was hope. The United Press reported that Japan's "high authorities advised against drastic procedure in Gibbon's case because it might react unfavorably abroad." The Japanese, not wanting to draw the United States into a war in the Pacific, were likely just as anxious as American officials to avoid a trial that would ratchet up tensions, the *New York Times* reported.

On April 26, after three days of captivity, Japanese officials ordered that no charges be filed. Gibbon was released that day into the care of American diplomats. A few days later he set out for Hawaii aboard the *President Taft.* With rumors that Japanese vigilantes might try to shoot him before he left Yokohama, the American diplomats were happy to see him go.

From Hawaii, Gibbon boarded the *Empress of Canada,* which finally took him to Seattle, where he was reunited with Toni at the dock. He recounted for reporters how the Japanese were "merciless in their grilling and kept repeating their threats. I was questioned on one occasion for 15 hours straight." During a stop at Honolulu, a reporter had tried to get to the truth behind the whole affair: "Did you shoot down any Japanese?" Gibbon demurred, "I better not say anything about that." Gibbon took a job as a pilot with TWA, and he and Toni settled into a quiet life in a cabin outside of Seattle.

Still, he kept up an occasional correspondence with Chennault. Despite the ordeal of his imprisonment, he missed the excitement of combat. Chennault's messages hinted at some cryptic plans about a project that might give him a chance to return to China later. "I can't divulge any of the details by letter and am not sure that the thing will materialize," he wrote. "If it does, I assure you that you will like it and that I'll count you in the outfit."

As the war dragged on, the United States was emerging as one of the last hopes for China. Hitler, eager to strengthen his relations with Japan, ordered the withdrawal of German advisers. Von Falkenhausen had grown attached to China's cause, but after some stalling decided that he would have to follow his orders. Still, "I feel sure of China gaining a final victory," he said. On July 5, 1938, twenty-eight German soldiers boarded a train that bore a large Nazi flag on the roof to keep it safe from Japanese bombers. Von Falkenhausen bent down through the window to shake hands with a Chinese officer standing on the platform and waved good-bye as the train pulled out of the station.

On the Fourth of July, the few Americans still in Hankow marked Independence Day. The "last ditchers," as they called themselves, gathered at the Hankow Race Club to grill hot dogs, drink Cokes, and play a game of baseball against the Brits. Chennault was the pitcher. He would spit on the glove and then go into an elaborate windup before throwing the ball. With the game on the line, an Englishman connected and sent the ball soaring deep into left field. A hapless outfielder ran to intercept the ball, but couldn't catch up, allowing three runs to score. Chennault let the player know his displeasure. He didn't like losing in war or in baseball.

The outfielder was a young missionary from Chicago, Paul Frillmann. Chennault wouldn't remember their brief encounter, but for the missionary it was a pivotal point, fated to change the course of his life in ways he couldn't see on that sunny afternoon.

Not long after, Chennault received orders from Madame Chiang to go to Kunming, deep in the mountains of Yunnan Province. Once again he would engage in what he called "the seemingly hopeless task of forging a new Chinese Air Force from an American mold."

As the Japanese army moved toward Hankow, Chiang Kai-shek understood his forces could not stop the onslaught for long, but he was grimly determined to keep true to his pledge of total resistance, whatever the cost. In a final desperate measure, he ordered the breaching of the dikes on the Yellow River, hoping the resulting floodwaters could wash away the Japanese advance. But the Japanese were still able to advance on Hankow, and the "drowned earth," as it came to be known, would remain a hushed topic in China for decades after. Contemporary estimates are that the floodwaters killed around half a million people and turned three to five million Chinese civilians into refugees.

As Japanese troops entered the suburbs of Hankow on October 24, Chiang Kai-shek and Madame Chiang had to evacuate once more. It was snowing as they lifted off from the airfield on a flight deep into China's interior. They would ultimately make their way to Chungking (modern-day Chongqing), the city that would be China's new capital.

The Chiangs and Chennault made it safely out of Hankow, but many others weren't as fortunate. Japanese forces took the city on October 25, 1938. The United Press reported "several cases of rape by Japanese soldiers," one involving the bayoneting of a Chinese woman trying to protect her fourteen-year-old daughter, and another in which "four soldiers successively raped a young girl."

Paul Frillmann had remained in Hankow. Horrified by the reports of rape, he crowded over five hundred women into a Lutheran mission. At night, he roamed the outer walls of the compound, looking for Japanese soldiers trying to climb over the barrier. He carried a broken .38 Luger pistol in his belt and kept his German shepherd close. If he encountered a Japanese soldier, he would brandish the pistol and point to the American flag overhead as the dog barked furiously. Even Frillmann was surprised when his bluff worked, and the Japanese soldiers left the mission and the women inside it alone.

Despite such small acts of resistance, the fall of Hankow underscored for many China's capitulation. Walter Lippmann, America's preeminent columnist, wrote: "The Japanese have won the war, and the operations from now on are likely to be not much more than the mopping up that follows any great victory." In Tokyo, a one-minute siren announced the capture of the city. A parade of unprecedented scope, with thousands carrying lanterns and singing patriotic songs, marched to the Imperial Palace. Emperor Hirohito, who rarely appeared in public, walked onto the bridge over the palace's moat as the crowd cheered ferociously. But no matter what anyone in Washington or in Tokyo thought, Chiang Kai-shek refused to consider the war over at all. The fall of Hankow marked the end of the first period in the hostilities, he said. The war "is only just beginning."

CHAPTER 5

EXILE IN THE CHINESE HINTERLAND

By the final months of 1938, Claire Chennault's new home, Kunming, would become one of China's last centers of resistance. The city was far up in the mountains, remote, and like no place Chennault had ever seen before. He took in the sights: creaking pony carts rattled and groaned over Kunming's cobbled streets, and water buffalo, cattle, and herds of fat pigs wandered among the pepper trees that lined the main street. But the pastoral calm was giving way to a feeling of rush and bustle. Refugees flooded in from the front but the city was transforming itself into an industrial center that could help keep China fighting. There was still hope. Out in the jungle along the Burma border, William Pawley's aviation company, the Central Aircraft Manufacturing Company, known as CAMCO, was assembling new fighter planes. The facility had been moved with the war, and this site came to be known as Pawleyville, named for CAMCO's owner. It was an important part of the strategy to replenish the depleted armaments of the Chinese Air Force.

Although Shanghai, Nanking, and now Hankow had fallen, the war seemed to have come to a stalemate. The mountains protecting Kunming made it difficult for Japanese armored units to advance rapidly, and the enemy appeared to be focused on maintaining control of the occupied territories. The Japanese bombed Chungking and sometimes even reached Kunming, but the stalled war on the ground gave the Chinese a chance to regroup for the long war ahead.

Chennault's job was formidable. He was the lead instructor at the Central Aviation School, which had been moved from Hangchow. This was the hub for teaching a new generation of Chinese pilots. The *New York Times* reported that hundreds of young men were receiving instruction in modern aerial warfare using scores of American and Russian training planes. Chennault noted in his diary that these new cadets were "below average, some were very bad," but he kept at it, and soon in the dusty streets of the old city, Kunming's residents could hear the drone of airplane engines and see the aircraft sweeping overhead, encouraging signs that the students were making progress.

Chennault had a group of approximately fifteen American pilots working at his side, including Billy McDonald, who wrote to his parents that "life now is rather tame in comparison with our earlier experiences at Nanking." For the first time since his arrival in China, Chennault could relax. He played tennis at the Kunming French Club and there were games of poker and cribbage with friends. The theater showed old movies, and that was where he spent his evenings.

Still, it was impossible to forget that there was a war going on. Chennault carefully logged each Japanese bombing raid in his diary. "23 Jap bombers came over about 3:00 P.M. in three units," he wrote on April 8, 1939. "None shot down." For now, Chennault couldn't muster the planes or pilots to turn back the bombers.

In early May 1939, Chennault traveled to Chungking, now the capital, and saw the resumption of Japanese air strikes. On the afternoon of May 3, he heard the air-raid siren ring out and grabbed his binoculars. He recounted standing on a hill, and seeing overhead a formation of twenty-seven Japanese bombers flying in a perfect V. For a moment they looked just "like Canada geese heading north from Louisiana in the spring." Their bomb bays opened and they unloaded their deadly cargo on the city. After the bombing, Chennault hurried to join the fire brigades as they battled the flames with hand pumps and bucket brigades. It was like "trying to quench a forest fire with a garden hose," he thought. Amid the "exploding bamboo sparks and crashing wooden walls," he would never forget the "sickeningly sweet stench" of corpses burning in the wreckage. The Japanese came back again the next day, May 4, and the results were even worse. "Large section of city set on fire and burned," Chennault wrote in his diary, "many people killed."

"Many" was an understatement. Approximately four thousand people were killed in those back-to-back raids, making them two of the most devastating air attacks in history up to that point.

"This is the most terrible thing I've seen in my life," Chiang Kai-shek wrote in his diary. "I can't bear to look at it." Madame Chiang despaired that the war was destroying China: "The bombs have reduced rich and poor, wise and stupid to one common level—pieces of burnt flesh which are extracted from the smoldering piles with tongs."

The war felt hopeless, and after more than two years in China, Chennault's longing for home was growing. The one connection the American pilots in Kunming had to the outside world was a radio kept in McDonald's apartment that would beam in music from stations in Manila, Hong Kong, and Hanoi. McDonald would fiddle with the channels to find the clearest signals amid the static. One day when he was scanning for new stations, he suddenly heard an American voice broadcasting from a station in California coming in loud and clear. "[My] hair just stood on end. Chennault and I got up and cheered mightily." He wrote to the station, thanking them and asking them to play the 1936 hit song "Is It True What They Say About Dixie":

> *Is it true what they say about Dixie?*
> *Does the sun really shine all the time?*

Chennault had a provision in his contract that allowed him to take a vacation, and he began to feel that the time had come. He decided he would try to make it home for Christmas, then return to Kunming in early 1940 to continue pilot training.

When Chennault returned to Chungking in September 1939 to meet with the Chiangs, he must have worried his employers would not want him leaving at such a critical time. But they saw an opportunity. Increasingly isolated from their allies in Italy and Germany, they believed Chennault could help persuade the United States to step up support of their struggle against the invading Japanese. His journey would become more than a trip home to see his family. He would be an emissary for China, pleading for assistance in a war they were on the brink of losing.

As the China Clipper went out into the bay in Hong Kong on the morning of October 19, 1939, the four Pratt & Whitney engines began to roar, pushing the plane's full weight of twenty-six tons against the water and slowly lifting it into the air to begin its multileg journey from Hong Kong to San Francisco. The largest plane of its day, the China Clipper was a Martin M-130. The Clipper was famous for its luxury: there was a lounge stocked with board games and a small library, and stewards in white suits served hot meals, like chicken fricassee. Chennault didn't fixate on the amenities, though. He cared more about the tremendous power of the airplane. He carefully tracked the plane's progress to each stop along its route: the Philippines, Guam, Wake Island, and Hawaii. The plane reached San Francisco after five days—a vast improvement in travel time over the weeks it would take on a ship. There Chennault boarded a Southern Pacific train crossing the Southwest. In Houston he transferred onto a train to Beaumont, Texas, where one of his sons was waiting to drive him to Waterproof.

"Home again," was all he wrote in his diary.

It had been over two years since Chennault last touched American soil, and now he reveled in the idyllic country life that he'd missed so much. His boys had grown to be young men, and Rosemary was now eleven. While her husband was away, Nell had a full life in the small town of just over five hundred. She had become involved with the Waterproof United Methodist Church, where she taught Sunday school, and was known for her quiet charm and friendliness. Life on the farm, which provided almost all of the family's food, kept her busy. While she looked forward to finding the occasional letter from her husband in the tin mailbox at the end of the dirt driveway, China was little more to her than a glimmer in her imagination. Her husband had increasingly become a distant memory during the years he was away. He arrived now seemingly out of nowhere. While Claire wanted to shape history on a grand scale in China, Nell was content to stroll through the orchard of pecan trees and fruit trees behind the house. Inevitably, the pair found their marriage in a precarious position now that they were reunited.

After only a few days at home, Chennault was off again, this time to observe the massive rearmament program that was under way and to try to press China's case. He first went to see his son John, who was stationed with the Army Air Corps at Selfridge Field, outside of Detroit. The new vigor in the Air Corps impressed him, and he was filled with fatherly pride to see his son follow in his footsteps. The droves of new pilots were a striking contrast to the cutbacks he'd seen when he was in the army.

Chennault alluded in his diary to working on "contracts" to get more aircraft for China, and now he wanted to get out and see the planes for himself. With new companies popping up across the United States and investment in military planes spurring innovation throughout the industry, the country was experiencing an aviation explosion. Chennault went to Buffalo, New York, to see his old friend Burdette Wright. One of the legends of early aviation, Wright had won a Distinguished Service Cross during the Great War for attacking enemy positions with his damaged plane and causing the Germans to abandon their posts. Burdette, who was not related to the famous Wright brothers, left the Air Corps after the war to become vice president of Curtiss-Wright, the premier airplane manufacturer in America, and to run their factory in Buffalo. The company churned out thousands of planes, including the Hawk 75, and the Buffalo plant was considered to be among the most advanced aircraft manufacturing facilities in the world. The factory was guarded like a military installation, and Chennault received a privileged view into an unparalleled technological marvel: new advances like automatic reaming machines and hydraulic presses manufactured plane parts en masse. Curtiss was planning to increase production to keep up with demand for fighters by the French Air Ministry, and Chennault could envision how much difference such fighters could make in the war against the Japanese if they could be sent to China.

To gin up support for China, Chennault traveled to Washington, D.C., to brief the staff of the Army Air Corps on developments in China. He knew it would be a hard sell, but even his low expectations weren't met. When he arrived for the meeting, it took over an hour for the officers to locate a large-scale map of China, and the one they did finally produce had such little detail that Chennault had to pencil in most of the locations where the war was actually being fought. He gave his presentation, but the officers showed little interest. Chennault thought it was his responsibility as an ex-army officer to warn the Air Corps about the capabilities of the Japanese planes, and he handed over his dossier of intelligence, but he felt it would be ignored.

Discouraged and disgusted, Chennault returned to Louisiana for Christmas, and though being home for the holidays was simple and inviting, he wasn't there to stay. He felt that China needed him, but it was equally true that he needed China. The war had given him a chance to be part of something larger than himself. "Nell seemed to have made a life for herself in Waterproof," biographer Jack Samson wrote, and "after the novelty of having their father home had worn off, his children had plunged back into the world of their friends and activities, jobs and school." Increasingly Chennault felt more of a foreigner in Waterproof than he had in Kunming. In January 1940, he bid farewell to his family with no indication of when he might return.

Before Chennault crossed the Pacific once more, he stopped in Los Angeles for a meeting with William Pawley. Southern California had emerged as an important area in America's aviation renaissance. Thanks to the dry, mild climate, planes could be built outside, and an array of companies had opened manufacturing facilities to keep up with the growing demand from the government. Pawley took Chennault to tour the Lockheed, North American Aviation, and Vultee factories in Los Angeles, then the Consolidated Aircraft and Ryan Aircraft factories down in San Diego. "No doubt [Chennault] was quietly and discreetly feeling out the prospects" of getting more planes for China, his biographer Martha Byrd wrote.

After the tour, Chennault flew to San Francisco, where he spent a couple of days socializing with some of the city's prominent Chinese residents, then boarded the China Clipper and headed across the Pacific once again. When they landed in Hong Kong after the endless blue of the Pacific, the winter air hung heavy. Madame Chiang was in Hong Kong to see a doctor and, according to one account, had dinner with Chennault the evening he arrived. If she hoped that he would have good news from the United States, she was disappointed; all he could tell her was that America seemed indifferent to China's plight. For now, China would have to continue to fight on its own.

Chennault arrived back in Kunming in February. During the quiet months of winter, thick fog shielded Kunming from enemy attacks, and Chennault could pass the time playing poker and tennis. There was a small social circuit in Kunming, and he got to know the wives of some of the men as well. A younger Chinese woman, Kasey Sutter, was married to Harry Sutter, a Swiss businessman in Kunming. Although Chennault had a friendly business relationship with Harry, he still invited Kasey to join him at social events. There may have been something more than a social relationship: Jack Samson has said that Chennault had affairs with Kasey and with another woman while he was in Kunming. In any case, his distance, physical and possibly emotional, from Nell and Louisiana had never been greater. He knew the bombings would return when the weather cleared and he had little idea when, if ever, he would make it home again.

With spring and the lifting of the fog, the bombing returned with a fury, bringing "thick columns of smoke, angry tongues of flames, the crackling of burning houses . . . and the incessant sputter of machine guns," as Madame Chiang described it. In the midst of a bombardment, Madame Chiang wrote to a Wellesley friend living in New York. "The bombers are circling overhead," she wrote. "They come in formation—in droves—looking like enormous black crows." She even described the dropping of the bombs: "Thud, thud, thud!" Chennault, too, was growing despondent over the situation. "We are not doing well out here," he wrote in a letter on July 24. "I can't win the d[amn] war alone and I am tired of fighting almost alone against such odds that we face."

Chennault's growing sense of isolation wasn't helped in April when Billy McDonald left to take a job as a pilot for CNAC in Hong Kong. "What I like about this job is that it has a future," he wrote to his father. Left unsaid, but implied, was the obvious contrast with fighting for China, which did not.

Worse was still to come. On September 13, a group of Chinese pilots flying Russian-made I-15 and I-16 fighters took to the air to fend off a raid. The Japanese bombers completed the run and then withdrew. Once the Chinese planes were in pursuit, Japanese fighters dove from out of the sun and opened fire. The Chinese pilots scrambled to defend themselves, but the enemy planes were faster and more agile than any the Chinese had ever encountered. Within half an hour, more than twenty Chinese planes had been lost—a massive blow to the Chinese Air Force. It was an unqualified disaster. Chennault mused that the Chinese had been shot down before they even knew what hit them. What had hit them was a new Japanese plane, the Mitsubishi A6M. It would come to be known by a simpler name: the Zero, and it would be feared not just in China, but throughout the Pacific.

Victory had never felt more distant. A mere two weeks after the rout, on September 27, 1940, Germany and Italy signed a new treaty with Japan, the Tripartite Pact, which cemented their military alliance with Tokyo. The geostrategic plates were shifting. By April 1941, the Japanese and the Soviets, both now aligned with Nazi Germany, would sign a nonaggression pact—a diplomatic shift that would leave China increasingly isolated on the world stage.

Meanwhile, as China struggled for its survival, Chiang Kai-shek knew he could no longer afford to rely on his old allies. Though he had received only a limited number of American planes, the United States increasingly appeared to be China's best hope. In Chungking on October 18, 1940, Chiang met with U.S. ambassador Nelson Johnson and begged for more planes. China needed, he said, five hundred to a thousand planes a year and "it is also hoped that American volunteers will be able to aid us in carrying on hostilities." He pleaded that the situation was dire. It wouldn't be long until "the people's spirit and sentiment might become so disturbed as to render the situation impossible of support." It was a stark warning, but one that went unheeded. Chiang had diplomats in Washington working on getting more aid for China, but he decided to add an American.

On October 20, Chennault received an urgent summons to come to Chungking. He flew in the next day and went to the Chiang residence. The Generalissimo launched into his plan: he wanted to buy the latest American fighters and hire American pilots to fly them. When asked his opinion, Chennault replied that he was pessimistic because of the overwhelming indifference most Americans felt toward China. Chiang was undeterred.

"You must go to the United States immediately," he ordered. "Work out the plans for whatever you think you need. Do what you can to get American planes and pilots." "Ordered back to the U.S. for duty," Chennault wrote in his diary. Once again, he boarded the China Clipper and the plane "settled down in a plume of spray at the now familiar milestones." The long trip gave him plenty of time to ponder his chance to shape history.

CHAPTER 6

AN AIR UNIT FOR CHINA

Washington, D.C., was cold when Chennault arrived on November 15, 1940. Storms had drenched the city for days. The city was abuzz over the upcoming inauguration of Franklin Roosevelt, who had just been reelected and would become the first U.S. president to be sworn in for a third term.

Chennault followed his instructions to report to Chiang's personal representative (and brother-in-law), T. V. Soong, at his stately home on Woodley Road. Soong explained to Chennault that they would be launching a lobbying campaign for planes and pilots for China.

Like his sister Madame Chiang, Soong spoke fluent English, though he had more of a Boston accent than a Southern one. He had been educated at Harvard and Columbia and had worked in a New York bank. "The Morgan of China," as *Time* magazine dubbed him, had a cosmopolitan sophistication that stood him well with Washington's elites.

Officially, China's embassy was at Twin Oaks, a mansion named for the two stately trees at its front. Just past Dupont Circle, the twenty-six-room white Georgian-style mansion was situated on an eighteen-acre estate and was a potent symbol of how seriously China was taking its investment in the capital's diplomatic circles.

Soong conducted most of the real lobbying, however, at the dining-room table at his home in Chevy Chase, where he hosted Washington's power brokers, including Supreme Court associate justice Felix Frankfurter and Treasury secretary Henry Morgenthau, Jr. His "elaborate Chinese dinners" were extolled in *Life* and his Peking duck was famous.

This informal lobbying had made him successful in securing huge loans for China, but he would turn to Chennault to come up with the plans for obtaining aircraft and pilots. He was convinced that the presence of an American pilot would help persuade American officials to provide China with military assistance.

On the night of Chennault's arrival, Soong hosted a small welcome reception at his home. He invited journalists he thought might be friendly to China's cause, including thirty-year-old Joseph Alsop. Despite his youth, Alsop was already a best-selling author with a nationally syndicated column. Educated at Groton and Harvard, he was well connected within Washington, and was known to visit his cousin Franklin Roosevelt at the White House frequently. Alsop could be a powerful ally for China, but Chennault first had to sell him on the plan.

As the group dined, the conversation turned to the war, and Chennault laid out his vision. He would use American planes and a nucleus of American pilots to build a fighting air force under the command of Chiang Kai-shek to blunt the advance of Japanese forces in China. Alsop initially rejected the idea out of hand as seemingly impossible. It was a reasonable position: Roosevelt was trying to build up America's own aerial arsenal and Britain was then being subjected to relentless Luftwaffe bombardment; any surplus American planes were needed to defend London. But over the course of the evening, Chennault and Soong persisted in stressing the gravity of the situation in China, and Alsop found something magnetic about Chennault, "a charismatic man and physically impressive." The journalist said that while China might not be able to get "the top-line equipment," he suspected that the White House would be amenable to supplying it with outdated planes. Chennault didn't like the idea of picking up Great Britain's leftovers, but he knew it was better than nothing.

Without mentioning his presence at Soong's dinner, Alsop penned one of his "Capital Parade" columns with Robert Kintner, presenting himself as a neutral observer. He wrote that "a powerful movement is afoot to give embattled China something more than empty goodwill and an occasional well-secured loan," and noted that China would need five hundred planes to start a counteroffensive and turn the war around. The numbers appear to be straight from Chennault's after-dinner talk.

Alsop's columns were widely read, and with his influential assistance Chennault and Soong soon began the work of assembling a small air force.

Chennault worked out of a nondescript two-story brick house owned by the Chinese embassy, at the corner of Sixteenth and V streets, a mile from the White House. He spent "many long and dreary days at my desk on V Street, ploughing through the myriad of details for these plans." Working late into the night, Chennault drew on his years of experience in China to draft a four-page memo outlining a proposal; though the memo was unsigned, it was clearly his work. "Japanese planes are much superior in quality as well as in absolute numbers, so that today no existing Chinese planes could take to the air," it read, and the solution was a "Special Air Unit" of five hundred planes, which could "contain an enemy air force of four times their number." This unit, which would consist of two hundred bombers and three hundred fighters, would have to be staffed by foreign pilots. The memo closed by making the case that China was fighting "in the common struggle for independence and democracy."

It was a fairly radical and even dangerous idea, for enlisting American pilots to fly American aircraft was a violation of the nation's neutrality. It could lead to war. Chennault understood that "there was no precedent for this kind of air force."

With the proposal in hand, Soong approached the Roosevelt administration, and he knew just the man to go to: Secretary Morgenthau. Soong had already turned to Morgenthau to secure loans for China and had come to consider him a close friend. Crucially, Morgenthau was a close confidant of Roosevelt, their relationship having begun decades before, when both had been gentleman farmers in the Hudson Valley and sold Christmas trees together. He had ridden Roosevelt's coattails into New York politics and then to Washington, D.C. He could weigh in with Roosevelt on pretty much any policy question he wanted, and had taken a special interest in China, believing that "the Chinese nation is actuated by ideals which we are proud to think have so much in common with those of the United States."

On December 8, Morgenthau and Soong had lunch at the White House and they discussed the idea. In his notes from their meeting,

Morgenthau wrote that he liked "the idea of sending long range bombers with the understanding that they were to be used to bomb Tokyo and other Japanese cities." But, he told Soong, "asking for 500 planes is like asking for 500 stars." Still, he was determined to do what he could. This idea had captured his imagination, and he believed his friend President Roosevelt would like it as well.

"I told [Soong] that I had not discussed this idea with the President but intimated it was the President's idea, which it is in part, because he has mentioned to me that it would be a nice thing if the Chinese would bomb Japan," Morgenthau noted. "I told [Soong] that if we let American planes be flown to Canada, I did not see why these bombers could not be flown to China via Hawaii and the Philippines. . . ." He was "convinced that overnight it would change the whole picture in the Far East." He told Soong he was going to raise this directly with the president and he was confident that not only would the bombers be sent over but that they could get American pilots as well.

Morgenthau called Roosevelt and said he needed to speak with him. Roosevelt inquired if it was something that could be done over the phone.

"No. It has something to do with a very secret message from Chiang Kai-shek," Morgenthau said.

"Is he still willing to fight?" Roosevelt asked.

"That's what the message is about," Morgenthau answered, adding that Chiang had drawn up plans to attack Japan.

"Wonderful. That's what I have been talking about for four years," Roosevelt said with obvious enthusiasm. They would talk more about it soon.

On December 19, the Cabinet met with the president at the White House and they discussed the war in Europe. Roosevelt asked about the German U-boats that were sinking supply ships en route to Great Britain and stressed the need to build new ships—he was still a navy man at heart. America was inching closer to war. Roosevelt had already permitted sending fifty old destroyers to Great Britain and was pushing for a "Lend-Lease" bill that would allow the United States to provide Great Britain and other Allied nations with arms and other supplies.

As the meeting was ending, Morgenthau said there was one more subject they needed to discuss. He, Secretary of War Henry L. Stimson, and Secretary of the Navy Frank Knox stayed behind as the others left. Morgenthau pulled out a map of China that Soong had given him; it showed Chinese air bases that were just 650 miles from Tokyo. He made the case for giving the Chinese the special air unit. Roosevelt was "simply delighted," Morgenthau noted, and gave his approval to the concept, though there was no consideration of the specific details regarding the kind of planes or their number. "Should we work it out and come back?" Morgenthau asked. That wouldn't be necessary, Roosevelt told them. Just "work out a program." Hinting at how ambitious he wanted this mission to be, the president turned to Stimson and asked, "How about that long distance bomber that you have?"

"I have good news for you," Morgenthau told Soong when they met. "The President was simply delighted" with the proposal. To figure out which planes they should press for, Morgenthau wanted to turn to an expert. "This Colonel Chennault, where is he?" he asked.

"He is here now in Washington," Soong replied.

Chennault and Soong went to Secretary Morgenthau's home on December 21 to discuss the plans. Chennault said they would need American pilots and crews, and they could be paid about a thousand dollars a month. They discussed more specifics for the plan—in addition to the bombers, China definitely needed a hundred fighter planes to help defend the Burma Road. As China had lost its access to the ports along its east coast, the transit route, which ran from Lashio in Burma to Kunming, was its last connection to the outside world. Supplies would arrive at the seaport in Rangoon, then be transported by rail to Lashio, and then be driven up the Burma Road into China. Keeping it open was crucial for China's long-term success in the war.

With Morgenthau's support and the president's blessing, everything seemed to be in place—China would be able to get U.S. bombers and fighters and ex-military pilots to fly both. Unfortunately for Chennault and Soong, Stimson was less enthusiastic. He wanted "to get some mature brains into this, before we are committed to do it." He considered the whole plan "half-baked."

The next day, Stimson met with Morgenthau, General George

Marshall, and others at his home. Marshall chimed in, "questioning the advisability of simply letting them have the bombers," Morgenthau wrote in his notes. The idea of sending over bombers was dismissed as foolhardy and dangerous.

The bombers seemed to be off the table for now.

While plans were being made, Chennault had once again set out to look at airplane factories and see if he could identify suitable planes for China. He returned to Buffalo to see Burdette Wright at the Curtiss-Wright factory. The plant was then producing an export model of the P-40 with "six assembly lines turning out P-40's for the British," Chennault recalled. Wright said he might be able to provide China with some of these aircraft. Chennault knew that the heavy craft with a slow rate of climb was "not an ideal airplane for the purpose required," but he couldn't afford to be too selective.

Before the new year, Chennault and a group of Chinese officials stood on the runway at Bolling Field, an army airfield just outside of the capital, where they could see the P-40 in action. Facing into the wind, the pilot throttled up the P-40 and took off, circling overhead. He came back around and then dove and sped past them, flying barely a hundred feet overhead. He tipped the right wing down, finishing the performance with a theatrical touch. The pilot climbed out of the plane after he landed and would recall that he could tell "by the smile on the face of the Curtiss salesman that he liked the demonstration. And the Chinese were excited." They wanted one hundred of those planes—and Chennault was sure to remind them that they'd also need one hundred of those pilots.

On January 1, 1941, Chennault and Soong went again to Morgenthau's house. Both Chinese and American officials seemed to be coalescing around an idea: "The idea of using these P-40s was to protect the Burma Road from Japanese raids," Morgenthau put in his notes. He explained that the "situation was a very complicated one" because the British had an order for the planes, but said he would work out an arrangement where the British would get more up-to-date planes at a later date.

Those diplomatic details weren't Chennault's concern, as long as

China got its planes. A company in New York, Universal Trading Corporation, had been set up to funnel U.S. aid to China, and they would use those funds to pay Curtiss-Wright for the planes. On paper, this would be a purely commercial business transaction.

Roosevelt "hankered after the near impossible, hurting Japan without provoking war," as historian Joseph Persico aptly put it. Roosevelt sensed that a war was coming, and he was becoming irate about Japan's indiscriminate bombing campaign in China. Though the public largely wanted to avoid entanglement in the battles raging across the Atlantic and the Pacific, Roosevelt increasingly came to see American involvement as inevitable. The isolationist Congress had tried to restrict the shipment of war materials abroad, but it didn't faze Roosevelt. He wanted to send planes to Great Britain for what he called "combat testing." These shipments of military material to Great Britain proved controversial—one general warned that "everyone who was a party to the deal might hope to be hanging from a lamp post."

As 1940 came to a close, it was increasingly clear that the conflicts across the two oceans were part of one war. The Japanese, Germans, and Italians had signed an alliance, the Tripartite Pact, in September 1940. As far back as 1937, Roosevelt had spoken out against the "epidemic of world lawlessness" as these nations launched aggressive attacks and called for their "quarantine." For some time, Roosevelt felt that he could only go so far. He told an aide, "It's a terrible thing to look over your shoulder when you are trying to lead—and finding no one there." Now, with his election to a third term in November 1940, Roosevelt was emboldened: he had accomplished a feat no president ever had before. Providing planes to China would undoubtedly stir the fury of Japanese leaders, but structuring it as a purely commercial transaction would give the White House some plausible deniability about the plan. This had to be done in such a way that the United States could deny any involvement in the whole operation. In one meeting, Morgenthau emphasized the secrecy of the arrangement: "As you know, Mr. Soong, if what I am saying to you now ever appears in the paper or you ever say you talked to me about it, I will just say I never saw you."

In fact, news of the negotiations had started to get out, threatening to blow up the agreement. The *New York Herald Tribune* ran a front-page story reporting that "Maj. General Peter Mow, head of the Chinese Air Force and China's outstanding pursuit pilot, is in Washington talking with those in charge of the defense program." The paper even reported that "Clare Chennault" was with him and they were having conversations with Morgenthau about getting planes for China—the sort of details that the reporter could only know from an insider who leaked them. Just weeks before, a Japanese spokesman had warned that any aid to the Chinese would "endanger the peace of the Pacific" and that the plan "would be very dangerous for both Japan and America; only god would know the fate of American planes and pilots if they flew over belligerent territory." The source of the leak had been Mow himself, who had come to the United States to help with these negotiations and had carelessly mentioned to the *Tribune* reporter why he was in Washington. Soong was said to have been so angry that he told the officer: "Here is a pistol. You are a soldier. You know what to do."

But concerned about the bad press that would come with a Chinese general killing himself in Washington D.C., Soong gave Mow a reprieve. Morgenthau was more amused about the leak than angry, and told the story to Roosevelt, who "liked it very much" and said he might start telling the tale.

The plan proceeded in secret, but Roosevelt had become increasingly vocal about his opposition to the Axis powers, and he was determined to signal in one of his Fireside Chats that America wasn't going to remain neutral forever. On the evening of December 29, 1940, the president was wheeled into the diplomatic reception room at the White House. Speaking to millions of listeners across the country, Roosevelt announced: "Never before since Jamestown and Plymouth Rock has our American civilization been in such danger as now. For us this is an emergency as serious as war itself. We must apply ourselves to our task with the same resolution, the same sense of urgency, the same spirit of patriotism and sacrifice as we would show were we at war." While his speech focused on the situation in Europe, he made certain to add that "in Asia, the Japanese are being engaged by the Chinese nation in another great defense." The address would be remembered for his description of America as the "arsenal of democracy," which could assist the Allies with "planes and ships and guns and shells."

Roosevelt mentioned "planes" five times during the speech.

In early 1941, the first batch of P-40s were crated at the Curtiss-Wright factory, moved onto railcars, and shipped to the harbor in Weehawken, New Jersey, where they were loaded on a Norwegian freighter. On Chennault's first night back in the United States, Joseph Alsop had said that the whole scheme was "impossible," but on February 19, the ship carrying the P-40s departed on its three-month trip to Rangoon, Burma. William Pawley's CAMCO would assemble them at a facility there and soon they'd be ready for battle in the skies of China.

Now that he had some planes, Chennault had to find pilots to fly them. The idea of recruiting U.S. military pilots was raised with Morgenthau. Chennault liked that idea—he didn't want another "International Squadron" of misfits. But that meant he needed to get approval from the generals. He recalled how "the military were violently opposed to the whole idea of American volunteers in China," not only because it risked inciting a war, but because the army believed it needed every airman it had in its ranks. Lieutenant General "Hap" Arnold, chief of the Army Air Corps, apparently told Chennault that it "couldn't spare a single staff officer then without endangering Air Corps expansion program."

Though there had already been some other discussion of the idea, Soong enlisted a friend to plead their case at the highest levels of government to try to close the deal. Thomas Corcoran was a Washington lawyer and former adviser to the president. He was known as "Tommy the Cork" because he knew how to float through the swampy morass of the capital to get things done. "He knew when to flatter, and he knew when to cajole and when to threaten," one profiler wrote of him. This was a task that would require both praise and oratory. As he recounted, he wrote directly to his old boss, President Roosevelt, and appealed to his sense of his place in history, and sent a copy of A. E. Housman's famous poem "Epitaph on an Army of Mercenaries." The poem praised British soldiers in World War I, whom the Germans had tried to label mercenaries because they were paid instead of being conscripted. Corcoran would speculate that Housman's words had been decisive in spurring Roosevelt to act. The proposal clearly violated the spirit and probably the letter of the Neutrality Acts passed by Congress between 1935 and 1939, but this wasn't an administration that felt constrained by the letter of the law. The president "had a tendency to think in terms of right and wrong, instead of terms of legal and illegal," as his attorney general, Robert Jackson, put it. The plan for military men to resign and join the special air unit was approved. The legend was that Roosevelt himself signed an "unpublicized executive order" on April 15, 1941, as Chennault put it, but Roosevelt would have been far too careful to put his signature on such an explosive document. Martha Byrd wrote, "No such order was signed by the President. His consent was verbal; specifics were handled" by aides. A few aides were dispatched to meet with the military brass and set up clearance for the pilots to leave for China. In a confidential March 1941 memo, Hap Arnold signed off on the proposal. The pilots would have one-year contracts with CAMCO, "an American firm," but this would be treated as akin to military service; "the year's absence will be considered as a year of duty as far as promotion is concerned."

The special air unit would recruit pilots and ground crews out of the U.S. military and then William Pawley's CAMCO would hire them to serve in "advanced training units" in China, in which they would be working for a "supervisor." That supervisor was Claire Chennault. Once again, the whole program was handled through a private company, a practical decision that would ensure that this was never traced back to the White House.

Soon, Thomas Corcoran would start another front, China Defense Supplies, to help handle the supply chain for the group. The board's chairman was T. V. Soong and their "honorary counselor" was an elderly man named Frederic Delano. (The Delano family had built its fortune on trade with China back in the 1800s, but Frederic's more immediate qualification was that his nephew, Franklin Delano Roosevelt, was the president.)

The nascent unit came to be known as the "American Volunteer Group," and the men would travel on Dutch-flagged ocean liners to Burma, where CAMCO would have the assembled P-40s waiting for them.

In April 1941, vague orders like this one went out to commanders at military bases: "This letter introduces Mr. C. L. Chennault, who has the permission of the Navy Department to visit your station. He will explain the purpose of his visit." To help with recruiting, Chennault and Pawley rounded up a crew of old friends to spread out across the seventeen military bases that had pilots. Chennault had "planned to give each pilot a final personal check, but in the hectic final rush to get the group under way, I had to abandon the idea."

Rumors about a secret operation in Asia began to spread around military bases.

It didn't take long for the press to pick up the story. *Time* magazine ran a piece on June 23, 1941, about these mysterious CONVOYS TO CHINA. "For the past few months, tall, bronzed American airmen have been quietly slipping away from east- and west-coast ports, making their way to Asia." So much for secrecy. But the piece was like an advertisement for the unit. One pilot at Randolph Field, R. T. Smith, read it and threw the magazine down on his coffee table, spilling his highball, and jumped up from the couch. "Holy jumpin' Jesus!" He told his squadronmate about it and they poured another round. "This screwball outfit" seemed like the ticket. Despite Chennault's insistence that the operation was a secret, the pilots were able to find a phone number for a recruiter and just call him up. Before long they were on their way to San Francisco.

Once recruiting was well under way, it was time for Chennault to make his way back to the Far East. He obtained a new passport. "Occupation: Executive," it said. Then he took a United Airlines flight to San Francisco. He arrived just in time to see off a large contingent of the American Volunteer Group—approximately fifty pilots and seventy-three ground-crew members as one pilot recorded in his diary—who would sail for Burma aboard the Dutch passenger ship the *Jagersfontein*.

A reception at the bar atop the Mark Hopkins Hotel on July 7, 1941, gave Chennault a chance to meet these young airmen. The pilots mingled over drinks, sharing stories about planes they'd flown. They had little notion of what to expect about the journey ahead of them. They may have heard stories about Chennault, the mysterious figure who'd be leading them, but here he was in the flesh. His face made quite the stark impression, his skin bronzed from years under the sun and covered with deep lines. *Time* would describe it as "scarred by razor-sharp lines that drop perpendicularly about his mouth. About the eyes sky-strain has woven a lacework of crow's-feet."

Chennault made the rounds with confidence. Whatever doubts he may have had about this "odd assortment of young men, looking slightly ill at ease and uncertain in their new civilian clothes," they were now his responsibility. Certainly, Chennault would recall, no one "could have possibly imagined that in a few months they would be making history."

Some of these men had undoubtedly enlisted for the money, but the bigger draw for most was the adventure. That was certainly the case for John Newkirk, a twenty-seven-year-old navy pilot who went by "Jack" or, in recognition of his hometown, "Scarsdale Jack." He viewed the assignment as a rebellion against the future that his father, an attorney in New York City, likely envisioned for him. Scarsdale Jack was an Eagle Scout from the posh suburb, but he wasn't your typical privileged suburban kid. The family lore was that as a child he became obsessed with shooting a bow and arrow, and became an excellent marksman. He brought down a sparrow in midflight, and then ate it, because that's what hunters do. His enthusiasm for adventure quickly turned toward flight. He went to Rensselaer Polytechnic Institute and then became a naval aviator. A handsome man with a wide smile, he had a penchant for living dangerously and boldly. His decision to sign up to fly combat planes in China surprised no one who knew him well.

Before he headed to San Francisco he stopped in Houston to see a girl. He'd met Jane Dunham in Galveston when he was on leave from the navy and was visiting his brother to go surfing. He'd been captivated by her immediately, and she by him. They kept the romance going after he returned to his aircraft carrier. He had written to her to inform her of his decision to join the American Volunteer Group and told her, "My deepest regret in my new capacity is that I will be compelled to be apart from you." When he arrived in Houston he announced that he wanted to get married before he left, and they were wed in a brief ceremony at the First Presbyterian Church. His trip to San Francisco to ship out to China became their honeymoon.

On July 10, Newkirk was part of a group of 123 who climbed aboard buses in San Francisco and made the trip out to the harbor. They carried bags crammed with the clothes and provisions they imagined they might need for the year they would spend in China. They carried new green passports with fictitious professions. Jane Newkirk and a few other girlfriends and wives came to say good-bye. At the docks, Jane held on to Jack's arm as long as she could. And then he was gone.

The *Jagersfontein* towered over the harbor, brimming with cars being shipped east and crates of cargo. The men wandered the narrow passages of the ship as they searched for their staterooms. After they dropped their bags, they crowded onto the rails to get one last look at American soil and their loved ones. Many of the men were wearing suits and ties for the occasion and one pilot captured the scene on his camera. Newkirk went up to the rail to wave good-bye to his new wife, who was easy to spot in her white head scarf. Many pilots, especially the married ones, felt regret as the ship started to pull away from the dock. "Words cannot tell the void this parting has left in me," one pilot in the same position would recall. The image of his wife "standing waving on the pier I will never forget."

At 1:20 P.M. the ship's horn let out a loud blast and the *Jagersfontein* departed from the pier. "As she passed under the Golden Gate Bridge it disappeared into a thick bank of fog, like a curtain falling on regrets and second thoughts. There was no turning back," another pilot remembered. The sea quickly turned rough, and some of the men hung above the rail, returning their good-bye luncheons to the sea.

Among those onboard were many young men, children of the Great Depression, who had scarcely left their hometowns before they joined the army. Frank Losonsky was one of them, a mechanic who had been recruited from Selfridge Field in Michigan.

His parents were Czech immigrants who struggled to make a living. During prohibition, they sold home brew and moonshine. His father was a barber and his stepmother worked at a factory that made metal springs. Frank remembered her "coming home with hands cut so bad they bled." Still, the two incomes weren't enough and in freezing Detroit winters Frank "stole coal from coal cars" to keep the house warm. He helped out in the barbershop that his father ran on the ground floor of their house, serving shots of booze to customers. Frank had a falling-out with his parents when he was in high school and he left home in ninth grade, living at first with an aunt, then any family that would take him for five or six dollars in rent a week. To keep a roof over his head he took any job he could get, including milking cows and working the beet fields.

He graduated from high school in June 1939 and knew what he wanted to do: he was going to join the Army Air Corps. It offered "independence, a steady job and a future in aviation," and left unsaid, it was a way to ensure he didn't spend the rest of his life milking cows and picking beets. He took the flight school exam, wanting to be a pilot, but failed the physics section. As a consolation prize, the army would train him to work on P-40 engines. He was determined to excel at the work, though flying would always remain an ambition for him.

He would fly as the passenger in a two-seater AT-6 with his friend piloting, and they would travel from Selfridge Field back to his hometown of Ashley to see his high school sweetheart, an athletic brunette named Nancy Trefry, whom he planned to marry. They would announce their arrival in spectacular form. As Nancy recalled, she was in study hall at school and "the airplane came in real low. We girls were quite excited as this crazy plane buzzed the high school. . . . I was thrilled." They once came by to buzz her house, and Nancy's father, as she recalled, "wanted to know what in the hell those idiots were doing up there." That was just her Frank.

Losonsky had wanted to fly but the AVG needed ground crew, particularly men like Frank who knew the P-40's Allison engine, and he signed up. "I wasn't motivated to save the world. Nor was I unhappy with the Air Corps. The reason was money, a subsidized trip to the orient and the promise of adventure," he recalled.

He spent the July 4, 1941, holiday with Nancy and her family and then it was on to San Francisco. He hadn't achieved his ambition of becoming a pilot, but this was pretty exciting and it was a chance to make something of himself. "I don't recall being nervous. Just a feeling of adventure," he wrote. Now, a few months shy of his twenty-first birthday, handsome in a still boyish way, he was looking forward to his $350 a month salary with the AVG, much more than what he had been making in the army. His plan was to save some money and see some of the world, then he would move back and settle down on a farm with Nancy. Everything had lined up sweetly. Even the rough seas couldn't knock down his optimism. "What a lark, I'm having a terrific time on this passenger liner, no work, eating like a king and I'm getting paid for it," Losonsky would recall. The journey was the first taste of real luxury for many of these men, who lounged in the sun on wooden deck chairs, only to be "interrupted around 11:00 for the morning cool, refreshing drink served by the barefooted turbaned Javanese boys" who served as the waiters on the ship, a pilot named Robert Brouk noted. Then lunch was "vegetable salad, soup, entrée, dessert and fruit," followed by coffee in the Social Hall. In the afternoon they read books, especially about China or Japan, and then it was time to commence the multicourse evening meal. Frank Losonsky found the Dutch cuisine somewhat intimidating and recalled that "it took the greater part of the ocean voyage to figure out which fork to use, when and where."

The night brought reminders of the war to which they were heading, as at sundown the *Jagersfontein* had to be blacked out to guard against hostile raiders operating in the Pacific—though the men seemed to be a bit confused about whether it was German or Japanese ships that they needed to fear. Portholes were closed, cutting off ventilation and leaving the rooms stifling. Because it was too dark to read, the men played bridge and drank rum collinses. Up on deck, a few men attempted to walk around and get some fresh air, only to blindly stumble into deck chairs in the darkness. They spent the evenings having sing-alongs.

Also aboard the *Jagersfontein* were members of a medical team Chennault had recruited for the American Volunteer Group. Led by an army flight surgeon, Dr. Thomas Gentry, the unit included two doctors, a dentist, and two female nurses. Chennault, concerned that the women might become romantically involved with his men, had specified to a friend who was helping out with recruitment: "I prefer female nurses (not too good looking) for the sake of morale but would require each one to sign an iron-clad agreement not to marry during year of duty out there." The results weren't quite what he had requested. While little is known about the older of the two women, Jo Stewart, the pilots found twenty-five-year-old Emma Jane Foster captivating. One pilot,

Jim Howard, recalled that she "looked ravishing, with tousled red hair reaching to her shoulder, deep blue eyes, and dressed in a simple white suit." Another pilot went so far as to say she was "the most beautiful girl I've ever seen." The men stared but she seemed to turn away from the attention. Foster wasn't particularly interested in a romance with any of her fellow passengers. For her, the chief allure of the mission was a chance to return to China, a country that she had grown to love as one of the first American women to study there. Growing up in Bellefonte, Pennsylvania, she had become enamored with the Far East after reading Pearl Buck's best-selling novels about China, *East Wind: West Wind* and *The Good Earth*. Her father took her to local Chinese restaurants, exotic dining choices in those days. While attending Penn State, she learned of a study abroad program at Lingnan University in Canton, and was not dissuaded by the fact that it was intended for male students only. If men could do it then there was "no reason why women can't go," she recalled. She didn't take no for an answer and she persuaded the administrators to let her attend Lingnan. That had been her first time traveling far from home. When she got on the train to the West Coast, the first leg of the long journey, she was "so homesick I cried all the way" across the country. Her pride kept her from turning back, and once settled into her new home at Lingnan, her fears dissipated.

She found the meals continually surprising and delightful, even when they included frog legs or chicken feet. When she bicycled into town men stopped in the street to watch her ride by, and her bright red hair and freckles soon made her into something of a local celebrity. She recalled that the Chinese called her a "foreign devil," but she'd understood their reaction to reflect a kind of awe, lacking animosity. She was quick to learn the Chinese language, and lectures left her wanting to know more about Chinese history. She traveled across the country and walked atop the Great Wall.

She returned to Pennsylvania and graduated from Penn State in 1937 with degrees in political science and sociology, then earned a master's degree from the Yale School of Nursing in 1940. She hoped her medical skills would lead her back to China, but those dreams were deferred after she took a nursing job in Minneapolis working with underprivileged women and soon found a serious boyfriend, Walt. She was on the verge of marrying him and settling down, but her desire to return to China hadn't completely died. Gentry learned of her on a recruiting trip to Yale. He immediately called her father and then tracked her down in Minneapolis. His invitation to take part in the mission seemed a kind of miracle to her and she accepted the offer, but almost as soon as she put the phone down she began to have second thoughts. At a time when the average age for a girl to marry was twenty-one, Foster was already twenty-five. She decided to press the issue. "If you marry me, I won't go," she recalled telling Walt during that fateful conversation. "I won't do that," he replied, "because you will regret it all your life."

"I knew he was right," she recalled, "I knew I had to go back, I knew I would be sorry if I didn't go." She packed her bags and headed for San Francisco the following day. On this trip west she boarded the train with no tears but only a sense of excitement.

Unlike the men on board, Foster immediately began her duties, starting with administering immunization shots. "These great burly men fainted way down on the deck," she remembered. "I just couldn't understand how a strong-hearted man could react so strangely to just a little old shot." She resisted the flirtations of her charges, many of whom looked as if they had barely left puberty. Despite her indifference, the men wanted a chance with "Red," as they nicknamed her, and some would venture up to the nurses' room on the upper deck. Some managed to get her to play deck tennis with them, or they'd sit and listen to records on her phonograph.

While listening to one of Tchaikovsky's piano concertos, she got into an argument with a handsome pilot named John Petach about whether it was the piano or the orchestra that made the piece so extraordinary. Despite her inclination to keep her distance from the, she found herself taking an interest in this more mature young man. They discovered they shared a love for music and could talk for hours on end.

Petach was an unlikely passenger on this ship to Burma. He had recently graduated from New York University with a degree in chemical engineering and could easily have found a job in New York City, or, as a talented singer in the glee club, could have followed in his father's footsteps and returned to Perth Amboy, New Jersey, to become choir-master at their church. Instead he announced to his parents that he had passed the exam to become a naval aviator. He went through training at Pensacola Naval Air Station and was soon flying from aircraft carriers. He was just shy of his twenty-third birthday when he signed up for the American Volunteer Group.

There was something about this "good-looking gentleman" that intrigued Foster. "I was impressed with him because he was so gentle and so understanding, so sensitive, which for a young man of his age, I thought was unusual." They soon became more intimate, holding hands and dancing on the ship's deck to one of her records. That was an adventure in itself. "When you put your foot down," she recalled, "you don't know whether the deck's going to meet you or whether it's way down below." But they made it through together. Petach was a good dancer, but it was his singing that really won her over. He had this "wonderful bass voice." Still, there were other men she danced with and it wasn't clear that this would be anything more than a fleeting flirtation.

On July 15, the *Jagersfontein* docked in Honolulu. The passengers spent a day sightseeing around the island and then the ship proceeded west.

When the boat reached the equator on July 21, the men who were crossing for the first time—a group that included Frank Losonsky—were subjected to a nautical hazing ritual, the King Neptune ceremony. "They forced us to eat raw fish," Frank Losonsky recalled, and then told them to strip. "Then they greased our bodies with some ungodly concoction of dough mixed with cod liver oil and milk." Breaded like veal, they were ordered to run across the deck, while they were spanked with paddles. Finally they jumped in the ship's pool, but even then the ordeal wasn't quite finished. The salt water and a rough bar of soap weren't much use in washing off the slime that had permeated their skin and scalp. It would take three days to feel like they were finally rid of the gunk. Still, "All had a good time," Frank Losonsky wrote in his diary.

Finally on August 15, 1941, they reached the mouth of the Irrawaddy River and sailed upstream toward Rangoon, encountering along the way a torrential rain that blacked out the sky.

Trailing the *Jagersfontein* were a number of other Dutch-flagged passenger liners carrying more members of the American Volunteer Group. On July 24, the *Bloemfontein* left San Francisco harbor.

One of the pilots aboard that ship was David "Tex" Hill, who, at over six feet, was almost too tall to fit in the cockpit of a P-40. Hill was "a lean, rangy blonde, with a permanent grin, outspoken and personable, the kind of guy who could charm the birds out of the trees," a friend recalled. Despite his nickname, Hill had been born in Korea to Christian missionaries. He'd always had an interest in the Far East, but more than anything else he loved to fly. He spent a year training as a pilot at Pensacola Naval Air Station, earned his wings in November 1939, and had been serving as a dive-bomber pilot on aircraft carriers in the Atlantic. He loved the navy, but this offer to go to China offered some "excitement and adventure," and a chance to return to the continent where he'd been born.

Hill's two best friends from the navy also joined the AVG. Like so many of his new colleagues, Ed Rector, a pilot from a small town in North Carolina, had dreamed of being a pilot since childhood. He spent all his allowance money on the pulp magazines that popularized aviation for kids of the 1920s and '30s. He memorized all the planes from the Great War and "by the time I was seventeen I knew what my future would be." He had fulfilled his dream by becoming a naval aviator, but having "read everything that Kipling had ever written twice over," he wanted to see the Far East for himself. Twenty-five-year-old Bert Christman was one of the most unusual recruits in the group. Originally from Fort Collins, Colorado, Christman received his degree from Colorado A&M in mechanical engineering, but knew he wanted to be an artist. He moved to New York City with some samples of his work and took whatever job he could find. The Associated Press soon hired him, and he got his big break when they asked him to take over the comic strip *Scorchy Smith*, which was syndicated across the country. *Scorchy Smith* recounted the adventures of a young pilot who traveled the world selling his services as a mercenary, including a stint in China. Christman soon began spending time at airports to get a better feel for his material. Intrigued, he took flying lessons himself, and was so taken with the experience that in 1938 he enlisted in the navy as a pilot. He kept up his art, and cocreated *The Sandman,* which first appeared in *Adventure Comics* in 1939. His next project, *The Three Aces,* ran in *Action Comics* as a backup to *Superman* and concerned three young pilots who became "winged soldiers of fortune" and traveled the world fighting evil. The friendship of Hill, Rector, and Christman seemed to be the basis for *The Three Aces,* and as Hill would later observe of Christman, "Really the whole reason he was a pilot and in the military was that he wanted to live the things he sketched out, the things he drew."

The *Bloemfontein* carried twenty-seven American Volunteer Group recruits, but the majority of the passengers were missionaries headed for the Far East, including a number of women. The ship's bar was well stocked, and there was always someone banging away on the piano in the passenger lounge. The "damn missionaries," R. T. Smith wrote, were "driving us nuts with their constant gatherings around the piano and singing hymns by the hour. So we drive them nuts by playing hot swing records on the phonograph; Goodman, Dorsey, Artie Shaw." The rumor was that Tex Hill had been able to "convert" one of the women missionaries on the way over.

When the *Bloemfontein* docked in Singapore for a few days, the Chinese consul hosted them for a lavish meal. Pilot George McMillan wrote to his mother: "You would be surprised how quick we caught on to using the chopsticks. The meal consisted of twenty some-odd courses and lasted over three hours. Some fun! Personally, I'd prefer bacon and eggs though." The recruits made the last leg of the journey to Rangoon aboard the *Penang Trader,* a small ship covered in "rusted metal and grime." They tried to sleep but they found that they weren't the only passengers on that ship, as Tex Hill recalled. "The cockroaches—My god!! That first night there were cockroaches running all over." They sought refuge from the insects up on the deck, breathing in the fresh air.

On July 8, Chennault had boarded the China Clipper once again. "As the big flying boat soared into the air over San Francisco," he recalled, "I settled comfortably in my seat, confident for the first time in my battle against the Japanese that I had everything to defeat them."

Chennault finally had his private air force, but it had taken longer than he hoped. The original plan was to send the unit to Kunming as quickly as possible, but if they'd arrived in spring 1941, they'd have landed in the midst of a renewed Japanese bombing offensive. Chennault knew the importance of careful training and wanted to instruct the pilots on the tactics he had soaked up in his four years fighting the Japanese. The plan had to change. He had to find a place where they could train in peace and quiet before throwing them into combat. Such a place was going to be hard to find in China, but the next-door neighbor, the British colony of Burma, fit that bill. CAMCO was assembling the P-40s in Rangoon, and it made sense to see if they could find a location in Burma. When Chennault landed in Rangoon, he worked with William Pawley to secure a location. They wanted to use a Royal Air Force base. Even though this risked upending Britain's uneasy peace with Japan, the British authorities approved the plan; the AVG would have access to a remote RAF base near the town of Toungoo. Like a landlord trying to control a potentially troublesome tenant, the British said that the AVG could use the base for training, but not for combat. Chennault agreed to the site despite its rustic qualities: he didn't care about the amenities. On July 28, 1941, a group of AVG mechanics arrived in Rangoon and Chennault greeted them and sent them on to Toungoo to get the base set up. This was supposed to be a secret mission but the men seemed to have problems keeping their mouths shut during a stopover in Singapore. The *New York Times* reported in July 1941 that "thirty United States airplane mechanics and maintenance men" were on their way to "aid the Chinese Air Force."

Chennault needed staff officers and he traveled around the Far East to hunt up "whatever American civilians happened to be available." During a stop in Hong Kong he found Harvey Greenlaw, a former army officer and West Point graduate who was selling aircraft. He offered Harvey a job as the executive officer, second in command for the unit, and Harvey brought along his wife, Olga, as the unit secretary. In August, at a small garden party hosted by Madame Chiang in a wooded area in the hills above Chungking, he found another American who he thought would be useful. The man looked familiar, and it was in fact Joe Alsop. Almost as if he were inspired by Chennault's example, Alsop had given up his column and joined the navy; he wanted to be a man of action, not just words. He was en route to Bombay, where he had been assigned to a somewhat unclear role as an intelligence officer, which "seemed to offer the prospect of much food and little work." It may sound like a dream assignment, but that had been Alsop's life in Washington, and he was hoping to "do something real under a real leader." He asked Chennault whether he could join the American Volunteer Group. He was an odd fit for the unit as he had no military background, but Chennault thought he could use him as a supply officer. Not long after, Alsop resigned his post and was on his way to join Chennault's unit in Burma. Years later, he would write that this would become "the greatest single adventure of my life."

Even after Chennault returned to the Far East in July 1941, his recruiters continued to search for more pilots. One of the recruiters was Richard Aldworth, an army pilot who'd taken part in the Great War in France. He liked to claim that he'd fought with the Lafayette Escadrille, but that was just for show. He'd retired from the army after a plane crash that almost killed him and had become a superintendent at Newark Metropolitan Airport. He could no longer fly, but for the moment at least, he was back in the game.

In August 1941 Aldworth traveled to Pensacola, Florida, where navy pilots were trained at the naval air station there. He made a beeline to the San Carlos Hotel, a premier seven-story hotel overlooking the sparkling waters of Pensacola Bay. Its elegant bar was a lure for pilots, who would congregate to drink and enjoy a respite from the heat in one of the few spots in town with air-conditioning. Aldworth sidled up to the bar and casually mentioned to some drinkers that he was looking for a few good volunteers for a mission to China. Anyone who wanted to hear more details, he told them, should come to his room for a private conversation.

On August 4, a twenty-eight-year-old Marine pilot, Greg Boyington, found himself wandering the sweltering streets of Pensacola, desperate for a drink and "looking for an answer." Boyington's drinking had helped him put on an extra thirty pounds, and it showed in how out of breath he was in the subtropical summer. He was the kind of guy, it was said around the base, who could "kill a fifth of whiskey before ten o'clock in the morning." His love for the bottle had taken him down some dark roads. Though he was married, one night he took another woman out for a drink at the Officers' Club. She sat down to play the piano and Boyington sat down next to her on the bench. The commanding officer sat down on her other side and nudged Boyington off the bench. Boyington stood up and told his date they were leaving, but the commanding officer said something to the woman like "I'll take you home." Boyington punched him in the face. The "unofficerlike conduct," as the report noted, led to Boyington being suspended for five days. Boyington's wife, Helene, had finally had enough and left for Seattle, taking their three children with her. Boyington said, "I drank more than ever."

By now he was also in thousands of dollars of debt. His creditors had contacted the Marine Corps, and he "had to account by mail to Marine Corps Headquarters each month how much money was being paid on each debt," he later wrote. He was worried that they might sideline him into a desk job and he desperately wanted to keep flying.

Though he had no way of paying for it, he took a seat at the San Carlos bar and ordered a drink. He wrote out a check for twenty dollars, certain it would bounce, but he'd be paid by the time they figured it out. He started talking to the patron seated next to him, confessing his woes.

"Boy, aren't you lucky," his fellow drinker said, "they're recruiting pilots to go over with Chiang."

"Well, how can you get out of the service?" Boyington wanted to know. He pounded back a few doubles and thought it over. Boyington was a native Idahoan who had never left the country, but at that moment the idea of fleeing to China sounded like just what he needed. "Where is this recruiting man?"

He found his way to Aldworth, who explained the mission in vague terms, telling him only that the group would be in China fighting to defend the Burma Road. But the monthly salary of $650 that he offered Boyington as a flight leader, and the $500 bonus for each kill, had Boyington's attention. "The Japs are flying antiquated junk over China," Aldworth told him. "Many of your kills will be unarmed transports. I suppose you know that the Japanese are renowned for their inability to fly. And they all wear corrective glasses." Boyington sensed there was something suspicious about the offer, but he was ready to seize any opportunity that would take him far away from his creditors and his estranged wife. He was "mentally calculating how wealthy I would be," he wrote in his memoirs. Aldworth promised him that he'd be able to get his Marine Corps commission back after his one-year contract ended.

Boyington didn't need the hard sell. His first love was flight and, more than anything, he wanted the chance to keep flying. He'd been hooked since he paid a barnstormer to take him up in a biplane as a kid. The incredible feeling of standing up in the cockpit as the wind whipped against his face while he helped the pilot drop handbills over the town of Coeur d'Alene imprinted itself on his brain. He had studied aeronautical engineering at the University of Washington and spent his summers working in mines to pay his tuition, all in hopes of becoming a pilot. If he had to go to China to keep flying, then that's what he was going to do. Though Boyington was worried that his personal problems would disqualify him from the unit, Aldworth signed off on the eager pilot. On paper at least, he was an experienced airman and his baggage could be overlooked if it meant adding some talent to this unit.

Later that week, Boyington packed up his sedan, stuffing it full of his uniforms and civilian clothes, and began the cross-country trek to San Francisco, taking his dog, Fella, with him. His parents came down from their apple ranch in Washington State to pick up the dog and the car, and his mother tried to talk him out of taking the job. "Oh, don't worry, Mom, I'll get by okay. I haven't got an enemy in the world," he assured her. He felt a stab of regret as he watched his parents drive away, the dog looking back at him forlornly as if to say "Why are you leaving me? What have I done wrong?"

Boyington followed Aldworth's instructions to check in at the St. Francis Hotel with the other recruits and noted in the registry that he was going to do missionary work, just like it said in his passport. If he was nervous, he decided to drink it away, as "there must have been a minimum of ten bars in each square block in downtown San Francisco, and each of us was in every one of them." On September 24, he took a taxi to the harbor and walked up and down the length of the *Boschfontein*, a ship that would ferry over twenty-six members of the American Volunteer Group, all under the guise of being missionaries. He was undoubtedly beginning to feel some jitters about the journey ahead and stationed himself at the ship's well-stocked bar. His shipmates would remember him being "plastered to the gills." The Americans carefully guarded their secret, which put Boyington in an awkward position when one of the actual missionaries onboard asked him to deliver the sermon at the Sunday morning service. Boyington politely declined.

These young pilots were filled with a "mingled feeling of sorrow at leaving the good old USA and joy at anticipating new lands and adventure," as John Donovan wrote to his mother just before the *Boschfontein* departed. As they crossed the Pacific, all they could see, as the Alabamian put it, was "WATER, WATER, WATER—you wouldn't believe it possible. Where does it all come from? All day long nothing but water."

As the Dutch ships began arriving in Rangoon in the fall of 1941, the members of the American Volunteer Group got their first glimpse of the Asian mainland. There was a "feeling of mystery as we sailed up the River through that new and strange country," as one pilot put it. There were rice fields and coconut trees. When they reached the harbor, there was chaotic small-boat traffic. As they neared the docks, their eyes were fixed on the gold-plated, jewel-encrusted dome of the Shwedagon Pagoda, a Buddhist holy site rising 325 feet over the city. "It looked like an immense gem set in the terraced hills."

Toungoo was a multihour train journey into the interior through fields studded with villages that were little more than bamboo huts connected by a mud road. They passed by water buffalo and statues of Buddha.

When the men reached Toungoo they piled into station wagons and drove the last few miles to the air base carved into the jungle.

The men had signed up for this mission without asking too many questions because they were inspired by the spirit of adventure. The cover stories and alibis had given them a rush, a sense that they would be like spies. But now they were in the jungles of Burma and realized they knew little about what exactly they'd signed up for.

Greg Boyington recalled being told by the recruiter: "You will be gentlemen in every sense of the word. Wherever you are stationed, you will have an interpreter who will act as a valet." Boyington would say that some of the men brought their dress clothes, golf sticks, and tennis rackets along with them. That was likely an exaggeration on Boyington's part, but if anyone had in fact put those items on their packing lists, it didn't take long to realize that they wouldn't be needing any of them. On their first night, the men laid down on straw mattresses on wooden bunks, closing the mosquito nets tightly around them. They dozed off to the strange sounds coming from the jungle.

When Chennault returned to Toungoo from a trip to Chungking on August 22, his new men were already encamped. Not all of them were happy campers: "My first business was to accept the resignations of five pilots who were eager to return to the United States," he recalled. Chennault took a long look around and was thoroughly unimpressed with the pilots. He couldn't help but feel that the "long boat trip and Dutch shipboard menus had left many flabby and overweight," and the men "appeared wilted during their introduction to the humid monsoon heat."

He wilted a little himself. His optimism that he was now prepared to take on the Japanese wavered as he wondered: Could these men really help him save China? Ultimately, the unit would come to just under three hundred people, and roughly a hundred of them were pilots (with resignations and later additions, the precise size constantly shifted).

If Chennault was uncertain about his new recruits, they had some questions about him as well. Just who was this Claire Chennault, "the Colonel"? He was wearing what looked like a costume, mixing Chinese insignia on his shirt with an old army cap. No one seemed to know the full story of the ex-army pilot. When he spoke to them, it was in a low voice with a Cajun drawl that almost made it sound like he was speaking in a foreign language. Despite his elusive qualities, Chennault was an impressive figure. He struck one pilot as "a man of vision who had the forcefulness to carry out his plans."

After the initial wave of resignations, Chennault decided he needed to draw a line in the sand, so to speak. He told the pilots, as one recalled: "If your hearts and minds are not in the proper place, we have no place for slackers." He didn't try to sugarcoat what they were up against: the Japanese "have had four years of combat experience. However, I think you and our P-40s will be a match for anything they throw at us." The pitch worked.

"Now there's a man I can follow," pilot Jim Howard whispered to a squadronmate. This wasn't going to be a vacation at a country club, but for men who had come to prove to themselves that they could really make it in combat, Chennault had struck all the right chords.

CHAPTER 7

TRAINING IN TOUNGOO

Back in the United States, leaves were starting to change colors and the World Series was heating up between the New York Yankees and the Brooklyn Dodgers. The baseball world was still buzzing about two magical deeds that summer—Joe DiMaggio's 56-game hitting streak and Ted Williams's incredible feat of finishing the season with a batting average above .400. Americans knew there were wars raging across both the Atlantic and Pacific oceans, but that all felt so far away. They were busy enjoying themselves once again, now that the worst days of the Great Depression had passed: they listened to Glenn Miller's smash hit "Chattanooga Choo Choo" and could go to the movie theaters to see *Citizen Kane* or *Dumbo*. Few Americans had traveled abroad, and though the wars in Europe and Asia were sparking considerable political debate, they could be ignored with the ease of throwing out the newspaper or turning off the radio.

As distant as war seemed to most Americans, developments in the States already felt remote to the men of the American Volunteer Group. Thousands of miles from home, they lived under constant attack from the mosquitoes and insects that infested their spartan bunkhouses in the Burmese jungle. The luxury of their Dutch ocean liners faded like a foggy memory. It didn't take long for these young men to miss the simple joys of home. "Right now—boy what I wouldn't give for a Coca-Cola," pilot John Donovan wrote in a letter. For R. T. Smith, it was a visit to the diner: "What I'd give for a Hamburger + a malt." Each day was a new adventure at the Toungoo airfield, and each morning began with the same ritual: at around 5:30 A.M. a Burmese man marched between their bunks banging a gong as loudly as he could. As soon as they hopped up, they'd feel the humidity envelop them. A water tank connected to bamboo rods served as their makeshift showers. The toilet was a "fourholer." When they got dressed, the men had to be careful to shake out their shoes in case a scorpion had crawled in during the night. They would then hustle to the mess hall and try to shield their plates from the insects competing for their rations. They'd find Chennault in the teakwood shack standing in front of a blackboard lecturing, just as he had in the small country schoolhouses where he'd taught back in Louisiana. Chennault knew that as much as the pilots may have wanted to get in a cockpit, they had to sit down and listen to what he had to say. They called this Chennault's "kindergarten," and for good reason.

He drew a Japanese plane, then used colored chalk to circle the spots the men should aim for: oil coolers, oxygen storage, gas tanks, bomb bays. Then he'd erase the circles, call upon a pilot, and ask him to draw them back on, reciting each part for the class. It was rote but he wanted these men to know the enemy aircraft like the back of their hands. Dutiful students, the pilots filled spiral-bound notebooks with copious notes. The strengths of the P-40, as Chennault put it, were "higher top speed, faster dive and superior firepower." Chennault reminded them, however, that the P-40 was a heavy, slow-climbing plane, and he didn't want them trying to challenge the Japanese fighters in a dogfight. They were to climb up into the sun and then dive down on the Japanese planes. "Hit and run! Hit and run, dive, and then come back to altitude," was one pilot's summary of Chennault's lectures. Unlike the chivalrous duels of the Great War, pilots in this new conflict needed surprise and overwhelming power, and he wanted his pilots to be accurate: "You need to sharpen your shooting eye. Nobody ever gets too good at gunnery. The more Japs you get with your first burst, the fewer there are to jump you later." He tried to cram years of experience into those lectures. "Each type of plane has its own strength and weakness," he told them. "The pilot who can turn his advantages against the enemy's weakness will win every time." Chennault would later say that some of the best teaching of his career was done in that shack.

As the pilots went to school, the armorers and mechanics swarmed over the planes. The P-40 had four .30-caliber guns in the wings and two .50-caliber guns mounted on top of the nose. The .50-caliber guns had to be synchronized to fire through the rotating propeller using an impulse generator. One armorer recalled that if a gun overheated or a bad cartridge hung in the chamber, a round could accidentally fire right into the propeller. After the guns were mounted, the armorers took the P-40 out to a makeshift range to make sure they'd gotten it right, bore-sighting the gun to converge at approximately three hundred yards.

Few of the pilots had flown a P-40 before, and because it didn't take much to turn a smooth flight into a fiery crash, Chennault wanted them to get some experience in the cockpit before they went into battle. The P-40 was an Army Air Corps plane, and for the recruits who had been flying big planes in the navy, this would be a new type of flying. "For the bomber and flying-boat pilots, the feel of a single-seat, single-engine plane would be a major adjustment," one historian wrote. A small mistake could be fatal.

Joe Rosbert was one of the navy pilots who knew this would be a challenge. The P-40 was "almost on ground level compared to the much larger" planes he was used to flying in the navy. Like all the new arrivals, he hadn't flown for a few months and he nervously adjusted his parachute and looked over the cockpit before checking out in the P-40 for the first time. A senior pilot came by to give him some final tips: "Careful when you taxi," he told Rosbert. "And don't land the thing thirty feet in the air, bring it right down on the ground." That wasn't reassuring, but he was in the cockpit and it was time to go.

"The engine started with a roar and I felt as though the plane was going to take off right then and there before I was ready," he recalled. The crew chief gave him the signal to proceed and as he taxied "the long, sharp nose blocked out vision straight ahead." He snaked along to avoid hitting the other planes on the runway. "Here we go," he said to himself, then "the plane lurched forward with a terrific burst of power, pushing me back against the seat." As if he were coaching himself, he said, "Tail up." He lifted off the ground. The wheels retracted and the plane "zoomed up at more than two thousand feet per minute." Finally, when he reached twelve thousand feet, he could get a feel for the plane. He took it into a steep dive and could feel the power as the "speed picked up almost at a frightening rate." That was what Chennault had been talking about. He looked down at the green jungle below. He did a few rolls and then tried a spin. "I was exhilarated beyond description."

He brought the plane down, and as the wheels touched the runway he said to himself, "This is what I came for." He taxied to a stop, and once the propeller stopped spinning another pilot came out to greet him, shouting, "How'd you like it?"

He smiled and replied, "Couldn't be better."

To a man, they were glad to be back in the air. "The sound heard in the cockpit of a P-40 under full power is awesome beyond description," pilot Erik Shilling would write. "To a fighter pilot's ear, the Philadelphia Philharmonic Symphony would fade in comparison."

"It even smelled good with that rich aroma found only in certain airplanes, a not-too-subtle mixture of hot metal, exhaust gases, and paint that most pilots preferred to Chanel No. 5," R. T. Smith remembered. As the men grew more confident in the cockpit, Chennault would send up two planes at a time in mock battle.

Chennault chose not to pilot a P-40 himself, but stood instead in a bamboo watchtower next to the field, observing his men through binoculars as they soared overhead. Sometimes he'd yell into the radio, giving instructions and corrections. The pilots came to feel a sense of intimacy with their aircraft as they learned to handle every knob and dial in the cockpit.

When the pilots landed, Chennault climbed down from the tower and debriefed their performance. Then it was time for P.T. The "Old Man," as the men took to calling him, prided himself on being in peak physical shape and he was determined to make the men shed the extra weight they'd gained from the food and drink on their transoceanic crossing. Paul Frillmann had been recruited as the unit's "chaplain," but he found himself taking on an assortment of tasks, including leading the men in calisthenics. There often would be baseball games as well, usually with Chennault pitching. The field was muddy and they would strip down to their shorts, or even their underwear, and splash in the mud as they dove for a fly ball or stole a base. Playing a familiar game could make the alien circumstances resolve to something almost ordinary, though for Chennault, having these American pilots with him was nothing short of extraordinary.

By day's end, the pilots were worn out. Dinner in the mess was another exercise in exotica—usually some sort of curried meat served with sides of potatoes and cabbage—but they got used to the mess hall dining soon enough. At least they ate it. After dinner Chennault would sometimes join them for a drink. They'd play cards and the commander would display the affable and talkative side of his personality. They were curious about what had brought him, and all of them, to the little airfield in the Burmese jungle. Chennault would regale them with stories and give them the "outline" of his life. He was something of an enigma to all his men, and they studied him closely. Even as he seemed to be letting his guard down a bit, there was still distance between them and this "gruff" man.

The only place Chennault seemed to let his emotions show was in letters to family members, few of which were saved. He had a new grandson, Claire Lee II, and he wrote to Nell that he was "look[ing] forward to teaching him to hunt and fish—and spoiling him, possibly." Whatever sense of homesickness may have plagued him, outwardly Chennault remained focused on the mission at hand.

Not too far from the airfield, Harvey and Olga Greenlaw lived in a small house where the men frequently stopped by for coffee. Thirty-one-year-old Olga became something of a surrogate mother to many of the young pilots, talking with them about their complaints or their homesickness. She would recall her husband pulling her aside one day to warn her about not "becoming too attached to any of these kids." He reminded her that they were "out here to fight a war—and you can't fight a war without somebody getting killed." They would not have to wait for combat for Harvey's warning to bear out. On a training flight on September 8, two P-40s engaged in a mock battle collided in midair. One plane lost a wing, and the pilot, Gil Bright, bailed out, narrowly escaping before his plane plunged down. The other pilot, John Armstrong, a graduate of Kansas State College, was found still strapped into his seat in the mangled wreckage of his plane. Jack Newkirk and John Petach were among the six pilots who served as the pallbearers, and Paul Frillmann conducted the funeral. After the service, he delicately pulled the American flag off the casket and folded it up; it was later shipped to the young man's mother. As they left the cemetery, dark clouds blocked out the sun, deepening the oppressive sense of gloom they already felt. Armstrong's was just the first in a series of fatal accidents for the American Volunteer Group. Pilot Maax Hammer lost control of his P-40 in a monsoon. Pete Atkinson tried to pull his P-40 out of a dive and the plane began to come apart, seeming to "disintegrate into a million pieces," as an onlooker put it. His body crashed through the tin roof of a house. Three had been lost in less than two months.

With their lives at stake, the pilots became obsessed with flight technique and theory. They talked endlessly about the specific quirks of the P-40, even mimicking dogfights with arms outstretched in the mess hall—Paul Frillmann thought it looked like a "gaggle of ballet dancers" as they played the part of their planes. No matter how silly it may have appeared, they wanted to be flawless when the shooting started.

Jack Newkirk had always prided himself on his fearlessness. He knew that not all the pilots would make it home alive, but this wasn't something he dwelled on in a letter to his new wife, Jane, who was waiting for him. On October 5, their three-month anniversary, he wrote her a letter: he wouldn't be back for their first anniversary, but "We will have our 2nd Anniversary together, won't we darling?" He promised her a "big reunion house party in Honolulu" to celebrate.

George McMillan, a dashing, six-foot-tall Floridian, wrote regular letters home to his mother telling her how much he missed her and that he wished he could be with her for Thanksgiving. The carefree days he would spend with his friends at Daytona Beach were long gone. Now, barely past his twenty-fifth birthday, he made out a will, leaving everything to his parents if he was killed. He would mail them a copy to keep in case something happened. The gloom seemed contagious. On the phonograph in the barracks, "I'll Never Smile Again" by Frank Sinatra and Tommy Dorsey was in constant rotation. Each man had to grapple with the knowledge of the suddenness, the randomness of mortality. They'd seen it with their own eyes, and understood there was no logical explanation for why one man died and the other did not. They pushed down the fear, though, and moved on.

They installed an old 16-millimeter movie projector in the mess hall. The sound was scratchy and out of sync with the screen—but going to the movies offered a precious few hours of thoughtless spectacle. During *The Ghost Breakers,* a Bob Hope comedy featuring former Ziegfeld dancer Paulette Goddard in various stages of undress, the moans and howls from those watching could be heard all over the base. The night that Pete Atkinson was killed the men gathered to watch *Flying High,* a 1931 musical about an inventor determined to fly his new "aerocopter." Frank Losonsky recalled "the movie took the edge off the day."

Unsurprisingly, the main thing they used to take the edge off was alcohol. Chennault demanded perfection of his men in the cockpit, but otherwise allowed them to party like they were at "a college campus on the eve of a homecoming football game." They drank whatever they could find—whiskey brewed by the natives, gin brewed by the nearby missionaries, and a potent mixture of rum that the Burmese called "Tiger Balm." If they were willing to bike the seven miles into Toungoo's tiny town center, they could have a meal and a drink at the small restaurant in the railroad station, a simple redbrick establishment. Anyone in search of a greater adventure on the weekends could take the train to Rangoon for a night out at the Silver Grill, a restaurant and nightclub popular with the British and other European expats, who would dance the night away in the back room. Into this relatively civilized assembly barged the brash American pilots, and in the recollection of Emma Foster, the British soldiers were "aghast at what these foolish Americans were doing." John Petach had been busy trying to court Foster ever since their romantic spark was lit aboard the ship. Emma, however, had been hesitant to get involved. She liked John but "wasn't all that enamored of getting serious," she recalled. Something started to change during those late nights at the Silver Grill. Decades later, she would recall, "The Silver Grill is where the romance took place so the Silver Grill has a special meaning for me and that's where all of it began to develop." She found herself dancing with John to the exclusion of the other eager young men. When a few of them made passes, she was "clear and decisive" that she was taken.

In the regimen of training and preparing, there was still time for Emma and John to get to know each other. They bought bicycles in Toungoo and put them to good use, going on long rides together. In the evenings, they explored their shared passion for music while listening to her records. He was thoughtful and really seemed to listen to her, and not only listen, but understand. "Bit by bit he got me," she said.

Foster could have stayed home in Minneapolis and gotten married. Instead she lived in a hut with rats crawling into her drawers and eating the buttons on her clothes, and it was exactly where she wanted to be. She was not only falling in love with John, but she believed in the mission and was eager to help the Chinese cause any way she could. Of course, she knew John would be in mortal danger once the fighting started. She would stand outside the hospital and observe the P-40s flying overhead. She always knew which plane was John's because he would fly right over the hospital and wiggle his wings. "Not very many women have had a courtship like that," she said. It was exhilarating, but she knew a safe landing was never guaranteed.

Despite the intense training, the American Volunteer Group didn't look much like a real military outfit. Since the men weren't enlisted in the army, there were no dress inspections—indeed, there were no uniforms—and the men grew out their hair and sported mustaches. The base didn't look like an army installation either. With monkeys living in the barracks as pets, the effect was something like a circus troupe mixed with a fraternity party. The men embraced their freedom, and with a bit of wanderlust they decided to explore the Burmese countryside. A group of pilots took a truck and drove deep into the mountains, where they found a little stream for swimming. Some even ventured into the jungles armed with shotguns and knives to go hunting, though they were more likely to catch malaria than a tiger. Chennault's laissez-faire discipline worked out fine for the most part. There was one notable exception: Greg Boyington.

Boyington was one of the last to arrive when his ship, the *Boschfontein,* reached Rangoon on November 12, 1941. It wasn't long before he developed a reputation in Toungoo, too, as a person who drank too much for his own good. He was a mean drunk, the kind who liked to fight. One pilot recalled him getting so drunk one night that he punched his fist through a bamboo wall. After another bender, he ran into a field and tried to wrestle a cow to the ground. Harvey Greenlaw told him that he needed to kick the habit, but Boyington replied, "Get lost,

Greenlaw, or I'll bend your teeth." Boyington was slow adjusting to the new lifestyle in the Burmese jungle. He forgot to shake out his shirt one morning and a scorpion left a bite on his back that "grew to the size of a cantaloupe."

To make matters worse, the brash pilot thought he was already an expert on the P-40, even though he had never flown the plane before. On his maiden flight, after bragging about his prowess, he landed so roughly he nearly wrecked the plane. As he stepped out of the banged-up aircraft he tried to maintain his composure, but the men on the ground mocked him as he walked away from the scene. The one place he found comfort was in talking to Olga Greenlaw. There were rumors that the two were having an affair, but she would mildly dismiss the specula-tion, later writing that he was simply a frequent caller who popped in "at odd times for coffee or whatever." Still, it is clear she admired him. When she first spotted him walking in the rain, she recalled "His waist and hips seemed much too slender for his massive torso and shoulders and his curly hair was wet. . . ." If someone wanted to speculate on the rumors, he wouldn't be alone. As one pilot put it, "There used to be a running gag: there's only two guys who didn't sleep with Olga, and I don't know who the other one is."

Whenever the men needed a wholesome touch of comfort in the Burmese jungle, they'd join an American missionary couple, Chester and Alice Klein, for Sunday-night dinners. They were homey affairs that would prove to be the setting for one of the more influential develop-ments in the identity of the American Volunteer Group. Chester had served in the U.S. Army in France during the Great War, and the Ohio native had later spent over twenty years in Burma before becoming fa-mous among Chennault's men for his homemade gin. After dinner one night in November 1941, their guests were sitting in the living room having a drink, when one of the pilots happened to pick up the Kleins' copy of an English-language newspaper, the *Illustrated Weekly of India,* which had an Australian P-40 on the cover. The nose of that P-40 was painted to look like it had the face of a shark, giving the pilots an idea for a redecorating project.

The next morning, a few of the pilots picked up some chalk from Chennault's classroom and headed down to the flight line on their bikes. They sketched the outline of what they'd seen across the nose of the P-40s in the photo—marking where the wide-open mouth and fearsome teeth would go—before asking Chennault what he thought. Not only did he like it, he wanted the design painted on the whole fleet as a distinct marker of the American Volunteer Group. They set about painting the side of every plane with a nose that looked like a shark's snout and a beady shark eye above the mouth. Head on, it looked like the plane was coming to eat you alive: the intake at the front of the nose was like the gaping maw that a shark's prey would disappear into. The pilots could never have imagined how iconic those faces would become in the months, years, and decades to come. Chennault couldn't wait to get his shark-nosed planes into battle.

The shark faces gave no indication of the nationality of the P-40, but the twelve-pointed star underneath the wings, the distinctive "Blue Sky with a White Sun," made clear that they belonged to Nationalist China.

Chennault was understandably worried that the Japanese—who had begun to amass troops in French Indochina after their initial September 1940 invasion—might launch a preemptive strike on his base. The British, who controlled Burma, and the Japanese were still at peace, but that was faint comfort for Chennault. Word of the mission had already leaked out from the beginning, and in June 1941, a Japanese spokesman had gone so far as to call it a "hostile act" on America's part. By November 1941, there were reports from the RAF about Japanese reconnaissance flights not far from the air base and Chennault was concerned that one day he would look up and see Japanese war planes overhead. Chennault sent a few of the P-40s on secret high-altitude reconnaissance missions over neutral Thailand in late October to look for dust clouds that would indicate the movement of Japanese forces below. He kept watch himself in the evening dusk, standing in a bamboo tower smoking his pipe. When darkness fell, he would climb down and get a few hours of fitful sleep before resuming his observation in the morning.

Training was coming to an end. Chennault had prepared for battle by dividing his men into three squadrons. Each chose its own nickname. The First Squadron nicknamed themselves the Adam and Eve squadron—after man's first pursuit—and decided to add a small red apple to the fuselage of their planes. Chennault reportedly told them that it would have to be a green apple to avoid any confusion with the Japanese red rising sun. The Third Squadron called themselves the Hell's Angels, after the 1930 Howard Hughes film, and used a scantily clad angel as their group insignia. But it was the Second Squadron, the Panda Bears, under the command of Jack Newkirk, that many agreed had the best designs on their planes. Bert Christman, the cartoonist, did sketches of pandas for the planes of his squadronmates. Tex Hill's was a panda cowboy wearing a ten-gallon hat and cowboy boots. John Petach's panda was riding a bicycle, a nod to the airman's cycling adventures with Emma Foster. John Newkirk's panda was in a tuxedo and wearing a top hat, a gesture that poked fun at Scarsdale Jack's reputation as the rich kid from New York.

The planes were painted and the pilots were ready, but there was just one problem: the ground crew needed additional spare parts to repair some of the damaged planes. Throughout the training, Chennault had pushed his men to fly as if they really were in combat. Aside from the three fatal accidents, there had been many more crashes in which the pilot had survived but the plane didn't make it. Landings frequently went awry: "Too much brake on a rolling aircraft stood it straight on its nose," crew chief Frank Losonsky recalled. The nose would come crashing into the ground, smashing the propeller. It would take mechanics half a day to replace the propeller, assuming they had a spare available. The totalled planes were piled up in a "boneyard" so the ground crew could salvage parts from the remnants, but they were always running short. One crew chief, J. J. Harrington, recalled the supply situation as "horrible." The rough landings and jungle heat had eaten away too many of their tires, and there weren't enough spark plugs for the planes. The plan was to have one hundred P-40s, but Harrington estimated they never had more than sixty that were flyable.

The supply situation concerned Chennault a great deal. He knew that the China Defense Supplies team in Washington, D.C., was working on getting spare parts that would eventually arrive, but none of that could be guaranteed. There were even plans for more planes and pilots to come in as reinforcements. In September, President Roosevelt directly signed off on plans for sending over another 100 pilots along with "269 pursuit planes and 66 bombers"—providing proof, if there had been any doubt, that the president was in the loop on this covert operation to assist China. Ultimately, plans existed for three American Volunteer Groups, but Chennault felt he needed to take his unit into action quickly.

Chennault had an idea to address the lack of spare parts. He would assign Joe Alsop—whose Harvard manners and lack of military experience had made him somewhat of an outlier in the Toungoo outfit so far—a task perfectly suited to his skills. In December 1941, Alsop embarked on a diplomatic mission: hunt up spare P-40 parts already in Asia. First, he flew to Singapore to meet with the British authorities, and then on to the Philippines to make his appeal for greater support directly to Lieutenant General Douglas MacArthur, the commander of U.S. Army Forces in the Far East. The general listened attentively and promised Alsop that he would do "everything possible" to support Chennault's outfit.

MacArthur's theoretical support didn't stop the ticking of the clock. There were rumors that the Japanese were going to launch a major attack on Kunming and try to cut off the Burma Road, China's last lifeline to the outside world. The time was coming for the AVG pilots to transfer to China and start doing what they'd come all this way to do. They were ready. "We'd like a change of scenery and a little excitement," George McMillan wrote in a letter home dated December 7, 1941. He cut the letter short, noting it was time to get to dinner.

Pilot John Donovan wrote to his parents in Montgomery, Alabama: "It seems that when you get near where danger is, you want to do something to relieve the danger." The relief he had in mind was fighting.

CHAPTER 8

WARTIME

December 6, 1941, was a Saturday and in Honolulu that meant it was a night for partying. Dive bars along Hotel Street were full of "drunken Army and Navy men," the Temperance League of Hawaii noted disapprovingly. For these young men stationed in paradise, it was another night out on the town. At midnight the bars closed, and the remaining sailors rushed to the buses waiting outside the YMCA. The buses dropped them off at the pier, where they boarded liberty boats that would take them back out to their vessels moored in the harbor. Not everyone would make it back to the ships that night—a few sailors from the *Arizona* drank so much champagne at the Halekulani Hotel that they passed out.

It was a beautiful night—"peaceful, so serene," as one sailor on the U.S.S. *Arizona* recalled—with a light breeze, full moon, and "stars shimmering in the night sky." The men got ready for bed, as they would have to wake in just a few hours. Some had plans to spend Sunday shopping in Honolulu, taking long hikes, or catching up on reading. At 5:30 A.M. reveille sounded over the intercom on the *Arizona,* and many of the crew donned T-shirts and shorts, a perk of being posted in the tropics in the wintertime. At 6:30 A.M. there was chow call and the men went to the mess hall for a breakfast of fried Spam, powdered eggs, and pancakes. On deck, sailors set up chairs for church services.

At 7:55 A.M. a white-and-blue flag was raised up the pole at the Pearl Harbor tower. That was the signal to the warships to raise their flags at precisely 8:00 A.M., and their color guards stood at the ready. At that moment, men in the tower saw lines of planes flying in from what seemed like every direction. The air seemed to vibrate. Lieutenant Commander Logan Ramsey sent an urgent message from Ford Island: "AIR RAID, PEARL HARBOR, THIS IS NOT A DRILL."

Suddenly the men below deck on the *Arizona* heard the distinct sound of airplanes buzzing and of explosions: "They're bombing the water tower on Ford Island!" someone shouted. The men ran to their battle stations on deck and looked up. On the underside of the swarming planes they could see big red "meatballs." They were Japanese. Some men made it to the antiaircraft guns, broke into the locked cabinets that held the ammunition, and got off a few shots at the Japanese dive-bombers, but they missed the planes. The blast and shock of explosions came from all around and smoke was turning the sky into an ugly black cloud. The ship's steel writhed under the force of the detonations, making "the most wretched sound, as if it were in agonizing pain."

At 8:06 A.M. the *Arizona* took a devastating blow when a 1,760-pound bomb landed on its deck, penetrating the ammunition magazine. An "expanding fireball shot five or six hundred feet into the air." The ship was ablaze, and so were many of the men. Of the men assigned to the *Arizona* that day, only 335 survived. The dead numbered 1,177.

It had taken only a few minutes for the first wave of 189 Japanese planes to hit the fleet. The tightly packed ships on Battleship Row had presented "a target that none could miss. A bomber could be pretty sure that he would hit a ship even if not the one that he aimed at," wrote Secretary of the Interior Harold Ickes. Ultimately more than twenty-four hundred Americans lost their lives at Pearl Harbor, and the Pacific Fleet was crippled. President Franklin Roosevelt was sitting in his study at the White House when he got the telephone call with the devastating news. He took the attack personally—he was a navy man, and as assistant navy secretary had overseen the ceremonial keel-laying for the *Arizona,* then Battleship 39, at the Brooklyn Navy Yard.

He also knew America wasn't ready for the war that had been thrust upon it. "We will have to take a good many defeats before we can have a victory," he said to Eleanor. Later that day, the White House butler overheard Roosevelt talking with Harry Hopkins, a close adviser, about a possible Japanese invasion of the West Coast—the president glumly calculated that the Japanese could make it as far as Chicago before their forces would become overextended and would be pushed back.

On the morning of December 8 Chennault rose and headed to the airfield to check on the planes. As he was walking across the field, he saw a figure running toward him, frantically waving a piece of paper bearing the awful news.

Chennault had expected the Japanese to launch a surprise attack against the United States, perhaps even on the American Volunteer Group at Toungoo, but Pearl Harbor was four thousand miles from the Japanese islands. How their planes and ships traveled that distance without having been detected was unfathomable to him. When he had been stationed at Pearl Harbor in 1924, he had prided himself on being diligent about placing sentries with binoculars to scan the skies for any unusual activity. Every officer should have been aware that his primary responsibility was "to take measures to ensure his own unit against tactical surprise by the enemy." For this failure there was "no excuse." If he had been the one "caught with my planes on the ground . . . I could never again have looked my fellow officers squarely in the eye." He would be ready if they came for the AVG next.

Word of the Japanese surprise attack traveled quickly about the base. The pilots and crew headed down to the flight line. Perversely, they were "laughing and kidding" about the news, R. T. Smith wrote in his diary, but it was "easy to see there was really plenty of tension" underneath that façade. George McMillan grabbed the letter he had written to his family the night before and added a P.S. in red ink: "Just received the news that the U.S. and Japan are at War. Anything can happen now! Will write whenever I get a chance, but my letters will be fewer. Don't worry—" That was easier said than done. In his diary, his excitement came through: "Received news today that Japan had bombed Pearl Harbor . . . Fine business! Maybe we'll see some action now. Everyone is getting tired of sitting around Toungoo."

The news was personal for many of the men. The navy recruits, in particular, felt certain that the names of friends would appear on casualty lists in the days to come. But for now, there was work to be done, and they knew that Toungoo was a vulnerable target. "If they don't bomb our field here before we get away, we'll be lucky," Smith added. Ed Rector recalled his impression of Chennault's state of mind: "There was a look of relief that even that taciturn man could not hide." For years, Chennault had wanted the United States to join with China in a war against Japan, and now it had finally come to pass.

The fraternity-party atmosphere that had prevailed among the American Volunteer Group before the attack on Pearl Harbor quickly disappeared as the base transitioned to a wartime footing. The men were instructed to wear their sidearms, and soon gas masks and tin helmets were distributed. An order was posted canceling all scheduled leave. The days of those wild hunting trips to the jungle were over.

Chennault ordered that the P-40s be fueled and ready to take off. The men prepared to "scramble into the air at the slightest hint of approaching enemy planes," as one recalled. A blackout was ordered, and a decoy airfield was set up a few miles away with lamps illuminating a deserted runway. They waited for the attack.

On December 10, the alarm sounded at 3:30 A.M. "We bolted out of the beds and ran as fast as we could," Frank Losonsky recalled. "Adrenaline was pumping like crazy." Planes scrambled into the air while the men on the ground sought shelter in trenches. Losonsky waited in the darkness, wondering, "What's a falling bomb sound like?" Tex Hill was on alert duty and raced to his P-40, taking off into the darkness. After patrolling long enough to realize that there was no enemy in sight, Hill brought the plane back down, guided by the kerosene lamps that had been rushed out to light the runway. Hill was a navy pilot and well versed in landing on the decks of aircraft carriers, but he overshot the runway and crashed. That error would have been fatal on a carrier, but he was able to walk away without serious injuries. One man recalled finding a dazed Hill walking around the airfield covered in gasoline and precariously holding an unlit cigarette in one hand and a match in the other. The episode was embarrassing for a man who considered himself to be one of the unit's best fliers, and he apologized to Chennault for the accident. Chennault was understanding about the incident, and Hill promised that he'd make it up to his commander in the battles ahead.

The men impatiently listened to KGEI in San Francisco for updates.

Olga Greenlaw wrote in the "official" AVG war diary on December 8: "Radio news: Japanese bombed Wake Island and Honolulu—results unknown. They also bombed Singapore but not much damage done there." It soon became clear that the Japanese offensive was far more extensive than just the attack on Pearl Harbor. In his address to Congress on December 8, 1941, President Roosevelt reported: "Yesterday the Japanese Government also launched an attack against Malaya. Last night Japanese forces attacked Hong Kong. Last night Japanese forces attacked Guam. Last night Japanese forces attacked the Philippine Islands. Last night the Japanese attacked Wake Island. And this morning the Japanese attacked Midway Island." With attacks on British colonies, including Hong Kong and Singapore, the British and Japanese were finally at war and the AVG men could no longer assume, if they ever had, that Burma was off limits to the Japanese bombers.

While the islands Roosevelt cited in his address meant little to most Americans, they were well known to Chennault and the men of the American Volunteer Group, as they were crucial links on the air and sea routes that connected their base in Toungoo with the United States. The men had stopped at many of them on their way to Burma, and only a few months had passed since they'd been carefree tourists swimming at Waikiki Beach. Now, with all these islands under attack, it quickly became apparent how isolated the AVG was from the United States. The Pacific Ocean had never seemed larger.

The war would throw a wrench into many of their plans. The Lockheed Hudson bombers that Chennault had been promised were still in California, and the plans for sending them over were scrapped. There was one ship in the Pacific carrying spare parts and tires for the P-40 and two more ships carrying the bomber pilots and crews for the Second American Volunteer Group, but none of them would ever reach Toungoo. The ships were diverted to Australia and the men were put back in the U.S. Army. The Pan Am Clipper bringing over tires and spare parts for the Flying Tigers was at Wake Island when the Japanese attacked. The plane was fueling when the captain heard the drone of airplanes in the distance, and within minutes, as one historian wrote, "the Clipper loading dock disappeared in a geyser of debris. A Japanese warplane strafed the [Clipper] stitching a line of bullets across the fuselage." Though damaged, the plane still seemed flyable. The order was given to strip it down, and the cargo, baggage, and even the furniture were thrown out—including the extra supplies for the AVG. Thirty-four people, including two wounded, were put on the plane. It took off, but now it turned back to Hawaii. The AVG supplies were left sitting in a pile on Wake Island, abandoned to the Japanese when the U.S. Marines surrendered on December 23.

President Roosevelt's approval in September of hundreds more pilots to assist China was off the table now. The whole purpose of the American Volunteer Group was suddenly up in the air—it had been intended as a way for the United States to secretly provide aid to China while maintaining official neutrality, but why bother now that there was a real war on? There was already discussion back at the White House about inducting the entire unit into the U.S. Army.

After Joe Alsop's successful meeting with MacArthur in Manila, he began the long trek back to Burma with the general's assurance of material support. But as Alsop's rickety transport reached Hong Kong, so did the Japanese. He'd barely breathed a sigh of relief on landing before he discovered the British colony was in the middle of a furious attack by the Japanese. He waited at the airport, hoping to get a seat on a departing flight, but all the planes leaving the island were full (he'd later claim that a seat he was supposed to get on the last flight had been taken by the large dog of a Chinese dignitary). Stranded, he tried to make the best of his situation. He thought about joining in the defense efforts, but found that no one was interested in a man who, as he put it, "had never shot a gun in his life." He spent his days with the St. John's Ambulance Corps, helping to carry the wounded to the hospital. As December, and the bombardment, dragged on, it was clear that Hong Kong would fall and he would be captured. He hoped that he could claim to be a newspaperman and avoid any connection to the Flying Tigers. As a soldier without a uniform, he ran the risk of being executed as a spy. He contemplated what life would be like in an internment camp. He had a few sapphires he'd bought in Burma and figured they might come in handy when he was locked up. He found a seamstress in his hotel and had her sew them into his jacket for safekeeping.

At 3:30 P.M. on Christmas Day, Hong Kong surrendered; it would be known as the "Black Christmas." Civilians who were deemed "enemy nationals" by the Japanese were required to report for internment. Alsop was locked up in a former brothel that was now a prison, and no one seemed to suspect that this plump aristocratic-sounding American had, just weeks before, been part of a covert mission to fight the Japanese. His ruse of posing as a newspaperman paid off. His captors accepted his claims that he was a civilian and shipped him across Hong Kong to the Stanley Internment Camp, where the Japanese would ultimately hold twenty-eight hundred British, American, and Dutch civilians who were unlucky enough to have been in Hong Kong when it fell.

The internment camp included what had been a prep school that the Japanese had seized, and Alsop was part of an advance party of prisoners sent over to help prepare the buildings to house the internees. The first place they went to was the home of one of the school's masters. When they entered they were greeted by his mutilated corpse—the man's head was across the room from his body. That was what you got for resisting the Japanese, Alsop concluded. While most of the men went to clean up the "frightful scene," he rummaged through the deceased's book collection, nabbing an eighteenth-century copy of the *Analects of Confucius,* which he considered a key part of the survival kit he would need in the camp.

In some ways, Alsop was more at home in Stanley than he had been with the AVG in Toungoo. He could return to long days of reading and thinking without having to worry about the mechanical needs of the airplanes. He even found a professor to teach him Chinese. That was the upside.

The downside was that he was a Japanese internee sleeping in a ratty barracks and surviving on pathetic rations of cold rice, condensed milk, and small servings of tinned beef. When he wanted to smoke he would roll cigarettes with toilet paper. Only a few short months earlier he had been one of the stars of the dinner circuit in Georgetown—that was how he had met Claire Chennault. He had been famous for his insatiable appetite, and had consequently struggled with his weight. Now he made do with what he had. What choice did he have?

His decision to identify himself as a newspaperman continued to pay off—in June 1942 he was sent back to the United States as part of an exchange of civilian prisoners, alongside the American diplomats who had been at the embassy in Tokyo when the war started. Back at his parents' home in Connecticut, he could tell the true story of what he had been doing in the Far East—a story that appeared in the *Hartford Courant,* making him something of a local hero, despite his utter lack of combat experience. Aside from coming home thirty pounds skinnier than when he'd shipped out, he was unscathed.

Within weeks he regained the weight, and then some.

After the "initial shock" of Pearl Harbor wore off, the pilots realized they were now on the front lines, "on the other side of the world from our friends." Japanese forces entered Thailand, a nation that would soon join Japan in declaring war against the United States. Japanese planes were amassing in Bangkok, and while that was still over four hundred miles from the AVG airfield in Toungoo, it was too close for comfort.

Chennault had to assess the Japanese buildup, and for that urgent task he turned to Erik Shilling. The twenty-six-year-old pilot had installed an aerial reconnaissance camera, courtesy of the Royal Air Force, in his P-40. Though not a combat mission, flying over Japanese-occupied territory was dangerous, especially now that the war was on. Two other P-40s, piloted by Ed Rector and Bert Christman, would accompany Shilling as escorts.

On the morning of Wednesday, December 10, the three planes stopped to refuel at the RAF base at Tavoy, Burma, and then flew over the Thai border. The escorts remained at a lower altitude as Shilling climbed to twenty-six thousand feet above Bangkok. The "makeshift camera system" was activated by remote control and the camera was soon "taking a continuous strip of photos." When they landed safely back in Rangoon, the images were developed and they revealed ninety-two Japanese airplanes parked wingtip to wingtip at just a single base. Shilling was certain there were even more aircraft parked in the hangars he'd seen.

He felt as if they were "facing the full weight of the Japanese Air Force." When they showed the photos to Chennault, the Old Man could scarcely believe the extent of the Japanese buildup under way, but reflected: "A dozen bombers could have wrecked the Japanese air offensive in twenty minutes." He didn't have a single bomber, however, much less a dozen, and would have to fight the enemy with his band of P-40s.

In the days that followed, the AVG pilots always seemed to be glancing up, half expecting a cluster of Japanese bombers to come into view. Even the slightest motion in the sky, a flock of birds perhaps, was enough to send jitters down their spines. But no Japanese planes ever appeared.

The uncertainty began to unnerve them. As Charlie Bond wrote in his diary, "We expect to be hit, but I presume they are working on Singapore right now. Who knows?" The twenty-seven-year-old Bond came from a working-class family in Dallas. He had spent some time helping his dad paint houses and put up wallpaper, but his dreams of becoming a military aviator eventually bore fruit. In the Army Air Corps, he was ferrying bombers to Canada, a job he found monotonous. When he got the AVG pitch, he eagerly accepted. Now, here was the excitement he'd been looking for, and maybe a little more than that. "We are very tense and prepared to do our best," he wrote, "but we have no replacements."

The attack on Pearl Harbor reinforced their sense of purpose. "This puts a totally different aspect or picture, our country is at war, so this is not to protect the Burma Road, this is all out," Ed Rector recalled. "So we were even more motivated, if that were possible." On December 19 Jack Newkirk wrote to his wife: "By now you know the President has declared war against the Japanese. My dear, you have no idea of what war really means back in the security of the States, and I hope you never will." He had originally joined Chennault's outfit with vague ideas about pursuing adventure, but now he was fighting for his country—and for her and the family they'd raise together someday. He continued: "There are certain things in every man's life which he cannot bear to leave undone if he is manly. . . . I dream that you and I shall someday raise our children to respect all men, but to fear no one."

Chennault found the transition to war invigorating. For months, he had anxiously expected a surprise attack on Toungoo, a sensation so intense he described it as "like the twisting of a turnbuckle, tightening nerves already taut and raw with uncertainty." But now that there was all-out war, he wrote, "For the first time since mid-October I breathed easier."

As much as the pilots wanted revenge for Pearl Harbor, the AVG was still under Chinese command. The Chinese were also cooperating with the British, which led to an unusual plan for the Americans: Chennault's men would split up to defend Kunming in China and Rangoon in Burma. Chennault would return as soon as possible to Kunming and with him the First and Second Squadrons of the AVG. The RAF had requested support for the defense of Burma, and the Third Squadron would join the Royal Air Force squadrons already in Rangoon. Protecting the two cities was a massive undertaking, but the Chinese couldn't ignore Rangoon. If it fell, then China would have no land-based supply route to the outside world.

At 9:30 A.M. on December 12, eighteen P-40s from the Third Squadron made the half-hour flight to the RAF's Mingaladon aerodrome at Rangoon. As soon as they landed, the air-raid siren sounded, but as it turned out the approaching planes were British. The pilots were pleased to discover that their new barracks and mess hall appeared to be a significant upgrade over those at Toungoo.

On December 18, three Douglas transports landed in Toungoo. The planes, flown by CNAC pilots, were to take Chennault, along with a number of his aides and supplies, to Kunming. Olga Greenlaw was scheduled to fly on a transport and showed up with her bags packed, carrying her small dog, Lucy. The CNAC pilot protested: "Now, look here, Olga. Don't tell me you're taking that rat along?" She insisted that the dog was a good-luck charm and that settled it; the dog was going, too. The long flight to Kunming would take them on a route over mountains to a city the Japanese had actively been bombing. Although the trip was fairly manageable for the Douglas transports that would shuttle Chennault, Greenlaw, and Lucy the dog, the P-40s would be pushed close to their limits on this long trek and the pilots weren't looking forward to it. It was, as Charlie Bond wrote in his diary, "a 670-mile flight over some awful-looking terrain and impossible in case of a forced landing."

Thirty-six planes had been scheduled to fly to Kunming, but before the squadrons even took off there were two accidents: one pilot taxied off the runway and destroyed his plane's landing gear, and another ran into a Studebaker that was parked nearby. The First Squadron made the flight nonstop, while the Second Squadron made the reasonable decision to refuel along the way at an airstrip at Lashio, Burma, before crossing the border into China. While they were flying at high altitude, one pilot's oxygen tube somehow came unfastened and he appeared to pass out. The plane began to lose altitude, but fortunately he regained consciousness before the dive was unrecoverable and rejoined the First Squadron's formation.

Charlie Bond finally spotted a field covered with what looked like "thousands of Chinese soldiers" and knew they had reached Kunming. The squadrons landed and quickly assessed their new living arrangements, hoping for an improvement from the dismal conditions they'd endured for months in Toungoo. They were pleasantly surprised to find they were being housed in conditions fit for visiting royalty. The AVG was given two converted university dormitories that would serve as their "hostels." Each room was furnished with a comfortable bed and a chest of drawers, a desk, and a table. After spending months in the teakwood barracks in the Burmese jungle, this was like checking in to a luxurious hotel. It was frigid in Kunming, in contrast to the tropical heat in Toungoo, but the pilots were provided with blankets and there was a small charcoal heater in each room. There were even flush toilets and another incredible luxury—showers with hot water. "Yeowee!!" Charlie Bond wrote in his diary. "I thought I would never get out of the shower."

After settling in, Tex Hill and a few other pilots decided to take a look around Kunming. There had been a Japanese air raid on the city just hours before they arrived, and the residents were still clearing up the debris and attending to the casualties. "That was my first indication of war, seeing all those dead and wounded people, with arms and legs blown off," Tex Hill recalled. "It was terrible." The Americans had spent their careers training for aerial warfare, but studying textbooks was different from witnessing the carnage up close. That night, they stayed up talking about the butchery in Kunming's streets. Bond hadn't accompanied them on the tour, but he remembered that it was "so easy after listening to such description of misery and woes to react violently and hate the guts of the Japs." They expected the Japanese air force would return the following day, and they'd have their own first taste of combat.

CHAPTER 9

LEGENDS IN THEIR OWN TIME

The pilots in Kunming rose before dawn on December 19 and made their way to the mess hall, where they devoured a breakfast of eggs and bacon, another welcome upgrade over the rations at Toungoo. Then they went out into the freezing morning air, heading across the ice-covered fields to the runway. When they encountered Chinese guards standing watch at the airfield they yelled out, "American! Friend! OK!" It didn't appear that the Chinese guards spoke English, but they seemed to understand and let the pilots proceed down to the waiting P-40s.

They inspected the planes, then gathered in the hut that served as the alert shack next to the airfield. They were to wait there until they got a signal to take off. "Sleepiness and excitement and the stimulus of being in a new country, a new climate, made everyone in the alert shacks light-headed," Paul Frillmann recalled. The men would occasionally step outside to gaze at the impressive expanse of Lake Kunming, dotted with small native craft, and the red mountains that rose up beyond the airfields. The cold winter air was "like a shot of iced gin after the Burma jungles," Frillmann recalled. As they nervously waited for the Japanese bombers to appear, there was plenty of horseplay and even a game of tag—anything that helped them to pass the time. But by sunset there had been no enemy activity.

The following day, December 20, started off much the same. Charlie Bond set off on a flight patrol at around 6:00 A.M. and saw nothing, so returned to the base. Chennault kept to his makeshift office, anxiously watching the telephone on his desk, which was connected to the

Chinese code room, which in turn was linked to the "warning net." At a time when radar was a recent invention and not yet widely used, many countries were employing warning nets of different varieties. Throughout Yunnan Province hundreds of Chinese soldiers were designated lookouts. Known by their station names (such as X-10, P-8, or C-23, as Chennault listed them in his memoir), they would call in a warning if aircraft were seen or heard overhead. The stations were spread out strategically; on a map they looked like a vast spiderweb that offered no way for bombers to sneak through undetected. The Chinese Air Force, now with the cooperation of the AVG, would plot the intelligence as points on a map, tracing the path of an incoming Japanese bomber formation. If an attack seemed imminent, a Chinese officer would call Chennault, who would quickly dispatch the P-40s.

At 9:45 A.M. the phone finally rang. A Chinese Air Force officer notified Chennault that "ten Japanese bombers crossed the Yunnan border at Laokay heading northwest." Chennault would have to wait for further updates from the warning net to map out the precise trajectory of the bombers. Additional stations soon reported in, with "heavy engine noise" indicated at one and "noise of many above clouds" at another. The nodes were carefully marked on the map in the command room, and it appeared that the Japanese bombers were headed to a spot about fifty miles east of Kunming. From there Chennault presumed they would "probably begin the circling and feinting tactics designed to confuse the warning net before their final dash to the target." For years, the Japanese had been striking Kunming at will with little or no opposition, but that was going to end today. Chennault had rehearsed this moment so many times in his head that by now it almost seemed like a dream. "The lines tightened about his mouth as he pulled a pipe from the pocket in his khaki jacket," the radioman sitting next to him observed. "I knew he was nervous by the way he crammed tobacco into it." Chennault radioed Sandy Sandell, the former army pilot who was leading the First Squadron, and told him to get his pilots ready. The First Squadron would take sixteen P-40s and try to intercept the Japanese bomber formation. The Second Squadron was ordered to fly out in two groups of four, one led by Jack Newkirk and the other by Jim Howard, and circle overhead in reserve duty. The pilots took to their cockpits wearing mittens, jackets, and heavy pants and waited for the signal to take off—a red flare darting across the morning sky. Chennault stepped outside and saw only puffball clouds. This was the moment he had been working toward for so many years, the moment when "American pilots in American fighter planes . . . [were] about to tackle a formation of the Imperial Japanese Air Force, which was then sweeping the Pacific skies victorious everywhere." He pulled out his flare gun, raised it, and pulled the trigger. The red flash arced across the sky and the P-40s raced down the runway, climbing quickly skyward.

Watching the planes depart, Chennault believed "that the fate of China was riding in the P-40 cockpits through the wintery sky over Yunnan." He drove over to the combat operations shelter next to the airfield, climbed into the "dark and dank" quarters. He may have thought of his days in the Flying Trapeze, when he had been the daring man in the cockpit, the one everyone said "laughed at death." At forty-eight, the Old Man wished he were "ten years younger and crouched in a cockpit instead of a dugout, tasting the stale rubber of an oxygen mask and peering ahead into limitless space through the cherry-red rings of a gunsight."

Instead he took his place at the radio. At first all he heard was the crackling of the static, but soon came the voices of pilots in their initial confusion: "There they are."

"No, no, they can't be Japs."

"Look at those rose balls."

"Let's get 'em."

That was all he could hear. Just "maddening silence."

Somehow, in the fog of battle, it was the reserve Second Squadron rather than the First that encountered the Japanese bomber group, a formation of ten Ki-48 bombers, or "Lily" bombers, as the Allies came to call them. Scarsdale Jack Newkirk's Second Squadron opened fire, but Newkirk was overeager and fired from too far away. His own guns seemed to jam, and he told his men to turn back. For the moment it seemed as if the enemy might get away. The bombers, retreating in the face of the American fighters, dropped their explosives without taking aim and began to pick up speed as they lightened their load, racing for their base at Hanoi.

But Charlie Bond and the First Squadron pilots were determined that the Japanese weren't going to escape unscathed. The First Squadron pilots had ascended and then turned southeast to locate the point outside of Kunming where they anticipated encountering the enemy. When it became apparent that the Japanese bombers weren't going to come to them, the Americans gave pursuit. After the endless patrols of the past few weeks, Bond was more excited than nervous. He took the P-40 to full throttle and used the thrust of its Allison engine to close the gap between him and the fleeing bombers. After ten minutes, which must have seemed like an eternity, the First Squadron pilots closed in. This was going to be a real fight—the Lily had a 7.7-mm machine gun in its nose, another on its back, and a third in the rear that could be lowered down, which enabled a tail gunner to lie prone and shoot. Charlie Bond could see them lower the rear "dustbin" guns, as they were called, but that would also slow them down.

The Americans split up to hit the Japanese from different angles, and Charlie Bond took his P-40 into an ascent, trying to get on top of them. He checked that his oxygen mask was on tight and turned on his gun switch—or so he thought. He was about a thousand feet above the Japanese planes and a few thousand feet to their left, so he rolled and then dove down until he reached a point where he had a clear shot and "the nearest bomber eased within the gunsight ring." He squeezed the trigger and waited for the flash from his machine guns. "Damn it, nothing happened!" He looked at his gun switch and realized that somehow, in his excitement, he had failed to turn it on. He pulled out of his strafing run, angry at himself for missing his first shot, and then climbed back on top and dove down again: "All guns were blazing this time. I saw my tracers enter the fuselage of the bomber . . . I attacked again and again. Two bombers began to lag behind, trailing smoke." He left them for others to finish off, keeping his focus on the group of Japanese bombers he saw in the main formation. The P-40s were attacking from all directions and they tried to avoid running into one another. Bond barely avoided a collision, but was "too keyed up to give it much thought." By now, the needles on the fuel dials began to tick ominously lower. Sandy Sandell finally called off the attack—but not before he saw a few Japanese planes go down, leaving trails of black smoke.

Chennault stood out on the airfield waiting for his pilots to return. He hadn't been able to hear anything further on the radio, and though there had been word from the warning net that Japanese bombers had crashed in the mountains, he needed to hear that verified by his men. The first to appear were some planes from the Second Squadron, but they were just "a dejected bunch of airmen," as Jim Howard put it, because they hadn't seen any action. Next in was Scarsdale Jack, who climbed out, complaining that his gun had jammed. They tested it out later, and when it fired successfully, the other pilots joked that it worked fine when someone else was shooting it. Chennault diagnosed the problem not as a mechanical one but as a case of "buck fever," which afflicts a new hunter when he gets nervous the first time the prey is in his crosshairs. Finally the shark-nosed P-40s from the First Squadron appeared overhead, doing victory rolls and looping over the field. As they landed, the men on the ground cheered. "It was our first taste of combat and our first test," Charlie Bond wrote. "It was the first time Japanese bombers have been turned back from bombing Kunming."

When Bond inspected his P-40, he found it full of bullet holes.

The pilots tallied four of the Japanese bombers downed for sure and considered a few more probables. To Chennault, though, the exact number of kills didn't matter if some of the Japanese bombers got away. He told the pilots, "Well, boys, it was a good job but not good enough. Next time get them all."

Before he dismissed them for lunch, he made the men report their experiences down to the most "minute detail." After each recounting Chennault would offer a detailed critique, suggesting how they could improve in their next encounter. Still, he was proud of how well they had worked together. He believed they had exhibited "the kind of teamwork that is so typically American, wherein there is plenty of scope for individual brilliance but everybody contributes toward a common goal. You can see it on an autumn Saturday afternoon in a top-notch football team."

That team was still waiting for one more of their players to return.

The last anyone remembered having seen of Ed Rector, one of the Second Squadron pilots, he was heading straight toward a Japanese bomber, but he hadn't been heard from since.

Rector had been delayed getting off the runway that morning because of a problem with his plane, so he arrived at the scene of the battle late. Taking stock of the situation, he thought, "I'm not going into that maelstrom." Instead he took his plane to a higher altitude, where he caught sight of a bomber on the edge of the Japanese formation. He rolled in, shooting as he dove, and then came "right up the tail of the [bomber]." His bullets were clearly hitting their mark, but still the bomber didn't seem to be going down. Rector soon succumbed to "target fixation," a phenomenon in which a pilot becomes so focused on the target that he risks flying directly into it. He held the trigger for five or maybe even seven seconds, a long burst, and was just "shooting the hell" out of the dustbin gunner. Only at the last second did he shove the stick forward to pass just beneath the Japanese plane, coming so close to it that he could make out the design of the camouflage and see the placement of the welding on the aircraft. But one aspect of that day would linger with him for decades to come: "As I went underneath, I saw, right in his face, the dustbin gunner hanging over his gun, and I had shot his lower jaw away." Rector took a few more shots at other Japanese bombers before realizing he was nearly out of ammunition. He tried to get his bearings, soon realizing that while he'd been so focused on the combat, he was now about seventy to a hundred miles from Kunming. That was too far. He wouldn't be able to make it back with the fuel remaining. He pulled out his map to look for a field where he could land safely.

He ran out of options when the red light flashed on his instrument panel, warning that he was nearly out of fuel. His only choice was to immediately drop down in the largest clearing he could find and hope for the best. He brought the P-40 down on its belly. It was a barely controlled crash. The plane slammed hard and skidded forward. When it finally came to a halt he pulled back the cockpit canopy and saw people rushing down a hill toward him—so many that they looked like an army. He pulled out his .45 pistol and knew that, if he had to, he could shoot a few of them before he was taken out. A six-foot-two former football player from North Carolina, Rector had been known for his confidence and his "cold fury" on the field, but he knew that this was a game he couldn't win. He thought: "What are you going to do? And I didn't know where I was. I didn't know whether I was in China or Jap territory or what. So I put the pistol back in my pocket, slid over the fuselage facing them, and I just stood up." He stood waiting, giving himself over to whatever fate awaited him.

As the group approached, one man stepped forward and, in halting English, invited him to lunch. The crowd consisted of Chinese villagers who "had heard the planes overhead [that day] and had for many years." Rector explained that he was an American who had come to help China, and, accepting their invitation, he joined them for a meal. Afterward, he returned to the P-40 with some Chinese mechanics to salvage the plane's radio and machine guns, which they loaded onto a villager's truck. He spent that night as a guest in the village and the following day he got a ride back to Kunming. His AVG squadronmates welcomed him back and could now officially claim that they hadn't lost a single man during their first battle.

The men who hadn't fired a shot in the fight, as Jim Howard wrote, were "itching for our chance to see the enemy in our gunsights." Greg Boyington, one of the handful of First Squadron pilots who hadn't been slotted to fly that morning, was forced to listen to the other pilots recall their glorious exploits. As the air-raid alarm had sounded, Boyington had run around the airfield "like a madman" trying to find a spare P-40. His hopes were raised when he saw some planes without pilots, but he discovered that these were the planes that were not flyable. He spent the battle on the ground, which to him had "lasted for an eternity." When the pilots finally returned, "How eagerly I listened to the[ir] accounts." They made it sound easy, and he was desperate for his chance.

The following day, when he responded to an alarm only to find that the attack consisted of a single Japanese plane that had turned back before he could attack, he reacted with bitterness, almost as if he felt there was a conspiracy afoot to keep him out of the fight.

There was no conspiracy, but there was a war, and a cruel one. Since 1937, the Japanese had focused their bombing raids on civilian

Claire Lee Chennault *(Courtesy of Ken Chennault)*

Chennault pictured with his two Flying Trapeze wingmen, John "Luke" Williamson (left) and William "Billy" McDonald (right), at the 1935 Miami airshow. It was after this performance that the trio were first approached by Chinese colonel P. T. Mow. *(Bettmann/Getty Images)*

Generalissimo Chiang Kai-shek addressing cadets of the Central Military Academy in Nanking, 1935 *(Library of Congress)*

Chiang Kai-shek and Madame Chiang in their home with a portrait of Franklin Roosevelt in the background *(Library of Congress)*

Japanese troops occupying a Chinese town in Anhui province *(National Archives)*

Smoke rises from a cluster of bombs dropped on Chungking by a Japanese bomber near a bend of the Yangtze River *(PF-(aircraft) / Alamy Stock Photo)*

A bird's-eye view of Shanghai burning after being bombed by the Japanese. Visible in the foreground are war vessels of the neutral powers anchored on the Huangpu River. *(Library of Congress)*

A Chinese baby in the ruins left after the bombing of Shanghai, 1937 *(National Archives)*

Street fighting in Shanghai, 1937
(Library of Congress)

Chiang inspecting cadets of
the Officers' Training Corps
in Hankow
(Library of Congress)

Chungking under a cloud of
smoke after the Japanese
bombing *(Library of Congress)*

The bombed-out ruins of
Chungking *(Library of Congress)*

Pan American Airways China Clipper over San Francisco, with the Coit Memorial Tower visible on the left *(Library of Congress)*

The Chennault family, pictured without Claire. Nell is second from the left. *(Courtesy of Ken Chennault)*

Swimming pool on the *Jagersfontein.* The Flying Tigers traveled to Burma on luxurious Dutch ocean liners, carrying passports that listed false professions to disguise their mission. *(Courtesy of the Losonsky family)*

The P-40 production line at the Curtiss-Wright plant in Buffalo, New York *(Courtesy of Buffalo History Museum)*

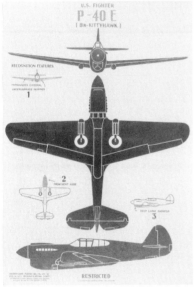

The P-40E "Kittyhawk"
(Library of Congress)

T. V. Soong and U.S. Treasury Secretary Henry Morgenthau sign a $50 million loan agreement in this photo that bears the inscription "For T. V. Soong, with best wishes and sincere regards, from his friend, Henry Morgenthau, 1942." *(T. V. Soong Papers, Envelope E, Hoover Institution Archives)*

American Volunteer Group (AVG) chaplain and later Office of Strategic Services (OSS) operative Paul Frillman *(Paul W. Frillmann Papers, Envelope A, Hoover Institution Archives)*

Joe Alsop standing with his brother and fellow newspaperman, Stewart *(Library of Congress)*

John "Scarsdale Jack" Newkirk with his wife, Jane, at the pier in San Francisco, 1941 *(Courtesy of Joseph W. H. Mott)*

Left to right, Charlie Bond, David "Tex" Hill, and Ed Rector pictured together in 1943 *(Courtesy of the Hill family)*

Frank Losonsky pictured in Toungoo in 1941 *(Courtesy of the Losonsky family)*

Inside the AVG living quarters in Toungoo *(Courtesy of the family of J. J. Harrington)*

A Bert Christman sketch of the exterior of the AVG barracks in Toungoo *(Courtesy of Audrey C. Smith)*

Aircraft parts at the CAMCO production facility in Loiwing, Burma *(Paul Fearn / Alamy Stock Photo)*

Inside the Loiwing CAMCO workshop in Loiwing, Burma *(Paul Fearn / Alamy Stock Photo)*

AVG members gather around the engine of a P-40 during training in Toungoo *(Courtesy of the family of J. J. Harrington)*

John Petach and Emma Foster riding their
bicycles in Burma
(Courtesy of the Yale Divinity School Archives)

Whiling away the time in Toungoo on the baseball diamond *(Courtesy of the family of J. J.
Harrington)*

A view of Kunming,
photographed by Frank Losonsky
(Courtesy of the Losonsky family)

The area where members of the AVG lodged while in Kunming *(Courtesy of the family of J. J. Harrington)*

Inside a P-40 cockpit,
photographed by Frank
Losonsky *(Courtesy of the
Losonsky family)*

The USS *Shaw* explodes during the Japanese raid on Pearl Harbor, December 7, 1941. The Flying Tigers were the unit best positioned to take the fight to the Japanese after the surprise attack in Hawaii. *(National Archives)*

An AVG P-40 taking flight, 1941
(Courtesy of the family of J. J. Harrington)

Imperial Japanese Army soldiers salute during a ceremony after the fall of Rangoon, March 13, 1942
(The Asahi Shimbun / Getty Images)

AVG P-40s on the ground *(Courtesy of the family of J. J. Harrington)*

Shark-faced P-40 in flight *(Courtesy of the family of J. J. Harrington)*

Chennault felt he faced a chronic shortage of planes throughout the Flying Tigers campaigns of 1941–1942. Crashes and damaged aircraft like the one above compounded the problem. *(Courtesy of the family of J. J. Harrington)*

Army Air Forces ground crews keep a P-40's engine tuned up, 1942 *(Library of Congress)*

John Wayne on the set of *Flying Tigers,* a Republic Pictures film directed by David Miller *(Republic Pictures/Sunset Boulevard/ Corbis via Getty Images)*

Left to right: British Field Marshal Sir John Dill, Brigadier General Claire Chennault, Lieutenant General Henry "Hap" Arnold, Lieutenant General Joseph Stilwell, and Brigadier General Clayton Bissell at an air base in China, 1943 *(Bettmann / Getty Images)*

A portrait of Major Greg "Pappy" Boyington as commander of the United States Marine Corps' Black Sheep fighter squadron, October 5, 1943, in the Russell Islands
(National Archives)

Brigadier General Claire Chennault relegated to desk duty, April 1, 1943
(National Archives)

Allied leaders at the Cairo Conference on November 25, 1943. Seated (left to right) are Chiang Kai-shek, Franklin D. Roosevelt, Winston Churchill, and Madame Chiang. *(Franklin D. Roosevelt Presidential Library & Museum)*

Wendell Willkie and Madame Chiang Kai-shek outside the generalissimo's official residence in Chungking, 1943 *(Library of Congress)*

A U.S. Army cargo plane flies over the snow-capped Himalayas along the borders of India, China, and Burma. More than 44,000 tons of war materials were flown over "the Hump" into China in January 1945 alone. *(PhotoQuest/Getty Images)*

An aerial reconnaissance photo of the Omori prisoner of war camp. "Pappy Boyington Here!" is visible on the buildings on the right. *(National Archives)*

Now Lieutenant Colonel Boyington (center) swaps stories with four other members of the Black Sheep squadron over drinks at the St. Francis bar in San Francisco. This photo appeared in an October 1, 1945, *Life* magazine feature on the former Tiger's homecoming. *(Nat Farbman/The LIFE Picture Collection/Getty Images)*

President Harry Truman presents the Medal of Honor to Lieutenant Colonel Boyington during Nimitz Day ceremonies at the White House, October 5, 1945 *(CORBIS/ Corbis via Getty Images)*

areas—their strategic objective seemed to be to make life unbearable for China's citizens. At that, they were threatening to succeed.

John Yee was a teenager when the attacks started. He would never forget one raid on "a sunny, warm, spring day" when the "Japanese bombers appeared out of nowhere. I ran fast . . . machine gun bullets ripped across the yard and almost hit me." There was a "deafening explosion and I was thrown on my face. I rose through a cloud of dust to find the bloody corpses of two young women and a little girl, lying in my yard." He saw that his neighbor's house was now nothing more than a crater, and the entire family of six was dead. The air raids turned Kunming into "a city of death and destruction."

John Yee had become one of the translators employed by the AVG after they arrived in Kunming, and he was in awe of the American pilots that day. When he looked upward he saw something he'd never witnessed before: a shark-nosed fighter plane "diving straight down out of the clear, blue sky. Its guns were blazing. Suddenly a Japanese bomber started smoking, and spiraled downward." A rush of excitement came over him as he realized, "By god, we got one of 'em." For the Chinese residents of Kunming, those shark-nosed planes represented a ray of hope after the years of siege. When the men later walked through Kunming and stopped at a store, children gathered just to catch a glimpse of them.

The American pilots were lauded by both Chinese officials and Kunming's residents. One official was quoted as saying that the AVG was "the most efficient combat group in the world today," and thanked them for "prevent[ing] hundreds of deaths in Kunming." A Chinese intelligence officer informed the Americans that Chiang Kai-shek himself wanted to extend his personal thanks.

Chinese dignitaries feted the pilots for their accomplishments. On December 23, they gathered at the airfield for a ceremony with the governor of Yunnan Province. The evening's program featured a Chinese band that played a questionable rendition of the "The Star-Spangled Banner" that seemed to include snippets of "Dixie" and "Yankee Doodle." After the governor gave a speech, the fourteen American pilots who had participated in the air battle were invited to stand, and each man was presented with a bright red silk scarf, representing joy, they were told. Fourteen Chinese girls—"really attractive young belles," in Charlie Bond's estimation—then pressed bouquets of flowers into their hands. For a man like Bond, who just a few years earlier had assumed that he would spend his life painting houses in Dallas, so grand a ceremony was especially stunning. More gifts appeared, including hams and fruit, and overhead thousands of firecrackers lit up the evening sky.

Then on December 29 local Chinese officials hosted a belated Christmas celebration in honor of the American pilots. Bond summoned the courage to try using chopsticks, but soon abandoned the effort and decided to stop eating entirely when he found a chicken foot in one dish he had been served. But he did enjoy the rice wine and toasted his new friends with *Ganbei!,* Chinese for "Bottoms up!" After dinner, they gathered to sing Christmas carols, and a Chinese general presented Chennault with a saber encrusted with gold and silver. Chennault gave a speech in which he promised victory even if it meant his death. However tough a critic he was of his men, moments like this guaranteed their unwavering loyalty to him.

It was Christmastime even if they were thousands of miles from home. The men exchanged gifts they had bought in the markets in Kunming. Charlie Bond received a saber from one of his friends, like the one given to his commander, minus the precious metals. The best present came from his Chinese hosts—a 6-x-10-inch white cloth printed with an image of the Chinese flag and a message in Chinese characters. The officials explained that the pilots should sew this cloth onto the back of their leather flight jackets, as the script on this "blood chit" identified them as friends of the Chinese people and would instruct anyone they might encounter to help them. If the Americans were shot down in some of the more remote areas of the country, the locals might not know how to treat them, or might even believe that they were the enemy.

Though the members of the AVG were largely unaware of it, their unit was also becoming somewhat famous back in the United States. YANKS SMASH ENEMY OVER CHINA read one headline the day after the December 20 raid. Some of the men's local newspapers ran brief profiles of them based on the telegrams they sent home, their victory hailed when there was little good news elsewhere about the war. A number of different names for the group began to appear in the press as journalists attempted to determine exactly who these young American pilots were and what they were doing in China. They were sometimes identified by their semiofficial title, the American Volunteer Group, but also came to be known by a catchier name: the "Flying Tigers." On December 29, 1941, *Time* ran a small piece with no byline titled BLOOD FOR THE TIGERS, which described how "the Flying Tigers swooped, let the Japanese have it" in the skies over Kunming. That laudatory article appears to be the first time that the term "Flying Tigers" was used in print as a name for the AVG. It was, on its face, somewhat incongruous, given that the P-40s were painted to look like sharks, not jungle cats. Chennault later claimed he had no knowledge of the origin of the name "Flying Tigers" and was "astonished" to see it in the press. Some would attribute the designation to the Chinese newspapermen who had watched the battle in Kunming and had used it as a term of praise. Others argued (and were likely right) that the term was a clever marketing ploy created by Thomas Corcoran and the team in Washington to gin up newspaper coverage for the group's exploits. Whatever its source, "Flying Tigers" would be the name by which the American Volunteer Group would now be known by the general public.

At a time when the navy was still clearing up the destruction at Pearl Harbor, Americans were desperate for stories that could give them some hope for the long war ahead. The triumph of these American pilots over the Japanese bombers in the skies of China provided much-needed inspiration, and their leader, the "lean, hardbitten, taciturn Colonel Claire L. Chennault," as *Time* described him, seemed just the hero they'd been looking for.

CHAPTER 10

CHRISTMAS IN RANGOON

In Rangoon, the pilots of the AVG's Third Squadron prepared for battle. On December 12, they had moved about 170 miles from the training base at Toungoo to the Mingaladon aerodrome, about a dozen miles outside of Rangoon. Mingaladon, the main RAF base in Burma, housed the pilots of the No. 67 Squadron RAF; it also served as the civil airport for Rangoon. It consisted of a few hangars and some barracks scattered around three 1,200-foot runways. Like the Americans, the RAF pilots were inexperienced in combat. They were young men, many from Great Britain and several from New Zealand, who had been stationed in this far-flung outpost of the British Empire while their nation was at war. Until December 8, Great Britain and Japan had been at peace, so these pilots had spent their time enjoying themselves, traveling the countryside by train and sailing the lakes around Rangoon.

Now things were changing. The Japanese had begun to move troops into Burma, but after the AVG squadron moved to Mingaladon, the pilots had been waiting for more than a week without seeing action. The news of the victory in Kunming on December 20 only fueled their impatience, and R. T. Smith summed up the sentiments of his squadronmates when he observed that his colleagues in China did "damn good work but we're all mad because they got into action before we did."

The pilots in Rangoon treated this downtime as a break, well aware that the time would soon come for them to fight. At the barracks, they napped, listened to phonograph records, and wrote in their diaries, waiting for the moment when they would take to the skies in their own P-40s. When they went into Rangoon to do some shopping, "Everything seemed as usual, nobody seemed terribly concerned about the war situation," Smith wrote. They enjoyed steak dinners at the Savoy Hotel and dancing at the Silver Grill.

One of the pilots waiting in Rangoon was Bill Reed. His friends back home back in Marion, Iowa, would describe him as "handsome" and a "fine gentleman," but he was no one's idea of patient. With his wide grin and thick head of slicked-back hair, he was almost a prototype of the classic all-American kid. At Marion High School, Reed had been not only a star athlete and honors student but had also served as the 1935 class president. After high school, he attended Columbia College in Dubuque, where he earned varsity letters in football and baseball and was again elected class president.

After college he could have returned to Marion, but with a population of just over four thousand, it was little more than a railroad depot, and didn't have much allure for the ambitious young man. He joined the Army Air Corps as a second lieutenant in 1940. This was a big step up and a chance to broaden his horizons. When he got wind of the AVG recruitment push in 1941, he signed up immediately. The chance to travel "half way 'round the world" was a dream come true. As his ship pulled out of San Francisco harbor and sailed beneath the Golden Gate Bridge, he thought "of home and how long it would be until I returned to those fading shores." Now, Reed's twenty-fourth birthday was coming up in January, and he wanted to celebrate by having proved himself in combat.

Just before 10:00 A.M. on December 23, Reed climbed into the cockpit of a P-40 to complete another routine inspection. He went through his checklist, assessing the oxygen equipment and the radio. Then, as he peered down the runway, he saw some of his squadronmates running to their planes—one more scramble to the skies for what was "probably another false alarm." Still, he started up the engine and followed the other aircraft as they climbed to seventeen thousand feet. He tried to make radio contact with the flight leader but could not reach him. He was in a cluster of six P-40s but didn't observe any Japanese planes. Then, up ahead, flight leader Parker Dupouy began violently rocking the wings of his P-40—the signal for an attack. Reed scanned the sky, and there they were: "A whole cloud of bombers headed for Rangoon!" Three P-40s were already rushing toward the enemy in pursuit.

Reed formed a string with two other P-40 pilots maneuvering to attack the leading Japanese bombers, while the other group of three launched its assault from the side. The Americans' formation soon broke up as each pilot looked for the best shot he could get. "I went in from every angle, raking the flanks with long bursts," Reed recounted in his diary. The bombers returned fire from their large-caliber machine guns. As he came in for another pass he saw Ken Jernstedt "pour a burst from close range. Apparently he found a bomb with one of his bullets, for the bomber burst into bright red flame and crashed right into Rangoon." Eager to score his own hit, Reed kept "pouring lead at them." Finally, one of the bombers he'd been raking pulled back in flames. With his first kill notched, he took the P-40 out over the Gulf of Martaban and observed fifteen Japanese planes heading back to Thailand. He could have chased them but decided he'd had enough for the day and turned back to Mingaladon.

As he passed over Rangoon, he looked down and was appalled by what he saw. Other Japanese bombers had hit their targets, leaving the city burning. Dust and smoke columns hung thousands of feet over the devastation. As he approached the base, he saw a gas depot burning, and the runway was pocked with bomb craters. Reed managed to land his P-40 on a damaged landing strip. As he climbed out of the cockpit, he saw a man lying on the grass waving a handkerchief in a desperate plea for assistance. His back was shredded by shrapnel and bleeding. Reed got a car and drove him to get help, but it was a brutal awakening to the realities of this war.

Another pilot getting his first taste of combat that day was Reed's good friend R. T. Smith. Just twenty-three, Smith had a typical small-town Nebraska childhood, playing on the high school football team and earning a dollar a week delivering milk. He had known since he was a child that he wanted to fly, and covered the walls of his room with posters of famous aviators. After dropping out of the University of Nebraska in 1939 to join the Army Air Corps, he signed up for the AVG.

As Smith rushed into his first contact with the enemy, he felt "the sudden and embarrassing urge to go to the bathroom." However frightened he was, he didn't think of turning back. He dove into battle to the "crackling sound" of the four .30-caliber machine guns on his plane's wings and the "slower, powerful thudding" of its twin

.50-caliber machine guns. The guns left the "smell of cordite filling the cockpit, a good smell." After the battle, he was grateful: "By God, I got one of the bastards whatever happens from now on!"

As Smith and Reed counted the planes making their way back to base, listening for the distinctive whine of the P-40s, they soon realized they were missing three men. One of them, Paul Greene, would soon turn up. His plane had been hit by enemy fire and he'd bailed out. As he drifted toward the ground, hanging exposed and vulnerable beneath the canopy of his chute, Japanese fighters came by to strafe him. He tried to accelerate his fall by tugging at the chute and hit the ground with a thud that knocked him unconscious. He eventually came to and seemed to be all right except for a torn neck muscle. Henry Gilbert wasn't so fortunate. His body was found in the cockpit of his downed P-40. From Lovell, Wyoming, Gilbert was just twenty-two years old when he was killed.

That left Neil Martin, a former army pilot from Arkansas, unaccounted for. It was devastating news for Reed, for not only were the two men roommates in Rangoon but they were also close friends. Another pilot had seen Martin dive in front of a Japanese bomber and get shot down, but lacking proof that he was dead, Reed continued to cling to the idea that Martin was only missing.

But Reed didn't have time to dwell on Martin's fate as he was summoned back into the air for a follow-up air patrol over Rangoon. There were concerns that the Japanese might return before sunset and, as Reed put it, the AVG "wanted to welcome them properly." As he flew above the city, he could see that the fires were still burning, but the Japanese didn't show.

The Japanese didn't return on December 24 either, and that night some of the men went into Rangoon to celebrate Christmas Eve. So many of its citizens had evacuated that they virtually had the city to themselves. The pilots walked the empty streets and headed to the harbor, where the American freighter *Tulsa* was docked. The sailors invited the American pilots and ground crew onboard, where they handed out cigarettes. It wasn't like Christmas at home, but it was nice to spend a few moments doing something that felt vaguely normal.

Bill Reed had been in the air for over six hours on Christmas Eve and he was so exhausted by the end of the day that he decided to remain at the barracks. He thought of his family back in Marion. He had been so excited to have this adventure and to leave the United States, but this night he wrote in his diary: "Would give a lot to be home just for tonight and tomorrow. Hope Mom isn't too lonesome and worried, and that the newspapers don't write up the raid too luridly." His fears were realized when the news came in that Neil Martin's corpse had been found. No festivities were held to celebrate the holiday at the barracks. There were reports on the radio that the Japanese were planning a major attack the following day as a Christmas gift.

As Christmas morning dawned, Reed took up his position in the alert tent near the airfield, awaiting reports from the warning net of the expected attack. As the hours passed it began to seem as if the threat of a Christmas-day raid was a bluff, but at 11:00 A.M. a call came from the warning net that Japanese planes had been spotted and the pilots should scramble. Reed hurried to his P-40 and started the engine but was abruptly told to shut it down, as the signal had apparently been just another false alarm. As soon as he dismounted from the cockpit and returned to the alert tent, the scramble was back on. "In a matter of a minute or two we were in the air and climbing as rapidly as a P-40 will climb," he wrote in his diary. The battle plan was issued over the radio: "Orbit Hometown Angels 15," which meant that his patrol of four P-40s should fly above Rangoon at fifteen thousand feet. They circled for thirty minutes without tracking anything. "I began to think people were just nervous," Bill wrote, "and we had another patrol for nothing." Then the plane ahead suddenly began rocking its wings. He anxiously scanned the sky. Some five thousand feet overhead a formation of about a few dozen Japanese bombers droned into view. Trailing them was a group of Japanese fighter planes "glinting wickedly in the sunlight."

Chennault had taught the AVG pilots to strike from above, but the squadron had no choice now but to climb to meet the enemy. Reed quickly gained altitude, aiming for the bombers, but found himself head-to-head with a Japanese fighter. He squeezed the trigger and "raked him with a long burst, and saw tracers rake him through the length of the fuselage." With that plane all but certainly dispatched, he engaged in an inconclusive exchange of fire with two more Japanese fighters, and then climbed in a steep ascent up to twenty thousand feet, hoping to catch the bombers. He "attacked [a formation] head-on, all guns blazing" and then flew past them. He hadn't succeeded in hitting any of his targets, but as he prepared to turn back for another pass, he caught sight of an American plane in a dogfight with Japanese fighters a mile ahead. He rushed into the fight, but "we went round and round, with no one getting in any very good bursts." He realized that he had flown far out over the Gulf of Martaban in the course of the battle, and headed for home. After linking up with the lone P-40 in sight, the pair flew over the open water and soon encountered three Japanese fighters heading to their base in Thailand. Despite the risk of running out of fuel in another dogfight, the two American planes pounced, dropping down on the fighters' tails. Reed opened fire, and one Japanese fighter "exploded right in my face." While he pulled up to avoid hitting the crippled craft, his squadronmate clipped the wing of another enemy plane, which "spun into the Gulf." Reed dove away from the remaining Japanese fighter. His gas meter was "damn low" and he was still out in the Gulf. He saw another group of Japanese fighters in the distance but had to ignore them. As he sped toward land, it felt as if "the coast would never show up." He made it to the base with a nearly empty tank. When he landed, he saw that he had taken his share of hits, but observed, "These P-40s absorb lead like a sponge does water."

By the end of the afternoon two pilots had not returned: Ed Overend from California and George McMillan from Florida. The other airmen "had given them up for dead," perhaps owing to the fact that much of the fighting had taken place far over the water. They sent back a message to Chennault in Kunming: "Two planes and pilots missing."

Before the fighting had started, McMillan had sent his will home to his parents. In another letter he told them how sad he was to be missing Christmas this year and how much he was looking forward to being home for the holiday the next year.

The men gathered together that night, and as armorer Chuck Baisden recalled: "If you've ever drank Australian ale on a hot day, it does leave an effect on you. But that was my Christmas dinner. We never even thought about Christmas really, Christmas just wasn't there, there was no feeling, my feeling was there was no Christmas at all."

At 9:00 P.M., a car drove up to the airfield and, to the group's astonishment, George McMillan stepped out. Not only was he alive, but he was carrying a Japanese saber. McMillan enjoyed the surprise as much as any of them, writing to his parents: "You should have seen them when I walked in!"

The excitement only grew as he related his harrowing story of survival. At a quarter past noon, McMillan was patrolling over Rangoon when he saw a formation of Japanese bombers. "We tore into them as soon as we caught them. They had dropped their bombs and were beating it for Thailand but we were too fast for them. I got one Jap bomber for Gilbert and then a second one for Martin," he told a reporter, referring to the pilots who had been killed in the last battle. He had pursued them about fifteen miles out over the Gulf of Martaban, but wanted to get one more. As he closed in, that bomber "poured everything he had into me . . . One .50-caliber bullet smashed the windshield just in front of me. I felt the shrapnel get me and swung away. I thought my plane was gone but I saw the Japs blow up at that moment." His sense of victory had to contend with the fact that his engine was shot up and his left arm was numb and more or less useless. He turned back toward the coast. The plane was barely staying in the air as he cleared the coastline. He knew he couldn't make it to the base, and took it down in a rice paddy.

As his plane skidded to a halt, McMillan opened the canopy and waited to assess his situation. After a half hour, a group of men appeared in the distance. He used his good arm to wave his handkerchief, a sign that he was a friend. The local Burmese approached, offered him water, and guided him on a four-mile walk to a town, where they bathed his wounds and fed him. They then put him on a horse, and a guide took him to another town, from which he was given a ride back to the base. Along the way he stopped to inspect a downed Japanese bomber, from which he retrieved the saber.

McMillan not only had survived a crash but was credited with having destroyed three bombers, more than any other AVG pilot in the air that day. He wrote to his parents: "While you were all eating turkey and cranberry sauce I led six men in an attack against thirty bombers and ten pursuit escort, ha! . . . Naturally we felt pretty good over Xmas' days work."

This was his first Christmas away from home, but he wasn't too sad to be missing out on the festivities back in Winter Garden, Florida. He told a reporter who was profiling the early AVG battles, "I'd rather fight them than eat any day."

At around eleven o'clock that night, the other missing pilot, Ed Overend, made a triumphant return. He, too, had been shot down and lived to tell his tale—he found a bicycle and biked ten miles and then hitchhiked the rest of the way. He had tried to pay the Burmese who rescued him but they wouldn't take the money. The men celebrated the day's victory and the incredible return of their squadronmates late into the night.

It was a somber Christmas in the United States, but the heroic exploits of these pilots provided a glimmer of hope. The *New York Times* ran a story on the "Christmas Day Raid," and said, "The American Volunteer Group is writing an amazing chapter in aerial warfare on a shoestring. Expert observers say that the work of these fliers has been a miracle." Chennault himself, the article said, "has whipped the AVG into a top fighting unit in only a few months." Leland Stowe, one of America's leading journalists, wrote in the *Boston Globe* that the victories above Rangoon were the "first walloping and crushing defeat the Japanese air force has suffered in 4½ years of war." The pilots of the AVG were "knock[ing] the living daylights out of the Japanese aircraft and veteran airmen."

The AVG's own initial estimate for the Christmas battle was that they had downed fifteen Japanese fighters and nine bombers. A few different totals were reported in the press, underscoring the fact that the number of Japanese planes actually destroyed was far from certain. No matter how many enemy aircraft they had brought down, the men were exhausted. "Even though we're getting good results we can't last thru more than a couple more raids," George McMillan noted in his diary. He had some wounds in his hand and shoulder but had recovered enough within a few days to be back on duty, and he was helping patch up holes and getting the planes ready for the next round of combat. But they needed a respite, and warily awaited alarms from the warning net. Bill Reed admitted in his diary, "I know I swallow hard every time the phone rings in the alert shack."

Chennault recognized that the Third Squadron had been through a trying ordeal in the skies over Rangoon and invited the men to join him in Kunming, which had not come under attack since the December 20 battle, for some time off as he sent new pilots down to Rangoon to take over. He had spent the first weeks of the war in Kunming largely bedridden. He had suffered another attack of his reoccurring bronchitis, which left him weak and coughing. He kept up with the news from Rangoon via a radio that had been installed next to his bed, as well as through a regular exchange of cables. Although he fashioned himself to his pilots as a man who was unafraid of the war ahead, he struck a different tone in a letter to Nell in January 1942, writing that he was "terribly worried" about what the war could bring for the family. "Try to get word to [our son] from me to take no unnecessary chances. . . . Tell the other kids to keep out as long as they can." It was different when it was your own boys.

At noon on January 3, 1942, Reed got into his P-40 and left from Lashio, Burma, for his first visit to China. After encountering "thick scattered clouds all trip, and the most wild and rugged terrain I ever hope to fly over," he finally spotted Kunming's landmark lake. He landed and quickly made himself at home in the luxury of the hostels, taking his first hot shower since September and then eating a hearty meal. The Third Squadron pilots quickly settled into a routine of easy living. On January 9 he wrote: "Threw the football around a bit, and then switched to basketball. Puttered around the room a bit and, after tea, Jernstedt and I had a long session of ping pong. By the time we finished it was time to clean up for dinner." A journalist for the *New York Herald Tribune* visited the pilots at their "secret base" in Kunming and reported that they "have the best living quarters in all this part of China. They have hot and cold running water. Their food is American. There are tennis and basketball courts and baseball diamonds here for them. They have their own bar, where they use American coins and bills to buy a drink. The bar is open only three hours, a day, however." The men did have one additional complaint. As one pilot told the reporter: "We love our work here and miss only one thing—American blondes."

For his part, Bill Reed thought the "only thing wrong was Neil's not being here."

CHAPTER 11

BURMESE DAYS

It fell to the men of the Second Squadron, who had been more or less idle in Kunming, to take up the battle in Rangoon as the Third Squadron pilots recuperated in China alongside the First Squadron. Tex Hill and Jack Newkirk were among those to arrive in Rangoon and were eager to prove themselves, while John Petach may have been more hesitant because it meant leaving Emma Foster behind in Kunming. Petach's only consolation was that he could send letters to her whenever a plane made a trip to Kunming.

The Second Squadron pilots arrived in Rangoon in time for New Year's Eve. They found a city that bore little resemblance to the one they had come to drink and party in just weeks earlier. In anticipation of further attacks, the dance halls and cinemas had been shuttered. Many residents had already fled. The only place that seemed still to be open was the Silver Grill, where they celebrated the new year. After spending the night partying, the men had stumbled out onto the dark streets of Rangoon at 2:00 A.M. and headed back to their barracks. In the days that followed they became regulars at the bar, and one pilot recalled Jack Newkirk putting together a singing group—the "Unholy Trio," as the manager dubbed them—that would commandeer the microphone and perform songs with more energy than skill, belting out familiar numbers like "I've Been Working on the Railroad."

Petach sent his first letter to Emma on January 1, 1942, writing in the glow of moonlight and rushing to finish the message so it could be dispatched on a plane the following morning. "Last night was New Year's Eve most of the boys celebrated by going to the Silver Grill and imbibing a few Bacchanalian Spirits," he wrote. It was fun but it felt "unnatural" to be back at the Grill, the place where their romance had blossomed, without her at his side. Petach began the new year, he wrote to Emma, with "the knowledge that the next year will find a closer relationship between us. Fact is, I got me some dandy plans for us."

For now, though, plans for the present had to take precedence. Jack Newkirk, still recovering from buck fever, soon became frustrated by waiting for enemy raids and decided that they should seize the offensive, striking at Japanese bases in Thailand. As squadron commander, and with Chennault hundreds of miles away, that seemed to be his decision to make. "Let's take the war to the enemy," one pilot recalled Newkirk saying. He chose one of a series of Japanese bases as their target.

Early on the morning of January 3, four P-40s sped down the runway at Mingaladon in what would be the first offensive mission for any U.S. airmen after Pearl Harbor. The pilots that day were Jack Newkirk, Tex Hill, Jim Howard, and Bert Christman, though Christman quickly developed engine trouble and had to drop out. Jim Howard had actually grown up in China while his father served as a doctor in Canton. He had graduated from Pomona College and nearly followed in his father's footsteps by applying for medical school, but he wanted some adventure. He became a naval aviator and, just like his old man, decided to serve in China. The three pilots, Newkirk, Hill, and Howard, flew their three shark-nosed P-40s across the jungle, illuminated by the glimmers of light from the rising sun.

Newkirk was in the lead as they approached the Raheng aerodrome from the southeast at 250 miles per hour. In the morning light, they could see the Japanese planes lined up on the field. They came in at ten thousand feet, and as they looked down they could see two Japanese fighters circling the field at a thousand feet. If they wanted to get in their strafing runs, they were first going to have to take out that pair of planes. Newkirk chose one of the craft beneath him and dove, his fingers closing on the trigger of his machine guns. As his P-40 bore down on the enemy, he blasted away, and in seconds the Japanese fighter was "streaming smoke, rolled over and crashed into the jungle."

It wasn't clear if Jim Howard hadn't seen the airborne Japanese fighters or if he simply ignored them. Diving over the field, he opened fire on the planes sitting on the runway. As he raced overhead, one Japanese fighter began to taxi down the runway, and he "gave it a five-second burst of .30- and .50-caliber fire. A sudden billow of orange flame swallowed the plane."

Spotting an enemy plane on Howard's tail, Tex Hill knew what he had to do, and swung his plane around to try to protect his squadron-mate. Without even enough time to look through his gunsights he closed in, fired, and watched the bullets pour out "just like a big hose." The Japanese fighter exploded into shards of metal and Hill narrowly missed flying into the pieces coming off like flak.

By now the Japanese troops had scrambled to man their antiaircraft guns. The Americans could see the sheets of deadly fire rising toward them. Glancing into the sun, Newkirk noticed four enemy aircraft ascending. They had lost the momentary advantage of surprise and now found themselves outnumbered and outgunned. But Jim Howard, determined to make one more strafing run, raced down the length of idling aircraft, admiring the "wonderful line of destruction" he left in his wake. When he heard a "dull thump" in his Allison engine, he feared it was dead. The engine began to sputter, and the cockpit began to fill with acrid black smoke. "I dropped my landing gear and nosed down to make a forced landing. I could also hear bullets hitting the plane, whether they were from another plane or from the ground forces I cannot tell," he wrote in a letter. He searched the patchwork of jungle for a place to land, a field or clearing where he could hop out of the plane and run into the trees to hide. He was all too aware that if he were captured it could mean torture or execution. He was only a hundred feet above the tree line when the engine coughed, showing signs of still having a bit of life. He touched the throttle and waited. "She caught again! COME ON!" The engine roared back to life, he pushed the throttle, and the plane shot up, banking for home, the Japanese airfield shrouded in flames and smoke behind him.

They landed safely back at Mingaladon and celebrated their successful attack. Newkirk and Hill still couldn't believe the risk Howard had taken by going on that strafing run with Japanese fighters in the air. As they inspected their P-40s they engaged in a somewhat morbid contest of assessing which of their planes had the most bullet holes. Howard came in with a respectable eleven, but Hill won with thirty-three. That explained why his plane had been violently vibrating on the way back. "By some miracle I was home," Howard wrote. "The moment was sweet, as only those who have come that close can know."

Whatever shame Jack Newkirk had experienced for his "buck fever" in Kunming, he could now claim to have led the first successful offensive mission of the Flying Tigers. The tally for that day noted that Newkirk had "destroyed 2 fighters in aerial combat." Hill had shot down one Japanese fighter, while Howard "destroyed 4 fighters on ground by burning." Howard "hoped it would be a long time before another hair-raiser like that" but that was out of his hands. The AVG pilots suspected that they had stirred the hornet's nest, and that the Japanese would probably strike back soon.

The following day, January 4, an alarm sounded, and six AVG P-40s scrambled to the air in two wings of three planes each. Bert Christman led one of the wings against a group of more than two dozen Japanese fighters swarming overhead. The Japanese dove down, guns blazing. Bullets pounded into Christman's P-40 as he "tried to evade the enemy by diving and turning." He managed to escape, but his plane was "riddled" with bullets and its controls were damaged. Smoke started to pour into his cockpit. The whole attack had lasted just ten seconds.

After a few minutes of flying, his engine died, and he knew he was going to have to bail. He pulled back the canopy, flipped the plane upside down, and let the airstream carry him into the sky. His parachute opened, and as he glided to earth he watched his P-40 crash and burn.

Bert Christman had joined the Navy and then the AVG because he wanted to participate in the heroism that was a staple of his cartoon strip characters. With this battle, he'd gotten his wish. He wrote a letter to a former colleague at the Associated Press, hoping that it might get published in a newspaper. It conveyed his longing for his earlier life as a cartoonist: "Things are getting hot here. Even Scorchy Smith would be satisfied," he wrote. Of course Christman understood that unlike Scorchy, if an enemy pilot put holes in him, he couldn't just erase the scene and start over. In the raid he'd learned quickly that his appetite for death-defying adventure had limits. "Flying has always been interesting to me," he wrote in the letter. "However, when 'this' is all over I'm sure I'll be content again to sit at a drawing board and pen my experiences and those of my friends in an authentic aviation comic strip." He had escaped the battle with plenty of bruises and splinters from his fall, but after a few days he was back at the flight line.

George Paxton, a pilot who had attended Yale and worked as a banker before becoming a naval aviator, also came under fire from the Japanese fighters during that battle. As bullets ripped through his fuselage he tried to steady the plane, but he knew the damage was too great. It was as if the "cockpit began falling apart." With the engine smoking, he tried to land the P-40 on the Mingaladon runway, and as his right wing dug into the ground, the plane spun until it finally came to a stop. The pilots rushed to pull him from the cockpit and found "a hole in his shoulder and belly and a plane full of holes." The legend was that just before he passed out, he said, "I still say those little bastards can't shoot!"

Jack Newkirk was proud of how his pilots had handled themselves. "The more hardships, work, and fighting that the men have to do, the higher morale goes," he wrote. "They seem to thrive on adversity. The squadron is becoming more unified every day."

The Japanese began attacking at night, which meant that the AVG had to remain on alert twenty-four hours a day. The fear of being bombed in their sleep led the men to abandon the housing provided by the RAF and instead choose to camp out in the open or sleep in "trucks or any place available."

There was a nighttime air raid on January 5, but the P-40 pilots who were in the sky didn't see the Japanese planes approach, and when they tried to pursue them, the enemy disappeared back into the darkness. The air-raid alarm sounded again in the early hours of January 8. Tex Hill gathered a few pilots into a car and raced to the runway. They got out to help but one exhausted pilot, Ken Merritt, stayed in the back to get some more sleep. Overhead a P-40 flown by Pete Wright circled under the moonlight, but after a while it became clear it was a false alarm. About 4:30 A.M., Newkirk gave the runway team instructions to prepare for Wright's landing. The whole base was blacked out, so after a nighttime scramble, the ground crew had to rush lights out to the runway and train a truck's headlights down the landing path to try to provide some illumination.

On this night the ground crew set out the runway lights, but the truck hadn't yet arrived. When Wright attempted to land, Newkirk signaled with his red flashlight that he continue to circle overhead and wait for the light from the truck.

As Wright began to lower his landing gear, a hydraulic line ruptured, spewing liquid into the cockpit and temporarily blinding him. As he came crashing down, the P-40 skidded across the runway, smashing into a parked car. The P-40 wasn't damaged too badly and Wright was able to walk away from the accident, but the car was smashed and Ken Merritt, who was napping inside it, was killed.

Just hours after the accident that killed Merritt, the AVG launched two raids into Thailand. The first of these missions was designed to be fairly small, with only four P-40s taking part and Charlie Mott designated as flight leader. Mott was one of the handful of Ivy League graduates in the AVG. He had received his degree from the University of Pennsylvania and worked as a civil engineer. He left behind a wife, and hoped to use his experience overseas as a path to a lucrative career in civil aviation.

That afternoon their target was the Mesoht aerodrome, which was little more than a landing field cut into the forest. The AVG crossed into Thailand and arrived at around eight thousand feet. They could see Japanese planes arrayed in a single long line on the ground. Mott led the P-40s down to the field, where they opened fire, their machine-gun rounds ripping into the enemy aircraft. Soon the row of neatly aligned Japanese fighters was ablaze.

After a few runs, the Japanese antiaircraft guns began coming to life, but Mott was undaunted. He caught a glimpse of two planes that had been off to the side, out of the formation, and as he flew over to strafe them he felt a tremendous thud rock the plane. An antiaircraft round had struck his engine. He was lucky to be alive, but knew he didn't have much longer in the cockpit. He looked out and saw "nothing but jungle in front of me."

His only option was to parachute directly into enemy territory. As he floated down, his parachute caught on a tree branch and he was left hanging in midair about twenty feet from the ground, "swinging like a big plum." He had a .38 pistol with him and thought he could make a run for it if he could only get down. There was a bush a bit to the side of where he was hanging, and he thought maybe he could aim for it as a cushion for his fall. He climbed out of his harness and dropped, missing the shrub and tumbling hard onto the ground, his right leg collapsing beneath him. Pain enveloped him, and he couldn't stand up. In the course of the fall he had also dropped his pistol, which now lay nearly fifteen feet away. As he remembered, "I lay there, immobilized."

The remaining three P-40s had no choice but to turn back for Rangoon without their flight leader. Based on the numbers alone, "it might have been considered a real successful mission," one of the pilots, Robert Moss, reflected, "but of course, there's nothing real successful if you leave one of yours on the other side." John Petach didn't take part in the raid but wrote to Emma about losing Mott a few days later: "Sure was a hell of a shame. We still have had no word and I am just about ready to give him up for lost. I hope I'm wrong."

Lying on the ground in the Thai jungle, Mott felt a prick on his left side, and when he turned his head he saw that it was a bayonet on the end of a Japanese rifle. He tried to stand but collapsed again. Soon a group of Japanese soldiers had gathered around him, all with bayonets fixed on their rifles. They were, he recalled, "running around like madmen, jumping like they had springs in their heels." Two of them took off their pants and used them to improvise a stretcher on bamboo sticks. They carried Mott back to the airfield, where he could see the smoke rising and tried to determine the number of planes that were burning. He thought he counted eight and smiled. A Japanese soldier slashed at him with a bayonet—Mott assumed his smirk had set off the Japanese soldier—and cut his scalp before another soldier stopped the attacker.

Mott was carried to a tent where a medical officer sewed up the cut on his scalp, put a splint on his broken left arm, bound up his foot, and gave him a shot of sedatives. Then a group of officers appeared and a standoff began: "They looked; I looked. They stared; I stared. They glowered; I glowered back. I could literally feel the tension building up." There had been warnings that any captured AVG pilots might be executed, and all Mott wanted was for "whatever was going to happen to me to be over with as soon as possible." But then one of the officers unexpectedly asked in English: "What can we do for you?"

Mott was shocked but thirsty, so he replied, "Do you have a bottle of beer?" They told him they had cider but the translation was off and they handed him two bottles of cherry soda. Then they began their interrogation. They wanted to know how many planes were in Rangoon. Mott sensed that his own role in the war was over, and that he now faced the prospect of many years in a Japanese prisoner camp, but he thought he could help out the Second Squadron by inflating their numbers. "Two hundred," he replied, multiplying what he thought was the real answer by a factor of five. After the questioning was over, he was loaded onto the back of a truck, which headed down a rough road.

The strike on the Mesoht aerodrome wasn't the main event the AVG had planned for January 8. The chief mission that day would be a joint raid conducted by AVG and RAF pilots. This would mark the first time in the war that American and British pilots would fly together in combat after Pearl Harbor and would christen the new alliance between Great Britain and the United States.

Though in command of the Second Squadron and the supervisor of much of the work at Mingaladon, Jack Newkirk wanted to get back in the air so he volunteered to lead the attack. The group chose a familiar target: the Japanese airfield at Raheng that they had hit back on January 3 (this was also known as Tak, a name they would use sometimes in their combat reports). The plan was for seven P-40s from the AVG and six Brewster Buffaloes from the RAF to carry out the raid.

At 4:35 P.M. Newkirk took off, followed closely by John Petach. As the planes neared their target, they split off into three groups and prepared to strike the airfield from different trajectories. Newkirk dove over the field and saw "four enemy aircraft, a few trucks, and several ground personnel," as he wrote in his combat report. He couldn't focus on a target on his first flyby but then swooped around for a second pass. This time he shot at a fighter that was "silver coloured and had branches on it." It went up in flames. He noticed a truck driving on the field and he fired on it as well, sending it swerving into the plane he'd just targeted. He dove once again over the field and was strafing another Japanese craft when he heard two "plunks." The plane had been hit—ground fire from Japanese troops, he thought. He pulled up and away from the field.

Petach came down to make his strike but by now the Japanese riflemen had assembled on the ground. "Well, as I made my approach and was looking for one of the planes to shoot at I saw a tracer streak past my right wing and looking dead ahead I saw a group of about twenty soldiers standing in a group, all firing at me," he wrote in a letter. He pulled the trigger and let out a two-second burst. The "compact group of riflemen" were no match for his .30-caliber and .50-caliber machine guns, and the men were "dispersed," as he euphemistically put it in his combat report.

It was almost dark when the combined force landed back at Mingaladon. "We caught the Japs flat-footed," Newkirk exclaimed to the men. "We cleaned that field mighty quick," another pilot boasted. Leland Stowe was on hand to record the scene and noted something remarkable as he listened to the cheering pilots. He heard accents that were "cockney, Texan, Yorkshire or Middle-Western American," but based on their natural camaraderie, Stowe felt like these pilots "might have been flying together for years." An RAF pilot yelled out "good show" and Stowe felt that was just the right description: "It had been a good show all right— just a new kind of British-American show, the kind where a dozen different varieties of English speaking accents do not matter in the least."

Time magazine praised the TIGERS OVER BURMA. It said that Jack Newkirk had destroyed eight Japanese planes and he then radioed his wife: "There aren't enough of them to keep us busy."

Though the raid was reported in headlines as a triumph, it left Petach disturbed. His combat report made a short reference to how he had shot at Japanese troops, but his conscience was bothering him, and he poured out his feelings in a letter to Emma. He recounted for her how "the last I saw of them, they were either well dispersed or were quite still on the ground. Personally, I hate that kind of fighting but GODDAMIT they fired on me first." He tried to look at the bright side, and made his intentions for their courtship clear: "Well, at least I can tell our children that I came into actual contact with the enemy and was directly responsible for destroying a few." With his lover so close but still out of reach, Petach was longing to return to Kunming. "Sweet One, I'm very much in love with you. Fact is, I miss you tremendously and only just about holding my own until I see you again," he wrote to her on January 17. Just the next day he wrote to her: "Sweet, have I told you that I'm in love with you?" He said he was "pestering Newkirk" for a transfer back to Kunming and was hoping to make it there by her twenty-sixth birthday on February 14—Valentine's Day.

If John Petach had some ambivalent feelings about the AVG mowing down Japanese soldiers on the runway, his countrymen didn't share them. AVG pilots in Rangoon were being hailed as among the first American heroes of the war. After his visit with them, Leland Stowe wrote in the *Boston Globe* that these "overnight warbird veterans in plain truth have hung up one of the most brilliant records of fighter squadrons anywhere since World War II began—genuinely comparable in many respects to the magnificent achievements of the RAF squadrons, which fought and won the Battle of Britain in September 1940." In a February 1942 statement, Prime Minister Winston Churchill shared that assessment, though he spread the praise to include his own RAF pilots in Rangoon as well as the Flying Tigers: "The victories they have won in the air over the paddy fields of Burma may well prove comparable in character if not in scale with those won over the orchards and hop fields of Kent in the Battle of Britain."

It was a great story for a journalist to tackle, if he could get to Rangoon. George Rodger had quickly risen to become one of the world's leading war photographers after publishing his searing portraits of Londoners enduring the Blitz. In January 1942, *Life* sent him to cover the Japanese invasion of Burma. His goal was to capture the human side of the war. He would leave it to others, as he put it, "to refight the battles, to criticize the strategy, and to forecast future effects of the campaign on the general picture of global war." There was no better story in Burma, perhaps in the entire war, than the Flying Tigers, and after he arrived in Rangoon he went to Mingaladon to document the by now almost mythic pilots flying the shark-nosed P-40s.

With his Rolleiflex camera, he spent two days capturing the everyday lives of the pilots. He photographed them eating lunch under a mango tree. He shot a picture of Tom Cole, a pilot from Missouri, leaning back in a wooden rocking chair in the alert tent. He took individual portraits of the pilots with their helmets on and their goggles resting on their foreheads. With an eye for drama, he also had the men pose for staged shots. Tex Hill and a group of pilots held up the rudder of a Japanese plane as a war prize. Rodger asked them questions; he wanted to learn where they were from, what they had left behind, what they dreamt about.

He also got a taste of the excitement of the war when an air-raid alarm sounded and the pilots dashed to their P-40s. One AVG pilot from Texas, Matthew Kuykendall, was "hit in the forehead and finger by Jap fire," as Rodger put it in a *Life* magazine article. Rodger took a photograph of him with white bandages wrapped around his head and his left pinky, and as if in contrast, photographed the corpses of Japanese pilots in the wreckage of their downed planes. Before he left Rangoon, he came back one last time and got devastating news: Tom Cole had been killed on a strafing mission. Rodger wanted to honor the young pilot's legacy, and he promised Jack Newkirk that Cole wouldn't be forgotten. He was going to make sure his portrait would be included in *Life*.

The March 30, 1942, edition of *Life* had Shirley Temple on the cover and inside it carried the feature on the FLYING TIGERS IN BURMA. George Rodger himself was pictured wearing a helmet, with a cigarette in his mouth, and the magazine hyped his quest to get these rare pictures: "Rodger has gone to more sweat and pain to get a few pictures in *Life* than any other *Life* Photographer . . . in Burma he has found a group of the best American fliers the U.S. will ever produce."

As Rodger had promised, the spread in *Life* included a photo of a young man reclining in a rocking chair and gazing off into the distance, as if preoccupied with something. Part of the caption read: "Tom Cole of Missouri . . . was killed soon after. He had parachuted but Japs machine-gunned him in the air."

On January 23, the Japanese hit Rangoon again. AVG pilots, including Bert Christman, scrambled to the air to defend the city. Daniel De Luce, a reporter for the Associated Press, was visiting the AVG that day and had brought good news for Christman—the censors had cleared his letter describing his experiences in battle for publication. De Luce waited for him to return after the air raid to deliver his message, but Christman's P-40 never came back. They later found him dead in his parachute on the ground with a bullet in his head. The only explanation was that he had bailed out of his P-40 after it was shot up, and a Japanese fighter strafed him as he fell. Technically, it wasn't unlawful to shoot a parachutist in his harness because the efforts to codify this rule in international law had failed after World War I. Still, there was something undeniably cruel about shooting a pilot as he hung defenselessly in his parachute.

Christman's death was like a gut punch to the AVG. "Christman displayed no lack of courage and was always eager to engage the enemy," Jack Newkirk wrote in a report, concluding that the pilot "was one of the highest assets that the squadron had and his death is a loss far more serious than the loss of his companionship."

The news of Christman's death made headlines in America. De Luce himself would write the moving eulogy: "None loved flying better than slender, blond Bert Christman, 26, of Fort Collins, Colorado, who at one time drew 'Scorchy Smith,' an Associated Press comic strip." He added that Christman "went on to greater adventure than any he drew with his pen." Newspapers reprinted one of the *Scorchy Smith* strips that Christman had done. Dated September 28, 1937, it showed Scorchy preparing for an air raid "somewhere in the Orient." Christman's letter, the one that he had written with hopes of publication, was finally printed after his death. It was full of a hope that would never be fulfilled: he would never get to "sit at a drawing board and pen my experiences and those of my friends in an authentic aviation comic strip." That privilege would be left to the new *Scorchy Smith* cartoonist, who drew a strip depicting Christman being shot by a Japanese fighter as he hung in his parachute.

He was buried in the Church of Edward the Martyr cemetery in Rangoon. The AVG shipped his personal effects home, including some of the sketches he had drawn in Burma. One depicted the shacks in Toungoo and another was of a water buffalo lying in a grass field. Some of Christman's *Scorchy Smith* comics were reprinted over the following year, but his art would be largely forgotten.

Greg Boyington had been waiting in Kunming for the call to go down to Burma and join the fight. Finally it came. He landed in Rangoon at dusk on January 25, excited about his chance to finally see some combat, but possibly a little nervous as well. He had some scotch before he went to bed that night.

The following morning the P-40s were scrambled in anticipation of a raid and Boyington ascended in his P-40 to face the Japanese. He would later write, "Boy oh boy, this was what I'd been waiting for." But things did not go as planned. As Boyington ascended in another pilot's wake he was nearly blinded by the sun. He knew the Japanese fighters were somewhere above him, but he couldn't see them. He was in trouble. As they dove toward him all he could see was "smoke and tracers from the Jap machine guns." They seemed to be concentrating on another plane, but he knew he would be dead if he didn't think fast. He put his plane into a steep dive. To pull out, he was "hauling back on my stick and turning with all my might, my neck muscles and breath locked," to keep from blacking out. He fought the g-forces and was able to maintain consciousness. When he leveled off, he looked back. No Japanese fighters in sight. When he landed he muttered to a colleague, "We sure screwed that one, didn't we?"

Boyington's relief at escaping was tempered by concern that there was no sign of Louis "Cokey" Hoffman, an experienced pilot from San Diego. Boyington had seen him under attack by the Japanese and feared the worst. At forty-four years old, Hoffman was probably the oldest Flying Tiger, and one of the few with a wife and children waiting for him back home. As expected, they found his "badly mutilated" body. Chennault awarded him a posthumous Citation for Bravery. Hoffman, the citation said, "was killed in action when he alone attacked several Japanese fighters in order to delay them from attacking the rest of the flight which was in a very disadvantageous position at the moment. All of the remaining pilots of the flight escaped this attack by the Japanese because of his disregard for his own safety. His action in this situation has demonstrated the greatest bravery and fearlessness, in that he sacrificed his own life in order to save his comrades."

The Flying Tigers gathered at the Church of Edward the Martyr cemetery for the funeral on January 28. Without any means of embalming the fallen, the stench of death was overpowering. Greg Boyington started to sweat as the English minister conducted the ceremony, praying that it would end soon. When they began to lower the coffin they discovered that the hole was too small, and the gravediggers had to return to widen it. Boyington was "nervous and perspiring," he recalled. He had signed up for the big paychecks, but realized that this war was "going to be a struggle for survival—not for money." After Hoffman's funeral, many of the pilots took part in a ritual they knew would cheer them up: a visit to the Silver Grill. The menu was sparse but they ordered ice cream topped with strawberries. They then drove around Rangoon in a Jeep and, like tourists, took photos of the Shwedagon Pagoda to take their minds off death.

"How these things happen, or even why they must happen, we can never know, for only God is answerable for the death of the brave," chaplain Paul Frillmann wrote to Hoffman's widow, "but of this I feel confident, that Louis Hoffman died honorably for a cause in which he believed. We, who are left behind, shall long remember with respect and admiration the man he was to us."

After spending a month in Rangoon, John Petach had wracked up a number of accomplishments in battle. He was credited in the AVG records for having taken part in the shared destruction of a bomber on January 19. Then on January 23 he destroyed a bomber on his own, and on January 29 he destroyed a fighter on his own.

Still, he was eager to get back to Kunming to see Emma Foster. His efforts to persuade Newkirk paid off and he was allowed to return at the end of January. He and Emma enjoyed the relative respite of the city and the luxury of the hostels, which made the war seem far away. Their passion for each other seemed so urgent in view of the daily threat of death that they decided to get married without delay. They had dinner with Chennault to seek his blessing despite the understanding that the nurses wouldn't marry the pilots. He consented.

At 5:30 P.M. on February 16, 1942, John and Emma gathered with a few friends in the garden at the American consulate. A consular officer conducted the wedding with a few friends as witnesses, followed by a large Chinese dinner to celebrate the occasion. John spent $7.50 to send a telegraph to his parents in New Jersey: "DEAR FOLKS MARRIED EMMA JANE FOSTER TODAY AM WELL AND HAPPY IN CHINA." The next morning, they took a car trip to the picturesque Dianchi Lake for a brief honeymoon.

When he returned to Rangoon, John composed a letter to his parents about the girl he'd just wed. The words didn't come easily and he simply described her as a "red-haired, blue-eyed nurse." He was looking forward to bringing her back to New Jersey: "I can't describe her much more but you will get a chance to see her when we get home. She certainly wants to meet you people and so do I." Though he was planning to honor his one-year commitment to the AVG, Petach's letters reveal a man who was eager to move on to the next chapter of his life with Emma by his side.

In Rangoon, the air-raid alarms never seemed to stop. The Japanese bombers attacked the city during the day and then throughout the night. Charlie Bond was finding it a difficult adjustment after the comforts of Kunming, recording in his diary on February 6 that there was "a big bombing effort last night. I nearly fell out of my bed, the bombs were so close. I thought they knew exactly where I was and were going just for me! It was the first time I got a bit scared of bombs." The next entry was much the same: "Man, they did it again last night, and hard!" In their sleep-deprived state the pilots would have to go out to the airfield and try to be alert for the daytime raids. One pilot drew a sketch in red ink on the reverse of his combat report of a heart being skewered over an open fire. Beneath it he wrote "Day + Night Night + Day."

By February 1942 it was evident that Rangoon was a doomed city. The pilots started making plans for an emergency evacuation, organizing trucks for a convoy. "We are just not too sure how long the Japs will be kept from swarming into Rangoon," Bond wrote in his diary. One night he sat outside on the lawn and looked up at the stars, wondering "about everything in general, life, death, love, Mom, and Dad." The war forced him to struggle with the question of what it meant to be "halfway around the world and involved in war where people are shooting at each other and trying to kill each other. And what for?"

The Americans continued to fly patrols over Rangoon, but the pilots were hoping it wouldn't be too long before they could evacuate back to the comfort of the hostels in Kunming. Bond tried to focus on staying busy during the day because it helped keep his nerves under control. But then night would come. After he closed his eyes he would dream about dogfights. Even on the nights the Japanese planes didn't come, they were there.

Although Rangoon's once-bustling streets had been largely abandoned, one more member of the AVG made the trek there in February. Paul Frillmann had been at Hankow when the city fell to the Japanese in 1938, and now, it seemed, he would once again become one of the "last-ditchers" as the Japanese army closed in. Frillmann had been assigned to catalogue all the belongings of the pilots who had been killed in the January fighting in Rangoon. He carefully counted their possessions, numbering everything down to their underwear and T-shirts, and then placed them all in boxes. Some were shipped home, while others were sold to the surviving pilots, the payments passed along to the next of kin. Frillmann took his job seriously, and he wrote personal letters to the families, in which he offered consolation and information about how he was planning to dispose of the personal effects of the dead.

Frillmann's other job was to help load trucks with the supplies that were piling up at the docks in Rangoon. Once the city fell, the AVG would have an even more difficult time obtaining provisions, so Frillmann and several ground crewmen were busy "smashing open crates and barrels, loading our trucks with spare parts for planes and vehicles, tires, tools, radio equipment, guns and ammunition." If this occasionally involved actual looting, it didn't bother their consciences too much.

The only bright spot in these increasingly desperate conditions was that the remaining AVG members had been invited to stay with some of the last of the British aristocrats who lived in grand homes in Rangoon. It was a welcome change from their sparse accommodations at the airfield and the chaos engulfing the city. When Frillmann returned to the palatial home where he was staying at the end of a long day, there was a servant "always waiting in the hall offering a silver tray with stiff Scotch-and-sodas to enjoy while we bathed and changed."

This particular residence belonged to a "Mr. Johnson," a man who worked for a British oil company. Mr. Johnson was helping destroy the British oilfields before the Japanese took over, and his family had already fled, so Frillmann and the pilots who were staying there had plenty of room. Frillmann made himself at home, checking out the "well-stocked wine cellar and library" and the "vast living room with splendid oriental rugs and a concert grand piano." After they dined and drank, Johnson would play Bach on the grand piano. For a moment Frillmann could forget about the war, but then reality intruded, like waking up from a pleasant slumber: "We always listened to the evening radio news, and every night it was worse. . . ." The Japanese captured Singapore, another British colony, on February 15, and it seemed like Rangoon wouldn't be far behind.

When it came time to evacuate the city, the pilots would fly out and the ground crew would drive out. When Frillmann passed the Buick agency, he went in to take a look at their inventory. The place was deserted, with debris scattered throughout the office, but three new cars were on display in the show window. He opened the door of one car and saw that the keys were inside. The Americans conscripted all three Buicks, looking forward to "driving a powerful smooth-riding car down empty streets." But as soon as they left the showroom, one driver crashed a Buick into a tree—not a good omen for the long trip ahead.

As the Japanese troops closed in on Rangoon in late February, the British made the necessary preparations to abandon the city. Precious silver was buried in gardens. Pets had to be taken to the veterinarian to be put down, and some owners just did the deed themselves and shot their animals. On February 20, an "E" sign was posted, indicating that only "essential" cars were allowed on the streets, which residents took as a compelling indication that it was time to evacuate. It was heartbreaking for these British colonials to vacate their grand residences, and one man described bidding farewell to his home as if he were leaving behind a family member: "The old clock was still ticking away and chimed the hour as I locked up the house for the last time." Mr. Johnson was ready to flee, but before he did he made one request of Frillmann: he wanted the house to be set afire before the Japanese captured the city, but he didn't have the heart to do so himself.

The Royal Air Force officers hosted a party toward the end of the month at which Frillmann had a "rip-roaring time." The men sang dirty songs and seemed intent on depleting the liquor supply before it, too, fell into the hands of the Japanese.

Not long after, Bob Neale, the commander of the First Squadron, decided it was time for the AVG to retreat. On February 28, the pilots ate a cold lunch of canned pork and beans before they took off from the Rangoon airfield for the last time. "Goodbye Rangoon!" Bond wrote in his diary. Neale, who was overseeing the evacuation, told Frillmann, "You're it. You are taking the first convoy up the road."

"You're out of your mind," Frillmann replied. "I'm the chaplain. I'm not taking any convoy anywhere."

Neale showed him a radio message that came directly from Chennault: "Convoys start this morning. Frillmann takes the first."

"Just get out," Neale commanded.

The convoy included eighteen trucks, twelve jeeps, and the two surviving Buicks. Some of the men had started dating women in Rangoon and had their girlfriends in the trucks with them. Frillmann knew they couldn't leave them behind and didn't object. He drove his Buick into the front and led them through the deserted streets. He couldn't help but marvel at the fires consuming the city, "full flame, crackling loudly in the empty sunlight." As the convoy passed by Johnson's home, Frillmann remembered his request. He could tell that the fire already raging farther down the block would eventually consume the house, so he avoided doing the deed. He looked longingly at the beautiful place and thought about running in and taking a stack of books, but there was no room in the packed trucks. Still, he stopped the car. There were stables out back and he went to drive the horses out so they could escape the fire. There was one black stallion, though, that he couldn't bring himself to leave to an uncertain fate in the burning city. Using a long rope, he tied the horse to the end of the last truck and then pulled his Buick behind, forming the end of the long convoy.

The sun beamed down on them as they set out, trying to create as big a gap as possible between themselves and the advancing Japanese forces. After a while Frillmann saw that the horse was terrified and had begun to stumble. He ordered the truck to stop and led the animal out into a field. After calming it and stroking its black mane, he pulled out a pistol and shot it. He felt that it was better than leaving it on the road, but admitted, "I had no idea whether I was doing right or wrong."

When evening came they pulled to the side of the road. Dinner was canned asparagus, washed down with some of their seemingly endless supply of Harvey's Bristol Cream. The sun began to set and bathed the clouds in red and purple. In a valley below, Frillmann could see "Buddhist shrines, clusters of bamboo and palms, busy farmers in the rice fields, elephants bathing in the river." It was like a scene from *National Geographic*, he thought.

Day after day the convoy made slow progress over the rough and winding road. Soon the trucks began to give out. The drivers would pour water into the overheated radiators, trying to resuscitate the vehicles, but when nothing would get them running again, they released the brakes and let them roll off the side of a cliff, watching them tumble and crash in the gulley below.

In mid-March, after more than two weeks on the road, what remained of Frillmann's convoy pulled into the hostels in Kunming. It was late at night, and the men scattered to find rooms. They were filthy and their clothes were tattered, but they were glad to be alive. In the morning, Frillmann went to greet Chennault and the Old Man was all business, asking about the condition of the trucks and the inventory of goods they'd brought with them. Frillmann's Buick now belonged to Chennault.

The drive had been harrowing for Frillmann, who felt the experience had left him a changed man. He had started in the AVG as a chaplain but always with an eye to proving that he could be something more than that—a man of action. He had resisted heading the first convoy because he didn't believe he could handle the task, but he had done so and could take pride in having led his men to safety. He had escaped just in time: on March 8, while the convoy was on the road to Kunming, the Japanese captured Rangoon.

"The battle of southern Burma was over," Claire Chennault would write. It was actually a battle that he never saw with his own eyes.

During those long months that the Flying Tigers had fought in Rangoon, Chennault had been back in Kunming. There were long periods where he was confined to his bed with his annual bout of bronchitis. He could read the cables, but those accounts of the battles were hardly a substitute for being able to see them with his own eyes. For years he had been on the front lines of this war, but now he had effectively been relegated to the sidelines. Even though he was away from the action, he took pride in what his men had accomplished. Writing to a friend in Louisiana in January 1942, he said, "No other group in history ever ran up such a score of victories in so short a time."

And though Chennault was not trading machine-gun bursts with Japanese pilots, he was fighting a battle of his own—this one with the bureaucracies in China and the United States. Rumors were circulating that the AVG was going to be inducted into the Army Air Forces, becoming part of the army's growing presence in the China-Burma-India Theater, as it came to be known. The idea revolted Chennault. He fired off radiograms to Madame Chiang, who was in Chungking, and warned that induction would weaken the ability of the AVG to defend China. He said the men would leave rather than be inducted into the army. He sent similar warnings to Lauchlin Currie, a White House economic adviser. Currie had gone from focusing on New Deal programs to becoming a leading adviser to the president on China policy, and Chennault had come to rely on Currie for ensuring continued support for the AVG back at the White House. Even though he didn't want to induct the AVG into the army, Chennault was lobbying Currie to send updated army planes for the AVG to use.

Since Chennault had arrived in China almost five years earlier, his devotion to the country was inseparable from his personal feelings of loyalty to Madame Chiang. After all that time spent fighting on her behalf, he had no desire to don his old army uniform and abandon China when it was at its hour of greatest need. The whole point of the AVG had been to protect China, and now the unit would face the challenge of stemming the tide of the Japanese invasion. In that respect the Burma fighting was essentially a warm-up round for the big show.

Chennault was nothing if not a man of vision, and his boldest dream was to change the course of the war. He felt that if he was provided with some additional planes he could seize the offensive and turn back the Japanese. For years he had preached the theory of defensive pursuit—the idea that fighters could stop bombers—rejecting the dogma that the bomber always gets through. Still, he had always maintained an interest in how you could wage a guerrilla-style offensive campaign. He saw himself as the heir to a tradition of cavalry officers that would use "surprise thrusts" to stay on the offensive. He wanted to use the tried-and-true strategy of launching sudden attacks, and update it for modern aerial warfare. He believed that "ordinary defensive tactics would have doomed us to extinction," and he was going to need to wage a war like an "aerial shell game" in which he would keep the AVG moving around to small forward operating bases from which they would strike with raids when the enemy least expected it. This may have been somewhat of a shift in emphasis away from his work at Maxwell Field on the value of defensive pursuit, but this wasn't an intellectual debate waged on blackboards and in academic journals—this was live combat and he was learning to fight the war that was in front of him.

This was "aerial guerilla warfare," as one historian put it.

Chennault had the chance to explain this offensive theory to a visiting reporter. In March 1942, the war correspondent Ève Curie was traveling across Asia on a trip to interview the region's leaders, including Chiang Kai-shek and Mahatma Gandhi, and she made a brief stop in Kunming to see Chennault. His office walls were covered with maps and charts, and young American men were busy at their typewriters or running around with papers. Chennault greeted her and took her over to one of the large maps. Speaking in a "low, intense voice," he explained that "we must get ourselves in shape to attack Japan constantly from the air." He pointed to a number of locations on the map and said, "There are many places . . . from which we can threaten the long supply lines of the enemy which, after his recent victories, extend over a dangerously vast area." He spoke about hitting targets in Indochina, Thailand, and Burma. He said that he needed more planes to take the offensive against the Japanese. Curie spent only a few hours with Chennault and the AVG pilots, but formed distinct impressions about them. Chennault struck her as being from another era entirely, an "aggressive-spirited" warrior who spoke in a language that sounded as if it had been used "centuries ago by adventuring navigators or bold buccaneers." As for the pilots, she concluded that it was unlikely that there was another group of airmen anywhere in the world who "have done a better and bolder job and gambled in a more dangerous way with their lives."

Despite the rumors about a potential induction into the Army Air Forces, the AVG was still part of the Chinese Air Force and under the authority of Chiang Kai-shek and Madame Chiang. En route to a wartime conference, the premier couple paid a visit to Kunming, where a banquet was held in their honor on February 28. The pilots dressed up in the finest uniforms they could find.

Chiang himself spoke to the airmen, with a Chinese officer translating. He knew that at least part of the reason these pilots had come to China was for the attractive salaries, and that many of the pilots had been killed. He wanted to reassure them that their widows and children wouldn't be forgotten. According to the official transcript of the speeches for the evening, he said, "I shall extend to those of your comrades who have given their lives the same mark of distinction and the same care for their families and children. For this I hold myself responsible. I trust that you will perform your duties free from any anxiety on this score." That may have offered some comfort to the pilots, but by this point in the war money was no longer their primary motivation. They had seen too many of their friends die in combat to believe that taking part in the conflict was worth it simply for the pay. Writing a check to their widow was a nice gesture, but they would prefer to make it back alive. Some were fighting out of loyalty to Chennault, others because America was now formally in this war, and still others out of a begrudging sense that this was what they had agreed to, while planning to return home when their yearlong commitment was over.

Chiang didn't want to emphasize their losses too much. He concluded: "When victory is ours I hope to celebrate together with you our successful issue of the war in Tokyo."

Then Chennault stood to address his men and introduce the main speaker: Madame Chiang. "Never before in history do I know of any military unit such as ours having been accorded the honour such as comes to us tonight. No matter how many decorations we may have bestowed on us in the future I am sure we will never receive more honour than we have received tonight," he said. Then he introduced Madame Chiang. Though the men may not have known of her long-standing friendship with Chennault and her role in organizing the AVG, he introduced her as the "Honorary Group Commander." It wasn't quite as over the top as calling her his princess, but he was certainly trying to shower her with praise.

Madame Chiang rose to speak. She spoke in English, and with her Southern twang she addressed her audience as "My boys!" She acknowledged the sacrifice the men were making, assuring them that the "whole Chinese nation has taken you to their hearts." She proposed a toast "to the two great sister nations of both sides of the Pacific. They now have a bond of friendship and sympathy which serves us well in the crucible of war and which will serve us equally well when victory has been won."

The gala included singing, and a play was performed, but as one pilot noted, "We could not very well understand it as it was all in Chinese." The evening was without incident until the predictably drunk Greg Boyington, along with another inebriated pilot, arrived at the dinner. They stumbled to their seats, causing a bit of commotion and upsetting Olga Greenlaw so much that she began ripping her scarf beneath the table.

When the Chiangs came back through Kunming once again in March, Boyington was chosen as one of the escorts for their DC-3. The pilots were supposed to put on an acrobatic routine and fly alongside the leaders' transport for the eighty-mile trip to Chanyi, at which point the Chiangs would carry on to Chungking. When one of the planes was forced to drop out almost immediately due to a malfunction, Boyington took his place leading the escort mission. As his biographer Bruce Gamble put it, Boyington now was "responsible for two of the most important people in China, and five P-40s. He was ill prepared." His radio wasn't working, he didn't know the route very well, and up ahead were powerful monsoon winds. To compensate for the weather the DC-3 altered course, and Boyington followed alongside without realizing he was now veering off the designated route. Another P-40 pilot tried to get Boyington's attention to signal that they should turn back, but he kept on in the same direction.

Finally, when he peeled off from the DC-3, the American pilots attempted to direct him west, but he put them on a southward course, leaving the others no choice but to follow along. "There's a cardinal rule," one of the pilots explained. "You don't leave your leader, you stick with him, right or wrong." By the time Boyington realized that he'd gone off course they were hopelessly lost and running low on fuel. In the unfamiliar hilly terrain, Boyington couldn't see any clearings for an emergency landing except for a small field atop a hill, which turned out to be a cemetery. It was not the best omen, but Boyington had no other choice. This was going to be a rough landing.

The plane hit the ground hard and skidded along the dirt. The wing ripped as it came to a stop next to some gravestones. When all the P-40s had landed, the men were miraculously uninjured but their planes were in various states of disrepair. Boyington used one undamaged radio to send an update on their condition. Harvey Greenlaw, who received the message, replied with sarcasm and anger: "Happy to hear from you fellows. We have made arrangements for you to stay in the bridal suite of the Grand Hotel, and God damn it, don't ever come back."

Local villagers began to crowd around the downed pilots. One of them spoke enough English to explain that they were still in China, but not far from the border with Japanese-occupied Indochina, so they were lucky to have avoided being captured by the enemy. They were led to the village of Wenshan, where the mayor hosted them for dinner and glass after glass of rice wine. The pilots felt odd celebrating, given that they had just lost a number of P-40s on a noncombat mission, but they drank anyway. The following day the obvious question loomed: How would they get out of this remote location? Boyington went for a hike to survey the area and discovered ancient stone towers that were lookout posts. He climbed to the top of one to survey the area but could see only mountains in every direction.

He'd have to think of something. Reunited with another one of the escorts who had crashed farther out, the downed pilots were taken by truck to another small village. Boyington thought the driver was going too fast over the rickety road, and as another pilot recounted the story, he pulled out his sidearm and demanded that one of the Americans be allowed to drive, but the others were able to calm him down. From the second village they were able to board a train that passed through only a few times a week. The locomotive was so old that the passengers had to occasionally get out and push it, but they finally made it back to Kunming two days later, on March 9.

Chennault was furious about the loss of the planes—he was focused on trying to get more P-40s and he couldn't afford to carelessly lose them like that. He insisted that they be examined to determine if any of them could be salvaged. That job fell to Frank Losonsky, the crew chief from Detroit, who was dispatched to the scene of the wreck to try to repair the damaged planes. Losonsky, another mechanic, and an interpreter loaded some tools and a case of sherry onto a truck and shipped out on a flatcar. When they went as far as they could by rail, they removed the truck and drove the last few miles to the hilltop, reaching the cemetery on March 11. The terrain was so rugged "it was a wonder the pilots survived," Losonsky thought. He could tell that two of the planes were wrecked beyond repair, but set to work on the two others that had crashed on the hilltop.

A crew chief like Frank Losonsky, a man who grew up scrounging for coal in Detroit, could take pride in what he was doing even if he wasn't getting fanfare in the press. These "minor miracles of repair," as one pilot called them, kept the Tigers flying. The pilots were grateful for the thankless job performed by the members of the ground crew. Bob Neale said, "Save some big words for our ground crew. They never get a break in the papers and they've gone through strafings, dodged bombs and always been there working at all hours to keep our planes flying."

And they'd do it again this time. They "replaced the props with spares and fixed the landing gear as best we could," though Losonsky had his doubts about whether the plane could get off the ground. The local villagers helped cut a takeoff strip that ran through the cemetery and ended at the precipice of a cliff. Losonsky appraised it and calculated that it was just long enough to be usable if they could strip the P-40 of all its extra weight. They got to work, pulling off the armor plate and everything else they could find on the craft that wasn't absolutely essential. Fittingly, it was Boyington himself who returned to the village to attempt the flight, and on March 16 he climbed into the cockpit, pushed the throttle forward, and the plane began to cut across the makeshift runway. As it neared the end it seemed to plummet off the edge, dropping fifty feet, but before it hit the ground, Boyington was flying once again, making it all the way back to Kunming. He came back to fly out the second craft that had been repaired, and when the ordeal was over, Losonsky and Boyington toasted their achievement with rice wine. Saving two of the planes didn't do much to redeem Boyington in the eyes of the AVG command, and Harvey Greenlaw gave him a hard time. Boyington wasn't the type to take responsibility for a mistake, and his sharp elbows only soured his relationship with the other members of the AVG. It was increasingly clear that his days in the outfit were numbered.

CHAPTER 12

AERIAL GUERRILLA WARFARE

After Rangoon fell on March 7, the AVG would make their last stand in Burma on a small, barren airfield near a town called Magwe, about three hundred miles north of Rangoon. The RAF had set up a small base there, but it was little more than a few hangars and planes on a dirt field. Pilots from the First Squadron manned the post in early March and then they were relieved by a group from the Third. Bill Reed, a pilot in the Third Squadron, arrived on March 14 and could tell immediately that he wasn't going to like this new posting. "So far there hasn't been any activity here except reconnaissance work. Magwe is very hot and dusty—living is quite makeshift," he wrote in his diary. To make matters worse, it didn't look like they were going to have the opportunity to do any fighting in this desolate outpost. "On alert today . . . Had one call for patrol duty today, but nothing developed." As he waited for the Japanese to appear, he ate the local watermelon and was "getting pretty tan again, and there is plenty of chance to read. Most of the time is spent in reading, sleeping, playing Acey-Deucey, etc." But Reed wasn't the sort of man who was content to spend his days reading and playing cards. "Action seems to make the days go by much more swiftly," he wrote, "which is a thing much to be desired."

Frustrated with waiting, he proposed a reconnaissance mission deep into Burma, where he could assess the Japanese forces. The mission was approved, and he persuaded Ken Jernstedt to join him. The twenty-four-year-old Jernstedt grew up on a farm in Yamhill, Oregon, where he shot gophers with a .22 rifle. He'd spent his whole life in Oregon until he signed up to become a Marine Corps aviator. When he heard about the secret mission in China, he signed on eagerly, like Reed, for the adventure of it all. The two pilots had become good friends. They played softball together during the training in Toungoo, they shared meals in Kunming, and they had fought together in the early battles over Rangoon in December. But this would be a challenge unlike anything they had done before—just the two of them flying deep into enemy territory.

Their first stop on the reconnaissance mission was an overnight rest at Toungoo. They arrived on March 17 and took a walk around places they had known well. If they assumed they would encounter the familiar setting from their days before the war, they were gravely disappointed. The town had been bombed by the Japanese and was "ruined," as Reed characterized it in his diary. A pile of corpses stacked in a field was a particularly gruesome sight. That night, they went back to their old barracks and went over their reconnaissance plan, though they may have discussed doing something more ambitious, as their .30-caliber and .50-caliber machine guns had plenty of ammunition. They even had been able to fit a couple of makeshift bombs into the flare chutes on their P-40s—an indication they were intending to do more than just look at the Japanese forces.

The two pilots awoke before dawn on March 18, 1942, and readied their P-40s. It was still dark as they prepared to depart, and the only light came from the North Star, visible on the horizon at the end of the runway. "I just kept my eye on the old North Star, and when I got up to flying speed, I pulled off," Ken Jernstedt recalled. The pair climbed to twenty thousand feet and flew along the Gulf of Martaban. They encountered a heavy rainstorm that forced them to descend to as low as seven thousand feet. When they were about twenty miles south of their objective, the Moulmein aerodrome, they caught sight of the railroad that would lead them straight to the airfield. As they were approaching their destination, they saw something unexpected—a landing strip with about thirty Japanese planes parked on it.

If this had ever been just a reconnaissance mission, those plans were shoved aside. This was an irresistible target, so the two pilots dove down to strafe the field. On the first few runs Reed initially scattered his shots but then found one plane to concentrate on. "[I] observed my fire going home and pieces of the ship flying off and the canopy smashed," he wrote in his combat report. Both pilots made six passes each, and when they left they could see five large conflagrations on the ground. Shockingly, it didn't seem as if the Japanese had put up any defense. "It was a complete surprise, for as far as I could see there wasn't even any ground fire," Reed wrote in his diary.

Emboldened by their success they decided to carry the attack to the main air base at Moulmein, just a few miles away. There they found more enemy planes arrayed beneath them. Jernstedt dove and "concentrated my fire on a fighter warming up and it immediately burst into flames." He released one of the bombs he'd packed in the flare case, aiming for the hangar. It missed but did "hit an Army 97 bomber parked in front of the hangar. This ship was soon ablaze." Reed dropped down with "all guns blazing at a field loaded with heavy bombers. This time we met pretty heavy antiaircraft, though, and as I pulled up and turned for another dive I saw [Jernstedt] crossing the field with little black mushrooms of smoke bursting all around him." Although he was concerned that "the antiaircraft fire was pretty heavy and too damn close," Reed made one final run. "On my last dive across the field I had only one [.50-caliber machine gun] and [two .30-caliber machine guns] firing, but I succeeded in setting what appeared to be an Army 98 fighter plane on fire," he wrote in his combat report.

Seeing that the Japanese planes were preparing to take off, and being almost out of ammunition, the Americans pulled out and followed the road back to where they had come from. "On the way back I strafed a boat, a Jap staff car, and some boxcars," Reed wrote in his diary. He also dropped a bomb on a compound. They landed at Toungoo, refueled with the assistance of some Chinese soldiers, and then returned to the field at Magwe.

"A pretty good day's work, so [we] took the rest of the day off," Reed added. They inspected their planes and discovered that each had only a single bullet hole. "It would be hard to estimate the amount of damage done to ther [sic] aircraft but I feel that it was considerable," Jernstedt wrote in his report. They were ultimately credited with taking out fifteen Japanese planes on the ground, many of which had been hidden under a camouflage net: seven by Jernstedt and eight by Reed. The impromptu raid was a massive success for the AVG, and Chennault would have been proud that his pilots were taking the offensive.

In Iowa, the *Des Moines Register* heralded the raid with a huge banner on its front page: IOWAN BAGS JAP PLANES. When an Associated Press reporter tracked down Reed's mother for a comment about her son, she was succinct: "Just say we are proud of him." *Time* magazine described how "Pilots Kenneth Jernstedt and William Reed popped out of a cloud into the hot blue sky over Burma" and left behind "a junk heap of burning, exploding Jap planes." The article added, "The AVG flyers were doing deeds that a movie director would reject, in a script, as too fantastic."

Although Reed had succeeded in breaking the monotony that had been plaguing him, he soon settled back into his old routine at Magwe. On March 19 he noted in his diary: "Not much doing in the way of alarms. Dust storms on the field that remind me of desert scenes in the movies. If it weren't for the watermelons, this place wouldn't be worth patrolling." Thinking about the surprise raid he'd just succeeded in carrying out, however, he assessed his own base and observed with some trepidation after a false alarm, "This field is too full of planes, though, to suit me."

As he had feared, while he was getting lunch on March 21, Reed heard the unmistakable buzzing of planes approaching. He ran to take cover in a trench, but Ken Jernstedt hurried to his P-40. He took to the air, and "went like a scared jack rabbit for miles, making sure no one was on my tail."

From his trench Reed peered out and watched as the Japanese bombers attacked their secondary field and "blew it sky high." When the raid seemed to be over, he emerged to assess the damage but saw another wave of Japanese aircraft approaching. "We ran until we heard the sound of the bombs falling and then fell flat." As *Time* later reported, "Bomb fragments wounded a pilot and two mechanics in a trench flanking the runway. An AVG doctor lugged the pilot to a jeep and drove it across the field to a hospital, with Jap bullets chasing him in the dust like puffs from his own exhaust pipe."

Jernstedt, meanwhile, had followed the Japanese bombers as they turned back to their base, and though he was only a single P-40 chasing a formation of enemy planes, he recalled that he "got into some skirmishing" and was "trying to close in on a kill" when his windshield was shot out. He had neglected to put on his goggles, and for a moment was blinded. But he quickly focused and was able to open his eyes against the streaming air, and landed safely.

The shooting was over but the toll from the raid had left the base in chaos. John Fauth, a mechanic from Red Lion, Pennsylvania, had been badly injured and would die later that night. Pilot Frank Swartz and ground-crew member Bill Seiple were flown to a hospital in India. It became clear to the AVG pilots that they were going to have to retreat, and they pulled back to a CAMCO factory in Loiwing, just over the border into China, on March 23.

The AVG wanted revenge. "We're going to make them pay," First Squadron commander Bob Neale said. Chennault was of the same mind, his anger compounded by guilt. The Americans suspected that the enemy planes were operating out of Chiang Mai, a key base in Thailand, and Chennault blamed himself for not conducting sufficient reconnaissance there. Now he didn't want to just spy on the base, he wanted to attack it with a surprise early-morning raid.

The squadrons were starting to mold together as numbers dwindled, and this plan would involve pilots from Neale's First Squadron and Newkirk's Second Squadron. Tex Hill, perhaps in deference to Newkirk's status as a married man, put himself forward for the dangerous job leading the raid. Hill wouldn't forget that conversation. "No, Tex," Newkirk replied. "I've got to do that. The guys might think I'm kind of chicken or something, you know." He had proved himself in battle time and again, but he may still have been worried about the reputation he'd got from his first encounter with the enemy. Coincidentally, on March 22 a full-page feature appeared in newspapers like the *Albuquerque Journal* profiling Jane Newkirk, one of America's "waiting wives." The feature described how she was "wistfully awaiting the day when, war clouds passed, reunion—and happiness" would return. Until then, she was volunteering for the Red Cross in Los Angeles and trying to keep busy reading, listening to the radio, and making a rug. She wore wings pinned to her dress as a reminder of her husband's absence and scanned the newspapers for any mention of Scarsdale

Jack. The feature said that Jane loved going out to dance but she was holding off until he returned, when "we'll make up for all the months we've been separated."

On March 22, on the other side of the world, a group of ten pilots, including Newkirk, Boyington, and Bond, took off from Kunming. They landed in Loiwing, directly across the border from Burma, and spent the night at the CAMCO facility there. They were pleased to discover that the luxurious facility included a clubhouse where the men could relax. Bond took a seat in one of its comfortable chairs and looked out the three windows at the "panoramic view of the distant mountains." The next morning, they woke up early and found that they had been joined by some of the survivors retreating from Magwe. "All of the men and pilots have been deeply affected by the bombing," Bond wrote in his diary. "They have a fear of bombing imprinted in their minds. I can understand it." Now, the Americans would try to carry out a retaliatory raid.

On March 23, the American pilots flew to a small Royal Air Force base near the Thai border around Namsang, Burma, where they would spend the night and review their plans one final time. They would take off in two groups before dawn the next morning. First up would be Bob Neale's men with six planes, after which Newkirk would advance with his group of four. All ten aircraft would rendezvous at a set point at ten thousand feet and would fly into Thailand in a single formation. They would then split up, with Neale's group striking the Chiang Mai airfield and Newkirk's a nearby military airfield at Lamphun. The surprise was key to their success—and their survival. If the Japanese had warning of the attack, they could overwhelm the Americans with superior force. One pilot called it "the most dangerous undertaking the AVG has done," adding that even if they didn't get shot down by ground fire or scrambling Japanese fighters, the pilots would be in "enemy territory where if you have to force land and the Japs don't get you the jungle will."

That night they placed trucks and lanterns around the runway to guide their predawn departure. They had dinner at the RAF barracks then prepared for bed. An RAF officer warned them that they could use the water to wash but not to brush their teeth. Boyington would recall that Newkirk ignored the advice, saying, "Well, after tomorrow, I don't think it'll make any difference."

"All right you curly-headed fellows, it's time," an RAF officer yelled as he barged into their room on the morning of March 24. They dressed in the darkness, had a quick breakfast, and gathered at the flight line, making jokes to keep their spirits up. The headlights of a truck parked on the end of the grass strip were turned on, toward which the planes would accelerate and then ascend. They began to warm up their fighters at around 5:25 A.M., and then, at 5:49, Neale was the first to take off, with Bond following closely behind.

Bond rose safely into the sky, but because he "couldn't see a thing" he flew based on his instruments. He was finally able to make out the navigation lights on Bob Neale's plane and followed him, wondering "how in hell those other guys will make it to rendezvous over the field at ten thousand feet." His concerns were well-founded, for while the six planes from Neale's group assembled successfully, Newkirk's contingent failed to appear at the rendezvous point. After waiting about twenty minutes, Neale decided to proceed without them. They couldn't afford to lose the cover of darkness for the mission. They formed two Vs of three planes each and turned to a course of 150 degrees. "What was passing by in the jungle below us, or how close we came to any mountains, was in my imagination only," Boyington would recall. The "early-morning haze hid any landmark that would have been helpful," but Bond could tell as they crossed over the Salween River that they were closing in. He had conducted a reconnaissance mission here once before and was hoping that his memory would help direct him. Recognizing a mountain off to the left, he knew that the field would be close by, but Neale didn't seem to be turning toward the target. Bond couldn't break their radio silence but took his plane next to Neale's, wagging his wings to signal that he knew where they were and that he would take over as leader for the final push. They had been in the air for more than an hour.

Bond took his P-40 into a "gradual descent," not knowing what he would find beneath him in the darkness. As he drew closer to the ground he finally made out something that looked like a "square shape." Pulling down lower he saw buildings that looked like hangars and spots on the field that had to be Japanese planes. When he descended to just a thousand feet he fired a burst into the darkness—the signal to the P-40s behind him that they had located their target. Another three P-40s dove down to join him in strafing the field, while Ed Rector and William McGarry remained above them to provide top cover.

"Now it was clear: we had caught them flat-footed without any warning," Bond would later recall. He made his first pass over the field, firing on a row of fighters. The planes were parked so close their wingtips were nearly touching. "Hell," he recalled, "I hadn't seen this many aircraft in years. Seemed like the whole Japanese Air Force had tried to crowd into this one little field. I couldn't miss." He made another pass and saw that fires had broken out. He was flying low enough to see details on the field: men running and propellers starting to rotate. As he turned, tracer bullets whizzed by his cockpit, and puffs of black smoke in the sky were signs that the Japanese had manned their anti-aircraft guns. He scanned the sky for Japanese aircraft, but there were none to be seen. Now that the base defense was heating up, he made what he thought would be his final run, but his aim was poor, so he came around for another one. As he came back for another strafing run, he spotted one large plane that "stood out from the others; perhaps it was a reconnaissance ship." Selecting this as his final target he fired, watching as the plane "seemed to shake itself to pieces." He considered going back again but decided against it, thinking, "To hell with pushing my luck."

"I looked back at the field as I rounded the southwest corner of the mountain, and it did my heart good," Charlie Bond wrote. "What satisfaction!" The attack had taken just seven or eight minutes.

Bond joined up with another pilot who had done strafing runs, William Bartling, and with Rector and McGarry. The four planes set a course back to Burma. The plan had been established: they would refuel at Namsang, then hopefully rendezvous with Newkirk's group at a farther airfield, and then they'd all head back to Loiwing. Bond could hardly wait to get word to Chennault in Kunming that they had pulled off a successful offensive strike. "It was a mission exactly according to Chennault's plan. How proud he would be. Hell, I was."

As they made their return flight, Bond could see that one of the P-40s was falling behind, dropping lower and wagging its wings as if to signal that it needed help. It was McGarry. He hadn't been on the strafing runs but must have been hit by one of the antiaircraft rounds as he circled up above. As his craft continued to lose altitude, he pulled the canopy open. A trail of smoke was now streaming from his plane. It was clear that the P-40 wasn't going to make it, but Bond, knowing it would be safer for McGarry to bail out over Burma than into the Japanese-occupied jungles of Thailand below, tried to direct him toward the Salween River, which was the border. It lay just ahead, but it seemed as if McGarry's plane was losing altitude too quickly to make it.

McGarry finally rolled his plane over and jumped from about a thousand feet while the others circled overhead and watched. He landed on a plateau, a short distance from where his plane crashed and burned. He stood and waved to the P-40s, but there was little they could do for him. Bond circled the spot where he thought they were on his map and marked the time, 7:41 A.M. He flew overhead and dropped the map down to McGarry, while Rector contributed a candy bar. The three remaining pilots then made their way back to Namsang, where they found that Boyington and Neale had already returned safely.

McGarry had been nicknamed "Happy-Go-Lucky" for his carefree attitude and "Black Mac" for his thick head of hair. Before joining the army, he had been an art student at Loyola University in Los Angeles, and had demonstrated his artistic talent in the AVG by helping to design the insignias. The RAF pilots at Namsang assured the Americans that they would do everything they could to assist with search and rescue. McGarry was only twenty-five or thirty miles from the border, and there was some hope that he could get out on his own. But given the "rough mountainous jungles," Bond had his doubts about McGarry's chances, and "couldn't get Mac off my mind."

Bond and his group then flew to another airfield where they had arranged to rendezvous with Jack Newkirk and his contingent of pilots. Once again they failed to appear, so the group went back to Loiwing. At least they could relax in those comfortable chairs while they waited.

Newkirk's group had gotten lost in the dark earlier that morning, and decided to head into Thailand on their own. They tried to find the city of Chiang Mai, knowing that the airfield wouldn't be far away, but they couldn't seem to locate it. After a while they were getting desperate enough that anything they saw started to look like a good target.

When they happened upon a railroad station they noticed what pilot Robert Keeton described as a "large building which was undoubtedly a barracks." It was set next to a grass field that appeared to be a small airfield. As Keeton, a former football player at Colorado College, strafed the barracks, he saw a row of wooden storehouses neatly lined up next to a rail track, and targeted them as well.

As he was finishing a strafing run, he glanced back and saw a "large ball of fire" in a field. The fire appeared to trail back over a hundred and fifty yards, and it looked as if his squadronmates had ignited some "gas dumps or oil tanks." He pulled up and was able to find two of the other three P-40s from their group. They flew on and eventually found the Chiang Mai airfield, and abundant evidence that their comrades had been there first. The airfield was covered in more fires than Keeton could count. Antiaircraft rounds were "popping all around" his plane, so Keeton turned back with the two other P-40s. He scanned the sky for the fourth plane in their group, but it was nowhere in sight. At 8:35 A.M. they landed at the airfield at Heho in Burma to refuel.

When Keeton stepped out of his cockpit to confer with the other two pilots, he was told why they were one plane short: Jack Newkirk had gone down. The fire Keeton had seen near the barracks, which he had thought was burning gas or oil, had in fact been Newkirk's P-40 incinerating as it skidded along the ground. Frank Lawlor, who had been flying alongside Newkirk, described what had occurred in his combat report: "Immediately after leaving the area of the barracks Squadron Leader Newkirk headed back up the road to [Chiang Mai]. He went into a dive to strafe what appeared to be an armored car and I sa[w] his plane crash and burn. Since by this time visibility had improved considerably and there appeared to be no unusual circumstances it was evident that Newkirk had been hit by enemy fire, possibl[y] from the armored car."

Over the decades, historians have not been able to establish with certainty what caused Newkirk to crash. Interviews with Thai eyewitnesses on the ground suggested that the "armored cars" were actually oxcarts carrying rice. Hank Geselbracht, a pilot accompanying Newkirk in those final seconds, was a bit hesitant in his own description of the "armored cars," perhaps a tacit acknowledgment that the pilots weren't sure what they were firing at. In fact, when he wrote the report in pencil he just called them "vehicles," and they became "armored cars" when it was typed up. The typed version reads: "The two vehicles we fired at were I believe armored cars. They were a camouflage brown and were squattish in appearance." He had fired on them and thought they had destroyed one, only to find that Newkirk was missing when they came up—realizing then that the "flash of flame" was his squadron leader.

After refueling, the three remaining members of the group set out to meet up with the rest of the pilots at Loiwing. It was only 10:45 A.M. when they reconvened and discussed the morning's events in detail. Bond listened to the account of Newkirk's crash and couldn't determine precisely what had befallen him: "We don't know whether he was hit and couldn't pull out or he waited too long to pull out."

As they were talking, the air alarm sounded. Bond took cover in a ditch while other pilots scrambled to their planes and took off, ready to face what they presumed was a retaliatory Japanese attack. But it was another false alarm, and the men returned in time for the lunch prepared by CAMCO's chef. Another CAMCO employee who played the role of bartender poured the pilots some much-needed drinks. Before long the whole group was at the bar "celebrating the day's work," as Bond described it.

Later in the day, Bond would return to the solace of his diary. He wrote a detailed narrative of the raid in line with the extensive combat report he filled out. In noting their celebration of the victory over drinks, he wondered whether it was the right attitude to strike: "It's surprising how quickly one gets over the horrible loss of his buddies in wartime and revels in the successes of the day. Everyone was laughing and enjoying the moment. Yet Jack [Newkirk] was gone and we weren't sure of [McGarry]. It makes one wonder about the nature of human beings. . . . Indeed, this was a great success for the AVG and the Allies. But can the AVG afford to lose such men as Jack Newkirk and Mac McGarry and two P-40 aircraft in these times? We wonder." Chennault, the old warrior, felt no such ambivalence. He was triumphant about the raid, and felt that the cost of losing two pilots "was more than justified from the tactical results obtained."

Americans mourned the loss of Scarsdale Jack. Obituaries were featured in papers across the country, emphasizing his all-American upbringing. He was described as a boy who had learned to shoot a bow and arrow, an Eagle Scout, and a young man who passed on an easy life of wealth because he wanted to serve his country. For months Americans had been reading about his exploits and had come to feel some degree of connection with him, as if he were a nephew or a neighbor. The *Honolulu Advertiser* ran a full-page ad invoking his legacy to sell war bonds: "He had a lot to live for. Ask his father . . . Ask his widow."

Newkirk's own family grieved the loss of a son, a brother, and a husband. His father, Louis, was devastated and couldn't bring himself to talk with reporters. He attended Saint Thomas Church in midtown Manhattan for a ceremony commemorating his son. The Reverend Roelif Brooks offered remarks on the solemn occasion: "There is something gallant about youth, and youth responds very quickly to a sympathy for the oppressed and downtrodden. Those who go perhaps have accomplished more than many of us who'll live to a ripe old age. Let that be a comfort when we remember this gallant young airman, who gave his life that others may live." On the other side of the country, Jane Newkirk struggled to come to terms with her widowhood. She was visiting a friend in San Francisco when she got the news. A reporter found her at the airport, waiting for a flight back to Los Angeles, and said she "became hysterical every time her husband's name was mentioned." An Associated Press photographer snapped shots of the bereaved widow with the wings pinned to her dress. She made it back to Los Angeles, but was despondent about her future: "I don't know what I'll do, now that Jack is gone." Eventually she decided to leave California and return home to Lansing, Michigan, and take time to mourn. Jack had promised her a reunion party in Hawaii, but now all she had were his letters and the framed picture of him she'd kept on her desk. She remembered waving good-bye to him on the dock in San Francisco. After his death she would say of his departure, "I had a premonition I'd never see him again when his ship sailed."

In the days after the Chiang Mai raid the men of the AVG heard the victory being cheered on the radio. Combined with the regular visits from reporters, the pilots were beginning to have a notion of the sensation they were becoming back home. But there were concerns arising in their ranks. They had signed up for a one-year commitment to CAMCO and then planned on heading home, with the assurance that they could take up their old commissions in the military. Many were set on returning to the Marine Corps or the navy. Their future felt uncertain.

Chennault called a meeting with the pilots in Kunming on the evening of March 26. He spent an hour with them discussing the rumors and found that there was overwhelming opposition to the idea of induction into the army. The pilots groused that the one-year contracts they'd signed with CAMCO were being abrogated, and there was some grumbling from men who wanted to resign immediately. Chennault assured them that he could find replacements if they weren't willing to stay for the long haul. For his part, he had committed his life to defending China and was planning to stay on no matter what—even if it meant having to put on an army uniform again.

However safe the hostels in Kunming felt from the bloody war raging in Burma, the Japanese were edging closer to the Chinese border. The army had sent Lieutenant General Joseph Stilwell to China to work with Chiang Kai-shek. He had visited Kunming and impressed upon Chennault the importance of the AVG's induction into the Army Air Forces. He thought that he had Chennault's acquiescence, but that would turn out to be a touchy subject.

Stilwell had been placed in command of the Chinese Expeditionary Force in Burma and was entrusted with halting the Japanese offensive, though he would lament that the Chinese troops wouldn't follow his orders. The mission wasn't going well. "The edge of war moved north with incessant air raids, villages in flames, more and more refugees choking the roads in a long frieze of bullock carts, heat and thirst and dust," historian Barbara Tuchman wrote. Stilwell was growing frustrated that the Chinese troops refused to go on the offensive as the Japanese closed in. Toungoo fell to the Japanese on March 30.

That same day, *Life* hit the newsstands with the article on the FLYING TIGERS IN BURMA. George Rodger's photographs were published two months after his photo shoot with the AVG. The article had a triumphant tone, noting: "One shining hope has emerged from three catastrophic months of war . . . [the AVG has] violently wrenched from the Jap Air Force control of the skies over Burma and southeast China." That was old news. The Flying Tigers had launched several successful raids, but by March 30, 1942, they had retreated across the border into China. They would use the CAMCO clubhouse at Loiwing as their new base.

It sounded like a mythical place.

In the press, the factory at Loiwing, the one the Americans had stayed at before and after the Chiang Mai raid, was known as Pawleyville, after the CAMCO executive who had designed it. Pawley seemed to have taken his inspiration from Henry Ford's Fordlandia in Brazil. Pawleyville was a remote outpost built deep in the jungles that had more luxurious accommodations than what you would encounter in most places in the United States. The public could hardly believe the reports. The *Honolulu Advertiser* told of a "famed but hidden city." It was a "mysterious workshop," the location of which "was a closely guarded secret." In 1939 *Time* described it as being "miles from civilization of any sort . . . a community of 15 U.S. experts, their families, nearly 1,000 Chinese workers, living in a modern town with electric lights, running water, bungalows, playgrounds, and a $4,000,000 plant of U.S.-owned Central Aircraft Co. which will produce fighting planes to help China win." Other accounts told of how Pawley's team had to overcome malaria, the bubonic plague, and Japanese air raids to build and maintain it. Pawley had originally housed his facility at Hangchow, where the American instructors taught Chinese pilots, but in the wake of the war it had been moved all the way to this remote outpost.

When the AVG pilots began to move into the CAMCO facility in late March 1942, they marveled at their lavish quarters, a remarkable upgrade from the dirt field at Magwe. "I certainly welcome the rest and relief from the tension," Bill Reed wrote in his diary. They could play pool or listen to phonograph records, and plans were made to screen movies. Best of all, there was "Ma," as the men took to calling her. Marion Davidson, the chef who had prepared lunch for the Chiang Mai raiders, cooked the men thick steaks and served up treats like fruit salad. "It's good for morale," she explained. When an American reporter visited, he said the pilots looked like "mild-mannered ex-college boys mothered by a plump dormitory manageress." Seated in the dining room beneath an eight-foot American flag, the men could escape from the war for the length of a hearty meal.

The pilots had been hardened by combat and the loss of their squadronmates, but they were still young men who wanted to have a good time. On April 1, they threw a party "for no reason at all + everyone cut loose," as R. T. Smith noted in his diary. The following night there was a wedding. Fred Hodges married an Anglo-Burmese woman he had met in Rangoon. The men didn't miss an excuse to enjoy a wild night, and the ceremony was followed by a bacchanalia. Greg Boyington attended wearing a bathrobe—he had recently crashed a plane on takeoff and explained that his knees were too swollen to wear slacks. Predictably he took things a bit far and got "full of whiskey." As the celebrating went on into the night, an air-raid alarm sounded and people ran outside to seek cover. Boyington wandered into the darkness in a drunken stupor and fell off the side of the hill. It was another false alarm, but his injuries, including a deep cut on his head, were severe enough to warrant his evacuation to Kunming, where he would recover in the hospital. By now he enjoyed little about the AVG except for Olga Greenlaw, who was in Kunming when he returned. She brought him a pack of Camels and kept him company. He complained that he felt dirty in his clothes so she brought him a pair of her husband's silk pajamas. As he recovered, he would go over to her place for tea and sympathy, and he talked about his growing unhappiness and his increasing certainty that his tenure with the group would soon be coming to an end.

The American pilots remained concerned about another Japanese attack, and for those who had survived the raid on Magwe, the idea of being caught in a surprise raid once again was terrifying. They would rather take cover or scramble their planes in response to any number of false alarms than find themselves again the victims of a surprise attack. "They should bomb this place any day now," Bill Reed wrote in his diary on April 2. Still, the Japanese bombers didn't appear.

April 5 was Easter Sunday, and services were conducted by an RAF chaplain after dinner. The musical accompaniment was less professional, as a drunken pilot, Duke Hedman, downed a few scotches and then tried a few tunes at the piano. Reed was overcome with a sense of wistfulness: "Nice services considering the circumstances, but I couldn't help thinking of Easter Sunday services at home." Afterward, the men played pool late into the night. The good news on the holiday was that eight RAF Hurricanes had landed on the Burma side of the border, an invaluable addition to the existing forces when the battle finally got started. A heavy rain on April 7 gave the pilots some assurance that it would be a quiet day for those on alert duty, and as expected there were no reports of Japanese planes.

Reed had planned to sleep late the next day, but was awoken at 9:00 A.M. by an air-raid alarm, and though it again turned out to be a false one, it ruined his morning: "My day off today, damn it!" At 12:30 P.M. three new planes—a revised version of the P-40—showed up as reinforcements. They had hardly landed when another air-raid alarm sounded. From a hilltop, Reed scanned the skies with binoculars and saw a cluster of enemy aircraft approaching.

Because they had little time to react after the air alarm sounded, the pilots took their P-40s into a "balls out" climb. R. T. Smith was leading the group, and he could tell that this battle was going to be the "damndest rat-race imaginable." He told the P-40 pilots to spread out, pick their individual targets, and hope for the best. When the Japanese planes approached to hit the planes still on the runway, the P-40s went into steep dives to hit them from above. Soon the American pilots could see smoke rising from their airfield and enemy fighters "buzzing around like flies."

Twenty-six-year-old Fritz Wolf was one of the airmen flying that afternoon. Though he had lost much of his bulk while overseas, he had been a fullback for Carroll College's football team, an All-Conference player, and had nearly gone on to try out for the Green Bay Packers, but instead decided to become a naval aviator. Wolf came out of his dive directly behind two Japanese fighters and began to shoot. They didn't go down, but when he saw another fighter doing a roll, he decided it would make a good target. He opened fire and watched as the bullet-riddled fighter plummeted, and then attempted to climb back up before finally crashing onto the field below.

The P-40s seemed to have the upper hand. Smith pulled in to the rear of a fighter that was completing a strafing run and kept his finger on the trigger until the Japanese plane went down in a ball of flames. The enemy planes still airborne seemed to be turning back. Smith was tempted to follow them but chose to return to the base, writing later in his diary that it had been "the most thrilling experience I've ever had." Wolf claimed two kills that afternoon, part of a total of ten that the AVG estimated for the day.

When the pilots landed they basked in the compliments of their squadronmates who had watched the fight from the trenches. It "looked just like a movie only better," one remarked. Reed had watched the dog-fight from the hill and then spent the rest of the afternoon walking around the field examining the downed Japanese planes. However celebratory the mood, some pilots privately expressed concerns about the enemy's capabilities. John Donovan, who had been in the air that morning, wrote in a letter home that "the Japs can afford to lose 10 out of 13 planes, because they always come back with a flock of new planes the next time . . you can depend they'll be here again." He added: "That red circle on their wings looks 'big' when they surprise you."

Throughout this period, Chennault, back in Kunming, had been working on plans to have the U.S. Army supply them with new and improved P-40s. He wanted the P-40E, or Kittyhawk, as it was called. The Kittyhawk would be an improvement over their older P-40, which was known as the Tomahawk. The Kittyhawk had six .50-caliber machine guns, an upgrade over the four .30-caliber and two .50-caliber machine guns on the Tomahawk. The Kittyhawk could hold a series of smaller bombs in underwing racks and a larger bomb on a centerline rack. Chennault and the pilots had spent months trying to build a makeshift bomb rack on the older P-40 but they hadn't had much success.

Claire Chennault's lobbying of Lauchlin Currie finally paid off. The White House adviser was able to free up some Kittyhawks for the AVG.

The planes were first shipped on a freighter to Accra. The problem then became getting them from the west coast of Africa to China—a daunting "ferry mission" to which Chennault assigned a group of six pilots led by George McMillan. In February the men hitched rides on CNAC and Pan Am transports to Accra. They saw this as "an unbelievable opportunity to see more of the world's exotic and mysterious places," R. T. Smith would recall. In Accra, they picked up the new P-40Es, which one pilot, C. H. Laughlin, described as "a bit bulkier than the B model we've been flying." There were small improvements—the instruments in the cockpit had a better layout, the iron ring sights were replaced with a reflector gunsight. It was like picking up a car from the dealer. The P-40E was like a "new Buick," he felt.

They turned back for Kunming, a trip that would take them across Africa, the Middle East, India, then a part of China itself. "Roughly the equivalent of a flight from New Orleans to the South Pole," R. T. Smith wrote. But he felt like Murphy's Law was governing the trip, as everything went wrong. The compartments on the P-40E were smaller than those on the Tomahawk, so they had to shove their clothes into parachute bags. They flew across endless miles of desert, enduring sandstorms, engine problems, and tire problems. But despite the taxing journey, they still took in the sights. McMillan rode a giraffe in the Sudan, and when they made it to Egypt they flew by the pyramids. The highlight of the trip, McMillan's diary reveals, was finding American beer and cigarettes at their hotel in Cairo. R. T. Smith bought a German Luger pistol there—"a honey of a gun"—that a British soldier had captured while fighting in North Africa. They continued on their journey, going across India, and finally arrived back in Kunming by March 22 to a hero's welcome. They were necessary reinforcements as the AVG was in the midst of intensive fighting. As they all knew, "new planes would add a good deal of much-needed firepower," R. T. Smith wrote. Though everyone wanted to know about their trip, the ferry pilots were exhausted when they got back. It was "the sort of thing you wouldn't trade for a million dollars, but wouldn't do again if paid a million."

Chennault had already dispatched another group of six pilots to pick up more P-40Es. The Kittyhawks could be used, Chennault believed, "to attack the enemy effectively." Loiwing needed reinforcements, so he sent three of the Kittyhawks down to the front lines on April 8, and they made it just in time for the air raid, during which one Kittyhawk was destroyed while it sat on the ground and another was damaged. On April 9, Tex Hill, John Petach, and seven other AVG pilots set out from Kunming to bring Loiwing more planes, goosing the total number to around twenty.

Once again war forced Petach to part from his wife. He kissed Emma Foster good-bye, with no certainty that he'd be back. She knew what combat could do to the pilots. She had seen it with her own eyes. "That fight was life or death," she recalled. "If I had seen it in a movie I would not have believed it, but I literally saw them go out as boys, and return with different faces, as men."

That same day, a CNAC transport brought Chennault to Loiwing. He hadn't seen actual combat since the December 20 battle over Kunming, and his arrival must have spurred rumors through the ranks about the reason for his appearance at the front lines. What the pilots didn't know was that he was carrying a secret that would essentially bring an end to the AVG. He had been facing continual pressure to induct the AVG into the U.S. Army Air Forces. He wasn't the type to defer to authority—a source of tension throughout his whole career in the army—and he guarded fiercely the independence of the AVG. But in early April he had gone to Chungking with Stilwell to attend meetings. U.S. diplomat John Davies, one of the State Department's original "China hands," assured Chennault that his work was appreciated but that he would have to "play ball" and join the Army Air Forces if he wanted to obtain additional planes. There was no denying that the AVG had been effective, but the army, and Stilwell in particular, wanted to take control. Chennault was determined to continue fighting, and if a change of uniform meant more planes, he figured it was worth it. The plan was signed off by the Chinese and American leadership, and as Stilwell noted in his diary, he was glad to "finish off the damn AVG thing."

Chennault's official induction took place the day he arrived at Loiwing. Though he had long been known as the "Colonel," this was just an honorary title, originally bestowed by the governor of Louisiana. Now he was designated a true colonel in the U.S. Army. He would soon be promoted to brigadier general, but that appointment was carefully dated one day behind the elevation of Clayton Bissell—a rival of Chennault's from his days at Maxwell, who was working for Stilwell—ensuring that Bissell was technically the senior aerial officer in the China-Burma-India Theater. The insult stung, but Chennault was all in, and a general himself now, so he simply took it. Going forward, the plan was for the AVG to focus on providing combat support for the Chinese troops that Stilwell was commanding in Burma—a task for which the new Kittyhawks were well suited.

But now, Chennault had to tell the men the news and explain their options: they would have the choice of applying to stay in the army, or they could return home after the date set for induction—the Fourth of July.

Chennault was welcomed to the front lines on the morning of April 10 by a surprise Japanese raid. The raid damaged almost half of the twenty planes on the runway, which were later taken to the CAMCO factory to be repaired. As John Petach recorded in his diary, the attack left them "not hurt but plenty scared."

Then Saturday night, April 11, the men gathered in the clubhouse to hear a speech by the Old Man. For many of the pilots, he had been a figure largely in the background during their service in the AVG, someone they had hardly seen for months. But they still knew that he was their ultimate boss. He announced that the AVG would become a fighter squadron in the Army Air Forces. The men could apply to join the army, but their acceptance wouldn't be guaranteed—an induction board would be established to assess what kind of commission they could receive. They were almost unanimous in their reaction to the news—they were going to leave for home on Independence Day, less than three months away.

Having been the first combatants in the war, they felt they had earned a break to see their families and luxuriate at home. John Donovan, who had fought in the April 8 battle, had written to his parents: "I admit to being lonesome and homesick. What a joy it would be to drive a car down a smooth American boulevard with modern stores and homes on both sides!" They were exhausted. The months of fighting "had taken their toll, and the signs of stress were apparent in gaunt faces, and bodies that had lost many pounds," as R. T. Smith said. They were ready to go home.

However loyal to Chennault the pilots may have been, that loyalty had its limits. To become just another fighter squadron didn't seem to suit men who had started the war as an independent unit. Although they admired Chennault, they did not share his deep desire to fight, and apparently even die, for China. "The demands made on him and the AVG are so great as to be absolutely impossible, except that Chennault will never admit impossibility," as one pilot put it. Chennault had given up everything—his wife, his children, his beloved backwoods in Louisiana—to devote his life to China. If he had longings for home, he had long ago learned to suppress them. He intended to keep at it until the end. But for his men, the end was in sight. Three months may have seemed like no time in the abstract, but they knew every day in this war could mean death.

In the meantime, the pilots found they had a new mission as the war continued to evolve. From the beginning of their service they had been primarily engaged in fighting air battles. Now they were tasked with providing aerial cover and conducting reconnaissance missions for General Stilwell, who needed intelligence on the deployment of Japanese forces. "God," Stilwell complained to an aide, "I feel like a blind man." Though it wasn't stated explicitly to them, they were effectively functioning as Stilwell's eyes in the sky.

They spent long days flying deep in Burma on these dangerous missions. To conduct reconnaissance, a pilot would place a map on his lap and try to mark down any sighting that looked like a troop movement, sometimes having no idea whether the troops he saw were Chinese or Japanese, as the front lines of the war were changing quickly. Forest fires were burning across the country, which left the pilots trying to navigate through smoke. "A thick layer of the stuff seemed to hang like a blanket over Burma, about like the smog in L.A. at its worst," R. T. Smith recalled. The conditions forced them to keep low to the ground, which exposed them to ground fire from Japanese troops, and they had to hope they wouldn't run into a formation of enemy fighters. Even landing at one of the Allied airfields was potentially perilous. A reconnaissance report reminded the pilots to wag their wings as they flew in to land or "it is probable that the ground forces will fire. Extreme caution must be exercised in landing at these friendly airdromes." Chennault knew these missions left the P-40s like "clay pigeons in a shooting gallery of Japanese flak gunners and fighter pilots," but he had little choice about the matter given that he was back in the army.

John Petach described a reconnaissance flight in a letter to Emma: "Yesterday I went with Rector and Ricketts to Toungoo again, we patrolled for 3 hours and landed at Pyawbwe [an Allied base] at 6:30 P.M. We stayed there overnight and took off at 05:30 A.M. this morning and patrolled for 3½ hrs more we didn't see any doggone Jap in all that time. . . . I imagine I'll go again tomorrow, they are rough! You come back feeling all washed out after concentrating so long. Maybe we'll have better luck next time." It could be worse than exhausting: during one flight, Petach had to make a forced crash landing in a dry riverbed. He was all right but the P-40's propeller was ruined.

The pilots were also required to fly along the front lines to provide aerial support to the Chinese troops. The men called these "morale missions" because they believed the entire point was to display the twelve-pointed Chinese star beneath their wings to the Chinese forces below. "Well, nobody wanted those missions. They really didn't," Tex Hill recalled. "Low-level operations are real dangerous, because some guy with a rifle, standing behind a tree, could knock you off, and you'd never see him."

Then there was a real "stinker" of a mission. On April 16, a request went out for eight pilots to volunteer as fighter escorts for RAF Blenheim bombers to attack the Japanese airfield at Chiang Mai the next day—the very spot where Newkirk had been killed less than a month before. "Volunteers were scarce as hen's teeth," Smith wrote in his diary, for the pilots knew that Chiang Mai was deep into enemy territory and was heavily defended by antiaircraft guns. The mission was ultimately called off due to bad weather, but the pilots had made it clear that they weren't going to fly assignments that they considered unreasonable. Disobeying orders was unthinkable in the army and sufficient cause for a court-martial, but Chennault had created a unit in which military discipline was lax, and now that was coming back to haunt him. Smith, who had become something of a ringleader in the opposition, wrote in his diary: "Now they intend to hold the line + want us to give them air support. Our twelve ships against the whole damn Jap air force. It seems mighty futile to all of us + we're wondering what's taking the U.S. so damn long to get something over here." Smith was no coward, but in his mind they had been asked to do the impossible, and he wasn't afraid to stand up to the Old Man.

Everything seemed to come to a head when Chennault called a meeting on Saturday, April 18, a week after he told the men about the upcoming induction. This gathering, though, had a far angrier tone. He announced that he was now a brigadier general (even though that promotion wouldn't go into effect for a few more days) and was taking orders from General Stilwell—which meant that the pilots were going to have to follow whatever orders were given. He described the upcoming missions and, as Smith put it in his diary, they "sounded pretty bad—suicide in fact." The men responded by taking a "load off our chest as to how we felt," insisting to Chennault they couldn't just keep fighting without reinforcements. Accounts of the heated argument differed, but Smith recalled Chennault's being clear that any pilot who didn't intend to obey commands should resign, as refusing to fly a mission would effectively be showing the "white feather" to the Japanese.

Smith leapt up and "told the old man that there was a hell of a big difference between common sense and cowardice, and after all we'd been through I couldn't believe he was now calling us cowards." When his protest was met with a "murmur of assent" from the men, Chennault insisted that wasn't what he meant, but he couldn't bring himself to apologize. The meeting wrapped up after that, but the pilots, still angry, assembled later that night at the alert shack to discuss their response. "It was almost like a union meeting, lots of arguments back and forth," Smith recalled. He asserted that they should call Chennault's bluff and resign, which was the only response that was appropriate to the disrespect they had been shown. Most of the men agreed, though they may have meant this more as a symbolic resignation to lodge their protest. "The guys were tired by that time . . . literally just living from hand to mouth going back up there," Tex Hill recalled. Still, he felt they should support Chennault and not question the orders. He was part of a small minority.

The men finally decided to draw up a petition: "We, the undersigned, pilots of the American Volunteer Group, hereby desire to terminate our contracts with the Central Aircraft Mfg. Co. and our services with the AVG." Chennault may have returned to the army, but the pilots were firm in their conviction that they had not. There had been a number of resignations throughout the AVG's tenure and the pilots felt that they could resign when they wanted to. The letter was typed up on First American Volunteer Group letterhead, the signatories trailing down the page in a long list. Twenty-six of the more than thirty pilots at Loiwing signed the document, with some notable absences—Tex Hill and, surprisingly, John Petach. He had spent much of the month writing love letters to Emma, and though he was eager to get home, loyalty to Chennault and Hill, or his sense of duty, kept him in the battle.

The resignation letter was presented to Chennault the following morning. He called another meeting for that night, and the group's existence "hung rather precariously throughout the day," as Bill Reed put it. Privately, Chennault sympathized with the pilots. He didn't approve of the aerial support missions or the escort service for the RAF, but as he wrote in his memoirs, "as long as these orders came down from my immediate superiors, the Generalissimo and Stilwell, I was obliged to execute them regardless of my personal feelings." But his conviction was more than a matter of simply following orders. He remained zealously committed to the cause of China, even if it meant the loss of his pilots. The pilots had increasingly come to reject that perspective. "Our main concern," Smith recalled, "was simply survival from day to day, each of us hoping his number wouldn't come up before it was time to head back for the good old U.S. of A." Chuck Older, one of the pilots who signed the letter, recalled explaining to Chennault: "We don't mind risking our lives but we just don't want to throw them away, that's the feeling."

That night the men gathered at 8:00 P.M. to hear Chennault address the matter of the resignation letter. His speech was blunt. He told the men that he would not accept their resignations and that "anyone leaving would be guilty of desertion etc.," as Smith summarized the warning in his diary. Chennault knew that others in the army had questioned the lack of formality with which he ran the unit, and if he were to allow the AVG to disband now, it would be judged as a black mark on his reputation. He had sought to lead without being the sort of domineering commander he had hated as a pilot, but now he felt he had little choice but to give forceful orders if he wanted to keep the unit intact. The pilots accepted their fate, hoping that their protest had at least made a point. Indeed, it seemed that Chennault at least reached out to Madame Chiang to ensure that the AVG wouldn't again be asked to escort the Blenheim bombers.

The men were all eager to put the Loiwing Revolt, as it came to be known, behind them. "So [Chennault] and all of us are forgetting the whole affair + carrying on as usual," Smith wrote in his diary. There were no mentions of the revolt in the newspaper articles that regularly celebrated the pilots' exploits. Neither Chennault nor his men wanted to tarnish the legend of the Flying Tigers by revealing how perilously close the entire operation had come to ending in a mass resignation. Chennault hoped that soon it would be "all but forgotten."

One signatory to the resignation letter, Robert Brouk, wrote in his diary that the pilots were going to "stick together and follow orders and see the thing out." Following orders actually came naturally for Brouk. The twenty-four-year-old had been participating in military organizations since his days in the Drum and Bugle Corps at Morton High School in Cicero, Illinois. After college, joining the army seemed like a better option than working for his father's sign-painting company; then in 1941 he signed up for the AVG.

On April 21, Brouk was back in his cockpit as one of four pilots on a patrol deep into Japanese-occupied Burma. As they flew over enemy territory, they saw puffs of black smoke from antiaircraft guns. To evade fire, they would "twist and turn, dive and soar, never flying the same pattern for more than four or five seconds." They survived the flight and spent the night at a remote outpost in Burma. The British had evacuated the site in advance of the Japanese attack, but Brouk found two cooks who prepared some food for the pilots. As they worked to get their planes ready for another patrol the following morning, Brouk discovered

some serious problems with his P-40, and decided he would have to return to Loiwing.

The next day, Brouk woke, had a quick breakfast, and got into his
plane. As he ascended, he saw that his oil temperature was too high, so
he decided to land and see if he could determine what was causing the
problem. He taxied back to the hangar that he'd just left. Suddenly, he
saw white flashes and felt a searing pain in his legs. A roar overhead
made him look up, and he saw a low-flying Japanese plane above him.
He was being strafed. His plane was barely moving, so he undid his
safety belt and jumped from the cockpit. As he ran, he was attempting
to pull off his parachute and struggling with its buckles when he saw a
bullet hole in his thumb just below the first joint. The Japanese fighter
was circling back, and he raced twenty feet toward a covered dugout,
diving in headfirst and landing between two Chinese soldiers. He saw
blood seeping from his left foot, and when he pulled off his shoe and
sock he found a "ragged wound." He had been shot in the leg, so he
pulled off his pants. A Chinese soldier helped apply handkerchiefs to
try to stanch the bleeding. On the runway, his P-40 was incinerating,
its .30-caliber and .50-caliber bullets cooking off as it burned. "Soon
the enemy planes left and only the flaming plane and shooting bullets
broke the stillness of the morning," he recalled in his diary.

Brouk needed a doctor and was fortunate that his squadronmates
tracked down the "Burma Surgeon," Gordon Seagrave. Educated at
Johns Hopkins Medical School, Seagrave was a surgeon-missionary
who had spent most of his life along the China-Burma border. Within
hours he was operating on Brouk, who, as he later described, had "six
holes in his leg and another in his thumb. I extracted three bullets and
some scraps of airplane metal." He saved Brouk's life but couldn't remember the young man's name when a reporter asked him about it.
Brouk was evacuated to Lashio, where medics took X-rays and then
operated again to remove more of the shrapnel. He was then flown
back to Kunming on a CNAC transport.

Word of Brouk's condition reached the men back in Loiwing, who
were reminded anew of the danger they faced. As it had become clear
that all of Burma would soon be in Japanese hands, the question for
many of the pilots was whether they could just stay alive until July 4.

Chennault would never accept defeat easily. He was determined to achieve one final victory over the Japanese in Burma. For the past months, the aerial combat in which the AVG had engaged had been on a small scale—nothing like the Christmas battle in Rangoon or the December 20 fight in Kunming. But Chennault believed that might be changing. Japanese reconnaissance flights had been spotted over Loiwing, and he predicted they would launch a major strike soon. He even had a hunch about the timing: April 29 was Emperor Hirohito's forty-first birthday, a day that would be marked by celebrations in Japan.

In 1938, Chennault had been advising the Chinese Air Force and had a hunch that the Japanese would want to launch a major strike on Hankow for the emperor's birthday. Chennault had tricked the Japanese the day before—instructing the Chinese pilots to take to the air in an apparent departure and then return at a low altitude just as the sun was setting. As he suspected, the Japanese spies reported that the planes had departed and launched a major raid. Once the Japanese planes had started the attack, the Chinese pilots swooped onto them in a surprise attack. It was a bizarre plan, but it had worked: "When the smoke cleared," historian John Pomfret wrote, "thirty-six of thirty-nine Japanese planes had been lost in the biggest pre-World War II battle in aerial history."

Chennault now wanted to replicate that feat. This time, however, he suspected that the Japanese bombers would strike a day before the emperor's actual birthday so that the commanders could relay the news of their victory in a communiqué that would reach the emperor in time to celebrate the occasion. Chennault was taking a risk putting so many Flying Tigers in the air on a single patrol, but he trusted his hunch.

The field at Loiwing was abuzz the morning of April 28 as a large group of P-40s took off at 9:30 for Burma. Tex Hill was flying cover at fifteen thousand feet with a small group of P-40Es, while a few thousand feet below was a larger group of P-40s, both the P-40E Kittyhawks and the P-40 Tomahawks. As they flew south one pilot suddenly "heard a strange tongue over the radio," and Hill saw a group of Japanese fighters overhead. He made radio contact with a squadronmate, then "turned my flight on an interception course of the enemy."

In addition to the fighters he had already identified, Hill found "a formation of 27 bombers," and then, farther away, what appeared to be around a dozen, maybe more, additional fighters. He flew up to meet them and knew he would have to choose his shots carefully. He focused on one Japanese fighter, firing off a series of short bursts. On the fourth burst, his target began to smoke, then plunged into the jungle below. The fight quickly devolved into a "rat race," with the combatants circling each other, each trying to get on the other's tail as if their lives depended on it, because they actually did. Lewis Bishop fired a "long burst" at a fighter that "had managed to get on Hill's tail," and the Japanese pilot bailed out of his smoking plane. Though the Japanese had the high ground and "engaged us heavily," they "seemed to be inexperienced as their defence [sic] was not coordinated," Hill wrote. The only P-40 lost that day was R. T. Smith's. But Smith wasn't shot down. He ran out of gas after the battle, landed in a field, and hitchhiked with some Chinese soldiers to regroup with his squadronmates. He was somewhat embarrassed about the incident, but everyone was in a triumphant mood.

However great the AVG victory that day, Japanese ground troops continued their push north, beating back Chinese and British resistance in northern Burma. On April 30, Lashio, the Burmese city where the Burma Road began, fell—a sign to Chennault that the CAMCO factory at Loiwing would soon follow. He had no choice but to order a retreat. The facility was a scene of chaos in those final days. There weren't enough planes for all the pilots to fly out so some of them would have to retreat up the Burma Road in a convoy of trucks. Hill selected who would fly and who would suffer the danger and discomfort of driving. Then he faced an even tougher decision. "Hell, I was the last guy out of [Loiwing], [and] had to make the call whether to burn the airplanes," Hill recalled. He knew what had to be done. The planes in the repair shop were ignited as the last Flying Tigers fled.

When the Japanese soldiers captured Loiwing, they saw those charred shark-nosed P-40s as a war prize. A Japanese newspaper printed a picture of the wreckage, evidence that the Japanese had the famed Flying Tigers on the run.

CHAPTER 13

LAST STAND

While the pilots in Loiwing had been flying reconnaissance and strafing missions into Burma in April, the men in Kunming were enjoying themselves. Charlie Bond was assigned a ferry mission to India to pick up additional P-40Es. This was an easy task compared to fighting on the front. On April 11, he and several squadronmates boarded a DC-3 transport for Calcutta. One of the other passengers was Clare Boothe, the wife of *Time* and *Life* owner Henry Luce, who had spent several days with the AVG in Kunming for a profile she was writing for *Life*. She would write that "the Flying Tigers were a blazing beacon of ultimate victory" but right then Charlie Bond was just looking forward to some R&R.

When they reached India, the Americans visited nightclubs, smoked American cigarettes, and even found a spot that served hamburgers and milk shakes for lunch. Bond met a pilot who told him that when he got out of the AVG he could make a small fortune flying for Pan Am, which was certainly an appealing prospect, given the uncertainty surrounding the AVG's future. Their only reminder of the war was when they went to check on Frank Swartz, one of the pilots who had been injured during the surprise raid on Magwe. He was still recovering in a Calcutta (modern-day Kolkata) hospital, and they could tell that his face would be deformed from the injuries, but he seemed happy to see the "old gang." Plans had been made for him to go back to the States for surgery, but he would soon die from an infection.

The next day they traveled to Karachi, which was filled with U.S. Army soldiers, and picked up the P-40Es. Bond himself was given a newer P-43. "It is a nice little plane," he decided. They flew back to Calcutta, and on April 21 left for Kunming, crossing over the steep peaks of the Himalayas. Chennault was there to greet them, fresh from returning after putting down the Loiwing Revolt.

On May 1, Bond saw a swarm of P-40s in the sky—the AVG forces retreating from Loiwing. When the pilots landed and stepped out of their cockpits, "they were an ugly-looking bunch—dirty and unshaven," but glad to be back. "It was good to get back to such civilization as we have here and enjoy clean clothing and such luxuries as showers and a barber shop again," Bill Reed wrote in his diary. John Petach and Emma Foster had been separated less than a month, and he had written to her about how he wanted to "crawl into our bed next to you, wrap my arms around you and give you a large hug and kiss." Now they could do that and forget, however briefly, about the war.

Chennault had grown increasingly concerned about the Japanese advance, especially now that Japanese forces were nearing the Chinese border. Stilwell had refused to evacuate from Burma on a plane that Chennault had sent for him, and instead set out to walk to India. Chennault couldn't understand why Stilwell didn't just fly out—and it was the sort of disagreement that would define the tense relationship between Stilwell the infantryman and Chennault the airman. Still, with his motley crew of 114, which consisted of a group as diverse as British commandos and an American war correspondent, Stilwell spent approximately two weeks making his way through the wilderness at his mandatory pace of 105 steps a minute. "Our people tired—damn poor show of physique," he noted in his diary. They all completed the journey successfully, and their endurance became a new touchstone for how Americans were defying defeat in the Far East—a harbinger of how the legend of the Flying Tigers was beginning to be eclipsed.

But Chennault couldn't spend too much time worrying about Stilwell's whereabouts. He had to focus on the war, scrambling for a plan to try to stem the imminent Japanese advance from Burma. His first step was to assemble some pilots from the First Squadron to go to Paoshan (modern-day Baoshan), a town close to the Burmese border. Charlie Bond was part of the contingent of eight who were selected to go to the front. It was a small group but their job was a formidable one.

They were, as Bond said, "to stop the Japanese from penetrating the southern tip of China and entering the back door." They landed on a grass runway, where they were met by Chinese soldiers. They were driven through the city en route to their new quarters. "The city streets were choked with refugees streaming up from Burma to get away from the Japs," Bond wrote in his diary. Earlier in the war, he had struggled to come to terms with exactly what they were fighting for, but now he could witness firsthand the importance of their efforts. He spent the next day on a reconnaissance flight, looking for enemy convoys in China, and though he spotted none, he knew they would be coming soon.

On the morning of May 4, Japanese reconnaissance planes appeared overhead. Bond scrambled to his plane, but by the time he ascended they were gone. He returned to the alert shack and waited, cleaning his pistol to keep himself occupied.

Bob Neale, the squadron commander, rushed in and shouted that Japanese aircraft were coming. The pilots all ran out and saw an enormous V formation that appeared to contain twenty-five Japanese bombers. Neale shot his pistol in the air and told them, "Too late, get in your ditches, get in your ditches!" But Bond was already in the cockpit of his P-40 with its prop spinning.

He sat there, hand on the throttle, and something just came over him: "Hell, I can make it." He raced his plane down the runway determined to get in the air before the bombs started to fall, barely clearing a rock barricade at the end of the field. He took the P-40 into a steep climb until the bomber formation was in sight. The enemy was targeting the urban area, which Bond knew was crowded with refugees, and he watched their efforts with a sense of awe: "The bombing was almost perfect—right in the middle of the city." As he scanned the sky he didn't see any Japanese fighters, but he did see some bombers in the distance and decided that would be his target for the day. Climbing to about a thousand feet above it, he set his sights on a bomber on the outside of the formation and fired a series of machine-gun rounds into its fuselage. The plane started to plummet and Bond kept on firing from behind. "I saw his right engine disintegrate," he recalled, "and ignite into a flaming torch. He went down and through the overcast."

He aimed at a second Japanese bomber but realized he was out of ammunition, so pulled out from the attack and followed the Burma Road back to Paoshan. He flew over the city and saw that it had been subjected to utter destruction. Buildings had collapsed and fires raged everywhere. The human toll must have been terrible.

Coming in to land, Bond was bringing his landing gear forward when he heard several loud explosions. He thought it was the landing gear malfunctioning, but then realized that the explosions were in the plane, behind the armor on his seat. His fuel tank was on fire and the flames were spreading into the cockpit. As he looked behind him he saw "three Jap Zeros right on my tail and firing like mad!" Closing his eyes as the smoke filled his cockpit, he recalled, "For a split second I considered giving up, but something wouldn't let me."

Cranking open the canopy with his right hand, he struggled to undo his seat belt with his left. He took the plane back up in a steep climb, then rolled it over and let the airstream pull him from the cockpit. As he tumbled downward he opened his eyes, searching for the metal ring on his parachute. He "jerked it wildly" until it opened. He was well aware that the Japanese had strafed parachuting airmen before, and he was terrified that he might suffer the same fate. "I prayed devoutly to God with my eyes closed," he remembered, "and then opened them to look for the Zeros." None came. He landed in a Chinese cemetery, amazed to be alive. He pulled his chute off and hid behind a burial mound. When no Japanese fighters appeared, his panic subsided and he suddenly felt the pain. His flying suit was on fire. He leapt into a nearby stream and reached a hand up to his head: it was covered in blood. Injured and wrung out, he lay still in the water. Chinese villagers must have seen the plane go down, because they soon approached to help him, taking him back to a nearby hut where they bathed his wounds. Lewis Richards, one of the AVG doctors, was summoned by telephone. He treated Bond's wounds with hydrogen peroxide. The doctor gave him some painkillers and loaded the wounded pilot into a jeep.

Bond looked around as they drove through Paoshan, horrified by the corpses and body parts that seemed to cover the streets, heads "burned so badly the teeth were showing from fleshless faces." There was a torso with no limbs and a mother on her knees grasping a dead child. The following day he was placed on a DC-3 back to Kunming, grateful that he had survived. But he could never forget what he had seen.

It was estimated that some ten thousand people were killed in the raid on Paoshan. Among the dead was Ben Foshee, a Flying Tigers pilot who had been driving a truck on the retreat from Loiwing. After the attack, Chinese villagers would find unexploded bombs that were filled with a "yellow waxy substance [with] many live flies struggling to fly away," as one Chinese witness described them. These "maggot bombs" were filled with the bacteria that carried cholera, and the bombers would return again to carry out more of these attacks. Historians estimate that around two hundred thousand people would ultimately die from the disease in Yunnan Province.

The AVG suspected that the Japanese would return. The following day, Tex Hill was assigned to a small patrol of P-40Es that would circle over Paoshan. Flying at eighteen thousand feet, they were alerted at around 12:15 P.M. that about sixteen Japanese fighters were heading their way. The pilots climbed into position at twenty-one thousand feet and waited, knowing that they would be outnumbered but confident that they had the high ground. Sure enough, the twin-engine Japanese bombers appeared below them and the P-40Es dove down. A group of olive-colored fighters with red suns on their wings intercepted the P-40Es in mid-dive. The bombers were able to proceed unimpeded to their target while the Tigers dueled in the sky with the enemy fighters. Hill thought he had a shot lined up but found himself under fire first—the kind of error that could be fatal, though he was eventually able to duck out of the attack. Other American pilots managed some successful shots. Frank Lawlor fired on a plane and saw it "burst into flames and pieces of it that were shot off filled the air with debris." Concerned that the Japanese fighters were going to strafe the airfield, the AVG fighters dove down to prevent it, only to have the friendly Chinese machine-gun crews mistake them for enemy planes and fire. Despite all the snafus, no AVG planes were lost that day, but they seemed unable to stop the Japanese assault that was driving into China.

"China faced its darkest hour since the fall of Nanking," Chennault would write.

As the Chinese forces retreated on the Burma Road, they blew up the 150-yard-long suspension bridge that spanned the Salween River. Chennault believed that the Japanese column, waiting for a pontoon bridge to be constructed to take its place, would be left exposed on a narrow series of switchbacks that descended into the gorge leading to the river. "On one side of the river stretched Japanese tanks, armored cars and lorries, packed close together and almost touching. On the other was a long column of stationary Chinese trucks," the *Boston Globe* reported.

Chennault thought that the Salween gorge offered his last chance to stop the enemy. "This was one of the few times during the war that I became greatly alarmed," he admitted. If China fell, the consequences could be grave. American policy was to ensure that China stayed in the war because Japanese forces might otherwise be freed to fight in the Pacific. The defeat of China might also give way to a Japanese invasion of India at a moment when Nazi forces could launch a successful campaign across North Africa.

On May 6, Chennault sent a message to Madame Chiang in Chungking:

> Latest reports say Japs on west bank Salween River 1400 hours 5 May stop Bridge destroyed stop Japs meeting no opposition anywhere as soldiers civilians panic stricken fleeing east along road stop Consider situation desperate and Japs may drive Kunming in trucks unless road and bridges destroyed and determined opposition developed stop Due to fact many Chinese trucks west of Salween presumably in hands of enemy request authority His Excellency the Generalissimo to attack targets between Salween and Lungling city.

Although Chinese civilians were trapped in the target area, Chennault felt he had little choice. "We had small stomach for bombing and machine-gunning those refugees on the west bank of the Salween, but if we were going to stop the Japs, we would have to slaughter some innocents along the way," he would write. This was just one of those "grim decisions that come to every military man so often in battle—issuing orders that meant the sacrifice of a few to save the many."

Madame Chiang replied:

> Generalissimo instructs you send all available AVG to attack trucks boats etc between Salween and Lungling city stop Tell AVG I appreciate their loyalty and redoubled efforts particularly at this critical juncture stop Please continue attacks especially boats and transports on Salween River stop Shall keep you informed immediately any change in situation.

Chennault didn't wait for the reply to give the orders for the first attack.

On the morning of May 7, 1942, four pilots climbed into the cockpits of their P-40Es. This was the group on whom Chennault was depending, as it would be the first into the Salween gorge and would thus determine whether this mission was even feasible.

Tex Hill was appointed leader of the mission. Years later he would recall that morning: "The monsoon season had already set in and we encountered some mighty rough weather before finally breaking out on the target side of the weather." When they emerged there were no Japanese planes in sight. The steep gorge with the Salween River snaking through it—his target—appeared below. They went in with heavy armaments. "We installed jury-rigged bomb racks to accommodate a new 570-lb. Russian high-explosive bomb on the bellies of our new P-40Es and fragmentation bombs mounted on the wing racks."

As the planes began to attack, he recalled: "The bombs we dropped impacted on the top of the Salween gorge, completely trapping some of the many pieces of armor and equipment, as well as personnel, at the bottom of the gorge. We knocked off some of the road there, and it blocked them, and then we were able to strafe them."

This first raid proved that the plan was effective, and in the coming days the AVG would launch additional strikes at the Salween, with the trucks that were thought to be carrying pontoon equipment a key target. Jim Howard was sent on the afternoon of May 8 to lead another attack: "We glided down and released our bombs in string along portions of the Jap side of the road. My bombs landed squarely along about 200 yds. of road with Jap trucks bumper to bumper to bumper." He looked down at the "black smoke and flame [that] showed the results" of the attack. Tom Jones, a pilot from Seattle, noticed trucks clustered close to the water and suspected that they were the vehicles transporting the pontoons, waiting to unload them until "night or when opposition from Chin[ese] soldiers across river should let up." He fired at them and, he wrote, the "destruction of these trucks, I believe, will hold up the Jap's plans for some time." As the raids continued, the Japanese troops seemed unable to muster significant resistance. Jones described them as being in a state of "general confusion," "[returning] fire with small arms after second pass by our planes."

Another pilot, C. H. Laughlin, observed "dispersed trucks [that] hid in brush on mountainside." He "dropped 2 bombs and observed large petrol fire" and watched "troops scrambling down side of hill away from trucks: dropped two more bombs and razed convoy with machine gun fire." He circled back twice more, strafing the "small units of cars and trucks."

The raids went on like this for days, as the AVG "threw everything we had against the Salween gorge and the Burma Road," as Chennault wrote. The Chinese troops launched a counterattack against the Japanese forces. R. T. Smith flew cover for a raid on May 10 and saw how they were "driving the Japs back down the road now. Hope it continues that direction." The *Washington Post* reported that "Chinese reinforcements were flung across the stream, and in a bitter struggle the main Japanese forces were thrust back . . . and the remnants . . . were wiped out." The tide of the invasion was shifting. The pummeling air strikes, combined with the Chinese counterattacks, helped to bring the invasion to a halt.

The sense that the AVG was making history was apparent in the hostels in Kunming, where a "paraphrased message" from Franklin Roosevelt had been posted on a wall: "The outstanding gallantry and conspicuous daring of the American Volunteer Group, combined with their almost unbelievable efficiency, is a source of tremendous pride throughout the whole of America. And the fact that they have labored under shortages and difficulties is keenly appreciated." It was little more than a sales pitch—a recruiting poster to motivate the men to sign up for the Army Air Forces. But still, the message resonated. The pilots themselves believed every word of the accolade. As Jim Howard wrote, their fight had been in the spirit of "Horatio's stand at the bridge over the River Tiber outside the gates of Rome or the stand made by the English against Germany's threatened invasion in 1940." Tex Hill was proud of what they'd done, believing the AVG "might have changed the course of history."

It wasn't just self-congratulation. With the perspective of decades, historian Duane Schultz wrote, "The victory at the Salween alone would have been sufficient to justify the Flying Tigers' existence. If not for the handful of tired American pilots and their maverick leader, the Japanese would have crossed the river and threatened China."

Those days "may have been their finest."

Chennault was now facing the end of his time with the Flying Tigers. A man of few words, he didn't share his pride in his pilots with them, though he poured out his emotions in a letter to a friend in Louisiana: "I've seen my companions die suddenly and violently . . . all of them are boys with whom I've worked and whom I'd grown to love as my own blood. . . . I am compelled to see them go out to meet death, but powerless to aid them to avoid it." He was indebted to these pilots, and later acknowledged that "the AVG gave me the greatest opportunity an air officer ever had—to collect and train a group like that with complete freedom of action. It afforded me enormous satisfaction."

He did think wistfully about a simpler life back home, but not seriously: "Right now, after five years of my work, I'd cheerfully trade my gun for a plow and hoe. However, being unable to do that and not knowing much about a plow anyway, guess I'll just go on using the gun until the affair is finished." A return to Louisiana for a retirement of hunting, fishing, and time with family wasn't imminent.

Still, it meant a great deal to Chennault that Louisianans were cheering him in fighting this war. A "Buy a Bomber for Chennault" campaign had been undertaken in the state. Though Chennault cabled that he "would be delighted to receive the Louisiana Bomber," the War Department informed the committee that the bombers had already been allocated, and that even a single plane cost far more than the paltry sum they could offer. Instead, they sent the money they raised to Madame Chiang to assist Chinese orphans.

Chennault found satisfaction in his growing fame, but he knew that reputation wouldn't help him much now that he'd given up his independence to once again be part of the army. He was already amassing a litany of grievances about how he was being treated by the army brass. His first major complaint was the Doolittle raid. On April 18, 1942, B-25s under the command of Lieutenant Colonel Jimmy Doolittle bombed Tokyo and then crash-landed in China. The Japanese had captured eight of the downed airmen. Three were ultimately executed and one died in captivity. Chennault was peeved that the B-25s had been lost and that he couldn't use them for his own missions. "If I had been notified," he later wrote, "a single AVG command ground radio station plugged into the East China net could have talked most of the raiders into a friendly field. My bitterness over that bit of bungling has not eased with the passing years." Apparently the Army Air Forces brass wanted to avoid notifying Chennault about the raid because of concerns that, given his close ties to the Chinese, word of the attack might be leaked.

Chennault was struggling to come to terms with the fact that he was losing his status as the foremost American military leader fighting in the China-Burma-India Theater. B-17 bombers had begun arriving for the Tenth Air Force based in India, which could carry out attacks that Chennault could only dream of with his P-40s, and which made him feel that he had been overlooked. "Apparently the only people who realized our acute need for bombers were my fellow citizens of Louisiana," he wrote.

As Chennault's spotlight faded, General Lewis Brereton supervised the buildup of the mighty Tenth. Now, as Clare Boothe reported in *Life,* "American bombers, flown by American pilots under American command and flag, [were striking] against the Japs in the China theater of war." By contrast, she said that Chennault had been operating "under Chinese operational direction." An awed Preston Grover wrote in the

Chicago Daily Tribune about how the Tenth Air Force pilots were "operating 10,000 miles from home in the most distant place from which an American bomber command ever has operated." Such praise had once been bestowed exclusively upon the Flying Tigers, but by now their feats had become old news.

In May, as the Japanese began to mop up their conquest of Burma, they attacked the site of the British civilian airlift. The air evacuation had to be called off, and thousands of British civil servants and colonials were forced to walk to India. Having planned on being evacuated by plane and not wanting to leave behind their best clothes, many had worn their formal wear and were ill-prepared for the trek. As historian Geoffrey Tyson wrote, "Not a few were found dead at lonely spots in the Naga country, clad in the fine evening gowns which in happier times they had purchased in London, Calcutta or Rangoon."

Safe in their "mountain hideaway" in Kunming "such grim news seemed unreal," Paul Frillmann recalled. For many of the Flying Tigers the war had begun to feel a part of the past. For the first time since Pearl Harbor, all the squadrons were reunited and the men could reconnect and relax. Chennault would order more raids, but for the most part, the weeks after the Salween gorge missions were fairly quiet. The men drank at the bars, played baseball, and ate the endless supply of scrambled eggs and fried rice that the cooks prepared for them. Frillmann led them on hikes into the countryside, where they would take off their shirts, lie down, and soak up the sun. They were mentally preparing for the trip home. Bill Reed was thinking about what souvenirs he would take back to Iowa and ordered material for a "complete Chinese outfit." Some had already departed. While the fighting had raged in Loiwing, many of the mechanics in Kunming had picked up and left. And there was one notable pilot who was gone—Greg Boyington.

There were different rumors going around the camp about what had set him off, but it was no surprise that Boyington had resigned. From the onset he had shown himself to be a drunkard and a brawler who didn't get along with the other members of the AVG. After his drunken fall down the hill and his two-week recovery in Kunming, he decided it was finally time to head home. Most suspected that it was because he had been accused of breaking into the bar and stealing booze, a charge that he vehemently denied. What no one knew was that he was eager to see his three children, after he received a letter from his mother reporting that his ex-wife had been neglecting them and Seattle's juvenile court had intervened, taking away her custody and sending the children to live with relatives. Boyington flew to India on a CNAC transport but from there getting home proved trickier. In order to get on a military transport he would need authorization from his commander. He knew he hadn't left on the best of terms but he figured this was the least the AVG could do. He recalled in his memoirs the reply that came from Chennault: "AM UNABLE TO GRANT PERMISSION FOR BOYINGTON STOP SUGGEST YOU DRAFT BOYINGTON INTO TENTH AIR FORCE AS SECOND LIEUTENANT STOP."

That moment, Boyington said, was "the closest I ever came to committing out-and-out murder," but he was on the other side of the Himalayas from the AVG so the homicidal urge dissipated. His disdain for Chennault, however, was lasting: "Who was this guy, God? . . . Why should he pick on me?" It wasn't lost on him that Chennault recommended him as a second lieutenant either. He felt for his experience he should at least be a major. Regardless, he wasn't drafted and though he was ultimately bound for Seattle he was relieved when he found a ship, the S.S. *Brazil,* that was going to New York City. The ship left Bombay in early June with Boyington on board. If he'd had a romance with Olga Greenlaw, as many of the other pilots suspected, he seemed to be moving on quickly. The ship had a wide array of male and female passengers and, other than the missionaries, they had "morals that suited my own," he wrote. "Many an orgy took place during the six weeks it was to take the S.S. *Brazil* to reach New York," he wrote, "And I was right in the middle of all I could handle." When he finally made it back to Seattle, he was able to win back custody of his kids, but his life seemed at a dead end.

Independence Day—July 4, 1942—was nearing. The pilots only had to survive until then. Whatever offer Chennault was going to make to get them to stay would have to be persuasive.

"I defy anyone to mention leaving the States again," George McMillan wrote to his parents back in Florida. "I've seen enough of this old world to last quite a while." To the exhausted pilots, "home" meant a number of things they were missing in China. To R. T. Smith, it was "American girls, an up-to-date movie followed by a hamburger with shoestrings and malted milk, and the chance to relax in a clean and peaceful atmosphere." "When I awoke this morning I lay there thinking of the trip home," Charlie Bond wrote in his diary as the day neared.

On May 21, a meeting was called in the hostel in Kunming. Brigadier General Clayton Bissell, the aviation adviser to Stilwell, was going to make a presentation to try to persuade the AVG pilots to apply for induction into the Army Air Forces.

Facing a tough crowd, he took an aggressive stance. "His tone and demeanor were belligerent as he stated that all of us should jump at the opportunity to be inducted, inferring that we would be guilty of disloyalty if we refused," Smith recalled. Bissell informed them that they would receive no help from the army's Air Transport Command in returning to America, that they would have to find their own way home. In addition, when they arrived home, they could be drafted immediately. When one of the men asked if they could take a few weeks of R&R first and then return to China, he dismissed the request, saying, "There's a war on, remember?"

However much Chennault wanted the pilots to stay on, he was almost gleeful watching Bissell fail so thoroughly with this pitch. He'd never liked the man when he knew him in the army before the war, and he hadn't gotten over how Stilwell slighted him by promoting Bissell a day before Chennault was promoted, making Bissell the senior officer. He was heartened when his pilots came up to him afterward and said, "If that's any sample of how the army is going to treat us, we want no part of it."

Chennault, however, wasn't going anywhere. There were rumors that the Japanese, who had begun to occupy Indochina in 1940, were amassing planes there, and he wasn't going to miss an opportunity to strike at a good target. He ordered a new round of air strikes in May, targeting the Japanese air base near Hanoi. It was the first American military action in what came to be known as Vietnam. It wouldn't be the last.

Tom Jones was eager to lead these attacks. He had spent much of the war sick with malaria and wanted a chance to see more action after participating in the Salween gorge raids. He had a wife back home and a baby who had been born after he left for China. He was considering applying to Harvard Law School when he got back and then trying to run for office. Taking the lead in raids could certainly provide material for a stump speech. A reporter was there to witness the preparations for the raid: "Tom Jones hunched over his maps and plotted courses to Hanoi for days, and every time he talked about it he got excited and his eyes sparkled like those of a schoolboy telling how the big football game was won." Flying four hundred miles into Japanese-held territory was a risky proposition, but there were still volunteers for this mission.

On the afternoon of May 12, Jones led a flight of six P-40Es to Hanoi. The clouds were thick, and they flew close to the ground at just three thousand feet. As they neared the city, they spotted Japanese fighters but continued to the target. The P-40Es dove at the airfield and strafed the enemy fighters parked on the runway. Large fires were breaking out, but "as the anti-aircraft fire was very intense we started back, still drawing fire from batteries along the river Northwest of the city," pilot Lewis Bishop noted.

Although the raiders had succeeded in reaching their target, John Donovan had been brought down by antiaircraft fire. The Alabama native had dropped out of law school to become a naval aviator and then signed up for the AVG. For months he had been sending home long letters to his family telling them that he couldn't wait for the war to be over and to come back home. His letters also expressed his anxieties about fighting, admitting that he felt "more helpless than a baby" during one battle. Before the mission in which he was killed, Donovan had given a handwritten note to Paul Frillmann, a message for his parents in the event he did not make it back safely:

Dear Folks: You must not feel badly about my death. The small part that I have played in the war, though it has cost me my life, I am glad to give. That life has meant much to me, but not so much that I am distressed at leaving and neither must you be. I had only a few things planned for the future, one of the most important was a nice home. Mamma will please me much if she will live in a more comfortable home with many flowers and trees. I am happy, and so must she be.

Claire Chennault wrote to Donovan's mother, saying her son had died "for a cause in which we still believe and for which we are fighting even now."

After leading the raid, Tom Jones told a reporter he "enjoyed that one" but admitted, "boy, was I scared." He wanted to go home to his wife and child but wasn't quite ready to leave. "Just one more strafing and then for home."

On May 16, a few of the pilots were finishing up lunch when word came in that a P-40E had crashed during a training flight. Bill Reed drove out to the site, pushing through the crowd of Chinese onlookers to find small pieces of the plane scattered around. "There wasn't a big enough piece to ever tell that it had once been an airplane," he wrote in his diary. "It was pretty nasty, and I won't go chasing wrecks again." The pilot of the doomed plane was Tom Jones, who had survived heavy antiaircraft fire in the attack he led on Hanoi only to die on a simple training run. "After the terrific mission just the other day," Charlie Bond wrote in his diary, "how awful." In less than two months, Jones could have gone home to his family.

On the following day Bill Reed was in the cockpit of a P-40E en route to an attack. His group followed the railroad into Indochina, looking for trains to strafe and hoping to bomb a freight yard. Reed and R. T. Smith broke off at one point to strafe a train they'd spotted, while the others, led by Lew Bishop, carried on. As they began dropping their bombs, they were met with antiaircraft fire. Whether it was a shell hitting his wing or the premature explosion of his own bomb, Bishop's plane was burning with "four feet of flame coming out of his tail," as a combat report stated. He parachuted and then disappeared into the trees.

It had been a wrenching week for the Flying Tigers. They had lost three pilots in five days. Then on May 22, Robert Little was killed on a follow-up raid at the Salween gorge. Many suspected that one of the bombs on his wing exploded. Charlie Bond couldn't believe it: "I had just seen him the day before at the field, and he was in his usual cheerful and kidding manner. . . . What a terrific person, and his contract was due to expire in forty days."

Chennault wanted to keep up the fight, but as the pilots neared the end, they found it hard to stomach that many deaths in the unit's final stretch. As R. T. Smith wrote in his diary about the Indochina mission that had cost John Donovan his life: "It wasn't worth it."

Before the Flying Tigers departed China, their hosts wanted to fete them with a ceremonial presentation of medals. On June 6, they assembled at the hangar in Kunming. A band played, and as each man's name was called, he stepped forward to receive his award from a Chinese colonel. Charlie Bond had recovered enough from his burns after being shot down at Paoshan to take part. When the colonel tried to pin the medal on his coveralls, it didn't seem to be sticking, "so he unzipped the upper part of my coveralls with the idea of pinning it on my undershirt. I had none on." The colonel laughed and then handed Bond his award and then another. The first medal was the Fifth Order of the Cloud and Banner. The second was the Chinese Ten Star Wing Medal, recognizing him for shooting down ten Japanese planes. Bond hadn't actually brought down that many, but he figured he could still keep it.

That night, some of the men celebrated in a restaurant in Kunming that they had been patronizing three or four nights a week. The place "had absolutely the finest Chinese food that I ever tasted, before or since," R. T. Smith recalled. They ordered champagne, which had been imported in large quantities from French Indochina. The bottles of Moët & Chandon or Piper Heidsieck were available for as little as six dollars, and the men had glass after glass. Induction day was still a few weeks off, but uniformed U.S. Army airmen were already showing up in Kunming and the AVG pilots felt like they had one foot out the door.

The Tigers' June diaries were filled with such comments as "another quiet day," "did nothing to speak of," as they passed the days "lounging around, gabbing about this or that, playing cribbage or Acey-Deucey, reading or strolling outside." Their war felt over, and the men could start packing and planning their next steps. Some would be making the long trip back to the United States, while others were joining CNAC, the civilian airline that was promising fat paychecks for flying transports across the Himalayas—and John Petach was one of them. Emma was pregnant and she was certain that "when our contract was over, we did not want to join the army." They would stay, go to India, and the soon-to-be family of three would start a new adventure.

With home calling so loudly, the war still kept getting in the way. On June 11, Charlie Bond, on Chennault's orders, flew with a group of AVG pilots from Chungking to Kweilin (modern-day Guilin), approximately four hundred miles to the southeast. It was like no place he had seen before—the airfield was "surrounded by high mountains that look like inverted ice cream cones." The base itself stood in a deep valley, and the Chinese were building mile-long runways that could support heavy bombers.

The following morning Bond was playing a game of cribbage when the alarm sounded. He and some other American pilots scrambled to their planes and took off. Bond spotted a group of Japanese bombers beneath him. Using his high-ground advantage, he dove down at them, firing short bursts on the bomber that was on the outside of the V formation, as the Japanese returned fire from mounted machine guns. In the midst of battle, Bond's guns began malfunctioning. Smoke seeped through the instrument panel. His plane had been hit. He pulled out of the attack and only at that instant saw two Japanese fighters coming up behind him. He dove and tried to stay ahead of them. The air speed indicator wound up until it hit 315 miles per hour. He hunched down, waiting for the "pings" from the Japanese machine-gun fire hitting the cockpit.

That fire never came, but before he could feel any sense of relief he caught sight of something that must have made his heart stop—a blade from his propeller was pointing straight up. The engine had died, and the P-40 started to fall. Bond struggled to keep control long enough to prepare for his second crash-landing in as many months. He found a field beneath him and aimed his failing plane at it. But he was coming in too hot. "I bounced out of one muddy rice paddy, sailed over a small dike and smashed down into another water-filled paddy." He had defied death once again, with little more than a wound on his head. A Chinese farmer guided him on a long hike to a village, where they cleaned and bandaged his wound. He was introduced to an American missionary, and after his rescuers fed him lunch the missionary escorted him to the railroad station. On his way, a crowd formed around him, and "little children tugged at my hands," he wrote. The missionary explained to him that the Flying Tigers had become local heroes. "I must admit that in spite of all my misery I felt very proud and honored," Bond recalled.

On June 20, the AVG pilots were introduced to a Japanese gunner who had been shot down during the battle and taken prisoner. They posed for pictures with him and, through a translator, found out that he had been a chicken farmer before the war. He didn't look like the imposing enemy they might have imagined they'd been fighting all these months.

That night, the AVG pilots were celebrated at yet another dinner, which Bond described as "the most elaborate affair I had attended since being in China." Cigars and whiskey were available in abundance, and everyone had a "rip-roaring time." Bond was introduced as a pilot who had been shot down twice, and he took two bows.

As July 4 approached, Claire Chennault and the induction board officers made the rounds to try to recruit the pilots and ground crew for the Army Air Forces. Wherever they went, the answer was the same: The men wanted to go home.

At Kweilin the meetings were held in a makeshift office built in a cave next to the airfield. The pilots were lined up, and each man could hear whoever was ahead of him speaking with Chennault and the board. By the time it was Charlie Bond's turn, he was already resolved that he was not going to accept any offer. When he entered, he met Colonel Homer Sanders, who asked him: "What are you going to do, Charlie? I'm sure you're going to stay with us, aren't you?" Bond said he would stay only if he got a highly desired "regular commission" in the Army Air Forces, but Colonel Sanders said that wouldn't be happening. Still, the colonel encouraged Bond to sign up. The army's refusal to accommodate the AVG veterans only stiffened the spine of the men. Sanders told Bond that he would be traveling to America on a ship that might well be sunk, and if he did make it home, he would be drafted immediately. "Colonel," he replied, "I assure you, that thought doesn't bother me after all I've been through!"

Only five pilots decided to accept induction. A handful of administrative staff and twenty-nine ground crew members agreed to stay on as well. Tex Hill was one of the few pilots who decided to remain. He was a bachelor without anyone waiting at home, and as he later put it: "We knew that [the army] had to have somebody there to take these new guys that were coming in and never had any combat experience at all."

Whatever disappointment Chennault felt about losing his pilots, he was overjoyed when a handful of B-25s from the 11th Bombardment Squadron finally began to arrive in China. He was eager to put these planes to use, operating from bases in Kweilin and Hengyang. Though the AVG pilots were still technically working on their CAMCO contracts, their unofficial induction seemed complete once they began escorting the B-25 bombers on raids in early July and intermingling with the new army fighter pilots. The United Press reported on July 6 that "since July 1 the AVG and United States Army fighters, now merged into one unit, have destroyed twenty-five Japanese planes." The AVG kept fighting right up until the last day, with pilots scrambling at Hengyang to take on a Japanese raid.

Chennault passed that final day, July 4, doing paperwork at an air base outside of Chungking. That night he and some of the remaining men drove to the palatial home of China's former president, Lin Sen, for a farewell dinner. It had been planned as an American-style barbeque, but rain forced them indoors to play musical chairs and sip the nonalcoholic punch. Chennault was presented with a portrait of himself with the Chiangs.

These were men disposed to action more than emotion, but the moment clearly touched them. "People don't seem to understand you got feelings," Tex Hill said. "When you work and fight together for a long time you hate to split up. It's like something going out of your life." At around 11:00 P.M. they walked through the mud back to their cars and drove through the rain to their barracks. "At midnight," Chennault would write, "the American Volunteer Group passed into history."

The Associated Press reported that in the course of their service the Flying Tigers had "shot down or burned on the ground 284 Japanese planes," with many more "probably destroyed." Some of their pilots were credited with as many as ten, or even sixteen, kills. CAMCO ultimately paid out the bonus of five hundred dollars per Japanese plane for 294 planes, including both those destroyed in the air and on the ground. Predictably, Chennault felt that he hadn't been given enough credit and that they had done even more damage than the official records reflected. "The group that military experts predicted would not last three weeks in combat had fought for seven months over Burma, China, Thailand, and French Indo-China, destroying 299 Japanese planes, with another 153 probably destroyed." Years later, some would suggest that these numbers were inflated, but the Flying Tigers stuck by their claims. These battles were fought well before the widespread use of gun cameras and any precise number was lost in the fog of war.

Whatever the true figure, such numbers couldn't begin to tell the full story of what they had accomplished. As Chennault would write, "The flashing shark's teeth of our P-40s and our trademark as Flying Tigers were world famous." After the attack on Pearl Harbor, in America's darkest hours, they had stood as a beacon of hope and proved that Americans could fight and win this war.

As the departing pilots said their farewells and hopped on planes headed out of China, Chennault couldn't seem to let go of his Flying Tigers just yet. He put out the word that he needed volunteers to stay for an extra two weeks. There had been reports that the Japanese were going to target army bases immediately after the transition, and he didn't think he could afford to lose so many of his pilots at once. Again he blamed the army, which was supposed to have sent more reinforcements, but they hadn't arrived yet.

His plea didn't sit well with his veteran pilots. "The Old Man is using this crutch," Charlie Bond said, referring to Chennault's argument that the new pilots hadn't shown up, and added, "Sometimes I wonder if he doesn't have more emotional problems than us pilots." Though he was "angry as hell," Bond couldn't turn his commander down. He agreed to remain until July 18. Tex Hill was going to stay on permanently and he asked John Petach to stay the extra two weeks. Petach probably felt the same pull of loyalty as Bond, even though he had a pregnant wife to consider. After seven months of fighting, what could be the harm in staying just two more weeks? He said yes.

Chennault was now placed in command of the U.S. Army's China Air Task Force (CATF), and was part of the Tenth Air Force, based out of India. What remained of the American Volunteer Group was folded into the 23rd Fighter Group, which much to the chagrin of the original group would paint their fighters with a shark-nose design. Pretty much any fighter pilot in China during World War II would end up saying they were a Flying Tiger. The AVG pilots, however, would insist that they were the only true Flying Tigers.

With eighteen of his battle-tested AVG pilots agreeing to stay for two more weeks, Chennault saw a narrow window of opportunity. July 7, 1942, would mark the fifth anniversary of this war, a date that was not lost on Chennault. After five years of being forced to retreat and fight for survival, he finally had the weapons to turn the tide of war.

On July 6, a formation of five B-25 bombers along with four P-40Es took off from Kweilin and made their way toward the Japanese-occupied city of Canton in eastern China. Hill, who had been made the commanding officer of the 75th Fighter Squadron, Petach, and two new army fighter pilots were in the cockpits of the P-40Es. They flew at thirteen thousand feet, slightly above the B-25s, and tried to keep a clear view for any enemy activity. Their job was to protect the bombers, ensure they reached the target, and fend off any Japanese attack. After an hour of flying, the B-25s arrived at Canton without incident. They dropped their payload, and the group turned back to Kweilin. Not more than five or ten minutes later the B-25s radioed that they had spotted Japanese fighters below. Petach dropped the belly tank on the P-40E to give him more speed and then dove.

Petach was alone when he saw the three Japanese planes strung out in a line in the distance. One of them fired a burst, and then all three headed torward him. Petach knew he had to be deliberate about what he did next. He lined up his nose in the path of one of the fighters, which "pulled into sight right in front of my nose so that my fire raked him as he pass[ed]." His bullets left large holes in the Japanese fighter's wing. With the other two Japanese craft now pursuing him, he climbed and managed to escape. When he scanned the sky, he saw two more Japanese fighters about three miles away. He sped toward them, focusing his aim on one and giving it "about a one second burst and he just burst into flame and was burning well." Hill radioed everyone to regroup. Their job was to focus on protecting the B-25s, not to go looking for trouble. They made it back to base with no losses.

On July 10, Hill organized a strafing run targeting Japanese military installations around Linchuan (modern-day Fuzhou). It wasn't a significant mission in terms of its objective, but they were eager to throw everything they had at the Japanese. Petach was once again in the cockpit of his P-40E, now with only eight days before he and Emma could finally start the next phase of their lives together. The four P-40Es reached their target at 12:03 P.M. They were at 6,500 feet, with no Japanese planes visible on the horizon. Petach was flying in the lead, and noticing something that appeared to be a Japanese military installation, dove down toward it. At 2,300 feet he released his bomb, but suddenly "his airplane went into a violent tumbling spin completely out of control," according to a combat report filed by another pilot, Ajax Baumler. Petach's plane had apparently been hit by antiaircraft fire, and part of his left wing seemed to have come off. The P-40 then "crashed in flames" alongside a river below. Baumler circled overhead, but it was unlikely that anyone could have survived the fiery crash. The mission was a disaster for the Americans—another two-week volunteer from the AVG, Arnold Shamblin, was shot down as well. He may have been captured by the Japanese. He was never seen again.

John Petach died just five days short of his twenty-fourth birthday. When the news of his death reached Tex Hill, he was overcome with guilt. Decades later he would remember how Petach "had his bag packed and suitcase, and sat down and was going to tell the old man goodbye," when Hill asked him for two more weeks. "God, it just killed me."

Death wasn't uncommon in the AVG: including the two killed in the July 10 raid, the AVG had lost twenty-six of its members. But when it happened to someone you loved, familiarity with death meant little.

Emma Foster was in Chungking when they told her the news. Her grief was crippling, though she had lived through the preceding months half expecting this dreadful news. "I always felt we were never coming back together," she would recall. "If I was going to lose him, I wanted part of him and that's why I was deliberately pregnant."

But she thought she had made it to the end, that her premonition had been wrong. Her understanding was that John would spend the additional two weeks waiting at the base in case there was a Japanese attack, not going on dangerous, low-flying attack missions. "I knew he could take care of himself in the air, I wasn't concerned about that. It never occurred to me they'd send him out on a bombing and strafing mission." So the news was even crueler.

If she blamed Chennault or Hill, she concealed it. But she was transparent about one thing: she didn't want to linger there another day. She wanted to go home. "There were no farewells, no parties, no nothing," she recalled. Chennault asked Charlie Bond and Bob Neale to go with her and make sure she got home safely.

That proved to be a tough assignment. They got as far as India, where their journey stalled. Transport flights were scarce, and the trio was encouraged to think of taking a ship home, but Emma didn't want to spend weeks lingering at sea with her heavy burden. Ultimately it took a cable to General Hap Arnold himself to get them on a plane home. Arnold designated the war widow and her escorts "highest priority" for military transport. Emma Foster was back at the hotel and Bond rushed to tell her the news: their plane was leaving the next day. He thought she would "break down and cry when we told her," but she was calm, with a sly sense of humor even in her grief: "If I can be ready by then," she said.

They started their journey on a DC-3 on August 1 and it took them nearly a week to island-hop across the Atlantic to South America, then finally reaching Miami on August 7. Even home at last, Emma had another injury to endure: "When we landed in the Customs Office, they treated the pilots like heroes, they went through with a breeze," she recalled. But the customs officer singled her out, and "treated me like I was a camp follower or a prostitute, and that really hurt."

Turning down the induction offer didn't endear the departing Flying Tigers to the army, and Bissell followed through on his threat—the army provided flights only as far as Calcutta. But that didn't concern the men.

"We were all in a carefree mood, happy to be out of China and heading for home despite the uncertainty of just how we'd manage that little trip amounting to halfway around the world," R. T. Smith recalled. Without access to the army's planes, they settled for berths on a transport ship sailing to New York—a voyage, Smith noted, "that would require weeks in traversing thousands of miles of submarine-infested waters," which he found about as appealing "as facing a firing squad, or playing Russian roulette." But they wanted to go home.

The S.S. Mariposa, formerly a cruise ship, was then en route to India carrying U.S. soldiers. It would be returning to the United States empty, and the Tigers were told they could purchase passage from Bombay (modern-day Mumbai) to New York City for about two hundred dollars. First, though, they would have to make their way from Calcutta to Bombay, an approximately 1,200-mile journey. Smith, Bill Reed, and their contingent booked a first-class compartment on a train for the two-day trip. The heat was so stifling that they filled the washtub in the center of their cabin with ice, but the only good that did was to keep their beer and scotch chilled. At each of the many stops along the way, they would dash out to buy more ice at the station's restaurant. When they finally reached Bombay, they were eager for a taste of luxury, so they checked into a suite of rooms at the Taj Mahal Hotel. They even hired servants to do their laundry and housekeeping. "I tell you, friends, we were living high on the hog and enjoying every minute of it," Smith wrote.

As they waited to board the Mariposa, more Tigers drifted into town. When three weeks later the Mariposa was ready for the homeward sail, over eighty of them were making the voyage, which felt oddly reminiscent of the one that had brought them from San Francisco just a year earlier. Other than a few missionaries and a small group of Chinese flying cadets being sent to the United States for training, they had the ship to themselves. They slept on triple-tiered bunks that had been set up in what had once been the cargo hold. The dining salon, meanwhile, had been converted to a mess hall run by army chefs who served "real honest-to-god American chow and we [ate] all we could eat," Smith recalled, and "in a matter of days our skinny frames began to regain the weight we'd lost over the past few months."

The *Mariposa* crossed the Indian Ocean and docked at Cape Town for a few days to refuel, after which they would cross the Atlantic Ocean, where Nazi U-boats were patrolling. Since January 1942, the U-boats had waged a campaign of destruction against cargo ships and fuel tankers, including launching attacks just outside of New York Harbor. Transport ships were safer if they traveled as part of an armed convoy, but the *Mariposa* would be alone. The crew maintained a speed of twenty knots to make the Atlantic crossing as swiftly as possible.

On a bright September morning, the now-former Flying Tigers stood at the ship's rails as it entered New York Harbor and passed the Statue of Liberty. "Some of the guys spoke of parents or grandparents who had been moved to tears as immigrants upon experiencing just such a moment," Smith recalled. None of the men admitted having tears of their own, but the fact that they were finally home affected them deeply.

Smith and Reed had never visited New York City and decided to stay a few days to top off their around-the-world adventure. They got a room at the Hotel Pennsylvania on Seventh Avenue, across from Pennsylvania Station, and called their parents to let them know that they had made it back safely.

Their arrival was announced by the *New York Herald Tribune* on September 9: FLYING TIGERS, IN CITY, TELL OF EPIC CAMPAIGN. These pilots from one of "the most famous fighting units" were "preparing to leave for their homes throughout the United States after seeing the sights of New York." But when the reporter interviewed Smith, the pilot seemed "reticent about his own exploits."

On the town, Smith and Reed discovered that everyone wanted to buy them a drink. They went to the Stork Club and the Copacabana, some of the city's most prestigious nightspots, and mixed with an elegant crowd. Even in this well-heeled company the pilots found themselves treated like celebrities. The fascination they excited apparently extended to quite a few "beautiful young ladies." One of them was Barbara

Bradford, a blond model who had done shoots for Coca-Cola ads and appeared on the cover of *Cosmopolitan*. She was already married to the famous vaudeville performer George Mann, but within a year she would become Mrs. R. T. Smith.

New York was only the beginning of their heroes' welcome. Across America, small towns took great pride in knowing that they had produced one of the famous Flying Tigers, and what better way to express civic pride than a parade? Perhaps no city went to greater lengths than Marion, Iowa, Reed's hometown. The *Marion Sentinel* featured his photo on the front page of the Thursday, September 10, edition under the headline SATURDAY IS 'BILL REED' DAY. A "royal welcome home" was planned for that weekend, complete with a parade and a speech by Governor George Wilson. "The whole world has given acclaim to the record of the little group of valiant flyers of which he was one," the *Sentinel* proclaimed. His accomplishments were shared by the entire community.

September 12 was a beautiful day, and thousands from across the state gathered in front of the bandstand in Marion's city park, where the governor and the mayor presided and the festivities kicked off with a performance by the high school band. A cleric from a local church led a prayer as a squadron of planes flew over the field. It was a spectacle unlike any Marion had experienced, but there was just one problem— Bill Reed was nowhere to be found.

He had missed his train and would blame his delay on getting lost in Grand Central Station, but that may have been a convenient excuse after a night out on the town. His train finally arrived and he jumped into a car that rushed him to his own celebration. He was just in time to make a dramatic entrance. He only had a few seconds to say hello to his mother and was thrust onto the stage.

"Some day the story will be told in detail," Governor Wilson announced to the crowd, of how "these AVG men from the American states, under General Chennault, showed the patriots of the oldest of the continents how to fight for freedom. They boldly met the challenge of the Japs. They shot them down one by one. The record of Lieutenant Reed is one of the best."

Reed stood to speak and grinned as he was applauded. He wore his uniform and he carried himself "with all the poise of a senator, an office for which he denied any aspirations," the *Sentinel* reported. For the moment, Bill Reed was just glad to be home, telling the crowd, "This is the most marvelous country between here and China, no matter which way you go."

Paul Frillmann avoided the long sea voyage and was able to lead a small group of Tigers on flights that crossed Africa and then traveled north through South America. At a stopover at Natal, Brazil, he met actor and director Orson Welles at their hotel. Welles was in Brazil to make a film and seemed to be in awe that he was in the presence of the real Flying Tigers. He knew his fellow Americans would be as well. "Just wait 'til you see what you're in for," the director told them.

On July 16, Frillmann and his group stepped off the plane in Miami. Boy Scouts and Girl Scouts crowded around to cheer, a band played and civic leaders pressed bouquets of flowers into their arms. Everyone wanted a photo with the Flying Tigers, and the reporters wanted stories. Frillmann was able to spoon out seamless quotes to the reporters who dogged their steps: "They were all adventurers. Most of them enlisted for excitement," he told one journalist. "They had no regard for personal danger. They had more than patriotism—they had plenty of nerve and loved a fight."

Predictably, when asked what they were most looking forward to back home, many of the pilots said they wanted dates with American girls. Other pilots were eager to taste home cooking. One said there was nothing he wanted more than a milk shake, as he had to start gaining back some of the forty pounds he had lost in China. As they prepared to go their separate ways, the men gathered for a last drink, taking over an office in the Pan Am terminal. VACATIONING HEROES, the newspapers described them, showing the men laughing and raising their glasses.

For George McMillan, the hero of the Christmas Day raid, home was just a short flight from Miami to Orlando. He stepped off the plane and saw his mother standing beside the tarmac. After writing her countless letters, he could think of just two words appropriate to the occasion: "Hi, mom." The crowd was silent as they embraced.

A reporter made his way forward and asked McMillan whether he'd return to the war. A few weeks earlier his answer might have been different, but now he replied, "Just let me get a little rest, some of my mom's meals, enjoy myself for a while, and I'll be ready to get back into the harness again."

In Chicago, Paul Frillmann's old church threw a welcome-home party. Nine hundred people crowded into a flag-filled St. Paul's Lutheran Church in Melrose Park to greet the "Fighting Parson." Frillmann soon settled into his role as a local celebrity, fulfilling duties like appearing as an honored guest at a parade in Chicago's Chinatown. He also had a more somber task. He had promised Chennault that he would write to the families of the deceased pilots, and he sent off notes telling them how brave their beloved had been and assuring the relatives that the men hadn't died in vain. Some of the bereaved came to visit him in Chicago, but most of them wrote back with simple gratitude. One woman from the South, however, responded that her son was certainly still alive and would soon return home to "go squirrel shooting with me like he did as a kid."

Given all the celebrity surrounding the return of the Flying Tigers, it was inevitable that Hollywood would view them as an inspiration for the country and, not incidentally, a way to fill movie theaters.

A movie titled *Flying Tigers* was already in the works. That spring, while the actual Flying Tigers finished up their hitches in Asia, Republic Pictures hired two former AVG clerks as consultants. The studio didn't know or didn't care that they were home early because Chennault had given them dishonorable discharges, as he had suspected that they were lovers. Now they were having the last laugh, attached to one of the most hotly anticipated films of the year, "the envy of every studio in town," as one paper said.

But who could they find to play the dynamic commander of the unit? There seemed to be only one man for the role: John Wayne. As one biography of Wayne said, "The film was an ideal vehicle for Wayne. The role of the solid, quiet leader around whom all the action and all other parts revolve played to [his] strengths." Historical accuracy wasn't the film's top priority—all the battles in the movie were depicted as having occurred before Pearl Harbor, though the AVG didn't actually see combat until almost two weeks after the attack. Military reviewers found fault with it for any number of other issues, including its failure to portray the Chinese, as well as attempting to simply do too much. But the box office verdict was clear: Americans were excited to see Wayne leading the Flying Tigers.

Everyone and everything connected to the Flying Tigers seemed to become famous almost overnight, especially Chennault himself. Writers flocked down to Louisiana hoping to interview his childhood friends and besieging Nell, working every angle to tell the story of the great man.

In 1943, without displaying the faintest hint of a smile, Chennault appeared on the cover of *Time* as the savior of the Allied war in the Far East, with a sketch of a tiger with wings behind him.

A man who had gone to China as a washed-up airman hoping for a second chance had become a legend, just as he'd always dreamed.

CHAPTER 14

BLACK SHEEP DOWN

While fame may have pleased Chennault, it didn't satisfy his sense of destiny, which had only grown more grandiose with each success in battle. He didn't want to be merely the man who had led a small group of plucky heroes. He wanted to be the man who played a decisive role in winning the war. That ambition was now being threatened by his new subordinate position in the army. And there still weren't enough planes.

On October 2, 1942, Wendell Willkie, who had been the Republican challenger to Roosevelt in the 1940 election, arrived in Chungking. After getting trounced in the polls, Willkie had agreed to serve as Roosevelt's envoy on a tour of the Far East. He brought with him the assistant director of the Office of War Information, Gardner Cowles, Jr., formerly a publishing magnate and something of a PR man for this "One World" tour, which was meant to show bipartisan support for the war.

As Willkie's car progressed through the city, thousands of Chinese children lined the street waving American and Chinese flags. "Any man who has run for President of the United States is used to crowds," he wrote, "but not this one." The receptions and banquets that followed were intoxicating, as was his hostess: Madame Chiang.

Cowles would recount a wild story about that evening.

At one point, standing in a receiving line with Chiang Kai-shek and Madame Chiang, the darkly handsome Willkie turned to Cowles and told him to keep the Generalissimo occupied while he slipped out with the lady. Cowles dutifully played wingman, pestering Chiang with questions. When the party petered out, Cowles went back to the guesthouse he was sharing with Willkie, but his friend was not there. It wasn't long until Chiang himself, accompanied by his entourage, came pounding on the door, demanding to know Willkie's whereabouts. The group searched the house, looking in closets and beneath the beds, and finding nothing, finally left. At around 4:00 A.M. Willkie came strolling in, bragging about the tryst he had just had with Madame Chiang. Cowles was furious, and told him, "Wendell, you're just a goddamn fool!" He was worried that Willkie might end up in front of a Chinese firing squad.

Whatever did happen that night, this was a business trip, and Willkie had a one-on-one meeting with Chennault during his visit. As expected, Chennault pled his case that Stilwell had been obstructing his mission and that he needed more airplanes. Willkie asked Chennault to write a detailed account that could be sent directly to Roosevelt, and Chennault obliged. He stayed up most of the night writing a letter. Historian Barbara Tuchman would call it "one of the extraordinary documents of the war."

In that document, Chennault listed a series of astounding claims:

1. Japan can be defeated in China.
2. It can be defeated by an Air Force so small that in other theaters it would be called ridiculous.
3. I am confident that, given real authority in command of such an Air Force, I can cause the collapse of Japan.

His hubris and insubordination caused a stir amongst officials back in Washington, D.C. However, his assurance that he could defeat Japan was greeted with some interest in the White House. Chennault soon had an opportunity to make his case in person.

At 2:00 P.M. on May 14, 1943, he attended a meeting with President Roosevelt, Prime Minister Winston Churchill, and the Combined Chiefs of Staff at the White House to discuss the war in the China-Burma-India Theater. Chennault repeated his plea for more planes, according to the meeting minutes, and his entreaty was at least somewhat successful, as new planes soon arrived to reinforce what had become the Fourteenth

Air Force (an elevation in status and title from the CATF in March 1943). But no number of planes would be sufficient to carry out Chennault's bold plans. Chennault didn't trust the generals back in Washington. He trusted his pilots. He wrote letters to some of the pilots from the AVG, imploring them to return to China.

The aerial war in China would never become the priority for Roosevelt that Chennault had hoped, and it receded from the front-page headlines as fighting picked up on other fronts. But the sense of duty to the Old Man drew some of the original Flying Tigers back to fight for Chennault, right until the bitter end of his campaign. George McMillan felt that he had to leave Florida and return to fight in China. "The AVG was hampered by a consistent lack of supplies," he told a reporter after he arrived. "Things are greatly changed now."

Chennault welcomed him back by giving him command of a fighter squadron. On June 24, 1944, McMillan led a formation of eleven P-38s on a raid. He saw a mass of troops on the ground but couldn't discern if they were Japanese or Chinese, so he circled and came in closer—a decision that would cost him dearly. The soldiers were, in fact, Japanese, and opened fire with their rifles, hitting his plane. He sent a distress call out over the radio and fled the target area, perhaps hoping for another miracle landing, like the one he had made on Christmas of 1941. As he headed over a river he radioed: "How do these things land on water?" Another pilot watched McMillan's damaged plane as the engine seemed to stop, it started to fall, and then it finally crashed in flames. "I saw no parachute in the area," his squadronmate reported.

Bill Reed returned to the Far East in 1943, first going to India then back to China itself. He was shot down in June 1944 but was able to make his way back to American lines after spending a few weeks in the wilderness, guided by Chinese fighters. He became known as one of the best pilots in China.

On December 19, 1944, Reed was returning from a nighttime mission when he discovered that his own base was being attacked and was under a blackout. His fuel was running low, and he circled overhead waiting for permission to land, but no clearance was granted. Several fighter pilots who were in the same situation bailed out, one man surviving without an injury, and another breaking his leg but surviving. But Reed was not so lucky. The next day they found his body. As he had bailed out, the tail of the plane had apparently struck him, leaving "a flap of hair loose on the back of his head that was scalped there." His hand was holding on to the ripcord, but he hadn't opened his parachute.

Congressman Mike Mansfield of Montana was in China around that time and when he returned to Washington, D.C., he conveyed the news of Reed's death directly to President Roosevelt. The *Des Moines Register*, published a letter, recalling how "two years ago the whole state rose to welcome him home from the war in China." But now, "word has been passed around that Bill Reed has flown his last flight."

Not all the AVG pilots who went back to China did so for Chennault, and others went on to become famous in their own right and in other theaters of war. Jim Howard, the Pomona graduate who had grown up in China, was flying a P-51 over Germany on January 11, 1944, when he got into a dogfight with Luftwaffe fighters that were targeting American B-17 bombers. He was credited with shooting down four Luftwaffe craft, and when he ran out of ammunition, he dove into a group of thirty Luftwaffe planes. Howard was credited with helping save the Flying Fortresses. "For sheer determination and guts, it was the greatest exhibition I've ever seen," said General Robert Travis, who personally led the bombers that day. "It was a case of one lone American against what seemed to be the entire Luftwaffe. He was all over the wing, across and around it. They can't give that boy a big enough award."

When Howard was awarded the Medal of Honor, he was celebrated as a hero in the press with journalists like Walter Cronkite and Andy Rooney writing profiles of the heroic pilot. But he downplayed his own bravery: "I seen my duty and I done it."

The story that most surprised the former AVG members was the second career of Greg Boyington. After leaving China, Boyington had returned to live outside of Seattle. He had applied to renew his commission with the Marine Corps but wasn't accepted, and he suspected that a negative review from Chennault was holding it up. He took a job parking cars at a garage in Seattle, the same job he had while attending the

University of Washington. He kept hoping that he would be accepted back into the Marine Corps but nothing came through. Finally, on November 8, 1942, he sent a cable to Washington: "HAVE BEEN STANDING BY FOR FOUR MONTHS PATIENCE EXHAUSTED WOULD LIKE TO BE ENLIGHTENED IMMEDIATELY PLEASE."

Boyington not only got his commission back, but in September 1943 was given command of Marine Fighter Squadron VMF-214. His pilots took to calling him "Gramps," because at thirty he was considered ancient. Though Chennault and Boyington had always had little respect for each other, now that Boyington had a squadron of his own he seemed to emulate the Old Man, as he had no use for wasting time with protocol. The pilots came to revere Boyington, who impressed them with his flying skills, and one night they discussed what their group's nickname should be. They were mostly "orphaned" from other squadrons, and one man joked that they were all pretty much bastards. Then someone suggested "Boyington's Bastards," which they submitted to a public relations officer, who rejected it as profane. They settled on another name with a B—Black Sheep. The Black Sheep Squadron under the command of Major Greg Boyington would become one of the most famous units of the war. They were stationed at an island close to Guadalcanal and flew Corsair fighters against the Japanese based on nearby islands.

Boyington took to battle in typical outrageous style, becoming famous for issuing radio challenges to the Japanese to come fight him. By December 1943, he had racked up an astonishing twenty-five enemy kills (though many have questioned the accuracy of his claims), only one short of the record set by Major Joe Foss in World War II and Eddie Rickenbacker in World War I. Boyington's numbers may have been inflated, but he desperately wanted to break that record. Coming back from one battle with no kills, he launched into a tirade. "Damn it," he said. "I couldn't hit the broad side of a barn with a brass viola today. I guess the tension was too great." It seemed like Greg "Pappy" Boyington, as the newspapers called him, wouldn't clear the record. His tour would be coming to an end in January 1944, and he, much like Chennault, had a sense that he was destined to make history no matter the cost. He was sure that he would survive. He was reported to have told the other pilots: "If you ever see me go down . . . I promise I'll meet you in a San Diego bar six months after the war."

When the daily schedule was posted for January 3, 1944, Boyington was slated to have a day off, but he didn't want a break. He knew that he might have only one or two more shots at breaking the record, and he wanted every chance to fly in combat. He volunteered to lead a "fighter sweep" over the island of Rabaul, one of Japan's fortified positions in the Pacific that hadn't yet fallen, and the request was granted. The night before the raid, the pilots moved to a forward operating base.

By 6:30 the following morning, Boyington was back in the cockpit of a Corsair, and he set off on a course for Rabaul. Mechanical problems forced several pilots to turn back, and by the time they arrived at the target at 8:00 A.M. Boyington was leading a force of four. If he was concerned, it was that he wouldn't encounter any Japanese planes. But at 8:15 A.M. he saw a formation of six Japanese Zeros glistening in the morning sun. He came in from behind, and overeager to land his kill he opened fire too early, still a quarter mile behind his target. That should have given the Zero enough notice to alter its course, but for some reason it didn't change its trajectory, and Boyington was able to close in. "The lightly built Zeke [Zero] shuddered under the impact of the slugs," Boyington's biographer, Bruce Gamble, wrote. The Japanese pilot bailed out, and the plane was ablaze. It was Boyington's twenty-sixth kill, and he had American pilots as his eyewitnesses. The record was now tied, and he had his eye set on beating it. Catching sight of a group of Zeros beneath him, he dove, but in his haste failed to spot another group of Zeros above him, which quickly came in pursuit. There were now only two Corsairs facing down a group of perhaps twenty Zeros. The other Corsair was soon hit and went crashing down in a ball of fire onto the island. Boyington was alone, and as machine-gun fire ripped into his plane, it was set ablaze. Boyington plummeted with the burning aircraft.

At the Allied base, word that Boyington hadn't returned spread "like the chill wind." Witnesses attested to the fact that he had achieved his twenty-sixth victory, but since then he had not been seen. His squadronmates, however, were confident that he had survived.

Bombers and fighters were sent out to search for Boyington but found no sign of the missing pilot. In April 1944, he was awarded the Medal of Honor in absentia. Officially, Boyington was still missing, but he was unofficially presumed dead. Still, his mother refused to give up hope. Invited to speak at a rally at the shipyard in Tacoma, Washington, to inaugurate a new warship by ceremonially breaking a bottle on its bow, she said, "When I dedicate this ship tonight, I'm going to make a little prayer. Just as the bottle breaks, I'm going to say, 'Ship go out and bring my boy back to me and his babies.'"

His three-year-old daughter, Gloria, went to live with her aunt. Before going to bed, she would pray: "Please, God, bring daddy back."

Sensing that he didn't have much time left in China, Chennault became focused on the idea of working with the OSS, the predecessor of the CIA, to help find and bring home the pilots who had bailed out in enemy territory as far back as 1942—Charlie Mott (the Penn graduate shot down in Thailand), William McGarry ("Black Mac," who had gone missing on the Chiang Mai raid in the jungles of Thailand), and Lewis Bishop (the pilot who had been shot down in Indochina).

In early 1945, Chennault met with OSS officer Nicol Smith, who was coordinating operations in Thailand with "Free Thai" resistance forces. He showed Smith a map of where McGarry had last been seen, and only a few days later Smith learned that he was, in fact, still alive. McGarry had wandered in the jungle for three weeks before the Thai police found and captured him. He had been interrogated by the Japanese and was held at a Thai-run facility under Japanese control. Chennault told Smith to "find out from McGarry if possible, whether he is in condition to leave and willing to attempt an escape." Free Thai fighters got in touch with the pilot, who confirmed that he was willing to try, even if he risked death. The original plan was for him to feign illness and be smuggled out to a hospital or even in a coffin, but that idea was eventually scrapped. Instead a Thai police officer working with the Free Thai drafted a fake release order. On April 14, 1945, McGarry was escorted out of the prison camp and taken to an OSS safe house. He was then smuggled out of Thailand by boat, lying below deck armed with a submachine gun in case a Japanese patrol boat decided to do an inspection.

Chennault was waiting, along with some of his old friends from the AVG, when McGarry arrived in Kunming. One of those present was Ed Rector, who had dropped the candy bar into the jungle when McGarry was shot down almost three years earlier.

Charlie Mott had been downed on January 8, 1942, during a raid on a Japanese air base and had been sent to one of the notorious prison camps along the River Kwai. As he recalled: "Almost everyone had malaria and dysentery. Small scratches got infected because of the lack of antiseptics and grew into great engulfing sores. The flesh rotted slowly away, leaving bones and tendons exposed. What kept us alive? Hope."

They were imprisoned not just by the Japanese guards, but by the dense jungle. "It was 600 miles through hostile territory to the nearest friendly line. The jungle was our keeper." In 1945, a Free Thai officer contacted some of the POWs when they were on a work detail and instructed Mott to walk out of the camp into the jungle, where a guide would take him to a hidden airfield that the OSS had helped set up. He put his faith in the plan and found, as promised, a Thai guide waiting for him. He rode a pony for the long trek to the airfield, where he was met by OSS agents and boarded a plane.

Lewis Bishop managed to escape from Japanese custody on May 10, 1945. He jumped from a moving train at night with four other American prisoners and then spent forty-seven days in the hands of Chinese Communist and Nationalist soldiers until he finally reached Kunming. Chennault was there to greet him, but the Old Man "looked much older, worn and tired," as Bishop put it. A celebratory dinner was held to welcome him back, and the former prisoner ate ice cream for the first time since he left the United States in September 1941. Chennault passed over his serving of dessert so that Bishop could have a second helping. As soon as he could, Bishop sent a message to his wife in Florida to let her know that he was alive and coming home. "The terrific urge to get home to my wife and little daughter, now three and a half years old, drove me on with more determination than ever," he would write of his escape. When he finally made it back to America his wife told him that during his three-year imprisonment she had met someone else and wanted a divorce.

Chennault was willing to work with almost anyone to rescue his downed airmen. "I dealt with Chinese of all political shades including

Communists, independent guerrillas and [anti-Chiang] dissidents. . . . The [Communists] rescued many of our airmen from under the noses of the Japanese, and we in turn supplied them with medicines, radio equipment, pocket compasses and watches." In March 1945, he met with a guerrilla leader who had been working with the OSS in Indochina to help rescue downed American pilots. The skinny man wore a khaki uniform. His name was Ho Chi Minh. In the meeting, he lauded Chennault's leadership of the Flying Tigers. Ho asked Chennault for a picture of the general as a keepsake and Chennault obliged, having his secretary bring one in and then autographing it with a fountain pen. Ho was known to display the picture of Chennault, proud of his friendship with the American people and one of its best warriors—a guerrilla fighter just like him.

Chennault's suspicions about his tenure coming to an end proved to be correct. In three years his Fourteenth Air Force had made considerable progress, despite the loss of the bases in East China to a Japanese offensive in 1944, but his successes did little to quiet the growing chorus of demands that he be relieved of his duties. He would ascribe this to personal grudges, particularly to Stilwell's reports in Washington, but the reality was that Chennault had always been out of step with the army, and now the war was racing past him.

In June 1945 General Hap Arnold, the chief of the Army Air Forces, wrote to General George Stratemeyer of the Eastern Air Command: "I firmly believe that the quickest and most effective way to change air warfare . . . is to change commanders. I would appreciate your concurrence in General Chennault's early withdrawal from the China Theater. He should take advantage of the retirement privileges now available to physically disqualified officers."

The news was delivered to Chennault in classic bureaucratic style: he wasn't being fired, but another layer of command would be placed above him, with Stratemeyer as the commander, and Chennault given an amorphous job. In 1937 Chennault had resigned from the army to go to China and now he would resign to head home. He replied: "I accepted active duty in China because of a desire to contribute my services in this war. . . . It has been indicated that my present job can be better done by another man. I therefore propose to request retirement a second time as soon as the transition to the new organization has been accomplished."

It was a devastating blow to Chennault, who wanted to stay on until the end, driven by the "natural desire to remain at the head of my command until victory was formally acknowledged and to taste of triumph after my long years of battle against odds."

Word of his leaving quickly got out, and the *Chicago Tribune* ran the headline GEN. CHENNAULT, SIDETRACKED BY CHIEFS, RESIGNS. There were calls in the Senate for an investigation into his mistreatment, but nothing could change the fact that he was leaving the service.

A farewell reception was held in Chungking. It was a foggy day, and Chennault spent the day seated on a platform as China's citizens presented him with any number of gifts, including everything from antiques and paintings to inscribed silken banners from cities and towns that were indebted to him. An official dinner was hosted by Chiang Kai-shek. Madame Chiang was out of the country, so Chennault didn't have a chance to say good-bye to his "princess."

In early August 1945, Chennault traveled the country to bid farewell to his airmen and to Chinese soldiers. American victory was on the horizon, especially after the Enola Gay dropped a nuclear bomb on Hiroshima on August 6. Chennault had been fighting the Japanese for eight long years, but he wouldn't get to see them surrender.

A young Chinese reporter, Anna Chen, just twenty, attended Chennault's final departure ceremony in Kunming on August 7, the night before Chennault was scheduled to leave. She had met him during the war when she interviewed him for a story. Afterward, he had invited her for dinner, and they'd become friendly. That final night, Anna detected "an undercurrent of sadness" to the celebration. "One by one during the evening, the 'boys' of the 14th [Air Force] sought brief moments with the General to give him their personal goodbyes." She wanted to bid him well, too, but the party seemed as if it would go on late into the night.

"I think I'd better go home, general," she said to him. "It's getting rather late." He told her that he would have his chauffeur drive her and walked her out to the parking lot, where his Buick was waiting. "I'll see you off tomorrow at the airport, General," she promised.

"Fine," he replied, "but that may not be the place to say goodbye." He held out his arms as if to hug her and when she stepped into his embrace he bent down and kissed her "long and tenderly." She opened her eyes and looked up. Chennault told her, "I shall be back."

The next morning, August 8, 1945, Chennault loaded all his gifts onto a C-47. The trip was planned with a few stops along the way, including a visit with the pope in Rome and with some RAF friends in London. As his plane lifted off the runway in Kunming, Chennault believed he might be leaving China forever, despite what he'd told the young reporter.

On August 15, as Chennault was taking a nap somewhere over the Mediterranean Sea, news came across the plane radio that the Japanese emperor had announced that Japan would unconditionally surrender. Chennault wasn't with his men to celebrate the victory.

After the official Japanese surrender, the U.S. Army Air Forces was faced with the issue of liberating the POW camps in Japan. Because there was concern that the American prisoners might starve to death before they could be rescued, U.S. bombers were sent to drop packages of food.

At a camp outside Tokyo called Omori, American B-29s opened the bomb-bay doors and released fifty-five-gallon steel drums to float down on parachutes. Sometimes the parachutes tore away from the barrels, which came crashing into the barracks. A container including Mounds bars landed in a latrine, but the prisoners retrieved it and ate them. The prisoners used white paint and even mixtures from tooth or foot powder to write messages on the rooftops that could be seen by the pilots: "500 MEN, OMORI CAMP, WE THANK YOU."

When a Corsair photographer with a Kodak camera took photographs of the camp and returned to the U.S.S. *Hancock* to develop them, he found a startling message written across the rooftops: "PAPPY BOYINGTON HERE!"

More than a year and a half had passed since Greg Boyington had been shot down and presumed dead. It seemed impossible that he could still be alive, but no other explanation could account for the message on the rooftops.

Late in the afternoon on August 29, Marines boarded a group of small Higgins boats, flat-bottomed vehicles that had been used for amphibious assaults like the one conducted on D-Day, and made their way through Tokyo Bay toward the camp. The prisoners had amassed on the shoreline, cheering them on. The men were wearing shorts, and many of them seemed little more than skeletons with loose flesh. They waved a makeshift American flag, which they had spent months sewing together from scraps of their bedsheets, using colored pencils to mark the red, white, and blue.

When the Higgins boats landed the Marines planted an American flag of their own, and one of the prisoners stood and saluted it. That man was Greg Boyington.

"God sakes, Pappy, we didn't know you were alive," the commanding officer told him. The formal surrender ceremony had yet to take place, and the Japanese commandant protested that he wasn't supposed to release the prisoners without a direct order from Tokyo, but the Americans paid him no attention. Boyington climbed aboard one of the boats, which took him to a hospital ship, aptly named the *Benevolence,* where he was given a disinfectant shower, some new clothes, and a meal of ham and eggs. Though some of the prisoners were so starved they could barely eat, Boyington helped himself to about five servings.

His liberation made headlines back home, and he told the story of his improbable survival, starting with how he'd escaped that burning plane. "I flipped my plane on its back and unfastened the seat belt" and then "dropped 100 feet to the water and was stunned by the impact." He hunkered down in the water as the Zeros strafed him. When they left, he inflated his rubber boat and sat bobbing in the swell until he saw a submarine rise to the surface. For a moment he hoped it was there to rescue him but the "red ball" indicated it was an enemy vessel. "I was blindfolded and handcuffed," he recalled. "My festering wounds smelled so foul I wondered how the Jap questioners could stand the stench."

At a prison camp at Ofuna, he was bound with his hands behind his back, and a guard took a baseball bat and "slugged the back of my legs and my backside as hard as possible." From there he was transferred to Omori, where he had been forced to bow to the vicious guards.

What had kept them alive? It wasn't just hope, but also memories. Boyington would go to sleep every night thinking in exquisite detail of the meals his mother used to make him. The famous runner Louis Zamperini would write down recipes on scraps of paper, recreating the Italian meals that he had cooked before the war. The prisoners would copy these down on scraps of paper, imagining the completed dishes. Boyington looked at the recipes and was certain this Zamperini was a better runner than he was a cook; he added potatoes to a dish at the same time as the tomatoes, an amateur mistake. Boyington was always something of a cynic, even when it came to hope.

At 5:46 A.M. on September 12, a navy transport plane carrying Boyington landed in Oakland. He walked out wearing a fresh uniform, and some of his old squadronmates from the Black Sheep Squadron who had gathered to welcome him lifted him up onto their shoulders and paraded him around. "This is the most wonderful thing that ever happened to me," the overjoyed Boyington yelled. He had promised them that he would see them at a bar in San Diego after the war, but they settled for a bar in San Francisco, and *Life* covered the momentous occasion, with a photo showing Boyington smoking a fat cigar at the hotel bar, looking supremely at home.

Chennault arrived in New Orleans on September 6. Nell was in the hospital, but his children came up to meet him. It was the first time he had seen them in two years, and the first time in over eight when he might be home to stay. Chennault had contemplated a retirement spent "hunting and fishing on the Tensas River," much as he had spent his youth. The generals had once again snubbed him, he believed, by failing to invite him to the Japanese surrender ceremony on the U.S.S. *Missouri,* an event he had understandably wanted to see after his many years fighting the Japanese. In Louisiana, however, Chennault had become something of a folk hero—the home-state boy who won the war in China. To celebrate his homecoming, New Orleans did what the city does best: it put on a parade. Tex Hill was back in Texas, and he flew a P-51 to greet the Old Man; the homecoming for Chennault was one "hell of a shindig."

On September 7 the crowds on Canal Street swelled fifteen rows deep. Young boys climbed up lampposts to get a better view. Confetti floated down from rooftops, and American flags billowed in the late-summer breeze. They had seen Chennault grace the covers of *Life* and *Time,* but here was the general in the flesh, perched atop a convertible in his khaki uniform, smiling and waving to the clamoring crowd. Children ran out into the street and sprinted alongside the slow-moving car. The crowd occasionally spilled so far into the street that the procession had to be stopped. No expense was spared: B-25 bombers and P-51 fighters swooped down low over the procession, and a float paid tribute to the Flying Tigers, its front shaped like the nose of a plane with the distinctive shark-nose design, and at its back a platform with a live tiger pacing inside a cage. When the procession reached City Hall, Chennault climbed down from the car, and the crowd surged around him. So many people wanted to shake his hand and touch his uniform that it took him almost thirty minutes to walk the ten feet to get to the stage.

A congressman presented Chennault with an American flag that had flown over the U.S. Capitol on V-J Day. Chennault stepped to the microphone and gave a few remarks: "I thank God it was our flag that flew over the Capitol and not the flag of the Rising Sun. I thank God we preserved our freedom. I hope it will be a symbol of a lasting peace and a world free from fear." While outwardly he looked and talked the part of a returning war hero, he was experiencing inner turmoil. As much as he had yearned for home during his years in China, he wasn't sure that a quiet retirement would fulfill him. His war wasn't yet over.

EPILOGUE

On June 26, 1952, a decade after the Flying Tigers disbanded, a C-54 cargo plane flown by a trio of former AVG pilots left New York and made its way to Los Angeles. A large "Flying Tigers Line" logo was painted on its side, but it wasn't embarking on a military mission. The plane belonged to the cargo airline started by a former AVG pilot after the war and was named for the old outfit, and it was making a special trip. The C-54 stopped in different cities to pick up former Tigers as it crossed the country, including Claire Chennault and his new young wife, Anna, the pretty Chinese journalist he had married in 1947 after a divorce from Nell.

The plane flew through the night, but no one slept as they reconnected with long-parted friends. On the morning of June 27, as they neared Los Angeles, four Air Force jets pulled up alongside as an honor escort for the final descent. Then a fifth plane flew alongside: a shark-nosed P-40.

After the plane taxied to a stop, the cabin door opened and Chennault walked down the staircase as an Air Force band played "Tiger Rag." The Tigers themselves rushed to meet their squadronmates waiting on the tarmac. "It is impossible to describe the emotional impact of this moment as once again we saw the familiar faces of buddies and friends from the old AVG days, many of whom we hadn't seen in ten years," reported an article in the *Tiger Rag,* an alumni newsletter that was launched a few months later.

The party continued at the Ambassador Hotel, where noontime cocktails were served and the men settled in for lunch. A *Los Angeles*

Times reporter noted that "the former combat pilots started swapping yarns immediately, wringing the hands of buddies they hadn't seen for years and shouting vociferous greetings across the table." Chennault gave some quick remarks and joked that he thought the food in Toungoo was better. There was a picnic the following day, where they were joined by their "mascot" for the weekend—an allegedly tame tiger lent by the Seattle Zoo. Its name was Toungoo.

Life had taken them in many directions: some had become lawyers, others had tried ranching or farming, and many were now military or commercial pilots. But having been a Flying Tiger was an honor that seemed to become only more meaningful as they aged. Many of the men were married and brought their wives and young children along, but one night had been set aside just for the men at the Hollywood Athletic Club. Thanks to sponsorships from companies like Lockheed and Texaco, they could live it up. There was a steak dinner, and they made good use of the open bar. They drank, danced, and partied like they were back in the Silver Grill.

The weekend culminated with a banquet on Sunday night. With guests, the crowd swelled to 350, filling the Blossom Room at the Roosevelt Hotel. Dinner was prime rib, followed by a brief ceremony. The first award was given to nine-year-old Joan Claire Petach, the daughter of John and Emma Foster Petach. Chennault presented her with a gold locket on behalf of the group, placing it around her neck. Its inscription read: "From all her dad's old buddies." The evening concluded with the Tigers honoring Chennault with a plaque marking the tenth anniversary of the AVG: "To Claire L. Chennault, our Beloved Leader and Friend."

If Chennault had considered settling down to a quiet retirement in Louisiana after the war, he didn't stick to those plans for long. As biographer Martha Byrd wrote, "He wanted to be part of what was happening . . . the idealistic yearning was still present; the instincts of the warrior who serves a noble cause still surged within him and demanded a means of expression."

After World War II, the civil war in China between the Nationalists and the Communists had resumed, and Chennault believed that the

Chiangs needed his help against the enemy forces. He returned to China in January 1946 and quickly drew up plans for procuring old U.S. Army transport planes—a mission that may have felt familiar—with which to start a new airline, Civil Air Transport, or CAT as it came to be known. The airline took part in the civil war but wasn't a combat unit, for the job of its pilots was to carry supplies to remote areas. Some of the CAT airmen had been members of the AVG, including Erik Shilling, the pilot who had flown the reconnaissance mission right after Pearl Harbor. There were, unsurprisingly, rumors that Chennault wanted to turn CAT into a new AVG, but he always firmly denied them, insisting that it was strictly a cargo airline.

There was little discipline in the group, and the pilots wore whatever they wanted when they flew, whether a tropical shirt or an old military uniform. They were creating one of the world's first freight airlines on the fly, and found themselves taking on any number of bizarre missions. They flew sheep to an area that had lost its livestock during the war. They flew an elephant that would tilt the plane if it stomped one of its feet. They flew whatever and wherever they were asked.

Chennault was reinvigorated by a new venture and a new wife, who worked for him as a publicist at CAT. But the company's fate was tied to the Chinese civil war, and it wasn't going well for the Nationalists. In 1949 CAT worked around the clock to help evacuate the Nationalists to Formosa (present-day Taiwan) as the Communists surged forward. By December of that year, the airline was nearly bankrupt and needed to find new sources of revenue. During a visit to Washington, D.C., Chennault met with officials from a new government body—the Central Intelligence Agency. What happened next would remain secret for years, but eventually the CIA disclosed: "On August 23, 1950, the Agency acquired the airlines' assets through a 'cut-out' (a Washington area banker) and the company was reorganized as CAT Incorporated, ostensibly a private enterprise, but actually CIA's new aviation arm." CAT was used to drop tons of supplies to U.S. troops during the Korean War and then, in 1954, it repainted some of its C-119 planes with French Air Force colors and started flying covert American missions to supply French troops besieged by the Viet Minh soldiers at Dien Bien Phu. The Eisenhower administration had declined to provide U.S.

military assistance to the French, but they could deny any involvement with the private airline—a strategy that paralleled the creation of the AVG. On May 6, one of CAT's C-119 transports was shot down, and two American pilots were killed. The names of these airmen were never listed on the Vietnam Veterans Memorial. Officially, America wasn't fighting in Vietnam in 1954. The day after their deaths, the French garrison at Dien Bien Phu surrendered, shocking the United States and Western powers. Chennault promoted the need for a new "International Volunteer Group" that would be composed of pilots from around the world and would take on the Viet Minh. His proposal made headlines: CHENNAULT WANTS TO REVIVE FLYING TIGERS. The idea was discussed at the White House, and when Secretary of State John Foster Dulles asked whether the president would control such a unit, an aide replied that it would be commanded by Chennault—just as the Flying Tigers had been. The plan never came to fruition but "in a broader sense Chennault's arguments carried" the day in the U.S. government, as Martha Byrd wrote. There would be more covert missions executed far from the scrutiny of Congress and the public. CAT would be used for some of them. William Pawley was friendly with CIA director Allen Dulles, and he suggested other clandestine schemes, including overthrowing the government in Guatemala and launching an invasion of Cuba. When the British started to raise questions about operations they believed the CIA was conducting in the Far East, the agency denied that they were its doing, and intimated that they might be the work of a group run by Chennault.

The reality was that Chennault was in declining health and finally was forced to consider something of a real retirement. He was still the chairman of the board of CAT, but it was effectively a figurehead position. He and Anna had two young girls, born in 1949 and 1950, and he wanted to spend more time with his family. They bought a house in Monroe, Louisiana, in 1954, and he would invite old friends over to have a bourbon on the porch. He would spend long days tending to his garden and his daughters. He had bought about seventy acres of rugged land on the Tensas River, where he "seemed to be most at peace," Byrd wrote. "He never outgrew his love for the outdoor life that had entered his blood when he was a boy." He built a cabin on a bluff that overlooked the river, explaining that he wanted it to be a memorial to his AVG pilots who had been killed, and a place where the AVG men could gather for reunions. Thomas Corcoran, the lawyer who had been responsible for helping to organize the AVG, came to visit Chennault there. They went hunting and, as the story is told, Chennault had a good shot at a deer but didn't pull the trigger. He explained to Corcoran that he no longer enjoyed killing deer. He wanted to let them live.

Chennault had suffered from bronchitis attacks for many years, and breathing became more difficult. Doctors treated him but he knew that the end might be near. His long career in the military had made him famous but it hadn't made him rich, and he worried about money. He was angry that some of his and Nell's children hadn't finished college, and he wanted to leave enough of an inheritance to his two young daughters. The Flying Tigers was still a well-recognized name, and Chennault decided he would cash in.

He did advertisements for a number of different companies, including, ironically, cigarette ads for Camel. The photo shoots would sometimes take him to New York City, and on one visit he decided to call up an old friend—AVG's chaplain Paul Frillmann.

It was something of a miracle that Frillmann was still alive. He had returned to China in 1943, this time as an army intelligence officer, in which capacity Chennault had quickly dispatched him to help call in air strikes on enemy positions. However, Japanese forces were closing in on the area in which he was based, in a town called Changteh, and Frillmann was forced to flee on foot. He and another army officer set out, avoiding open spaces and staying close to the underbrush in case there was an assault. In the afternoon they climbed up a dike and "in horror discovered right below us more than a dozen Japanese soldiers lounging in a circle of sandbags while food cooked over a campfire. A big black machine gun stood among them and other weapons were stacked at hand." His American comrade raised up his rifle to shoot. "Don't be a damn fool," Frillmann told him, and as they fled Frillmann lost his shoes in the muddy paddy, but there was no time to find them. With four or five Japanese soldiers in pursuit they didn't stop "until the darkness was so thick we couldn't see to run."

Frillmann ultimately found himself with the OSS and was sent deep behind Japanese lines to live in the wilderness and report back his observations. By V-J Day he had been promoted to running the OSS office in Peking. The key question that hung over China's future was whether the Nationalists led by the Chiangs would continue to rule or whether the Communists would prevail. Frillmann had spent months in the countryside and came to believe that the Nationalists "seemed to regard the peasants as nothing but an endlessly exploitable source of money, food and conscripts." In the closing days of World War II, he wrote a secret memo to higher-ups in the OSS stating that "it is extremely important that definite overtures be made to contact the Reds."

After the war, Frillmann became a U.S. diplomat, serving in posts throughout Asia, but was forced out in 1953 on suspicions that he had been friendly with Communists during his service in China—this was during the time when Senator Joseph McCarthy was holding hearings into un-American activities. Frillmann moved to New York City without much idea of what he would do, but ended up becoming a PR man. His apartment was soon a crash pad for former China hands, and "at odd hours we would be telephoned by former missionaries, AVG pilots, spies and the like, asking if we had a bed or a patch of floor where they might sleep."

When Chennault came to New York, Frillmann would go to the Old Man's hotel, where they would spend hours talking about the old days. During one trip Chennault invited Frillmann to come to the photo shoot he was doing for a cigarette advertisement. Frillmann was horrified to see how the young photographers treated Chennault, shouting out orders: "Look there! Look here! Hold your hands this way! Blow the smoke that way!" Frillmann could tell that Chennault hated every second of the ordeal and afterward asked him about it. Chennault said he needed the money and that "despite popular opinion, he was not a wealthy man," as Frillmann recalled. It would be the last time the two men saw each other.

In 1956 Chennault was diagnosed with lung cancer. He was treated at Walter Reed Hospital and was then transferred to the Oschner Foundation Hospital in New Orleans. He was determined to beat the disease; he still had a young wife and children to live for. But the radiation treatments were wearing him down, and he felt increasingly alone. "No one paid much attention to me," he wrote one day in his diary. He was "nervous, almost jittery."

Madame Chiang was in the United States at the time and went to New Orleans in July 1958 to see Chennault for what she must have known would be their last reunion. When she arrived at the hospital, he was gaunt and exhausted. "I can't talk very well," he said in a low voice. "Well," she consoled him, "you always talked too much. I want to do the talking this time. You have this wonderful fighting spirit. You were never defeated. Certainly not by the Japanese."

On July 27, 1958, Chennault passed away. Anna wrote a note that day: "I lost my dearest one and the world lost a great leader. I wish I could die with him."

There was one final flight for him to take. His body was placed in a flag-draped casket, and a Fourteenth Air Force transport plane flew him to Washington, D.C.

Six black horses pulled the caisson up the hill at Arlington Cemetery, where Chennault was laid to rest on the grass down the slope from the former mansion of another legendary general. It was a strange twist of fate that Claire Lee Chennault was buried in what had been the rose garden of his ancestor Robert E. Lee. Madame Chiang Kai-shek and T. V. Soong attended the funeral, representing the Chinese people. Tex Hill attended along with other Flying Tigers. Madame Chiang bowed her head beside the casket as an Air Force squad fired three volleys and a bugler played taps. Anna Chennault wept as she bade farewell to her husband.

"The flight of another airman is over," the chaplain said, and Chennault was lowered into the earth. On his gravestone his name is inscribed in English on the front, and on the back, in Chinese.

The memory of World War II, and the young men who fought in it, receded as the decades wore on. New wars came to claim new warriors, and those from the Greatest Generation grew gray, paunchy, and arthritic. And like their old leader, they passed away, one by one. Their obituaries were featured in publications like the *Washington Post* and the *Los Angeles Times*, reminders of when young Americans had dared to undertake bold deeds.

But the last of the Flying Tigers wanted one final victory—recognition that they had been on active duty and were not just mercenaries, as many had considered them. Finally, in 1991, a Pentagon special service board reviewed the old documents and concluded that the AVG members had indeed qualified as a bona fide part of the American war effort. They found a secret army report from 1942 that explained: "To avoid a breach of international law, the entire project was organized as a commercial venture." The lawyer representing the AVG vets put it in terms that could be more easily understood: the AVG "makes the Iran-Contra affair look like a small-scale operation."

Tex Hill was as proud as ever of what they had accomplished. "We have a record that is second to none," he said. "Nobody will ever match that again."

At the 1996 AVG reunion in Dallas, each pilot was awarded a Distinguished Flying Cross, and all the ground crew received Bronze Stars. As the surviving Tigers slowly made their way across the stage to receive their long overdue medals, some needed canes or walkers, but the eighty-one-year-old Hill walked without assistance. Air Force Chief of Staff General Ronald Fogleman pinned a medal on each man's lapel. One pilot who attended was Ken Jernstedt, who had been a state senator in Oregon after the war. He had lost his vision, and as he told an interviewer: "I've got to be the only person to get one of those [medals] 55 years late and with a seeing eye dog."

They grew old, but they didn't forget. Emma Foster married a former CNAC pilot she met at a reunion in the 1960s, their marriage grounded in shared memories of China. By 2000 she was in "God's Waiting Room," as she put it, but she wanted to go back to see China one last time. She returned to the places she had first visited when she was an exchange student in 1937, but nothing was familiar. The cities "are like New York, traffic jams, cars, cars, cars, and more cars." Her time with the Flying Tigers had been filled with love and loss but still, she "wouldn't change that year for anything." She never forgot about John, saying, "I had the kind of romance that girls would dream of." She passed away in 2009.

By the 2012 reunion marking their seventieth anniversary, only six former AVGers remained, and only four of them made it to the reunion in Columbus, Georgia. It was an easy trip for AVG crew chief Frank Losonsky, who had retired to Columbus after a long career with General Motors' Allison Division. He grew old with his wife, Nancy—the high school sweetheart he left behind when he joined the AVG and then married when he got back. In his nineties, Losonsky would spend hours at home looking over his wartime diary and old photos of his squadronmates, staring at the faces and trying to recall distant memories. "I just remember that we were doing what we really had to do," he told a reporter.

In September 2016 the Flying Tigers Association hosted its reunion for the seventy-fifth anniversary in Atlanta in conjunction with the Commemorative Air Force, an organization that maintains World War II–era planes. At ninety-six years old, Losonsky was one of only three living former Tigers, and one of only two who were able to attend. After the war he had spent a few years as a commercial pilot, but he had never achieved his original dream of flying for the army, having failed the physics section of the test for flight school. He had dutifully accepted his career working on planes. Not long before the reunion he got a call asking if he would participate in a special activity there, one that might be a bit risky for a man pushing the century mark. He didn't hesitate to say yes.

On a crisp fall day, Losonsky was driven to the DeKalb-Peachtree Airport. There, poised in front of a large American flag, was a P-40, complete with the shark-nose design and an added rear passenger seat. With the assistance of his son, Frank climbed into the back seat and settled in. The engine roared to life, and the plane sped down the runway and lifted off.

Frank looked out the cockpit and watched as the ground fell away; the runway, people, vehicles, and buildings seemed to disappear below. The plane rose ever higher, reaching the clouds.

"It felt," Frank said, "like I was starting all over again."

Acknowledgments

Writing this book and telling the story of the Flying Tigers has been the privilege of a lifetime, and I am thankful to everyone who made this possible. I am indebted to my grandfather Herman Kleiner for sparking my early interest in World War II as he told me about serving as a navigator on a B-25 in the Pacific. He and my grandmother Barbara Kleiner were invaluable supporters of my interest in history, taking me on countless visits to Fort Nisqually when I visited them in Tacoma. My other grandfather, Otis Miller, taught me about history through his passion for stamp collecting. I am grateful to them all.

I was fortunate to grow up in a family that nurtured my love for history: my parents, Jan and Rick, packed our vacations with visits to museums and battlefields. As a monthly pilgrimage, they'd take me to the used bookstore Bookmans on Campbell Avenue in Tucson and would encourage me to pick up out-of-print tomes on one subject or another. I was lucky to grow up with a sister, and best friend, Emma Kleiner, who shared my love of reading. Thanks also to our family dog, Soda, who provided many years of support and love to us all—we miss her dearly.

I grew up attending great schools in Tucson and then was fortunate to go to Northwestern University, the University of Oxford, and Yale Law School, where I learned from amazing professors. I will never forget my first visit to an archive as part of an American studies course in college—I've been addicted ever since.

I'm grateful to have the best agent in the business, Gail Ross. She saw something in my ruminations about the Flying Tigers long before there was a book. Along with her colleagues Dara Kaye and Howard Yoon, she helped me develop this into a real book project. I was fortunate to have Rick Kot as an editor: he believed in this book even at moments when I struggled to, and he had a real vision for what this story was about. Viking has an incredible team that I was privileged to work with. Assistant Editor Diego Núñez was an invaluable guide on this journey, not only ensuring that the project made it to the finish line, but answering my endless questions along the way. The cover is thanks to the incredible Colin Webber and the layout is thanks to Nancy Resnick. Senior Production Editor Ryan Boyle did a phenomenal job transforming the manuscript into these finished pages. I'm grateful to Jeff Ward for helping to give this far-flung story a sense of place through his cartography. Tony Forde from Viking's publicity team has done a fantastic job of ensuring this story gets told to new audiences. Jane Cavolina was a wonderfully detailed fact-checker and copy editor on this project. I am thankful to Dan Jackson, one of the best historians of the aerial war in China, for reviewing the manuscript. Of course, all errors are my own. Independent editor Tom Shroder was an invaluable colleague in developing the narrative for the book and ensuring that the story was being told in an artful way. Thank you to Grant Giles, for his many years of friendship and for designing the exceptional website. These brief acknowledgments fail to do justice to how much I relied on this team.

As I was working on this book, I had the incredible fortune of being invited to attend the Flying Tigers Association reunions, and I owe a great deal to that incredible group of men and women who are keeping the memory of the Tigers alive. They shared documents and photographs that allowed me to bring this story to life. Having the privilege to deliver the keynote to their 2017 reunion was one of the highlights of the book-writing process. I could go on for pages to thank each and every individual I met through these reunions and other relatives of the Tigers who helped me along this journey, but I wanted to mention a few: Billy McDonald III, Ed Boyd and the Harrington family, Reagan Schaupp, Edward Reed, Janet Alford, Lou Hoffman, Jr., Brad Smith, Ed and Nancy Stiles, Amelia Smith Lucas, Shiela and George Irwin, Audrey C. Smith, Tripp Alyn, Nancy and Mike Engle, Lydia Rossi,

Ward Boyce, Lee and Michelle Clouthier, Keith Lee, and Joseph W. H. Mott. I'm especially grateful to Frank Losonsky, the last surviving Tiger, and his son Terry Losonsky. I had the privilege of interviewing Frank at the 2015 reunion, and when Terry started to tell me that we were discussing aspects of the Flying Tigers that "Pops" had never mentioned before, I knew that I had to write this book. Nell Calloway, the director of the Chennault Aviation and Military Museum, shared a great deal about her grandfather and was a major believer in telling this story. I'm thankful to Cynthia and Anna Chennault, as well as Roger Waddell, for providing access to the papers at the Chennault Foundation. These individuals, and many more, helped me to envision this tale as one that involved real people and drove me to tell the human story of the Flying Tigers. I am also indebted to the other World War II veterans who were gracious enough to tell me about their experiences: Chuck Baisden (who was an armorer in the AVG), Abe Schumer (who was stationed in India), Paul Crawford (who was shot down in China) and Fiske Hanley (who was imprisoned at Omori). I want to thank the many archivists who helped to make researching this history a joy, especially the staffs at the Yale Divinity School, Winter Garden Heritage Foundation, Grand Valley State University, and the San Diego Air & Space Museum.

I am fortunate to have wonderful colleagues at Boies Schiller Flexner LLP, and I am grateful for their support as I completed this book.

Lastly, I couldn't have finished this book without Laura Temel. Even when our dining table was covered with notes and every surface in our apartment was overflowing with volumes on World War II, she was excited about this project, and that meant everything to me. Laura, I am lucky to have you as a partner—not only on this book, but also in life.

Notes

Introduction

1 fifty-five thousand football fans: Steve Twomey, *Countdown to Pearl Harbor: The Twelve Days to the Attack* (New York: Simon & Schuster, 2016), 284.

1 "There was a sudden, startled buzz": Tommy Holmes, "Giants Champ in East But Not in Brooklyn!," *Brooklyn Daily Eagle*, December 8, 1941, 15.

2 HAVOC IN HONOLULU: "Havoc in Honolulu," *Time*, December 29, 1941, 15.

2 A hangar at the army's Hickam Field: Ibid.

2 INVASION OF THE U.S.?: "Invasion of the U.S.?," ibid., 18.

2 "plants, aircraft factories": "Big Man, Big Job," ibid., 48.

2 "At forest-fire lookout towers": "The West at War," Ibid., 9.

2 "the dusty remnants": Ibid., 10.

2 "Last week ten Japanese bombers": "Blood for the Tigers," ibid., 19.

3 "A hundred American": Clare Boothe, "Life's Reports: The A.V.G. Ends Its Famous Career," *Life*, July 20, 1942, 7.

3 "a movie director would reject": "20 for 1," *Time*, April 6, 1942, 20.

Chapter 1: Dancing in the Sky

5 a modest abode: Martha Byrd, *Chennault: Giving Wings to the Tiger* (Tuscaloosa, AL: University of Alabama Press, 1987), 9; Ernest M. Chennault, National Register of Historic Places Inventory—Nomination Form, Chennault House, May 23, 1983.

5 "roaming the oak woods": Claire Chennault, *Way of a Fighter: The Memoirs of Claire Lee Chennault*, ed. Robert Hotz (New York: G. P. Putnam's Sons, 1949), 3.

5 Tensas River basin: William Smith, "Claire Lee Chennault: The Louisiana Years," *Louisiana History: Journal of the Louisiana Historical Association* 29, no. 1 (Winter 1998): 51.

5 frying catfish and bream: Chennault, *Way of a Fighter*, 4; Byrd, *Chennault*, 9–10.

5 one of his favorite books: Byrd, *Chennault*, 12.

6 The woods were always: Smith, "Claire Lee Chennault: The Louisiana Years," 51.

6 "Although I had no idea": Chennault, *Way of a Fighter*, 5.

6 descendant of General Robert E. Lee: Smith, "Claire Lee Chennault: The Louisiana Years," 50.

6 signed up for ROTC training: Ibid., 51–52.

6 "I continued to walk my post": Chennault, *Way of a Fighter*, 6.

6 He racked up forty demerits: Byrd, *Chennault*, 13.

6 "you will never make a soldier": Chennault, *Way of a Fighter*, 7.

7 "trying to eke a living": Ibid., 30.

7 infestation of boll weevils: Byrd, *Chennault*, 14.

7 "The future seemed": Chennault, *Way of a Fighter*, 7.

7 state's agricultural traditions: "Fine Weather and Large Crowd Mark Second Day of State Fair," *Shreveport Times*, November 4, 1910, 1.

7 "Last Days of Pompeii": Ibid.

7 few Americans had actually seen: The first air shows in Louisiana were held in January 1910.

7 "astonish the people": "A Trial Flight by Airship Yesterday," *Shreveport Times*, November 2, 1910, 7.

7 "like a duck": "Aeroplane Fell with a Smash," *Shreveport Times*, November 4, 1910, 1.

7 Vaughn "stepped out": Ibid.

7 machine would be ready: "Aviator Comes Tumbling Down," *Times-Democrat* (New Orleans), November 4, 1910, 10.

7 "Sunday was a big day": "Big Day at Fair," ibid., November 7, 1910, 13.

8 "the sky was perfectly clear": "State Fair Visitors Have a Perfect Day," *Shreveport Times*, November 7, 1910, 1; Smith, "Claire Lee Chennault: The Louisiana Years," 49.

8 "the whir of the engine": Ibid.

8 "eyes were strained": Ibid.

8 "a new frontier": Chennault, *Way of a Fighter*, 7.

8 the end of the disciplinary problem: Byrd, *Chennault*, 15.

8 "annual crop of oversize farm boys": Chennault, *Way of a Fighter*, 7.

9 "like any other graduation": Keith Ayling, *Old Leatherface of the Flying Tigers: The Story of General Chennault* (New York: Bobbs-Merrill, 1945), 38.

9 "impressed by her independence": Byrd, *Chennault*, 15.

9 he and Nell were wed: There is some disagreement over Claire Chennault's birthday, but I'm using the generally recognized date of September 6, 1893. Nell Chennault was older than Claire, born on January 11, 1893.

9 moved to New Orleans: Smith, "Claire Lee Chennault: The Louisiana Years," 53.

9 YMCA in Louisville: Ibid.

9 He rented the attic: "Chennault, Famed 'Tiger' Chief, Once Lived in Akron Attic Rooms," *Akron Beacon Journal*, September 9, 1945, 4.

10 the balloon-production line: Anna Chennault, *Chennault and the Flying Tigers* (New York: Paul S. Eriksson, 1963), 24–25; "Press Writer Flies in Uncle Sam's First 'Blimp,'" *Binghamton Press*, July 30, 1917, 2.

10 fifteen dollars a week rent: "Chennault, Famed 'Tiger' Chief, Once Lived in Akron Attic Rooms," *Akron Beacon Journal*.

10 "energetic and forceful": "Sky Pilots Are Needed by Sam," *Daily Commonwealth* (Mississippi), November 9, 1917, 1.

10 "quick, and determined": Hiram Bingham, *An Explorer in the Air Service* (New Haven, CT: Yale University Press, 1920), 17.

10 Ivy League campuses: Samuel Hynes, *The Unsubstantial Air: American Fliers in the First World War* (New York: Farrar, Straus & Giroux, 2014), 21.

10 "Applicant does not possess": Chennault, *Way of a Fighter*, 7.

11 Kelly Field, where the army was training: Ibid., 8–9.

11 "the roar of their motors: Ayling, *Old Leatherface*, 43.

11 an unauthorized lesson: Ibid.

11 "jumped in and": Chennault, *Way of a Fighter*, 8.

11 still an infantryman: Ibid., 10.

11 "hit me hard": Ibid., 9.

11 "isn't dead yet": Ibid.

12 he applied again: Ibid., 10.

12 "kaleidoscope of sky": Ibid., 10–11.

12 "like a Tensas River bass": Ibid., 10. Chennault notes a brief discharge during this period; he returned to Louisiana to await his regular commission.

12 "I had the taste": Ibid., 11.

12 Twelfth Observation Squadron: Smith, "Claire Lee Chennault: The Louisiana Years," 55–56.

12 "He made time": Ibid., 56.

13 "Spectators gasped as the runaway plane": John W. Zischang, Letter to the Editor, "'Grandma' Chennault," *Life*, August 3, 1942, 4.

13 "a boy with his first love": Chennault, *Way of a Fighter*, 13.

13 "best fighter-pilot tradition": Ibid.

14 "Our team was picked": Ibid., 25.

14 "the outstanding thrill producers": "Miami Air Race Interest Rises," *Miami News*, December 26, 1934, 17.

14 "Wrigley's the best": William C. McDonald III and Barbara L. Evenson, *The Shadow Tiger: Billy McDonald, Wingman to Chennault* (Birmingham, AL: Shadow Tiger Press, 2016), 41.

14 "It is true that": David. F. Kerby, "Jests for Fun," *Popular Aviation*, March 1935, 186.

14 with five hundred planes: "Fastest Planes en Route Here for Air Races," *Miami Daily News*, January 9, 1935, 1.

15 Miamians paid sixty cents: "Starting Tomorrow, Air Races," *Miami Daily News*, January 9, 1935, 22.

15 "thrills of a lifetime": Ibid.

15 the municipal airport: Reginald M. Cleveland, "Army Air Armada Opens Miami Meet," *New York Times*, January 11, 1935, 11.

15 contingent of Chinese officers: Anthony R. Carrozza, *William D. Pawley: The Extraordinary Life of the Adventurer, Entrepreneur, and Diplomat Who Cofounded the Flying Tigers* (Washington, D.C.: Potomac Books, 2012), 39–40.

15 There would be parachutists: "Aviation Meet Closes Today with Big Show," *Miami Daily News*, January 12, 1935, 1–2.

15 "wing tips seemed to overlap": Reginald M. Cleveland, "Army Air Armada Opens Miami Meet," *New York Times*.

15 "a perfection that seemed": Ibid.

15 "Indiana Jones and Donald Trump": Carrozza, *William D. Pawley*, 6.

16 "a young country": "Chinese Air Chief Finds Things 'Just Lovely' in Miami Area," *Miami Daily News*, January 9, 1935, 11.

16 Some formed the Kościuszko Squadron: William M. Smith, "Mercenary Eagles: American Pilots Serving in Foreign Air Forces Prior to United States Entry into the Second World War 1936–1941" (PhD diss., University of Arkansas, May 1999), 45.

16 turned them down: Chennault, *Way of a Fighter*, 17; Smith, "Claire Lee Chennault: The Louisiana Years," 58.

16 "You will hear": "Denied Commissions in Air Corps Williamson and McDonald, Flying Trapezers, Are on Way to China," *Index-Journal* (South Carolina), July 12, 1936, 12.

16 bombers were the future: Carrozza, *William D. Pawley*, 39.

16 "the bomber will always get through": Stephen L. McFarland and Wesley Phillips Newton, *To Command the Sky: The Battle for Air Superiority Over Europe, 1942–1944* (Tuscaloosa, AL: University of Alabama Press, 1991), 24–25.

17 aerial finesse as "convincing proof": Chennault, *Way of a Fighter*, 26.

17 "Who is this damned fellow": Jack Samson, *The Flying Tiger: The True Story of Claire Lee Chennault and the U.S. 14th Air Force in China* (Guilford, CT: Lyons Press, 2012), 11.

17 "The personal battles": Smith, "Claire Lee Chennault: The Louisiana Years," 60.

17 irritated his lungs: Ibid, 61.

17 diet of raw liver: Chennault, *Way of a Fighter*, 29.

17 "Lying on a hospital bed": Ibid., 30.

17 "When you're thwarted": Smith, "Claire Lee Chennault: The Louisiana Years," 62–63.

17 a personal rebuke: Chennault, *Way of a Fighter*, 30.

18 embark on an adventure: McDonald and Evenson, *Shadow Tiger*, 41.

18 going to see his family: "John 'Henry' Luke Williamson," South Carolina Aviation Association, scaaonline.com/?hall-of-fame=john-henry-luke-williamson.

18 "the busiest place": Sebie Smith with Thayne Redfort Short, "My Quest to Fly: Memories and Photographs of My Experiences with the American and Chinese Air Force" (unpublished manuscript, courtesy of Amelia Smith Lucas), 89.

18 From their new home: Ibid., 108.

18 Fourth of July celebration: Ibid., 116.

19 "the successive flybys": Ibid., 117.

19 "the ships came roaring": Ibid.

19 a suitable pilot: McDonald and Evenson, *Shadow Tiger*, 67.

19 a survey of the Chinese Air Force: Chennault, *Way of a Fighter*, 31.

19 at a thousand dollars a month: Ibid.

19 "hundreds of years": Claire Chennault, letter to Bill Chennault, March 15, 1937, Chennault Aviation and Military Museum, Monroe, Louisiana (hereafter "Chennault Museum").

20 "whip h[ell] out of Japan": Ibid.

20 She would sit on the front: McDonald and Evenson, *Shadow Tiger*, 27.

20 outside of Birmingham, Alabama: Ibid.

20 being "sucked under": Chennault, *Way of a Fighter*, 30.

20 on the children: Byrd, *Chennault*, 63.

20 send to college: Ibid., 64.

20 be gone long: It's still unclear whether this was initially just a three-month contract, as Chennault described it, or whether it was intended as a longer two-year contract. Byrd, *Chennault*, 63.

20 "to prove his theories": Smith, "Claire Lee Chennault: The Louisiana Years," 62.

20 longer two-year contract: Byrd, *Chennault*, 61.

20 farm in rural Louisiana: Chennault, *Way of a Fighter*, 31.

20 a town called Waterproof: "Life Goes Calling on Mrs. Chennault," *Life*, March 15, 1943, 98.

20–21 "ill several months": "Army Officer to Be Retired," *Shreveport Times*, March 13, 1937, 2.

21 May 1 for San Francisco: Chennault, *Way of a Fighter*, 31.

21 "a compulsion to go": Byrd, *Chennault*, 63.

21 the "great adventure": Diary of Claire Lee Chennault, May 8, 1937, Chennault Foundation, Washington, D.C. (hereafter "CLC Diary").

Chapter 2: Meeting the Princess

22 "showers, wind and considerable sea": CLC Diary, May 8, 1937; Jack Samson, *The Flying Tiger: The True Story of Claire Lee Chennault and the U.S. 14th Air Force in China* (Guilford, CT: Lyons Press, 2012), 3.

22 his actual mission: Samson, *Flying Tiger*, 5.

22 "working on my plans": CLC Diary, May 10, 1937.

22 "voyage continues uneventfully": Ibid., May 9, 1937.

22 "uniformly uninteresting": Ibid.

22 "Tried to dance": Ibid., May 13, 1937.

22 Alexander Young Hotel: Ibid., May 15, 1937.

23 an old fraternity brother: William C. McDonald III and Barbara L. Evenson, *The Shadow Tiger: Billy McDonald, Wingman to Chennault* (Birmingham, AL: Shadow Tiger Press, 2016), 73.

23 Japan's rapid industrialization: Claire Chennault, *Way of a Fighter: The Memoirs of Claire Lee Chennault*, ed. Robert Hotz (New York: G. P. Putnam's Sons, 1949), 32.

23 "Industry seemed to be expanding": Ibid.

23 find the country "very attractive": CLC Diary, May 28, 1937.

23 its "beautiful scenery": Ibid., May 29, 1937.

23 this new land fascinated him: Samson, *Flying Tiger*, 15.

23 "the weather was perfect": Sebie Smith with Thayne Redfort Short, "My Quest to Fly: Memories and Photographs of My Experiences with the American and Chinese Air Forces" (unpublished manuscript), 156–57.

23–24 "At last I am in China": CLC Diary, May 31, 1937.

24 Holbrook was an American: Ibid., June 3, 1937; Anthony R. Carrozza, *William D. Pawley: The Extraordinary Life of the Adventurer, Entrepreneur, and Diplomat Who Cofounded the Flying Tigers* (Washington, D.C.: Potomac Books, 2012), 37.

24 "Madame Chiang, may I present": Chennault, *Way of a Fighter*, 34.

24 "I am a southerner": Barbara A. Brannon, "China's Soong Sisters at Wesleyan," *Wesleyan Magazine*, Fall 1997, www.wesleyancollege.edu/about/soongsisters-home.cfm.

24 Tau Zeta Epsilon: Laura Tyson Li, *Madame Chiang Kai-shek: China's Eternal First Lady* (New York: Atlantic Monthly Press, 2006), 37.

24 After graduation and a tearful: Ibid., 41.

25 she "loved power": Ibid., 1.

25 "When we need a friend": Ibid., 77.

25 first meeting with Chennault: Chennault, *Way of a Fighter,* 35.

25 As secretary general: Li, *Madame Chiang Kai-Shek,* 133–34.

26 "I reckon you and I": Hannah Pakula, *The Last Empress: Madame Chiang Kai-shek and the Birth of Modern China* (New York: Simon & Schuster, 2009), 284.

26 "a princess to me": CLC Diary, June 3, 1937.

26 "I never recovered": Chennault, *Way of a Fighter,* 35.

26 six hundred aircraft: Rana Mitter, *Forgotten Ally: China's World War II, 1937–1945* (New York: Houghton Mifflin Harcourt, 2013), 178.

26 like those in Rome: "Italians Man China Bombers," *Daily Boston Globe,* May 30, 1937, B5.

26 Colonel P. Y. Shu: McDonald and Evenson, *Shadow Tiger,* 77.

26 "felt good to be in the air": Chennault, *Way of a Fighter,* 35.

27 "really China below": Ibid.

27 "roared through the streets": Ibid., 37.

27 "to sabotage China": Ibid.

27 "glad we did not have motor trouble": McDonald and Evenson, *Shadow Tiger,* 77.

27 "Am appalled by situation": CLC Diary, June 25, 1937.

27 "2000 years old here": McDonald and Evenson, *Shadow Tiger,* 79.

28 It took a couple of days: It wasn't immediately clear that this was going to develop into a full-scale war. McDonald and Evenson, *Shadow Tiger,* 86.

28 "never run from a fight": Chennault, *Way of a Fighter,* 39

28 "acid test in combat": Ibid.

28 "services gratefully accepted": Ibid.

28 gasping for air: Ibid.

28 "is terribly unprepared": CLC Diary, July 19, 1937.

28 he and Mow drank cold beer: Chennault, *Way of a Fighter,* 39.

28 "the Generalissimo turned to Mow": Ibid., 40.

29 "The Generalissimo has threatened": Ibid., 41.

29 "shortness of temper": Alden Whitman, "The Life of Chiang Kai-shek: A Leader Who Was Thrust Aside by Revolution," *New York Times,* April 6, 1975, 6.

29 "Chiang's temper was": Pakula, *The Last Empress,* 384.

29 "figures are correct": Chennault, *Way of a Fighter,* 41.

29 "laid the foundation": Ibid.

29 just an observer: In addition to these meetings, Chennault describes the myriad number of responsibilities and travels he had during this early period of the war. Chennault, *Way of a Fighter,* 42–44.

29 "We will fight": Ibid., 44.

29 eight-inch and six-inch guns: Peter Harmsen, *Shanghai 1937: Stalingrad on the Yangtze* (Havertown, PA: Casemate Publishers, 2013), 45.

30 "poring over maps": Chennault, *Way of a Fighter,* 45.

30 "playing for keeps": Ibid.

30 "Technique poor, Dive shallow": Diary of William McDonald, July 30, 1937. Transcript provided from the personal collection of William C. McDonald III, Birmingham, AL (hereafter "McDonald Diary").

30 "The [Chinese] attackers": "Chinese Bomb Japanese Flagship in Air Raids in Heart of Shanghai; Chapei Set Afire by Artillery Duel," *New York Herald Tribune*, August 14, 1937, 1a.

30 "one of the most frightful holocausts": John R. Morris, "Dead Litter Streets in Shanghai Building," *Los Angeles Times*, April 15, 1937, 2.

30 The dead numbered over: Harmsen, *Shanghai 1937*, 62.

Chapter 3: The Rape of Nanking

31 "might have been a boardinghouse": Carl Randau and Leane Zugsmith, *The Setting Sun of Japan* (New York: Random House, 1942), 144.

31 "It was still inconceivable": Sebie Smith with Thayne Redfort Short, "My Quest to Fly: Memories and Photographs of My Experiences with the American and Chinese Air Forces" (unpublished manuscript), 213.

31 "Sharp machine-gun reports": Ibid., 214.

31 Chennault ran toward a dugout: Jack Samson, *The Flying Tiger: The True Story of Claire Lee Chennault and the U.S. 14th Air Force in China* (Guilford, CT: Lyons Press, 2012), 31.

31 "funeral on a large scale": Iris Chang, *The Rape of Nanking: The Forgotten Holocaust of World War II* (New York: Basic Books, 2011), 65.

32 "Water and mountain provided": Ibid., 62.

32 "a bristling ring": "Nanking Defense," *South China Morning Post*, August 14, 1937, 14.

32 the roofs themselves painted gray: "Nanking's Air Defense Steps Are Inspected," *China Press*, August 12, 1937, 2.

32 "get louder and louder": Smith, *Quest to Fly*, 220.

32 "The sound of whining": Ibid., 221.

32 "Who will it be this time?": "Reminiscences of Sebie Biggs Smith: Oral History, 1981," Columbia University Oral History Research Office Collection, Columbia University, New York, 79.

32 "terribly handicapped by": William Wade Watson, ed., *High Water, High Cotton and High Times* (Pittsburgh, PA: Dorrance Publishing, 2007), 133.

32 organize a "warning net": Ray Wagner, *Prelude to Pearl Harbor: The Air War in China, 1937–1941* (San Diego, CA: San Diego Aerospace Museum, 1991), 9; Claire Chennault, *Way of a Fighter: The Memoirs of Claire Lee Chennault*, ed. Robert Hotz (New York: G. P. Putnam's Sons, 1949), 39.

33 incredible 1,250 miles: Peter C. Smith, *Dive Bomber!: Aircraft, Technology and Tactics in World War II* (Mechanicsburg, PA: Stackpole Books, 1982), 132.

33 they were vulnerable: Mark Peattie, *Sunburst: The Rise of Japanese Naval Air Power, 1909–1941* (Annapolis, MD: Naval Institute Press, 2001), 109–10.

33 If a few Chinese fighters: Martha Byrd, *Chennault: Giving Wings to the Tiger* (Tuscaloosa, AL: University of Alabama Press, 1987), 77.

33 "all the tricks I've learned": Watson, *High Water*, 133.

33 "The Japanese can't survive": Smith, *Quest to Fly*, 236.

33 "The Jap has the upper hand": William C. McDonald III and Barbara L. Evenson, *The Shadow Tiger: Billy McDonald, Wingman to Chennault* (Birmingham, AL: Shadow Tiger Press, 2016), 117.

33 "the Chinese pilots swarmed": Royal Leonard, *I Flew for China* (Garden City, NY: Doubleday, Doran, 1942), 178.

33 One of them, Arthur Chin: Chris Dickon, *Americans at War in Foreign Forces: A History, 1915–1945* (Jefferson, NC: McFarland & Company, 2014), 133.

34 "Sir, can I have": Chennault, *Way of a Fighter*, 68.

34 "wine-shops, steaming noodle vendors": Ibid., 55.

34 "China will not": "China Will Not Be Cowed," *China Press*, September 25, 1937, 4.

34 "Bad weather," McDonald wrote: McDonald Diary, September 24, 1937.

34 "the most terrible air raid": "Air-Raid Plans," *The Age* (Melbourne, Australia), September 22, 1937, 13.

34 pair of thousand-pound bombs: Minnie Vaughn, *Terror in Minnie Vautrin's Nanjing: Diaries and Correspondence, 1937–1938,* ed. Suping Lu (Urbana, IL: University of Illinois Press, 2008), 21.

34 "gallons of civilian blood": Peter Harmsen, *Nanjing 1937: Battle for a Doomed City* (Havertown, PA: Casemate Publishers, 2015), 61.

34 "fight to the last man": McDonald Diary, September 25, 1937.

34 "What time do you think": McDonald and Evenson, *Shadow Tiger,* 116.

34 he had soiled: Smith, *Quest to Fly,* 231.

35 "Our visit to the shop": McDonald Diary, September 28, 1937.

35 "How wonderful it would be": Smith, *Quest to Fly,* 239.

35 "Only a few planes left": McDonald Diary, September 23, 1937.

35 The "lack of equipment": Ibid., September 29, 1937.

35 "the end of its rope": Chennault, *Way of a Fighter,* 59.

35 watch the battle unfold: Harold J. Timperly, "Mme. Chiang Making Air Defense Plan," *Hartford Courant,* September 3, 1937, 8.

35 "five out of eleven planes": Chennault, *Way of a Fighter,* 55.

35 "What can we do": Ibid.

35 Chennault prepared to get: There is uncertainty about whether Chennault actually participated in conflict in this period. Chennault always denied it. For further discussion, see McDonald and Evenson, *Shadow Tiger,* 96–105.

35 He stripped the plane: Chennault, *Way of a Fighter,* 57.

36 "spotted troop movements": Ibid., 59.

36 "get some guns": Chennault claims that he flew an observation flight after the *Izumo* raid. Chennault, *Way of a Fighter,* 46.

36 "mystery surrounded his activities": "Mystery Surrounding Louisiana's Activities," *Weekly Town Talk* (Alexandria, Louisiana), July 31, 1937, 1.

36 "Colonel Chennault, retired": U.S. Department of State, *Foreign Relations of the United States, Diplomatic Papers 1937, Vol. III: The Far East* (Washington, D.C.: Government Printing Office, 1954), 406.

36 "round-shouldered from a life": John Paton Davies, Jr., *China Hand: An Autobiography* (Philadelphia: University of Pennsylvania Press, 2012), 22.

36 Hirota gave a speech: "Jap Official Cites Reports," *Des Moines Tribune,* August 6, 1937, 5.

36 Secretary of State Cordell Hull: Guangqiu Xu, "The Eagle and the Dragon's War Wings: The United States and Chinese military Aviation, 1929–1940" (PhD diss., University of Maryland College Park, 1993), 263.

36 "This passport is not valid": Ibid.

37 "intimated a court-martial": Chennault, *Way of a Fighter*, 51.

37 Fifteen of the civilian pilots: Ibid., 52; Crouch, "Fleeing Shanghai, August 1937," author's website, August 20, 2013. http://gregcrouch.com/2013/aug-1937 -bixbys-last-ditch-effort.

37 Luke Williamson left: Chennault, *Way of a Fighter*, 52.

37 "Though so far away": Watson, *High Water*, 133.

37 "baseball progress, motorcycle maintenance": Smith, *Quest to Fly*, 287.

37 "Guess I am Chinese": CLC Diary, September 21, 1937.

37 "All my life": Chennault, *Way of a Fighter*, 53.

37 "of all the Pacific nations": Ibid., 52.

37 what was to come: F. Tillman Durdin, "Japanese Atrocities Marked Fall of Nanking After Chinese Commander Fled," *New York Times*, January 9, 1938, 38; Harmsen, *Nanjing 1937*, 51.

38 "We cannot abandon Nanking!": Harmsen, *Nanjing 1937*, 155.

38 "It was impossible to find": Ibid., 109.

38 The Chiangs fled: Ibid.

38 "apologized, more or less": Smith, *Quest to Fly*, 258.

38 "final warning to all Americans": "Embassy of the United States of America," December 2, 1937, "Circular to All Americans in Nanking," The Nanking Massacre Archival Project, Yale University Library, divinity-adhoc.library .yale.edu/Nanking/Images/NMP0130.pdf.

38 American journalists packed their bags: Norman Alley, *I Witness* (New York: W. Funk, 1941), 245.

38 "go to hell if you must": Ibid., 230.

38 Before dawn on December 4: This is the date according to Smith; Chennault doesn't date their departure. Smith, *Quest to Fly*, 262.

38 fire was too close for comfort: Ibid., 263.

39 "prophetic bloody red": Chennault, *Way of a Fighter*, 60.

39 the ensuing bloodshed: Durdin, "Japanese Atrocities Marked Fall of Nanking After Chinese Commander Fled."

39 Minnie Vautrin, an American missionary: Vautrin, *Terror in Minnie Vautrin's Nanjing*, xxiv.

39 A soldier slapped her: Ibid., xxv.

39 "Tonight a truck passed": Ibid., 137.

39 "raping a poor girl": Ibid., 87. She describes how in this instance she was able to get the soldiers to leave.

39 called "sexual torture": Chang, *The Rape of Nanking*, 95.

39 "The Japanese drew sadistic pleasure": Ibid.

39 unleashed German shepherds: Ibid., 88.

40 massive Nazi flag: Ibid., 114.

40 Rabe put on his Nazi armband: Ibid., 120.

40 "I saw the victims": Ibid., 119.

40 "the men were lined against a wall": F. Tillman Durdin, "All Captives Slain," *New York Times*, December 18, 1937, 1.

40 "We may have suffered": "Guardian Correspondent Finds China's Leaders Unshaken in Confidence," *China Press*, January, 16, 1938, 1.

40 contend with worsening bronchitis: Claire Chennault letter to John Chennault, March 30, 1938, Chennault Museum.

41 a group of German advisers: "China's German Military Advisers Go Home," *Life*, August 1, 1938, 18.

41 instructing China's soldiers: "German General Still Aiding China," *New York Times*, May 20, 1938, 12.

41 "Olive-drab Russian planes": Edward L. Leiser, "Memoirs of Pilot Elwyn H. Gibbon: The Mad Irishman," *Journal of the American Aviation Historical Society* 23, no. 1 (Spring 1978): 6.

41 "Russians enforced iron discipline": Chennault, *Way of a Fighter*, 62.

41 effort to enlist Western pilots: Smith, *Quest to Fly*, 270; Leiser, "Memoirs of Pilot Elwyn H. Gibbon," 4.

41 true "mercenary pilots": Smith, *Quest to Fly*, 270.

41 a "young lad who exhibited": Chennault, *Way of a Fighter*, 70.

41 "I've never flown": Ibid., 71.

42 "Hired abroad at fabulous salaries": Mark J. Ginsbourg, "China's New Wings," *Washington Post*, May 11, 1938, x9.

42 "He has no military training": Leiser, "Memoirs of Pilot Elwyn H. Gibbon," 4.

42 a "valuable man": Ibid.

42 "we are the oddest part": Elwyn Gibbon, "Commuting to War," *Collier's*, November 12, 1938, 72–73.

42 the "Mexican revolutionary war": "Raid on Formosa: Attack Directed by American Aviator Vincent Schmidt," *South China Morning Post*, February 26, 1938, 15.

42 "fight with the underdog": "Raider?," *Daily Review* (California), March 3, 1938, 7.

Chapter 4: The International Squadron

43 "not a sound was heard": "First Air Raid Since Removal of Seat of Government," *China Press*, January 5, 1938, 1.

43 "I keep my foot on the gas": Elwyn Gibbon, "Combat" (unpublished essay), Elwyn H. Gibbon Collection, San Diego Air and Space Museum (hereafter SD Gibbon Collection), 2. Gibbon doesn't provide a specific date for this but it is apparent that this is on January 4 because he refers to the death of "the German" and Kreuzberg (who was American though known as "the German") was killed during that raid.

43 "the motor catches": Ibid., 4.

44 "red rising suns": Ibid., 7.

44 "I looked through": Ibid., 8.

44 "as though some giant": Ibid., 9.

44 "I climb out": Ibid., 11.

45 "I think I got one": Ibid.

45 "believed he was shot down": "American Flier Killed," *New York Times*, January 7, 1938, 11.

45 "Foreign pilots have become": "Foreign Pilots Aid Chinese in Defense Against Japanese Air Raids," *China Weekly Review*, February 5, 1938, 274.

45 "I can't really believe": Elwyn Gibbon, "Commuting to War," *Collier's*, November 12, 1938, 71.

45 "crazy kind of fear": Ibid., 72.

45 "I've been scared green": Ibid.

45 **"each burst of noise"**: Toni Gibbon letter to "Bobby," August 30, 1938, SD Gibbon Collection. This letter was sent after Gibbons returned to Seattle.

46 **"unpleasant things might happen"**: Gibbon, "Commuting to War," *Collier's,* November 12, 1938, 44.

46 **"modern war being waged"**: Ibid., 71.

46 **"Swing music is an anticlimax"**: Ibid.

46 **"refused to pay the prize"**: "Parting Shot: American Flier Unburdens Himself," *South China Morning Post,* April 20, 1938, 15.

46 **"on high-octane beverages"**: Claire Chennault, *Way of a Fighter: The Memoirs of Claire Lee Chennault,* ed. Robert Hotz (New York: G. P. Putnam's Sons, 1949), 71.

47 **"farming and country life"**: Claire Chennault letter to John Chennault, March 30, 1938, Chennault Museum.

47 **Canadian passenger liner**: Edward L. Leiser, "Memoirs of Pilot Elwyn H. Gibbon: The Mad Irishman," *Journal of the American Aviation Historical Society* 23, no. 1 (Spring 1978): 12. Some accounts have this ship as the *Empress of India,* others the *Empress of Asia.*

47 **"foreign legion of the air"**: "Foreign Legion of Air Disbanded by China," *New York Times,* March 24, 1938, 14.

47 **The Japanese police seemed**: "New Yorker Questioned by Japanese for 3 Hours," *New York Herald Tribune,* April 23, 1938, 5.

47 AMERICAN IS HELD: "American Is Held in Japanese Jail," *New York Times*, April 24, 1938, 33.

47 **eight by twelve feet**: "Elwyn Gibbon Finds That Japanese Jails Are Not So Bad, at Least at Yokohama," unidentified newspaper article, SD Gibbon Collection.

48 **fought for an enemy power**: "Japan Holds American," *New York Times,* April 23, 1938, 7.

48 **"my number was up"**: "Gibbon Tells of Torture," *Alton Evening Telegraph* (Illinois), May 19, 1938, 1–2.

48 **"ELWYN TAKEN BY JAPS"**: Leiser, "Memoirs of Pilot Elwyn H. Gibbon," 12.

48 **"high authorities advised against"**: "Japan May Free Flyer," *Des Moines Tribune,* April 26, 1938, 11.

48 **just as anxious**: "Japanese Continue to Question Gibbon," *New York Times,* April 25, 1938, 5.

48 **no charges be filed**: According to Leiser, the Tokyo Court of Appeals dismissed the case.

48 **happy to see him go**: "U.S. Flier Jailed by Japan Arrives on President Taft," *Honolulu Advertiser,* May 12, 1938, 7.

48 **"merciless in their grilling"**: "Gibbon Tells of Torture," *Alton Evening Telegraph.*

48 **"I better not say"**: "U.S. Flier Jailed by Japan Arrives on President Taft," *Honolulu Advertiser.*

49 **"I'll count you in"**: Leiser, "Memoirs of Pilot Elwyn H. Gibbon," 14.

49 **"I feel sure"**: "Falkenhausen Says China Will Gain Final Victory," *New York Herald Tribune,* July 6, 1938, 2.

49 Von Falkenhausen bent down: "China's German Military Advisers Go Home," *Life,* August 1, 1938, 18.

49 let the player know: Paul Frillmann and Graham Peck, *China: The Remembered Life* (Boston: Houghton Mifflin Company, 1968), 19.

49 to go to Kunming: Chennault, *Way of a Fighter,* 73.

50 "the seemingly hopeless task": Ibid.

50 the floodwaters killed: Rana Mitter, *Forgotten Ally: China's World War II, 1937–1945* (New York: Houghton Mifflin Harcourt, 2013), 163.

50 on October 24: "Chiang Escapes Hankow as Foe Enters Suburbs," *New York Herald Tribune,* October 25, 1938, 1. For further description of the evacuation, see Mitter, *Forgotten Ally,* 163.

50 "several cases of rape": "Hankow Outrages," *South China Morning Post,* November 8, 1938, 12.

50 he roamed the outer walls: Frillmann, *China,* 28.

50 "The Japanese have won": Walter Lippmann, "The Foundation of Another Empire," *Washington Post,* October 27, 1938, x11.

51 the Imperial Palace: "Tokyo Celebrates," *South China Morning Post,* October 31, 1938, 16.

51 "is only just beginning": "Chiang Confident," *South China Morning Post,* December 15, 1938.

Chapter 5: Exile in the Chinese Hinterland

52 Chennault's new home, Kunming: Claire Chennault, *Way of a Fighter: The Memoirs of Claire Lee Chennault,* ed. Robert Hotz (New York: G. P. Putnam's Sons, 1949), 73.

52 known as CAMCO: Anthony R. Carrozza, *William D. Pawley: The Extraordinary Life of the Adventurer, Entrepreneur, and Diplomat Who Cofounded the Flying Tigers* (Washington, D.C.: Potomac Books, 2012), 53–54.

53 American and Russian training planes: "Chinese Aviators Train at Kunming," *New York Times,* March 29, 1938, 14.

53 were "below average": CLC Diary, January 30, 1939.

53 "life now is rather tame": William C. McDonald III and Barbara L. Evenson, *The Shadow Tiger: Billy McDonald, Wingman to Chennault* (Birmingham, AL: Shadow Tiger Press, 2016), 156.

53 He played tennis: Chennault, *Way of a Fighter,* 85.

53 "None shot down": CLC Diary, April 8, 1939.

53 "like Canada geese": Chennault, *Way of a Fighter,* 88.

53 "trying to quench": Ibid.

53 "sickeningly sweet stench": Ibid., 89.

53 "many people killed": CLC Diary, May 4, 1939.

54 four thousand people were killed: Rana Mitter, *Forgotten Ally: China's World War II, 1937–1945* (New York: Houghton Mifflin Harcourt, 2013), 4.

54 "the most terrible thing": Ibid.

54 "pieces of burnt flesh": Hannah Pakula, *The Last Empress: Madame Chiang Kai-shek and the Birth of Modern China* (New York: Simon & Schuster, 2009), 354.

54 Chennault's longing for home: Chennault, *Way of a Fighter,* 80.

54 "hair just stood on end": McDonald and Evenson, *Shadow Tiger,* 149.

55 Chennault boarded a Southern Pacific: CLC Diary, October 27, 1939.

55 "Home again," was all he wrote: Ibid., October 31, 1939.

56 working on "contracts": Ibid., April 22, April 25, and May 1, 1939. Chennault discusses working on contracts for more planes, making clear his role as a strategic adviser. The decisions over which planes to buy were contentious. Carrozza, *Pawley*, 55.

56 new advances like: Wayne Thomas, "Curtiss Plants Speed Building of War Planes," *Chicago Daily Tribune*, December 3, 1939, 10.

57 handed over his dossier: Chennault, *Way of a Fighter*, 94.

57 "after the novelty": Jack Samson, *The Flying Tiger: The True Story of Claire Lee Chennault and the U.S. 14th Air Force in China* (Guilford, CT: Lyons Press, 2012), 62.

57 "No doubt [Chennault] was": Martha Byrd, *Chennault: Giving Wings to the Tiger* (Tuscaloosa, AL: University of Alabama Press, 1987), 107.

57 had dinner with Chennault: Ibid., 63.

58 Chennault had affairs: Samson, *Flying Tiger*, 346.

58 "thick columns of smoke": "China Carries On: Madame Chiang's Speech," *China Critic*, August 8, 1940, 89.

58 "enormous black crows": Thomas A. Delong, *Madame Chiang Kai-shek and Miss Emma Mills: China's First Lady and Her American Friend* (Jefferson, NC: McFarland Company, 2007), 134.

58 "I can't win": William Wade Watson, ed., *High Water, High Cotton and High Times* (Pittsburgh, PA: Dorrance Publishing, 2007), 137.

58 "What I like about this job": McDonald and Evenson, *Shadow Tiger*, 173.

59 more than twenty Chinese planes: There are different accounts of the numbers from this battle, though it is regarded as a massive blow to the Chinese Air Force. Craig Nelson, *Pearl Harbor: From Infamy to Greatness* (New York: Simon & Schuster, 2016), 57; Roy M. Stanley, *Prelude to Pearl Harbor: War in China, 1937–41: Japan's Rehearsal for World War II* (New York: Scribner, 1982), 148.

59 the Mitsubishi A6M: For further information on the introduction of the Zero into China in 1940, see Daniel Ford, *Flying Tigers: Claire Chennault and His American Volunteers, 1941–1942* (Washington, D.C.: Smithsonian Institution Press, 1991), 39–41.

59 "American volunteers will be able": U.S. Department of State, *Foreign Relations of the United States, Diplomatic Papers, 1940, Vol. IV, The Far East* (Washington D.C.: Government Printing Office, 1955), 673.

59 "the people's spirit": Ibid., 674.

59 an urgent summons: CLC Diary, October 20–21, 1940.

60 "You must go ": Chennault, *Way of a Fighter*, 90.

60 "Ordered back to the U.S.": CLC Diary, October 21, 1940.

60 "now familiar milestones": Chennault, *Way of a Fighter*, 90.

Chapter 6: An Air Unit for China

61 Chiang's personal representative: Claire Chennault, *Way of a Fighter: The Memoirs of Claire Lee Chennault*, ed. Robert Hotz (New York: G. P. Putnam's Sons, 1949), 91.

61 "The Morgan of China": Hannah Pakula, *The Last Empress: Madame Chiang Kai-shek and the Birth of Modern China* (New York: Simon & Schuster, 2009), 362; James Bradley, *The China Mirage* (New York: Little, Brown, 2015), 148.

61 "elaborate Chinese dinners": Ernest O. Hauser, "China's Soong," *Life*, March 24, 1941, 93.

62 an American pilot would help: Martha Byrd, *Chennault: Giving Wings to the Tiger* (Tuscaloosa, AL: University of Alabama Press, 1987), 106.

62 Chennault laid out his vision: Joseph W. Alsop with Adam Platt, *I've Seen the Best of It* (New York: W. W. Norton, 1992), 147.

62 Alsop initially rejected the idea: Chennault, *Way of a Fighter*, 93.

62 "a charismatic man": Alsop, *I've Seen the Best of It*, 147.

62 need five hundred planes: Joseph Alsop and Robert Kintner, "Powerful Move Afoot to Give China Something More than Goodwill and Occasional Loan," *Daily Boston Globe*, November 19, 1940, 15.

63 "many long and dreary days": Chennault, *Way of a Fighter*, 98.

63 it was clearly his work: Byrd states that "Chennault was without doubt the author of the proposals." Byrd, *Chennault*, 110.

63 "Japanese planes are": Secretary Henry Morgenthau, "Diary: Book 342-A, China: Bombers, December 3–22, 1940," Franklin D. Roosevelt Library, 5, www.fdrlibrary.marist.edu/_resources/images/morg/md0452.pdf (hereafter "Morgenthau Diary 342-A"). This was an unsigned memorandum that T. V. Soong presented to Morgenthau at a meeting on November 30, 1940. Chennault references drafting "strategic plans" along these lines in his memoir. Chennault, *Way of a Fighter*, 97.

63 "in the common struggle": Morgenthau Diary 342-A, 7.

63 "there was no precedent": Chennault, *Way of a Fighter*, 98.

63 "the Chinese nation": Bradley, *China Mirage*, 193.

64 "the idea of sending": Morgenthau Diary 342-A, 2.

64 "asking for 500 planes": Ibid.

64 "I told [Soong] that": Ibid., 2–3.

64 Morgenthau called Roosevelt: Ibid., 12.

64 Roosevelt asked about the German U-boats: Henry Stimson with McGeorge Bundy, *On Active Service in War and Peace* (New York: Harper, 1948), 367.

65 "How about that long distance bomber": Morgenthau Diary 342-A, 18. There is some degree of hearsay about this conversation because this is how Morgenthau recounts the story to Soong.

65 "I have good news": Ibid.

65 Secretary Morgenthau's home: Ibid., 24.

65 "to get some mature brains": Joseph E. Persico, *Roosevelt's Centurions: FDR and the Commanders He Led to Victory in World War II* (New York: Random House, 2013), 146.

66 "questioning the advisability": Morgenthau Diary 342-A, 27.

66 "P-40's for the British": Chennault, *Way of a Fighter*, 100. The British had taken over the French order after the fall of France. No dates are provided for this trip in Chennault's memoir or in his diary.

66 "not an ideal airplane": Ibid.

66 "the Chinese were excited": John Alison, untitled essay in Oliver L. North with Joe Musser, *War Stories II: Heroism in the Pacific* (Washington, D.C.: Regnery Publishing, 2004), 139. See also "Oral History of John Alison," National Museum of the Pacific War, 2004.

66 one hundred of those pilots: Chennault, *Way of a Fighter*, 101–2.

66 was "to protect the Burma Road": Secretary Henry Morgenthau, "Diary: Book 344, January 1–3, 1941," Franklin D. Roosevelt Library, 12, www .fdrlibrary.marist.edu/_resources/images/morg/md0454.pdf (hereafter "Morgenthau Diary 344").

67 Universal Trading Corporation: Universal Trading Corporation was a "Chinese government front" that received funds from the Export-Import Bank based on loans that Secretary Morgenthau had negotiated. Michael Schaller, *The U.S. Crusade in China, 1938–1945* (New York: Columbia University Press, 1979), 25. The question of who "paid for" the planes is thus somewhat ambiguous: the underlying funds were part of American aid to China, but they were now being diverted from economic aid to military aid. For further information on Soong, Universal Trading Corporation, and these diplomatic negotiations, see Tai-chun Kuo and Hsiao-ting Lin, "T. V. Soong in Modern Chinese History: A Look at His Role in Sino-American Relations in World War II" (Stanford, CA: Hoover Institution Press, 2006), 4–17.

67 Roosevelt "hankered after": Joseph E. Persico, *Roosevelt's Secret War: FDR and World War II Espionage* (New York: Random House, 2001), 60.

67 what he called "combat testing": Persico, *Roosevelt's Centurions*, 42.

67 "from a lamp post": This was General Walter Bedell Smith's warning regarding sending 75-mm guns to Great Britain. Doris Kearns Goodwin, *No Ordinary Time: Franklin & Eleanor Roosevelt: The Home Front in World War II* (New York: Simon & Schuster, 1994), 65.

67 "epidemic of world lawlessness": Franklin Roosevelt, "Address at Chicago," October 5, 1937. This was known as the "Quarantine Speech." The public reaction to the speech had been negative and Roosevelt felt he may have gone too far. Robert Dallek, *Franklin D. Roosevelt: A Political Life* (New York: Viking, 2017), 291.

67 "It's a terrible thing": Ibid.

67 Roosevelt was emboldened: Goodwin, *No Ordinary Time*, 191.

67 plausible deniability about the plan: The strategic rationale for the plan was the "plausible deniability" that the United States had committed an act of war. I address this more fully in an article: Sam Kleiner, "Erik Prince's 'New Band of Flying Tigers' Is a Sequel We Don't Need," *Just Security*, September 11, 2017, www.justsecurity.org/44864/erik-princes-new-band-flying-tiger-sequel.

67 "I never saw you": Morgenthau Diary 344, 35.

68 "Maj. General Peter Mow": Ansel. E. Talbert, "China May Get 400 of Newest U.S. Warplanes," *New York Herald Tribune*, December 30, 1940, 1.

68 "endanger the peace": Joseph Newman, "Tokio Says Aid to China Puts U.S. Near War," *New York Herald Tribune*, December 5, 1940, 10.

68 told the story to Roosevelt: Morgenthau Diary 344, 36.

68 "Never before since Jamestown": Franklin D. Roosevelt, Fireside Chat, December 29, 1940, the American Presidency Project, www.presidency.ucsb.edu /ws/index.php?pid=15917.

69 the ship carrying the P-40s departed: Anthony R. Carrozza, *William D. Pawley: The Extraordinary Life of the Adventurer, Entrepreneur, and Diplomat Who Cofounded the Flying Tigers* (Washington, D.C.: Potomac Books, 2012), 76; Daniel Ford, *Flying Tigers: Claire Chennault and the American Volunteer Group* (Washington, D.C.: Smithsonian Institution Press, 1991), 52–53.

69 "were violently opposed": Chennault, *Way of a Fighter,* 101.

69 "couldn't spare a single": Ibid.

69 some other discussion: Pawley had been involved in discussions about this idea "as early as December 1940, but serious recruitment for the AVG did not begin until late March." Byrd, *Chennault,* 117. It appears that Chiang and CAMCO were both pushing similar, if not intertwined, proposals in late 1940 and their strategic and commercial interests would ultimately merge into the AVG when Pawley was tapped as the civilian front for the group. Ibid., 116.

69 "He knew when to flatter": Justin Pritchard, "The Power Broker," *Brown Alumni Magazine,* September/October 1998, www.brownalumnimagazine .com/content/view/1773/40.

69 "Epitaph on an Army": A. E. Housman, "Epitaph on an Army of Mercenaries," in Michael Harrison and Christopher Stuart-Clark, eds, *Peace and War: A Collection of Poems* (Oxford, UK: Oxford University Press, 1989), 88.

69 Corcoran would speculate: Ford, *Flying Tigers,* 54. See Thomas Corcoran, "Rendezvous with Democracy," Thomas Corcoran Papers, Box 586, Library of Congress, Washington, D.C.

70 president "had a tendency": Robert Jackson, *That Man: An Insider's Portrait of Franklin D. Roosevelt,* ed. John Q. Barrett (New York: Oxford University Press, 2003), 74.

70 "unpublicized executive order": Chennault describes an "unpublicized executive order [that] went out under [Roosevelt's] signature" issued on April 15, 1941. Chennault, *Way of a Fighter,* 102.

70 "No such order": Byrd, *Chennault,* 107.

70 "the year's absence": This memo is reproduced in full in Lewis Sherman Bishop and Shiela Bishop Irwin, *Escape from Hell: An AVG Flying Tiger's Journey* (self-published, 2004), 107–8.

70 "advanced training units": Chennault, *Way of a Fighter,* 102.

70 handled through a private company: Byrd, *Chennault,* 116.

70 China Defense Supplies: Pakula, *The Last Empress,* 362–63.

71 "This letter introduces": Frank Beatty, "Memorandum for Commanding Officer, Naval Air Station, Jacksonville," April 14, 1941, National Museum of Naval Aviation, collections.naval.aviation.museum/emuwebdoncoms/objects /common/webmedia.php?irn=16015371.

71 "planned to give each pilot": Chennault, *Way of a Tiger,* 103.

71 "For the past few months": "Convoys to China," *Time,* June 23, 1941, 34.

71 "Holy jumpin' Jesus!": R. T. Smith, *Tale of a Tiger* (Van Nuys, CA: Tiger Originals, 1986), 15.

71 "This screwball outfit": Smith, *Tale of a Tiger,* 16. This description is attributed to Paul Greene.

71 "Occupation: Executive," it said: Claire Chennault Passport, June, 23, 1941, Chennault Family Papers, Louisiana State University (Baton Rouge) Special Collections.

71 approximately fifty pilots: Jennifer Holik with Robert Brouk, *To Soar with the Tigers: The Life and Diary of Flying Tiger, Robert Brouk* (Woodbridge, IL: Generations, 2013), 19.

72 "scarred by razor-sharp lines": "When a Hawk Smiles," *Time,* December 6, 1943, 26. There is no byline on the article but it likely was written by Theodore White.

72   "would be making history": Chennault, *Way of a Fighter*, 104.

72   He brought down a sparrow: "Scarsdale Jack Knew He Would Never Return," *News-Messenger* (Ohio), March 24, 1942, 14.

72   then became a naval aviator: John J. Newkirk, *The Old Man and the Harley* (Nashville, TN: Thomas Nelson, 2008), 16.

72   "My deepest regret": Ibid., 184.

73   one pilot captured the scene: *Fei Hu: The Story of the Flying Tigers*, directed by Frank Christopher (1999; Fei Hu Films), www.flyingtigersvideo.com/about.

73   "standing waving on the pier": Larry M. Pistole, *The Pictorial History of the Flying Tigers* (Orange, VA: Publishers' Press, 1995), 49.

73   "There was no turning back": James H. Howard, *Roar of the Tiger: From Flying Tigers to Mustangs, A Fighter Ace's Memoir* (New York: Pocket Books, 1991), 66.

73   returning their good-bye luncheons: Frank S. Losonsky and Terry M. Losonsky, *Flying Tiger: A Crew Chief's Story* (Atglen, PA: Schiffer Publishing, 1996), 44.

73   "coming home with hands cut": Ibid., 9.

74   "independence, a steady job": Ibid.

74   "the airplane came in": Ibid., 44.

74   "what in the hell": Ibid.

74   "I wasn't motivated: Ibid., 11.

74   "don't recall being nervous": Ibid., 12.

75   "What a lark": Ibid., 15.

75   "interrupted around 11:00": Holik, *To Soar with the Tigers*, 19.

75   "vegetable salad, soup, entrée": Ibid., 20.

75   "it took the greater part": Losonsky, *Flying Tiger: A Crew Chief's Story*, 13.

75   whether it was German or Japanese: Robert M. Smith, *With Chennault in China: A Flying Tiger's Diary* (Blue Ridge, PA: Tab Books, 1984), 18.

75   drank rum collinses: Ibid.

75   stumble into deck chairs: Holik, *To Soar with the Tigers*, 20.

75   evenings having sing-alongs: Losonsky, *Flying Tiger: A Crew Chief's Story*, 15.

75   "I prefer female nurses": Nancy Allison Wright, *Yankee on the Yangtze: Romance and Adventure Follow the Birth of Aviation* (self-published, 2011), 203.

76   she "looked ravishing": Howard, *Roar of the Tiger*, 70.

76   "the most beautiful girl": Ibid., 68.

76   she seemed to turn away: Ibid., 70.

76   "no reason why women can't go": Much of the information on Emma Foster's early life is from her oral history in the Library of Congress. See Emma Jane Foster Hanks Collection (AFC/2001/001/10697), Veterans History Project, American Folklife Center, Library of Congress (hereafter "Foster Oral History, Library of Congress).

76   "so homesick I cried": "Oral History of Emma Jane 'Red' Petach," Fei Hu Films research and production files (RHC-88), Special Collections & University Archives, Grand Valley State University Libraries (hereafter "GVSU Collection" and for consistency Emma's maiden name, Foster, will be used: hereafter the "Foster Oral History"), digitalcollections.library.gvsu.edu/files/original/460b2917fdbfebdc40c28497f39835e1.pdf. (Only some of the GVSU collection has been digitized).

77   "I knew he was right": Ibid.

77 "a strong-hearted man": Ibid.

78 "good-looking gentleman": Ibid.

78 "When you put your foot": Ibid.

78 "Then they greased our bodies": Losonsky, *Flying Tiger: A Crew Chief's Story,* 18.

78 "All had a good time": Ibid.

78 a torrential rain: Howard, *Roar of the Tiger,* 76.

79 "a lean, rangy blonde": Smith, *Tale of a Tiger,* 35.

79 "excitement and adventure": Oral History of David Hill, conducted by Reagan Schaupp, San Antonio, February 2000. Major Schaupp conducted an oral history of Hill (his grandfather) while working on their book, and he has generously shared the edited transcript that he prepared. Direct quotations from Hill are from the oral history. Also see: David Lee "Tex" Hill with Reagan Schaupp, *"Tex" Hill: Flying Tiger* (Spartanburg, SC: The Honoribus Press, 2003).

79 "by the time I was seventeen": Ed Rector Oral History, GVSU Collection, 1.

79 "read everything that Kipling": "Edward Rector; Fighter Ace with 'Flying Tigers,'" *Los Angeles Times,* May 3, 2001.

79 *Scorchy Smith* recounted: *Scorchy Smith* was created by Noel Sickles, who left in 1936; Christman succeeded him.

80 "winged soldiers of fortune": For further information on Christman's background see Andrew Glaess, "Remembering Bert Christman," Warbird Forum, 2014, www.warbirdforum.com/scorchy.htm.

80 "the things he drew": Glaess, "Remembering Bert Christman."

80 "driving us nuts": Smith, *Tale of a Tiger,* 46.

80 had been able to "convert": Ibid., 48.

80 "You would be surprised": George McMillan letter to family, September 6, 1941, Winter Garden Heritage Foundation, Winter Garden, Florida.

80 "rusted metal and grime": Smith, *Tale of a Tiger,* 53.

80 "The cockroaches—My god!!": Oral History of David Hill, National Museum of the Pacific War, 2001.

80 "As the big flying boat": Chennault, *Way of a Fighter,* 104.

81 not for combat: Ibid., 107.

81 a group of AVG mechanics: The first ship to go over transported a group of mechanics led by the chaplain Paul Frillmann. See Paul Frillmann and Graham Peck, *China: The Remembered Life* (Boston: Houghton Mifflin Company, 1968), 49–65.

81 "aid the Chinese Air Force": "U.S. Mechanics Reach Singapore," *New York Times,* July 10, 1941, 3.

81 "whatever American civilians": Chennault, *Way of a Fighter,* 107.

82 "much food and little work": Alsop, *I've Seen the Best of It,* 167.

82 "a real leader": Ibid.

82 "greatest single adventure": Ibid., 150.

82 "looking for an answer": Bruce Gamble, *Black Sheep One: The Life of Gregory "Pappy" Boyington* (New York: Ballantine Books, 2000), 132.

83 "kill a fifth of whiskey": Ibid., 126.

83 The "unofficerlike conduct": Ibid., 126–27.

83 "I drank more than ever": Ibid.

83 "had to account": Gregory Boyington, *Baa Baa Black Sheep* (New York: Bantam Books, 1977), 5.

83   "Where is this recruiting man": Gamble, *Black Sheep One*, 133.

83   "The Japs are flying": Boyington, *Baa Baa Black Sheep*, 4.

84   He was "mentally calculating": Ibid.

84   "Oh, don't worry, Mom": Ibid., 7.

84   "a minimum of ten bars": Ibid., 8.

85   "plastered to the gills": Gamble, *Black Sheep One*, 139.

85   "mingled feeling of sorrow": Susan Clotfelter Jimison, *Through the Eyes of a Tiger: The John Donovan Story* (Athens, GA: Deeks Publishing, 2015), 18.

85   "WATER, WATER, WATER": Ibid., 23.

85   "feeling of mystery": C. Joseph Rosbert, *Flying Tiger Joe's Adventure Story Cookbook* (Franklin, NC: Giant Poplar Press, 1985), 59.

85   "an immense gem": Ibid.

86   "You will be gentlemen": Boyington, *Baa Baa Black Sheep*, 7.

86   dress clothes, golf sticks: Ibid.

86   "My first business": Chennault, *Way of a Fighter*, 109.

86   the men "appeared wilted": Ibid., 110–11.

86   a low voice with a Cajun drawl: Smith, *Tale of a Tiger*, 71.

86   "a man of vision": Rosbert, *Flying Tiger Joe's*, 64–65.

87   "no place for slackers": Howard, *Roar of the Tiger*, 83.

87   to a squadronmate: Ibid.

Chapter 7: Training in Toungoo

88   "Right now—boy": Susan Clotfelter Jimison, *Through the Eyes of a Tiger: The John Donovan Story* (Athens, GA: Deeks Publishing, 2015), 84.

88   "Hamburger + a malt": R. T. Smith, *Tale of a Tiger* (Van Nuys, CA: Tiger Originals, 1986), 83.

89   was a "four-holer": Ibid., 85.

89   "higher top speed,": Claire Chennault, *Way of a Fighter: The Memoirs of Claire Lee Chennault*, ed. Robert Hotz (New York: G. P. Putnam's Sons, 1949), 113.

89   "Hit and run!": Charles R. Bond, Jr., and Terry H. Anderson, *A Flying Tiger's Diary* (College Station: Texas A&M University Press, 1984), 46. This diary is referred to as an "edited document," so it is possible that alterations were made during the publication process, xiii.

89   "sharpen your shooting eye": Chennault, *Way of a Fighter*, 113.

89   "win every time": Ibid.

89   the best teaching: Ibid., 112.

89   four .30-caliber guns: There was the additional problem that the .30-caliber machine guns had been set for a British order to size .303, and procuring the correct ammunition was difficult. Ibid., 100.

90   if a gun overheated: Charles Baisden, *Flying Tiger to Air Commando* (Atglen, PA: Schiffer Military History, 1999), 30.

90   approximately three hundred yards: Ibid. This is Baisden's estimate, though he acknowledges that there are some discrepancies regarding the distance. Furthermore, because these P-40s had originally been intended for the RAF, a number of adjustments had to be made to allow them to function properly. See Daniel Ford, *Flying Tigers: Claire Chennault and the American Volunteer Group* (Washington, D.C.: Smithsonian Institution Press, 1991), 74–75.

90   "For the bomber and flying-boat": Bruce Gamble, *Black Sheep One: The Life of Gregory "Pappy" Boyington* (New York: Ballantine Books, 2000), 155.

90   "almost on ground level": C. Joseph Rosbert, *Flying Tiger Joe's Adventure Story Cookbook* (Franklin, NC: Giant Poplar Press, 1985), 66–67.

91   "The sound heard": Erik Shilling, *Destiny: A Flying Tiger's Rendezvous with Fate* (self-published, 1993), 93.

91   "It even smelled good": Smith, *Tale of a Tiger,* 68.

91   sense of intimacy: Shilling, *Destiny,* 93.

91   Paul Frillmann had been recruited: See Paul Frillmann and Graham Peck, *China: The Remembered Life* (Boston: Houghton Mifflin Company, 1968), 71–72.

92   this "gruff" man: Smith, *Tale of a Tiger,* 71.

92   "look[ing] forward to": Claire Chennault to Nell Chennault, October 25, 1941, Chennault Family Papers, Louisiana State University (Baton Rouge) Special Collections.

92   "becoming too attached": Olga Greenlaw, *The Lady and the Tigers* (Durham, NH: Warbird Books, 2012), 24.

92   As they left the cemetery: Ibid., 27.

93   "disintegrate into a million pieces": Jennifer Holik with Robert Brouk, *To Soar with the Tigers: The Life and Diary of Flying Tiger, Robert Brouk* (Woodbridge, IL: Generations, 2013), 42.

93   "gaggle of ballet dancers": Frillmann, *China,* 86.

93   "We will have our 2nd": John J. Newkirk, *The Old Man and the Harley* (Nashville, TN: Thomas Nelson, 2008), 199.

93   "big reunion house party": Ibid.

93   George McMillan, a dashing: George McMillan letter to family, November 27, 1941, Winter Garden Heritage Museum, Winter Garden, Florida.

94   During *The Ghost Breakers:* Bond, *A Flying Tiger's Diary,* 45.

94   "the movie took the edge": Frank S. Losonsky and Terry M. Losonsky, *Flying Tiger: A Crew Chief's Story* (Atglen, PA: Schiffer Publishing, 1996), 55.

94   "a college campus": Chennault, *Way of a Fighter,* 116.

94   "these foolish Americans": Foster Oral History, GVSU Collection.

94   "wasn't all that enamored": Ibid.

94   "began to develop": Ibid.

94   "clear and decisive": Ibid.

95   "Bit by bit": Foster Oral History, Library of Congress.

95   "Not very many women": Ibid.

95   monkeys living in the barracks: Losonsky, *Flying Tiger: A Crew Chief's Story,* 42.

95   wrestle a cow: Bond, *A Flying Tiger's Diary,* 49.

96   "bend your teeth": Gregory Boyington, *Baa Baa Black Sheep* (New York: Bantam Books, 1977), 32.

96   "the size of a cantaloupe": Gamble, *Black Sheep One,* 151.

96   the men on the ground mocked: Ibid., 158.

96   "for coffee or whatever": Ibid., 162.

96   "His waist and hips": Ibid.

96   "a running gag": Ibid.

96   a redecorating project: This is the story of the origin as presented by Erik Shilling. Shilling, *Destiny,* 107. However, there is considerable debate about this. See Terrill Clements, *American Volunteer Group "Flying Tigers" Aces*

(Seattle: Osprey Publishing, 2001), 30. There also was debate about whether the design came from an RAF P-40 or a German Messerschmitt Bf 110. Shilling, *Destiny*, 113.

96 **picked up some chalk:** Ibid., 108.

97 **on the whole fleet:** Ibid.; Bond, *A Flying Tiger's Diary*, 49. Originally it seems to have been proposed as a squadron emblem.

97 **a "hostile act":** "American Pilots and Mechanics for China," *China Weekly Review*, June 7, 1941, 22.

97 **reconnaissance missions over neutral Thailand:** Chennault, *Way of a Fighter*, 122; Ford, *Flying Tigers*, 83.

97 **He kept watch himself:** Chennault, *Way of a Fighter*, 122.

98 **Bert Christman, the cartoonist:** Clements, *American Volunteer Group*, 38.

98 **"Too much brake":** Losonsky, *Flying Tiger: A Crew Chief's Story*, 44.

98 **The totalled planes:** Clements, *American Volunteer Group*, 94.

98 **supply situation as "horrible":** Oral History of Lt. Colonel Jasper J. Harrington, 1981, United States Air Force Oral History Program, Air Force Historical Research Agency, Maxwell Air Force Base, Alabama.

98 **never had more than sixty:** Ibid.

98 **The supply situation concerned:** Chennault, *Way of a Fighter*, 117.

99 **"269 pursuit planes":** President Franklin D. Roosevelt, "Memorandum for the Secretary of the Navy," September 30, 1941, National Museum of Naval Aviation, NNAM.1997.269.014, collections.naval.aviation.museum/emuweb doncoms/pages/common/imagedisplay.php?irn=16015381&reftable=ecatalogue &refirn=16037479.

99 **three American Volunteer Groups:** Ford, *Flying Tigers*, 93–94.

99 **do "everything possible":** Joseph W. Alsop with Adam Platt, *I've Seen the Best of It* (New York: W. W. Norton, 1992), 181.

99 **cut off the Burma Road:** William H. Stoneman, "Jap Thrust at Burma Lifeline Looms," *Star Tribune* (Minnesota), November 5, 1941, 2.

99 **"a little excitement":** George McMillan letter to family, December 7, 1941, Winter Garden Heritage Foundation, Winter Garden, Florida.

99 **"It seems that when":** Jimison, *Through the Eyes of a Tiger*, 70. This letter was dated November 16, 1941.

Chapter 8: Wartime

100 **"drunken Army and Navy men":** Thurston Clarke, *Pearl Harbor Ghosts: The Legacy of December 7, 1941* (New York, Ballantine, 2001), 89.

100 **champagne at the Halekulani Hotel:** Craig Nelson, *Pearl Harbor: From Infamy to Greatness*, (New York: Scribner, 2016), 181.

100 **"stars shimmering in the night sky":** Donald Stratton with Ken Gire, *All the Gallant Men: The First Memoir by a USS Arizona Survivor* (New York: HarperCollins, 2016), 74–75.

100 **fried Spam, powdered eggs:** Ibid., 80.

101 **"AIR RAID, PEARL HARBOR":** Clarke, *Pearl Harbor Ghosts*, 104.

101 **"They're bombing the water tower":** Stratton, *All the Gallant Men*, 85.

101 **ran to their battle stations:** Shaun McKinnon, "USS Arizona: The Attack That Changed the World," *Arizona Republic*, December 4, 2014.

101 "the most wretched sound": Stratton, *All the Gallant Men*, 89.

101 "expanding fireball shot": Ibid., 93.

101 The dead numbered 1,177: There are some discrepancies in the number of survivors, likely because some sailors were away from the ship that morning. This figure is used by the National Park Service.

101 "a target that none could miss": Doris Kearns Goodwin, *No Ordinary Time: Franklin & Eleanor Roosevelt: The Home Front in World War II* (New York: Simon & Schuster, 1994), 288.

101 "We will have to take": Ibid., 290.

101 White House butler overheard: Ibid.

102 "to take measures to ensure": Claire Chennault, *Way of a Fighter: The Memoirs of Claire Lee Chennault*, ed. Robert Hotz (New York: G. P. Putnam's Sons, 1949), 124.

102 "laughing and kidding": R. T. Smith, *Tale of a Tiger* (Van Nuys, CA: Tiger Orginals, 1986), 144.

102 "Just received the news": George McMillan letter to family, December 7, 1941, Winter Garden Heritage Museum, Winter Garden, Florida.

102 "Received news today": Diary of George McMillan, December 7, 1941, Winter Garden Heritage Foundation, Winter Garden, Florida. This should have been dated December 8, when they received the news of the attack.

102–3 "If they don't bomb": Smith, *Tale of a Tiger*, 144.

103 "There was a look of relief": Ed Rector Oral History, GVSU Collection, 29.

103 The men were instructed: First American Volunteer Group Diary, December 8 and December 12, 1941, Microfilm Reel 863.305, Air Force Historical Research Agency, Maxwell Air Force Base, Alabama (hereafter "AVG Diary"). This was the group diary that Olga Greenlaw kept for the AVG for a time.

103 "scramble into the air": James H. Howard, *Roar of the Tiger: From Flying Tigers to Mustangs, A Fighter Ace's Memoir* (New York: Pocket Books, 1991), 98.

103 "We bolted out": Frank S. Losonsky and Terry M. Losonsky, *Flying Tiger: A Crew Chief's Story* (Atglen, PA: Schiffer Publishing, 1996), 68.

103 "What's a falling bomb sound like": Ibid.

103 light the runway: AVG Diary, December 8, 1941.

103 an unlit cigarette: Daniel Ford, *Flying Tigers: Claire Chennault and the American Volunteer Group* (Washington, D.C.: Smithsonian Institution Press, 1991), 103.

103 apologized to Chennault: Oral History of David Hill, conducted by Reagan Schaupp, San Antonio, February 2000.

104 "Radio news: Japanese bombed": Olga Greenlaw, *The Lady and the Tigers* (Durham, NH: Warbird Books, 2012), 40.

104 "Yesterday the Japanese": Franklin Roosevelt, "Pearl Harbor Address to the Nation," December 8, 1941, www.americanrhetoric.com/speeches /fdrpearlharbor.htm.

104 Lockheed Hudson bombers: Ford, *Flying Tigers,* 102–3.

104 diverted to Australia : Ibid., 103.

105 "geyser of debris": Robert Gandt, "Pan Am at War," Pan Am Historical Foundation, 2015, www.panam.org/images/Stories/Pan-Am-at-War.pdf.

105 inducting the entire unit: Ford, *Flying Tigers,* 103.

105 large dog of a Chinese dignitary: Hannah Pakula, *The Last Empress: Madame Chiang Kai-shek and the Birth of Modern China* (New York: Simon & Schuster, 2009), 369.

105 "never shot a gun": Joseph W. Alsop with Adam Platt, *I've Seen the Best of It* (New York: W. W. Norton, 1992), 185.

106 the "frightful scene": Ibid., 188–89.

107 a story that appeared: "Alsop, Long Jap Captive, Comes Home," *Hartford Courant*, August 27, 1942, 1.

107 "other side of the world": Howard, *Roar of the Tiger*, 96.

107 an aerial reconnaissance camera: Erik Shilling, *Destiny: A Flying Tiger's Rendezvous with Fate* (self-published, 1993), 116.

107 "continuous strip of photos": Ibid., 117. For a fuller description of the photo strip, see 102.

108 "facing the full weight": Ibid., 118.

108 "A dozen bombers": Chennault, *Way of a Fighter*, 126.

108 "We expect to be hit": Charles R. Bond, Jr., and Terry H. Anderson, *A Flying Tiger's Diary* (College Station: Texas A&M University Press, 1984), 52.

108 "we have no replacements": Ibid.

108 "we were even more motivated": Rector Oral History, GVSU Collection, 29–30.

108 "I hope you never will": John J. Newkirk, *The Old Man and the Harley* (Nashville, TN: Thomas Nelson, 2008), 204.

108 "There are certain things": Ibid., 204–5.

109 "like the twisting": Chennault, *Way of a Fighter*, 120.

109 "I breathed easier": Ibid., 127.

109 an unusual plan: Though the AVG was a Chinese unit, most of its battles would occur in the British colony of Burma, stemming from joint Sino-British defense plans. See Ford, *Flying Tigers*, 54. Chennault wasn't focused on the defense of Burma, and pushed to send the AVG to China. See Chennault, *Way of a Fighter*, 125–26.

109 RAF's Mingaladon aerodrome at Rangoon: Smith, *Tale of a Tiger*, 148.

109 "Now, look here": Greenlaw, *Lady and the Tigers*, 46.

109 "a 670-mile flight": Bond, *A Flying Tiger's Diary*, 58.

110 ran into a Studebaker: Ford, *Flying Tigers*, 109.

110 one pilot's oxygen tube: Bond, *A Flying Tiger's Diary*, 58.

110 "thousands of Chinese soldiers": Ibid.

110 "Yeowee!!" Charlie Bond wrote: Ibid., 59.

110 "That was my first indication": Di Freeze and Deb Smith, "Tex Hill: The Richest Kind of Life," *Airport Journals*, December 1, 2007, airportjournals.com /tex-hill-the-richest-kind-of-life-2.

111 "hate the guts": Bond, *A Flying Tiger's Diary*, 59.

Chapter 9: Legends in Their Own Time

112 "American! Friend! OK!": Charles R. Bond, Jr., and Terry H. Anderson, *A Flying Tiger's Diary* (College Station: Texas A&M University Press, 1984), 68.

112 "Sleepiness and excitement": Paul Frillmann and Graham Peck, *China: The Remembered Life* (Boston: Houghton Mifflin Company, 1968), 91.

112 "like a shot of iced gin": Ibid.

112 following day, December 20: Bond, *A Flying Tiger's Diary*, 60.

113 **Known by their station names:** Claire Chennault, *Way of a Fighter: The Memoirs of Claire Lee Chennault,* ed. Robert Hotz (New York: G. P. Putnam's Sons, 1949), 128; Jack Samson, *The Flying Tiger: The True Story of Claire Lee Chennault and the U.S. 14th Air Force in China* (Guilford, CT: Lyons Press, 2012), 117.

113 **"ten Japanese bombers crossed":** Chennault, *Way of a Fighter,* 127–28.

113 **"I knew he was nervous":** Daniel Ford, *Flying Tigers: Claire Chennault and the American Volunteer Group* (Washington, D.C.: Smithsonian Institution Press, 1991), 111.

114 **"American pilots in American fighter planes":** Chennault, *Way of a Fighter,* 128–29.

114 **"There they are":** Ibid., 129.

115 **racing for their base:** Ford, *Flying Tigers,* 112.

115 **The First Squadron pilots:** Ibid., 111.

115 **excited than nervous:** Bond, *A Flying Tiger's Diary,* 60.

115 **the Lily had a 7.7-mm machine gun:** "KI-48 'Lily' Japanese Light Bomber," *Pacific War Online Encyclopedia,* http://pwencycl.kgbudge.com/K/i/Ki-48 _Lily.htm.

115 **"the nearest bomber":** Bond, *A Flying Tiger's Diary,* 61.

116 **trails of black smoke:** AVG Diary, December 20, 1941.

116 **"a dejected bunch of airmen":** James H. Howard, *Roar of the Tiger: From Flying Tigers to Mustangs, A Fighter Ace's Memoir* (New York: Pocket Books, 1991), 101.

116 **a case of "buck fever":** Chennault, *Way of a Fighter,* 129.

116 **"It was the first time Japanese":** Bond, *A Flying Tiger's Diary,* 62.

116 **a few more probables:** Ibid.

116 **"Next time get them all":** Chennault, *Way of a Fighter,* 130.

116 **most "minute detail":** Ibid.

116 **"the kind of teamwork":** Ibid., 137.

117 **having seen of Ed Rector:** Ibid., 129.

117 **"I'm not going into that maelstrom":** Ed Rector Oral History, GVSU Collection, 36.

117 **"right up the tail":** Ibid.

117 **"shot his lower jaw away":** Ibid., 37.

118 **his "cold fury":** "Flying Tiger: Catawba Star Went on to Become WWII Hero," *Salisbury Post* (North Carolina), July 17, 2014.

118 **"I just stood up":** Rector Oral History, GVSU Collection, 41.

118 **Chinese villagers who "had heard":** Ibid.

118 **"itching for our chance":** Howard, *Roar of the Tiger,* 102.

118 **"like a madman":** Gregory Boyington, *Baa Baa Black Sheep* (New York: Bantam Books, 1977), 38.

119 **"a sunny, warm, spring day":** Peter Mertz, "Last Flying Tiger Recalls WWII Experiences," *Xinhua Net,* September 24, 2015. The precise timing of Yee's work as a translator isn't clear but his quotes indicate that he was with the AVG by December 20.

119 **"diving straight down":** Ibid.

119 **"we got one of 'em":** Sara Burnett, "WWII Chinese Translator Denied U.S. Veterans Status but Says Record Speaks for Itself," *Denver Post,* May 28, 2011.

119 **glimpse of them:** Ford, *Flying Tigers,* 118.

119 "deaths in Kunming": "U.S. Air Volunteers Praised by Chinese," *Pittsburgh Press,* December 23, 1941, 2.

119 Chiang Kai-shek himself: Bond, *A Flying Tiger's Diary,* 63.

120 "really attractive young belles": Ibid., 65.

120 Chennault gave a speech: Ibid., 68.

120 "blood chit" identified them: Ibid., 67.

120 becoming somewhat famous: "Yanks Smash Enemy Over China," *San Bernardino County Sun,* December 21, 1941, 2.

121 "the Flying Tigers swooped: "Blood for the Tigers," *Time,* December 29, 1941, 19.

121 was "astonished" to see it: Chennault, *Way of a Fighter,* 135.

121 a term of praise: "Labels Americans 'Flying Tigers,'" *New York Times,* January 26, 1942, 10.

121 clever marketing ploy: Anthony R. Carrozza, *William D. Pawley: The Extraordinary Life of the Adventurer, Entrepreneur, and Diplomat Who Cofounded the Flying Tigers* (Washington, D.C.: Potomac Books, 2012), 96; Ford, *Flying Tigers,* 120.

121 "lean, hardbitten, taciturn": "Blood for the Tigers," *Time.*

Chapter 10: Christmas in Rangoon

122 was at war: For more on the base and the RAF in Burma, see Neil Frances, *Ketchil: A New Zealand Pilot's War in Asia and the Pacific* (Masterton, New Zealand: Wairarapa Archive, 2005), 38–42.

122 "damn good work": R. T. Smith, *Tale of a Tiger* (Van Nuys, CA: Tiger Orginals, 1986), 157.

122 "Everything seemed as usual": Ibid., 158.

123 "handsome" and a "fine gentleman": Cary J. Hahn, "Reed Remembered as Distinguished Pilot, Commander," *Marion Times* (Iowa), May 20, 2009.

123 "half way 'round the world": Diary of Bill Reed, December 4, 1941 (hereafter "Reed Diary"). The [transcript of the] diary of Bill Reed was made available through a website maintained in Reed's memory. I am grateful to family member Edward Reed for providing greater background on Reed. For more on Reed see E. Bradley Simmons, "William Reed, Fighter Ace and Hero," *Marion Times,* November 10, 1994, 1, 10.

123 "probably another false alarm": Reed Diary, December 23, 1941. All subsequent descriptions of this battle are from Reed's diary entry from this day. The diary entry is similar to and consistent with Reed's combat report; see W. N. Reed, "Substitute Combat Report Form," December 23, 1941.

123 "A whole cloud": Ibid.

124 posters of famous aviators: Kate Burke, "York Native Was a Flying Tiger," *York News-Times* (Nebraska), March 17, 2009.

124 "the sudden and embarrassing urge": Smith, *Tale of a Tiger,* 31.

124 the "crackling sound": Ibid.

125 "By God, I got one": Ibid., 160.

125 missing three men: Reed Diary, December 23, 1941.

125 torn neck muscle: Daniel Ford, *Flying Tigers: Claire Chennault and the American Volunteer Group* (Washington, D.C.: Smithsonian Institution Press, 1991), 131–32.

125 **From Lovell, Wyoming:** Gilbert is sometimes identified as from Wyoming and sometimes from Washington State.

125 **"wanted to welcome them properly":** Reed Diary, December 23, 1941.

125 **American freighter *Tulsa*:** Smith, *Tale of a Tiger*, 162.

126 **"Would give a lot to be home":** Reed Diary, December 24, 1941.

126 **"In a matter of a minute":** Ibid., December 25, 1941. The diary entry is similar to and consistent with Reed's combat report; see W. N. Reed, "Substitute Combat Report Form," December 25, 1941.

127 **"had given them up for dead":** Smith, *Tale of a Tiger*, 163.

127 **"Two planes and pilots missing":** Ford, *Flying Tigers*, 150.

127 **"no Christmas at all":** Oral History of Chuck Baisden, GVSU Collection, 41. Some have suggested that Pawley brought a feast for them that night. Although it is possible, it doesn't appear in contemporaneous accounts.

128 **"You should have seen them":** George McMillan letter to family, April 15, 1942, George McMillan Collection, Winter Garden Heritage Foundation, Winter Garden, Florida.

128 **"We tore into them":** Leland Stowe, "American Flyers Describe Death of 92 Japanese in Air," *Los Angeles Times*, January 4, 1942, 1.

128 **"Xmas' days work":** McMillan letter, April 15, 1942.

129 **"I'd rather fight them":** Stowe, "American Flyers Describe Death of 92 Japanese in Air," *Los Angeles Times*.

129 **"has whipped the AVG":** "3 U.S. Fliers Attacked 108 of Foe at Start of Air Battle at Rangoon," *New York Times*, January 8, 1942, 4.

129 **"knock[ing] the living daylights":** Leland Stowe, "American, British Flyers Give Japs First Trouncing in 4½ Years of Warfare," *Boston Globe*, January 3, 1942.

129 **they had downed fifteen:** AVG Diary, December 25, 1941. The estimate was fifteen bombers and nine fighters, "but confirmation as per Olson's radiogram, above, only thirteen fighters and four bombers were confirmed."

129 **"Even though we're getting":** Diary of George McMillan, December 25, 1941, George McMillan Collection, Winter Garden Heritage Foundation, Winter Garden, Florida.

129 **"I know I swallow hard":** Reed Diary, December 27, 1941.

130 **he was "terribly worried":** Claire Chennault letter to Nell Chennault, January 12, 1942, Chennault Museum. This letter refers to "Buck" but it is not clear which of the sons had this nickname.

130 **"thick scattered clouds":** Reed Diary, January 3, 1942.

130 **"Threw the football around":** Ibid., January 9, 1942.

130 **"have the best living quarters":** Karl Eskelund, "Chinese Idolize U.S. Defenders of Burma Road," *New York Herald Tribune*, February 13, 1942, 3.

130 **"only thing wrong":** Reed Diary, January 3, 1942.

Chapter 11: Burmese Days

131 **the "Unholy Trio":** "U.S. Ace, Killed in Thai Raid Proved He Was No 'Sissy,'" *St. Louis Star and Times* (Missouri), March 25, 1942, 1.

131 **"Last night was New Year's Eve":** John Petach letter to Emma Foster, January 1, 1942, Emma Jane Foster Petach Hanks Papers, Yale Divinity School, China Record Project Miscellaneous Personal Papers Collection, Record Group 8, Box 353 (hereafter "Foster Papers, Yale Divinity School").

132 "the knowledge that": Ibid.

132 "Let's take the war": James H. Howard, *Roar of the Tiger: From Flying Tigers to Mustangs, A Fighter Ace's Memoir* (New York: Pocket Books, 1991), 109.

132 approached the Raheng aerodrome: Raheng was a forward airstrip used by the Japanese. Daniel Ford, *Flying Tigers: Claire Chennault and the American Volunteer Group* (Washington, D.C.: Smithsonian Institution Press, 1991), 124.

132 "streaming smoke, rolled over": Jack Newkirk, "Report on Activities of This Squadron," January 13, 1942, Chennault Foundation, Washington, D.C. (hereafter "Second Squadron Report, January 13, 1942"). All combat reports are from the collection in the Chennault Foundation's papers. The full combat reports for the Second Squadron's activities for early January 1942 were not found in the collection, but Jack Newkirk did prepare a summary of all the Second Squadron missions on January 13, 1942, which included some reports in full and excerpts from others.

133 "gave it a five-second burst": Howard, *Roar of the Tiger*, 4.

133 "just like a big hose": Oral History of David Hill, conducted by Reagan Schaupp, San Antonio, February 2000.

133 four enemy aircraft ascending: Second Squadron Report, January 13, 1942.

133 "wonderful line of destruction": Howard, *Roar of the Tiger*, 4.

133 he heard a "dull thump": Ibid. In his memoir, Howard implies this was from antiaircraft fire but in a February 1942 letter he states that it was probably from a malfunction in the plane's electrical system.

133 "I dropped my landing gear": "St. Louis 'Flying Tiger' Writes of Battles Over Burma Road, Death of Clayton Flyer," *St. Louis Post-Dispatch*, May 10, 1942, 13. This article contained Howard's letter dated February 17, 1942, in which he described the January battle.

133 "She caught again! COME ON": Howard, *Roar of the Tiger*, 4.

134 most bullet holes: Wanda Cornelius and Thayne Short, *Ding Hao: America's Air War in China, 1937–1945* (Gretna, LA: Pelican Publishing Co., 1980), 122–23.

134 "By some miracle": Howard, *Roar of the Tiger*, 5.

134 "destroyed 2 fighters": Untitled AVG Battle Record, Chennault Foundation. The "First American Volunteer Group" prepared a document that listed credits allotted to individual pilots for Japanese planes destroyed (both on the ground and in the air). This document was untitled and undated, though it appears to have been made just after the AVG's induction because it includes battles as late as July 6, 1942 (hereafter "AVG Battle Record").

134 "destroyed 4 fighters": Ibid. However, Japanese records indicated that only one Japanese fighter was shot down in the air and two more were damaged on the ground. See Ford, *Flying Tigers*, 163.

134 "hoped it would be": Howard, *Roar of the Tiger*, 5.

134 "tried to evade the enemy": Second Squadron Report, January 13, 1942.

134 he glided to earth: Ibid.; Bert Christman, "Combat Report," January 4, 1942. This combat report was dated "4/1/42," but that was meant as 4 January; by April 1, 1942, Christman was dead.

134 letter to a former colleague: "A Last Letter from Ragoon [*sic*]—How Bert Christman Died," *Casper-Tribune Herald* (Wyoming), February 18, 1942, 3. Christman's letter was to former colleague M. J. Wing, who seems to have solicited it.

135 "when 'this' is all over": Ibid.

135   **back at the flight line:** Jack Newkirk, "Report of Activities of 2nd Pursuit Squadron on Detached Duty," January 13, 1942. This is a separate report detailing matters outside of air activities conducted by the AVG. It should be noted that some First Squadron pilots also joined the AVG in Rangoon during this period and they are accounted for in the roster in this report.

135   **"cockpit began falling apart":** Second Squadron Report, January 13, 1942.

135   **"a hole in his shoulder":** John Petach letter to Emma Foster, January 7, 1942, Foster Papers, Yale Divinity School.

135   **"bastards can't shoot":** Oral History of David Hill, conducted by Reagan Schaupp.

135   **"The more hardships":** Newkirk, "Report of Activities of 2nd Pursuit Squadron on Detached Duty," January 13, 1942.

135   **"trucks or any place available":** Ibid.

135   **nighttime air raid:** C. D. Mott, "Report of Night Flight," January 5, 1942.

136   **target was the Mesoht aerodrome:** Mesoht is the name used in the AVG records, but it is also referred to as Mae Sot, a location that the Japanese were using as a forward airfield. Ford, *Flying Tigers,* 169. This account uses the AVG records for establishing the targets; there is some uncertainty about precisely which airfields the AVG attacked in the course of these raids.

136   **AVG crossed into Thailand:** Second Squadron Report, January 13, 1942.

136   **"nothing but jungle":** Charlie Mott Oral History, GVSU Collection, 29.

137   **"a big plum":** Ibid., 30.

137   **"I lay there, immobilized":** Bob Bergin, "Charlie Mott: Flying Tiger Caged," Warfare History Network, October 10, 2016, www.warfarehistorynetwork .com/daily/wwii/charlie-mott-flying-tiger-caged.

137   **"a real successful mission":** Robert Moss Oral History, GVSU Collection, 23.

137   **"Sure was a hell of a shame":** John Petach letter to Emma Foster, January 13, 1942, Foster Papers, Yale Divinity School.

137   **"running around like madmen":** Bergin, "Charlie Mott: Flying Tiger Caged."

138   **also known as Tak:** Ford, *Flying Tigers,* 170. As noted above, this account uses the AVG records for establishing the targets, though there is some uncertainty about precisely which airfields the AVG attacked in the course of these raids.

138   **saw "four enemy aircraft":** Second Squadron Report, January 13, 1942.

139   **"as I made my approach":** John Petach to Emma Foster, January 13, 1942, Foster Papers, Yale Divinity School.

139   **"compact group of riflemen":** Second Squadron Report, January 13, 1942.

139   **"flying together for years":** Leland Stowe, "Allied Teamwork on Burma Front," *St. Louis Post-Dispatch*, January 12, 1942, 4.

139   **RAF pilot yelled out "good show":** Ibid.

139   **"There aren't enough of them":** "Tigers over Burma," *Time,* February 9, 1942, 26.

139   **"the last I saw":** John Petach to Emma Foster, January 13, 1942, Foster Papers, Yale Divinity School.

140   **"Sweet One, I'm very much":** Petach to Foster, January 17, 1942, ibid.

140   **"Sweet, have I told you":** Petach to Foster, January 18, 1942, ibid. Petach would write these letters successively and then they were sent together when a plane could take them.

140 "overnight warbird veterans": Leland Stowe, "Jap Air Losses as Told by AVG Flyer's Own Reports," *Daily Boston Globe,* February 1, 1942, b38.

140 "The victories they have won": "Churchill Acclaims Exploits of Flyers Defending Rangoon," *Los Angeles Times,* February 3, 1942, 2.

140 "to refight the battles": Carole Naggar, *George Rodger: An Adventure in Photography, 1908–1995* (Syracuse, NY: Syracuse University Press, 2003), 89.

140 he arrived in Rangoon: The precise dates of Rodger's photoshoot are somewhat unclear but it was in late January. See Terrill Clements, *American Volunteer Group "Flying Tigers" Aces* (Seattle: Osprey Publishing, 2001), 67.

141 *Life* magazine article: "Flying Tigers in Burma," *Life,* March 30, 1942, 28.

141 Tom Cole had been killed: Naggar, *George Rodger,* 91.

141 "the best American fliers": "Life's Pictures," *Life,* March 30, 1942, 25.

141 "Tom Cole of Missouri": "Flying Tigers in Burma," *Life.*

142 strafed him as he fell: AVG Diary, January 23, 1942.

142 "Christman displayed no lack": Clements, *American Volunteer Group,* 39. Newkirk's "Personnel Report" is reproduced there.

142 "None loved flying better": Daniel De Luce, "Adventure Strip Artist Is Killed While Fighting Japs," *Sheboygan Press* (Wisconsin), February 17, 1942, 13.

142 sketches he had drawn in Burma: I am indebted to Christman's relative, Amelie Smith, for sharing these sketches.

143 He landed in Rangoon: AVG Diary, January 25, 1942. In his memoir, Boyington places this on February 2, but it would have been earlier because Hoffman was killed on January 26. Boyington had gone to Rangoon earlier in January but was quickly sent back to Kunming.

143 "Boy oh boy": Gregory Boyington, *Baa Baa Black Sheep* (New York: Bantam Books, 1977), 45.

143 "smoke and tracers": Ibid., 46.

143 "hauling back on my stick: Ibid., 47.

143 "We sure screwed that one": Ford, *Flying Tigers,* 205.

143 "badly mutilated" body: Charles R. Bond, Jr., and Terry H. Anderson, *A Flying Tiger's Diary* (College Station: Texas A&M University Press, 1984), 83.

143 "was killed in action": Claire Chennault, "Citation for Bravery," February 19, 1942, Collection of Louis Hoffman, Jr., Placerville, California.

144 gravediggers had to return: Bond, *A Flying Tiger's Diary,* 85.

144 "nervous and perspiring": Boyington, *Baa Baa Black Sheep,* 48.

144 "not for money": Ibid., 51.

144 ice cream topped with strawberries: Bond, *A Flying Tiger's Diary,* 85.

144 "Louis Hoffman died honorably": Paul Frillmann letter to Alys Hoffman, January 27, 1942, Collection of Louis Hoffman, Jr., Placerville, California.

144 credited in the AVG records : AVG Battle Record.

144 conducted the wedding: John Petach letter to family, February 19, 1942, "The Flying Tigers, Johnnie Petach," johnniepetachavg.com/2012/01/20/uncensored-letter-to-family.

145 "HAPPY IN CHINA": Petach "Postal Telegraph" to family, undated, "The Flying Tigers, Johnnie Petach," johnniepetachavg.files.wordpress.com/2014/01/johnnie-petach_avg_161.jpg.

145 "red-haired, blue-eyed nurse": Petach letter to family, February 19, 1942.

145 "a big bombing effort": Bond, *A Flying Tiger's Diary,* 93.

145 "Man, they did it again": Ibid., 95.

145 "Day + Night Night + Day": Frank L. Lawlor, "Combat Report," January 23, 1942. The sketch is on the reverse side of this combat report, undated and unsigned.

145 "We are just not too sure": Bond, *A Flying Tiger's Diary*, 96.

146 he would dream about dogfights: Ibid., 100.

146 had been largely abandoned: Paul Frillmann and Graham Peck, *China: The Remembered Life* (Boston: Houghton Mifflin Company, 1968), 114.

146 "smashing open crates": Ibid.

146 "always waiting in the hall": Ibid., 109.

147 "We always listened": Ibid., 115.

147 "driving a powerful": Ibid.

147 an "E" sign was posted: Felicity Goodall, *Exodus Burma: The British Escape Through the Jungles of Death 1942* (Stroud, UK: History Press, 2011), 61.

147 "The old clock": Ibid., 65.

148 a "rip-roaring time": Frillmann, *China*, 116.

148 AVG to retreat: Bond, *A Flying Tiger's Diary*, 95. The original commander of the First Squadron, Sandy Sandell, was killed in an accident in Rangoon on February 7.

148 "Goodbye Rangoon!" Bond wrote: Ibid., 115.

148 "Just get out": Frillmann, *China*, 117.

148 "full flame, crackling loudly": Ibid.

149 "doing right or wrong": Ibid., 118.

149 "Buddhist shrines, clusters of bamboo": Ibid., 120.

149 the convoy made slow progress: Ibid., 130.

149 Frillmann's Buick now belonged: Ibid., 134. Frillmann acknowledged that there were "black market intrigues" involving some of the goods; these rumors would damage the reputation of the AVG.

149 "The battle of southern Burma: Claire Chennault, *Way of a Fighter: The Memoirs of Claire Lee Chennault*, ed. Robert Hotz (New York: G. P. Putnam's Sons, 1949), 139.

150 "No other group in history": William Wade Watson, ed., *High Water, High Cotton and High Times* (Pittsburgh, PA: Dorrance Publishing, 2007), 137–38.

150 inducted into the army: Ford, *Flying Tigers*, 195.

151 use "surprise thrusts": Chennault, *Way of a Fighter*, 185. Chennault is discussing Confederate cavalry attacks from the American Civil War.

151 "aerial shell game": Ibid.

151 was "aerial guerilla warfare": Martha Byrd, *Chennault: Giving Wings to the Tiger* (Tuscaloosa, AL: University of Alabama Press, 1987), 114.

151 "low, intense voice": Ève Curie, "Eve Curie Finds AVG Flyers Eager to Smash Japanese Lines," *New York Herald Tribune*, March 23, 1942, 13.

151 "aggressive-spirited" warrior: Ibid.

152 Chiang himself spoke: Olga Greenlaw, *The Lady and the Tigers* (Durham, NH: Warbird Books, 2012), 86.

152 "I shall extend": London Office Chinese Ministry of Information, *The Voice of China: Speeches of Generalissimo and Madame Chiang Kai-shek Between December 7, 1941, and October 10, 1943* (London, UK: Hutchinson, 1944), 14–19. This volume published by the Chinese Ministry of Information

includes transcripts of speeches by Chiang, Madame Chiang, and Chennault from the February 28, 1942, dinner.

153 **"it was all in Chinese":** Ford, *Flying Tigers*, 249.

153 **the predictably drunk Greg Boyington:** There is some uncertainty about whether Boyington's disturbance took place at the February 28 gala or at a later one on March 4, but it seems likely to have been at the main event on February 28. Greenlaw, *Lady and The Tigers*, 85–86. Greenlaw references Madame Chiang's language from the February 28 speech.

153 **"He was ill prepared":** Bruce Gamble, *Black Sheep One: The Life of Gregory "Pappy" Boyington* (New York: Ballantine Books, 2000), 204.

154 **"You don't leave your leader":** Ibid., 205.

154 **"don't ever come back":** Boyington, *Baa Baa Black Sheep*, 69.

154 **Boyington went for a hike:** Ibid., 70.

155 **he pulled out his sidearm:** Gamble, *Black Sheep One*, 206.

155 **made it back to Kunming:** Ibid., 206–7.

155 **"it was a wonder":** Frank S. Losonsky and Terry M. Losonsky, *Flying Tiger: A Crew Chief's Story* (Atglen, PA: Schiffer Publishing, 1996), 86.

155 **"minor miracles of repair":** Clements, *American Volunteer Group*, 68.

155 **"Save some big words":** Maj. George Fielding Eliot, "Japan's Dispersal of Its Fighting Forces Improves Prospects for Allied Offensive, Maj. Eliot Says," *St. Louis Post-Dispatch*, March 8, 1942, 22.

155 **"replaced the props":** Losonsky, *Flying Tiger: A Crew Chief's Story*, 86.

156 **Boyington was flying:** Boyington, *Baa Baa Black Sheep*, 73; Losonsky, *Flying Tiger: Crew Chief's Story*, 86.

156 **Losonsky and Boyington toasted:** Losonsky, *Flying Tiger: Crew Chief's Story*, 87.

Chapter 12: Aerial Guerrilla Warfare

157 **Pilots from the First Squadron:** Daniel Ford, *Flying Tigers: Claire Chennault and the American Volunteer Group* (Washington, D. C.: Smithsonian Institution Press, 1991), 254. By that point, the three squadrons were increasingly blending together.

157 **Magwe is very hot:** Reed Diary, March 14, 1942.

157 **"On alert today":** Reed Diary, March 15, 1942.

157 **"Action seems to make":** Reed Diary, March 4, 1942.

158 **A pile of corpses:** Reed Diary, March 17, 1942.

158 **"I just kept my eye":** Bob Bergin, "Tiger Attack at Moulmein," *Air Classics* 45, no. 3 (March 2009): 15.

158 **"observed my fire":** Bill Reed, "Combat Report," March 18, 1942.

159 **"It was a complete surprise":** Reed Diary, March 18, 1942.

159 **"concentrated my fire":** Kenneth Jernstedt, "Combat Report," March 18, 1942.

159 **with "all guns blazing":** Reed Diary, March 18, 1942.

159 **"On my last dive":** Bill Reed, "Combat Report," March 18, 1942.

159 **"On the way back":** Reed Diary, March 18, 1942.

159 **"It would be hard to estimate":** Kenneth Jernstedt, "Combat Report," March 18, 1942.

160 IOWAN BAGS JAP PLANES: "Iowan Bags Jap Planes," *Des Moines Register*, March 27, 1942, 1.

160 "we are proud of him": "AVG Hero Is Iowa Native," *Mason City Globe-Gazette,* March 27, 1942, 2.

160 "a junk heap": "20 for 1," *Time,* April 6, 1942, 20.

160 "Not much doing": Reed Diary, March 19, 1942.

160 "went like a scared jack rabbit": Ron Blankenbaker, "This Walter Mitty Tale Is True," *Statesman Journal* (Oregon), April 24, 1977, 1–2.

160 "blew it sky high": Reed Diary, March 21, 1942.

160 "Bomb fragments wounded a pilot": "20 for 1," *Time,* April 6, 1942, 20.

160–61 "got into some skirmishing": Ron Blankenbaker, "This Walter Mitty Tale Is True."

161 John Fauth, a mechanic: Other accounts vary from the *Time* version of how the three were shot. One witness said that these men ran out to help an RAF pilot. See Ford, *Flying Tigers,* 264.

161 pulled back to a CAMCO factory: Ibid., 269.

161 "make them pay": Charles R. Bond, Jr., and Terry H. Anderson, *A Flying Tiger's Diary* (College Station: Texas A&M University Press, 1984), 130.

161 Chennault blamed himself: Claire Chennault, *Way of a Fighter: The Memoirs of Claire Lee Chennault,* ed. Robert Hotz (New York: G. P. Putnam's Sons, 1949), 147.

161 "No, Tex," Newkirk replied: Oral History of David Hill, conducted by Reagan Schaupp, San Antonio, February 2000.

162 "we'll make up for": "And Women Must Wait!," *Albuquerque Journal,* March 22, 1942, 17.

162 "panoramic view of": Bond, *A Flying Tiger's Diary,* 131.

162 "the jungle will": Ford, *Flying Tigers,* 271.

162 "it'll make any difference": Gregory Boyington, *Baa Baa Black Sheep* (New York: Bantam Books, 1977), 83.

163 "you curly-headed fellows": Bond, *A Flying Tiger's Diary,* 132–33.

163 "What was passing by": Boyington, *Baa Baa Black Sheep,* 83.

163 "early-morning haze hid": Bond, *A Flying Tiger's Diary,* 133.

163 a "gradual descent": C. R. Bond, Jr., "Low Flying Attack Form," March 24, 1942.

164 "Now it was clear": Bond, *A Flying Tiger's Diary,* 134–35.

165 A trail of smoke: W. E. Bartling, "Low Flying Attack Form," March 24, 1942.

165 Bond circled the spot: E. Rector, "Combat Report," March 24, 1942; Bond, *A Flying Tiger's Diary,* 135. There is a small discrepancy over the assistance to McGarry: Bartling says in his combat report that he dropped the map.

165 McGarry had been nicknamed: Myrna Oliver, "William McGarry, 74, of World War II Flying Tigers Fame," *Los Angeles Times,* April 13, 1990.

165 "couldn't get Mac off my mind": Bond, *A Flying Tiger's Diary,* 136.

166 "undoubtedly a barracks": R. B. Keeton, "Low Flying Attack Form," March 24, 1942.

166 "large ball of fire": Ibid.

166 "Immediately after leaving": Frank L. Lawlor, "Low Flying Attack Form," March 24, 1942.

167 oxcarts carrying rice: Bob Bergin has written extensively on this topic. "Scarsdale Jack Newkirk's Crash at Lamphun," Warbird Forum, www.warbird forum.com/jackcra3.htm. He concluded that Newkirk was hit by ground fire and was trying to find a place to land.

167 "The two vehicles": H. M. Geselbracht, Jr., "Low Flying Attack Form," March 24, 1942.

167 "We don't know whether he was hit": Bond, *A Flying Tiger's Diary*, 137.

167 "celebrating the day's work": Ibid.

167 "It's surprising how quickly": Bond, *Flying Tiger's Diary*, 137.

168 "was more than justified": Chennault, *Way of a Fighter*, 148.

168 "Ask his widow": "He Gave More than 10%—What About You?," *Honolulu Advertiser*, December 5, 1942, 7.

168 "There is something gallant": "Newkirk Memorial Rites Are Held at St. Thomas," *New York Herald Tribune*, March 28, 1942, 8.

168 "became hysterical every time": "On Verge of Hysteria, Mrs. Newkirk L.A. Bound," *Oakland Tribune*, March 26, 1942, 4.

168 "now that Jack is gone": "Death Premonition Told by Widow of AVG Ace," *Los Angeles Times*, March 26, 1942, 1.

169 cheered on the radio: Bond, *A Flying Tiger's Diary*, 146.

169 General Joseph Stilwell: Barbara W. Tuchman, *Stilwell and the American Experience in China, 1911–1945* (New York: Macmillan, 1971), 260.

169 "The edge of war": Ibid., 275.

170 "One shining hope": "Flying Tigers in Burma," *Life*, March 30, 1942, 27.

170 "famed but hidden city": "Mayor: William Pawley," *Honolulu Advertiser*, March 21, 1940, 8.

170 "closely guarded secret": "Pawleyville, Burma! China's Plane Mart," *Honolulu Advertiser*, November 29, 1939, 1.

170 "miles from civilization": "China. New Route, New Factory," *Time*, November 13, 1939.

170 Pawley's team had to overcome malaria: "U.S. Plane Plant in China Defies Japan's Bombs," *New York Herald Tribune*, November 22, 1940, 6.

170 "I certainly welcome the rest": Reed Diary, April 2, 1942.

171 "It's good for morale": "Flying Tigers Are Mild Youths, Cared for at Night by Widow," *News Journal* (Delaware), April 24, 1942, 6.

171 "for no reason at all": R. T. Smith, *Tale of a Tiger* (Van Nuys, CA: Tiger Originals, 1986), 265.

171 "full of whiskey": Bruce Gamble, *Black Sheep One: The Life of Gregory "Pappy" Boyington* (New York: Ballantine Books, 2000), 219.

172 "They should bomb": Reed Diary, April 2, 1942.

172 a drunken pilot, Duke Hedman: Smith, *Tale of a Tiger*, 268.

172 "Nice services considering": Reed Diary, April 5, 1942.

172 eight RAF Hurricanes: Smith, *Tale of a Tiger*, 268.

172 "My day off today": Reed Diary, April 8, 1942.

172 "balls out" climb: Smith, *Tale of a Tiger*, 272.

172 "damndest rat-race imaginable": Ibid.

173 Wolf came out of his dive: F. E. Wolf, "Combat Report," April 8, 1942.

173 Smith pulled in: Smith, *Tale of a Tiger*, 272.

173 "most thrilling experience": Ibid., 271.

173 Wolf claimed two kills: F. E. Wolf, "Combat Report," April 8, 1942. Some accounts refer to ten Japanese planes being shot down, though the AVG Battle Record counts only nine. The RAF may also have participated in this battle but the AVG records don't comment on their role.

173 "like a movie": Smith, *Tale of a Tiger*, 271.

173 "the Japs can afford": Susan Clotfelter Jimison, *Through the Eyes of a Tiger: The John Donovan Story* (Athens, GA: Deeks Publishing, 2015), 159.

173 P-40, which was known as the Tomahawk: There is some ambiguity about whether the earlier P-40s should be classified as P-40Bs, or due to alterations that were made to them, P-40Cs. Pilots appear to generally refer to the P-40 as a "B model." See C. H. Laughlin, "Ferry Flight," *Journal of American Aviation Historical Society* (Spring 1979): 52.

173 underwing racks: J. J. Harrington photographed these bombs extensively. The bombs were oftentimes Soviet built. Terrill Clements, *American Volunteer Group "Flying Tigers" Aces* (Seattle: Osprey Publishing, 2001), 81.

174 a freighter to Accra: Ford, *Flying Tigers,* 154.

174 "an unbelievable opportunity": Smith, *Tale of a Tiger,* 219.

174 "new Buick": Laughlin, "Ferry Flight," 52.

174 "Roughly the equivalent": Smith, *Tale of a Tiger,* 233.

174 American beer and cigarettes: George McMillan Diary, March 8, 1942, Winter Garden Heritage Foundation. Winter Garden, Florida.

174 "a honey of a gun": Smith, *Tale of a Tiger,* 245.

174 "new planes would add": Ibid., 250.

174 "the sort of thing": Ibid., 255.

175 "to attack the enemy effectively": Chennault, *Way of a Fighter,* 164. The P-40Es first saw combat in the defense of Loiwing.

175 one Kittyhawk was destroyed: Ford, *Flying Tigers,* 285.

175 "If I had seen it": Mike Barber, "Before the U.S. Entered WWII, The Flying Tigers Were Already in the Fight," *Seattle Post-Intelligencer,* May 25, 2001.

175 would have to "play ball": John Paton Davies, Jr., *China Hand: An Autobiography* (Philadelphia: University of Pennsylvania Press, 2012), 46–47.

175 "finish off the damn AVG thing": Diary of Joseph Stilwell, April 1, 1942, Joseph Warren Stilwell Papers, Hoover Institution Archives, Stanford University (hereafter "Stilwell Diary"), digitalcollections.hoover.org/images/Collections/51001/1942_stilwell_diary_rev.pdf.

175 just an honorary title: William Smith, "Claire Lee Chennault: The Louisiana Years," *Louisiana History: Journal of the Louisiana Historical Association* 29, no. 1 (Winter 1998): 61.

176 return home after the date set for induction: Martha Byrd, *Chennault: Giving Wings to the Tiger* (Tuscaloosa, AL: University of Alabama Press, 1987), 146. The precise date was the subject of some negotiation.

176 "not hurt but plenty scared": Diary of John Petach, April 10, 1942, Foster Papers, Yale Divinity School (hereafter Petach Diary).

176 "I admit to being lonesome": Jimison, *Through the Eyes of a Tiger,* 144.

177 "had taken their toll": Smith, *Tale of a Tiger,* 284.

177 "The demands made on him": Byrd, *Chennault,* 147.

177 "I feel like a blind man": Tuchman, *Stilwell,* 282.

177 "A thick layer of the stuff": Smith, *Tale of a Tiger,* 261.

178 "it is probable that": F. Schiel, "Reconnaissance Report," April 14–15, 1942.

178 "clay pigeons in a shooting gallery": Chennault, *Way of a Fighter,* 154.

178 "we patrolled for": John Petach letter to Emma Foster, "Monday," Foster Papers, Yale Divinity School. No date is provided on this letter but presumably it was written on Monday, April 13, 1942, about his mission the day before, as detailed in the diary.

178 "Low-level operations are": Oral History of David Hill, conducted by Reagan Schaupp, San Antonio, February 2000.

178 real "stinker" of a mission: Smith, *Tale of a Tiger*, 281–84.

179 lodge their protest: Reed Diary, April 18, 1942.

179 "The guys were tired": Oral History of David Hill, conducted by Reagan Schaupp, February 2000.

180 "We, the undersigned": Untitled document, Headquarters First American Volunteer Group, April 19, 1942 (Collection of Brad Smith, Berkeley, California).

180 some notable absences: There were a number of edits to the document, so it is hard to confirm the original list of signatories. Smith places the number at twenty-six. See *Tale of a Tiger*, 284.

180 "hung rather precariously": Reed Diary, April 19, 1942.

180 "as long as these orders": Chennault, *Way of a Fighter*, 156.

180 "Our main concern": Smith, *Tale of a Tiger*, 289.

180 "We don't mind risking our lives": Oral History of Charles Older, GVSU Collection, 39.

180 "anyone leaving would be": Smith, *Tale of a Tiger*, 285.

181 escort the Blenheim bombers: Chennault, *Way of a Fighter*, 156; Smith, *Tale of a Tiger*, 285.

181 "carrying on as usual": Smith, *Tale of a Tiger*, 285.

181 "all but forgotten": Chennault, *Way of a Fighter*, 156.

181 "see the thing out": Jennifer Holik with Robert Brouk, *To Soar with the Tigers: The Life and Diary of Flying Tiger, Robert Brouk* (Woodbridge, IL: Generations, 2013), 79.

181 "twist and turn": Ibid., 80.

182 a "ragged wound": Ibid., 81.

182 "six holes in his leg": Daniel De Luce, "Missionary Surgeon Races in Truck to Beat Japs to Burma Base, Save Nurses," *St. Louis Post-Dispatch*, April 29, 1942, 21. Though Seagrave didn't identify Brouk by name, the description of the wounds and the timing match Brouk's account.

183 "thirty-six of thirty-nine": John Pomfret, *The Beautiful Country and the Middle Kingdom: America and China, 1776 to the Present* (New York: Picador, 2016), 258.

183 time to celebrate the occasion: Chennault, *Way of a Fighter*, 149.

183 "heard a strange tongue": A. E. Olson, Jr., "Combat Report," April 28, 1942.

183 "turned my flight": D. L. Hill, "Reconnaissance Escort and Combat Report," April 28, 1942.

184 "a formation of 27 bombers": Ibid.

184 a "long burst": L. S. Bishop, "Reconnaissance Escort and Combat Report," April 28, 1942.

184 "seemed to be inexperienced": D. L. Hill, "Reconnaissance Escort and Combat Report," April 28, 1942.

184 Smith wasn't shot down: Smith, *Tale of a Tiger*, 294–96.

184 "Hell, I was the last guy": Oral History of David Hill, conducted by Reagan Schaupp, February 2000.

184 Japanese newspaper printed: Ford, *Flying Tigers*, 323.

Chapter 13: Last Stand

185 that "the Flying Tigers were": Clare Boothe, "Life's Reports: The A.V.G. Ends Its Famous Career," *Life*, July 20, 1942, 7.

185 the "old gang": Charles R. Bond, Jr., and Terry H. Anderson, *A Flying Tiger's Diary* (College Station: Texas A&M University Press, 1984), 130.

186 "It is a nice little plane": Ibid., 155.

186 "they were an ugly-looking bunch": Bond, *A Flying Tiger's Diary*, 161.

186 "It was good to get back": Reed Diary, May 1, 1942.

186 "hug and kiss": John Petach to Emma Foster, April 25, 1942, Foster Papers, Yale Divinity School.

186 105 steps a minute: Barbara Tuchman, "The Retreat from Burma," *American Heritage*, February 1971, www.americanheritage.com/content/retreat-burma.

186 "Our people tired": Stilwell Diary, May 8, 1942.

187 "entering the back door": Charles Bond Oral History, GVSU Collection, 63.

187 "The city streets": Bond, *A Flying Tiger's Diary*, 162.

187 "Too late, get in your ditches": Charles Bond Oral History, GVSU Collection, 63.

187 "I can make it": Bond, *A Flying Tiger's Diary*, 163. The remainder of the combat scene is from Bond's May 4, 1942, diary entry, 163–69. In his combat report, Bond specifies his injuries as "burns about the face, neck and shoulders and both hands." C. R. Bond, Jr., "Reconnaissance Escort and Combat Report," May 4, 1942.

189 "yellow waxy substance": Jeffrey A. Lockwood, *Six-Legged Soldiers: Using Insects as Weapons of War* (New York: Oxford University Press, 2009), 115.

189 Hill thought he had a shot: D. L. Hill, "Reconnaissance Escort and Combat Report," May 5, 1942.

189 "burst into flames and pieces": Frank Lawlor, "Reconnaissance Escort and Combat Report," May 5, 1942.

189 AVG fighters dove down: F. I. Ricketts, "Reconnaissance Escort and Combat Report," May 5, 1942.

190 "China faced its darkest hour": Claire Chennault, *Way of a Fighter: The Memoirs of Claire Lee Chennault*, ed. Robert Hotz (New York: G. P. Putnam's Sons, 1949), 161.

190 "On one side of the river": W. S. Mundy, "Chinese Smash Japs as A.V.G. Shows Way," *Daily Boston Globe,* May 18, 1942, 1.

190 "I became greatly alarmed": Chennault, *Way of a Fighter,* 163–64.

191 On the morning of May 7: Unfortunately, the only combat report on record is a sparse one by Tom Jones. Thomas A. Jones, "Reconnaissance Escort and Combat Report," May 7, 1942. The report notes that they strafed the Japanese position and dropped a "560 lb." bomb.

191 "The monsoon season": Oral History of David Hill, conducted by Reagan Schaupp, San Antonio, February 2000.

191 "The bombs we dropped": Ibid.

192 "We glided down": J. H. Howard, "Reconnaissance Escort and Combat Report," May 8, 1942.

192 until "night or when opposition": Thomas A. Jones, "Reconnaissance Escort and Combat Report," May 8, 1942.

192 observed "dispersed trucks": C. H. Laughlin, "Reconnaissance Escort and Combat Report," May 8, 1942.

192 "threw everything we had": Chennault, *Way of a Fighter,* 166.

192 "continues that direction": R. T. Smith, *Tale of a Tiger* (Van Nuys, CA: Tiger Originals, 1986), 307.

192 **"Chinese reinforcements were"**: "Japs Driven from Bank of Salween," *Washington Post*, May 19, 1942, 1.

192 **The tide of the invasion**: Though Chennault and many of the AVG pilots would portray this as a victory won by airpower alone, that would overstate their role in the battle. The counterattacks by Chinese troops played a decisive role in helping to turn back the invasion, and the two attacks should be understood as acting in concert. See Daniel Jackson, *Famine, Sword and Fire: The Liberation of Southwest China in World War II* (Atglen, PA: Schiffer Publishing, 2015), 25–26.

192 **"The outstanding gallantry"**: "Notice," May 6, 1942, Chennault Foundation, Washington, D.C.

193 **"invasion in 1940"**: James H. Howard, *Roar of the Tiger: From Flying Tigers to Mustangs, A Fighter Ace's Memoir* (New York: Pocket Books, 1991), 148.

193 **"might have changed"**: Oral History of David Hill, National Museum of the Pacific War, 2001.

193 **"The victory at the Salween"**: Duane Schultz, *The Maverick War: Chennault and the Flying Tigers* (New York: St. Martin's Press, 1987), 255.

193 **"I've seen my companions"**: William Wade Watson, ed., *High Water, High Cotton and High Times* (Pittsburgh, PA: Dorrance Publishing, 2007), 138–39.

193 **"the AVG gave me"**: Chennault, *Way of a Fighter*, 174

193 **"Right now, after five years"**: Watson, *High Water*, 138.

194 **"the Louisiana Bomber"**: "Bomber-for-Chennault Drive Gets Under Way," *Shreveport Times*, February 16, 1942, 2.

194 **assist Chinese orphans**: Chennault, *Way of a Fighter*, 165.

194 **"If I had been notified"**: Ibid.

194 **avoid notifying Chennault**: Craig Nelson, *The First Heroes: The Extraordinary Story of the Doolittle Raiders—America's First World War II Victory* (New York: Penguin, 2002, 165).

194 **"American bombers, flown by"**: Clare Boothe, "General Brereton," *Life*, June 1, 1942, 66.

194 **"under Chinese operational direction"**: Ibid., 67.

195 **"operating 10,000 miles"**: Preston Glover, "8 Raids by U.S. Pilots in India Bag 75 Planes," *Chicago Daily Tribune*, May 13, 1942, 6.

195 **forced to walk to India**: "'Dunkirk of the East': How Thousands of Brits Travelled the 'Road of Death' in Burma," *Independent*, March 17, 2012.

195 **"Not a few were found dead"**: Geoffrey Tyson, *Forgotten Frontier* (Calcutta: W. H. Targett & Co., 1945), 23.

195 **"such grim news"**: Paul Frillmann and Graham Peck, *China: The Remembered Life* (Boston: Houghton Mifflin Company, 1968), 146–47.

195 **"complete Chinese outfit"**: Reed Diary, May 15, 1942.

195 **the mechanics in Kunming**: Charlie Bond saw many of them during his ferry mission to India.

196 **eager to see his three children**: Bruce Gamble, *Black Sheep One: The Life of Gregory "Pappy" Boyington* (New York: Ballantine Books, 2000), 221.

196 **"AM UNABLE TO GRANT"**: Gregory Boyington, *Baa Baa Black Sheep* (New York: Bantam Books, 1977), 98.

196 **"closest I ever came"**: Ibid., 99.

197 "I've seen enough": George McMillan letter to parents, March 13, 1942, Mc-
     Millan Papers, Winter Garden Heritage Foundation, Winter Garden, Florida.
     He wrote this letter from Cairo during his ferry mission trip.
197 "American girls, an up-to-date movie: Smith, *Tale of a Tiger*, 321.
197 "When I awoke": Bond, *A Flying Tiger's Diary*, 182.
197 "His tone and demeanor": R. T. Smith, "After the Tigers," 2 (unpublished
     undated essay, courtesy of Brad Smith, Berkeley, California).
197 "we want no part of it": Chennault, *Way of a Fighter*, 172.
198 "Tom Jones hunched over": "Aviator Never Quite Reached His Goal of Down-
     ing 12 Japanese, but 'Crazy' Feat Won Promotion from Chiang
     Kai-shek," *New York Times*, May 19, 1942, 8.
198 "as the anti-aircraft fire": Lewis S. Bishop, "Reconnaissance Escort and Com-
     bat Report," May 12, 1942.
198 "more helpless than a baby": Susan Clotfelter Jimison, *Through the Eyes of a
     Tiger: The John Donovan Story* (Athens, GA: Deeks Publishing, 2015), 157.
198 "Dear Folks: You must": Ibid., 183–85.
199 died "for a cause": Ibid., 192.
199 "enjoyed that one": "Aviator Never Quite Reached His Goal of Downing 12
     Japanese, but 'Crazy' Feat Won Promotion from Chiang Kai-shek," *New York
     Times*.
199 "It was pretty nasty": Reed Diary, May 16, 1942.
199 "After the terrific mission": Bond, *A Flying Tiger's Diary*, 177.
199 "four feet of flame": Peter Wright, "Reconnaissance and Combat Report,"
     May 17, 1942. There is some uncertainty about the cause of the fire. See Lewis
     Sherman Bishop and Shiela Bishop Irwin, *Escape from Hell: An AVG Flying
     Tiger's Journey* (self-published, 2004), 5–6.
200 "I had just seen him": Bond, *A Flying Tiger's Diary*, 179.
200 "It wasn't worth it": Smith, *Tale of a Tiger*, 309. A small discrepancy: Smith
     states there were only five pilots on this mission, but Bishop's combat report
     says that there were six.
200 "so he unzipped": Bond, *A Flying Tiger's Diary*, 184.
200 Fifth Order of the Cloud: Ibid., 184–85. For more on the specific awards con-
     ferred to the AVG, see Terrill Clements, *American Volunteer Group "Flying
     Tigers" Aces* (Seattle: Osprey Publishing, 2001), 84.
200 "had absolutely the finest": Smith, *Tale of a Tiger*, 329.
200 The bottles of Moët: Ibid., 329, 334. Smith says six dollars in his diary but
     twelve dollars in added commentary—either way, a good deal.
200 "another quiet day": Smith, *Tale of a Tiger*, 339.
200 "nothing to speak of": Ibid., 331.
200 "lounging around, gabbing": Bond, *A Flying Tiger's Diary*, 185.
201 "when our contract": Emma Foster (Hanks) letter, August 30, 2000, Foster
     Papers, Yale Divinity School.
201 "surrounded by high mountains": Bond, *A Flying Tiger's Diary*, 185.
201 "I bounced out": Ibid., 188.
202 "little children tugged": Ibid., 190.
202 introduced to a Japanese gunner: Ibid., 196.
202 "the most elaborate affair": Ibid.
202 "What are you going to do": Ibid., 197.
203 "We knew that": Oral History of David Hill, GVSU Collection, 32.

203 "since July 1 the AVG": Robert Martin, "U.S. Pilots Blast Japs in China," *Arizona Republic,* July 6, 1942, 1.

203 The AVG kept fighting: Ford, *Flying Tigers,* 265–66.

203 sip the nonalcoholic punch: Chennault, *Way of a Fighter,* 173.

203 "People don't seem to understand": "End of the A.V.G.," *Time,* July 13, 1942, 25.

203 "passed into history": Chennault, *Way of a Fighter,* 174.

204 "shot down or burned": "Epic Story of America's Flying Tigers Finished," *Herald and News* (Oregon), July 4, 1942, 3.

204 CAMCO ultimately paid out: Ford, *Flying Tigers,* 388.

204 "destroying 299 Japanese planes": Chennault, *Way of a Fighter,* 174.

204 numbers were inflated: There was hostility among some former Flying Tigers toward Daniel Ford's claim in his book, *Flying Tigers: Claire Chennault and the American Volunteer Group,* that these numbers were inflated. See: Flying Tigers Collection, Box 8, Folder 7, San Diego Air and Space Museum. San Diego, California. Though Ford disputed the original number, he states there isn't "an equally precise number" that can be put forward. Ford, *Flying Tigers,* 369.

204 "flashing shark's teeth": Chennault, *Way of a Fighter,* 174.

204 "Sometimes I wonder": Bond, *A Flying Tiger's Diary,* 200.

205 the only true Flying Tigers: In a 1976 interview, Tex Hill expressed this sentiment. See Dan M. Huff, "Every Man a Flying Tiger? Depends on When He Flew," *Tucson Daily Citizen,* July 30, 1976, 12.

205 "pulled into sight": J. E. Petach, "Reconnaissance Escort and Combat Report," July 6, 1942.

206 "violent tumbling spin": Ford, *Flying Tigers,* 371.

206 "had his bag packed: Oral History of David Hill, GVSU Collection, 29.

206 had lost twenty-six of its members: Ford, *Flying Tigers,* xiii. The twenty-six does not include Alsop, who was captured in Hong Kong. Ultimately, three of the captured pilots would be rescued, bringing their losses to twenty-three killed or missing in action.

207 "I always felt": Foster Oral History, Library of Congress.

207 "bombing and strafing mission": Foster Oral History, GVSU Collection.

207 "There were no farewells": Ibid.

207 "If I can be ready": Bond, *A Flying Tiger's Diary,* 210.

207 "When we landed": Foster Oral History, GVSU Collection.

208 "to halfway around the world": Smith, "After the Tigers," 4.

208 "playing Russian roulette": Ibid.

208 "I tell you, friends": Smith, *Tale of a Tiger,* 356.

209 FLYING TIGERS IN CITY: "'Flying Tigers' in City, Tell of Epic Campaign," *New York Herald Tribune,* September 9, 1942, 3.

209 "beautiful young ladies": Ibid., 357.

210 "The whole world": "Saturday Is 'Bill Reed' Day," *Marion Sentinel,* September 10, 1942, 1.

210 "Some day the story will be told": "A Flying Tiger Comes Home," *Marion Sentinel,* September 17, 1942, 1, 4. The newspaper account suggests the governor waited for Bill Reed to arrive but there is some ambiguity regarding the schedule.

211 "This is the most marvelous country": "Thousands Cheer Bill Reed Home," *The Cedar Rapids Gazette,* September 13, 1942, 1. For more on the event see

Cary J. Hahn, "Reed Remembered as Distinguished Pilot, Commander," *Marion Today*, May 20, 2009.

211 "Just wait 'til you see": Frillmann, *China*, 168.

211 "They were all adventurers": "Flying Tigers in City Itch for More Adventure," *The Miami News*, July 16, 1942, 7.

211 there was nothing he wanted: Ibid.

211 raising their glasses: "Vacationing Heroes," ibid.

211 words appropriate to the occasion: "Hi, mom": "Flying Tiger McMillan Home Safe from Air Battles Against Japanese," *Orlando Reporter-Star*, July 16, 1942, 1.

212 "some of my mom's meals": John Forney Rudy, "George McMillan, AVG Ace, Home from Burma to Rest Up After Thrilling Experiences," *Orlando Morning Sentinel*, July 17, 1942, 1.

212 the "Fighting Parson": "Friends Hold Reception for Fighting Parson," *Chicago Daily Tribune*, July 25, 1942, 7.

212 "go squirrel shooting": Frillmann, *China*, 170.

212 that they were lovers: Little is known about these two men, Larry Moore and Ken Sanger. It's reported that Chennault wrote letters to Republic when he heard they were involved in the movie and they were subsequently fired. Ford, *Flying Tigers*, 361.

212 "the envy of every studio": "Anna Lee Girl Star for 'Flying Tigers,'" *The Philadelphia Inquirer*, April 22, 1942, 19.

212 "The film was an ideal vehicle": Randy Roberts and James S. Olson, *John Wayne, American* (New York: Simon & Schuster, 1995), 218.

213 Military reviewers found fault: Ibid., 219.

213 Chennault appeared on the cover: *Time*, December 6, 1943.

Chapter 14: Black Sheep Down

214 serve as Roosevelt's envoy: Hannah Pakula, *The Last Empress: Madame Chiang Kai-shek and the Birth of Modern China* (New York: Simon & Schuster, 2009), 405.

214 "not this one": Ibid., 406.

214 a wild story: Cowles would recount this story but there is still debate over its accuracy. It has been cited in contemporary biographies of Madame Chiang. For further information, see Herbert Strentz, "Compatriots: Wendell Willkie, the Press, and the Cowles Brothers, an Introductory Survey, including Willkie's 'One World' Trip with publisher Gardner (Mike) Cowles," paper presented at the Association for Mass Education in Journalism Conference, July 1988, 34–41.

215 "a goddamn fool": Pakula, *The Last Empress*, 410.

215 "one of the extraordinary documents": Barbara W. Tuchman, *Stilwell and the American Experience in China, 1911–1945* (New York: Macmillan, 1971), 337.

215 "Japan can be defeated": Claire Chennault, *Way of a Fighter: The Memoirs of Claire Lee Chennault*, ed. Robert Hotz (New York: G. P. Putnam's Sons, 1949), 212–13.

215 the meeting minutes: U.S. Department of State, *Foreign Relations of the United States, Conferences at Quebec and Washington* (Washington: Government Printing Office, 1970), 66–77 ("Combined Chiefs of Staff Minutes" from May 14, 1943).

216 "greatly changed now": "George McMillan Returns to China to Complete Jap Mopping-Up Job," *Orlando Reporter-Star,* November 3, 1943, 1.

216 "How do these things": Daniel Jackson, *The Forgotten Squadron* (Atglen, PA: Schiffer Publishing), 66.

217 "a flap of hair": Carl Molesworth and Steve Moseley, *Wing to Wing: Air Combat in China, 1943–45* (New York: Orion Books, 1990), 115.

217 Congressman Mike Mansfield: Drew Pearson, "More Favorable Report on China, Chiang Is Cleaning Up Bad Spots," *News-Journal* (Ohio), January 17, 1945, 4.

217 "the whole state rose": Walter Abel, "Tribute for Iowan from Hollywood," *Des Moines Register,* January 16, 1945, 6. Abel was one of a few Hollywood celebrities who met Reed on a war-bonds tour.

217 "a big enough award": Stephen Frater, *Hell Above Earth: The Incredible True Story of an American WWII Bomber Commander and the Copilot Ordered to Kill Him* (New York: St. Martin's Press, 2012), 120.

217 "I seen my duty": Wolfgang Saxon, "Gen. James Howard, 81, Dies; Medal Winner in Aerial Combat," *New York Times,* March 22, 1995.

217 a job parking cars: Gregory Boyington, *Baa Baa Black Sheep* (New York: Bantam Books, 1977), 103.

218 "HAVE BEEN STANDING": Bruce Gamble, *Black Sheep One: The Life of Gregory "Pappy" Boyington* (New York: Ballantine Books, 2000), 233.

218 another name with a B—Black Sheep: Ibid., 261.

218 "tension was too great": James Lowery, "American Flier Out After 26th Victory," *Tampa Bay Times,* December 29, 1943, 1. This article refers to Boyington as "Pappy."

219 "six months after the war": "'Pappy' Boyington Comes Home," *Life,* October 1, 1945, 29–31.

219 "The lightly built Zeke": Gamble, *Black Sheep One,* 325.

219 "like the chill wind": Ibid., 339.

220 "When I dedicate": "Grapevine Reports Boyington Is Alive, Hidden by Native," *Brooklyn Daily Eagle,* June 11, 1944, 1.

220 "bring daddy back": "Marine Ace Missing in Raid," *St. Louis Star and Times,* January 7, 1944, 2.

220 pilots who had bailed out: Another downed pilot, Arnold Shamblin, was never found. He was presumed to have died in Japanese captivity.

220 "find out from McGarry": Bob Bergin, "OSS and Free Thai Operations in World War II," *Studies in Intelligence,* Vol. 55, no. 4 (Extracts, December 2011), 17.

221 "Almost everyone had malaria": Bob Bergin, "Charlie Mott: Flying Tiger Caged," Warfare History Network, October 10, 2016, warfarehistorynetwork .com/daily/wwii/charlie-mott-flying-tiger-caged.

221 "looked much older": Lewis Sherman Bishop and Shiela Bishop Irwin, *Escape from Hell: An AVG Flying Tiger's Journey* (self-published, 2004), 68.

221 "The terrific urge": Ibid., 51.

221 "I dealt with Chinese": Chennault, *Way of a Fighter,* 241.

222 lauded Chennault's leadership: William J. Duiker, *Ho Chi Minh: A Life* (New York: Hyperion, 2000), 291.

222 display the picture: Ibid., 292.

222 **"I firmly believe"**: Martha Byrd, *Chennault: Giving Wings to the Tiger* (Tuscaloosa, AL: University of Alabama Press, 1987), 279.
222 **"I accepted active duty"**: Ibid., 280.
223 **"natural desire to remain"**: Chennault, *Way of a Fighter,* 351.
223 *Chicago Tribune* **ran:** "Gen. Chennault, Sidetracked by Chiefs, Resigns," *Chicago Tribune,* July 15, 1945, 1:7.
223 **calls in the Senate:** "Senator Desires Account of Chennault Removal," *Salisbury Times* (Maryland), August 4, 1945, 5.
223 **A farewell reception:** Chennault, *Way of a Fighter,* 352.
223 **"their personal goodbyes"**: Anna Chennault, *A Thousand Springs* (New York: Paul S. Eriksson, 1962), 109.
224 **"long and tenderly"**: Ibid., 110.
224 **including Mounds bars:** Gamble, *Black Sheep One,* 372.
224 **"WE THANK YOU"**: Ibid., 371.
224 **"PAPPY BOYINGTON HERE"**: Ibid.
225 **a makeshift American flag:** "Symbol of Patriotism Made by Richmond Native in POW Camp," WTVR, Richmond, Virginia, April 9, 2014.
225 **That man was Greg Boyington:** Boyington, *Baa Baa Black Sheep,* 312.
225 **"God sakes, Pappy"**: Ibid.
225 **"I flipped my plane"**: Frank H. Bartholomew, "Boyington Tells of Jap Torture," *The Philadelphia Inquirer,* August 31, 1945, 2.
225 **the "red ball"**: Boyington, *Baa Baa Black Sheep,* 221.
225 **"My festering wounds"**: "Bartholomew, "Boyington Tells of Jap Torture."
225 **forced to bow:** Ibid.
226 **famous runner Louis Zamperini:** Boyington, *Baa Baa Black Sheep,* 221.
226 **the overjoyed Boyington yelled:** Jean Kapel, "Colonel Boyington, Yank Air Ace in Pacific, Reaches California, Gets Welcome of Hero," *Bend Bulletin* (Oregon), September 12, 1945, 1.
226 **supremely at home:** "'Pappy' Boyington Comes Home," *Life,* October 1, 1945, 29–31.
226 **home to stay:** "Gen. Chennault Joins Family in New Orleans," *Weekly Town Talk* (Alexandria, Louisiana), September 15, 1945, 5.
226 **contemplated a retirement:** Chennault, *Way of a Fighter,* 355.
226 **"hell of a shindig"**: Oral History of David Hill, conducted by Reagan Schaupp, San Antonio, February 2000.
226–27 **fifteen rows deep:** "New Orleans Hails Return of Chennault," *Salt Lake Tribune,* September 8, 1945, 10.
227 **"I thank God"**: "Capitol V-J Flag Given Chennault at Home-coming," *Los Angeles Times,* September 8, 1945, 5.

Epilogue

228 **"It is impossible"**: "The Flying Tigers Reunion," *The Tiger Rag,* Vol. 1, no. 1, (October 1952): 2.
229 **"the former combat pilots"**: "Chennault Blasts State Department," *Los Angeles Times,* June 28, 1952, 2:1.
229 **"To Claire L. Chennault"**: "The Flying Tigers Reunion," *The Tiger Rag,* Vol. 1, no. 1, (October 1952): 7.

229 "a means of expression": Martha Byrd, *Chennault: Giving Wings to the Tiger* (Tuscaloosa, AL: University of Alabama Press, 1987), 284.

230 "new aviation arm": "CIA Acquires CAT," CIA News & Information, August 24, 2005. For more on CAT and the CIA, see William M. Leary, *Perilous Missions: Civil Air Transport and CIA Covert Operations in Asia* (Birmingham, AL: University of Alabama Press, 1984).

231 Vietnam Veterans Memorial: Richard Sisk, "Honors for War Pilot Lost in Bureaucracy," *New York Daily News,* May 29, 2007, www.nydailynews .com/news/world/honors-war-pilot-lost-bureaucracy-article-1.249071.

231 take on the Viet Minh: Byrd, *Chennault,* 356.

231 REVIVE FLYING TIGERS: Douglas Larsen, "Chennault Wants to Revive Flying Tigers," *Port Huron Times Herald,* 6.

231 "in a broader sense": Byrd, *Chennault,* 356.

231 William Pawley was friendly: Anthony R. Carrozza, *William D. Pawley: The Extraordinary Life of the Adventurer, Entrepreneur, and Diplomat Who Cofounded the Flying Tigers* (Washington, D.C.: Potomac Books, 2012), 198–200, 238.

231 When the British started: Byrd, *Chennault,* 356.

231 "He never outgrew": Ibid., 362–63.

232 enjoyed killing deer: Ibid., 363.

232 "couldn't see to run": Paul Frillmann and Graham Peck, *China: The Remembered Life* (Boston: Houghton Mifflin Company, 1968), 184.

233 "regard the peasants": Ibid., 261.

233 "to contact the Reds": Paul Frillmann, "Report on Third War Area Activities," Office of Strategic Services China Theater, May 12, 1945, Hoover Institution Archives, Stanford University, https://digitalcollections.hoover .org/images/Collections/75056/HIA-FRILLMAN-3-B-1-1-4.pdf.

233 "at odd hours": Frillmann, *China,* 288.

233 "Blow the smoke that way": Ibid., 289.

233 "not a wealthy man": Ibid.

233–34 "No one paid much attention": Chennault diary, May 6, 1958, Chennault Foundation, Washington, D.C. This is a separate diary from the one that Chennault maintained in 1937–1941.

234 "nervous, almost jittery": Ibid., April 15, 1958.

234 "You were never defeated": "Madame Chiang Sees Chennault," *Monroe Morning World* (Louisiana), July 12, 1958, 1.

234 "die with him": Chennault diary, July 27, 1958 (note from Anna Chennault in the diary kept by Claire Chennault).

234 one final flight: "Gen. Chennault Burial Set for Arlington," *Tampa Times,* July 29, 1958, 7.

234 "The flight of another airman": "Flying Tigers Chief Is Buried in Arlington," *Arizona Daily Star,* July 31, 1958, 3.

235 "To avoid a breach": Ralph Vartabedian, "One Last Combat Victory," *Los Angeles Times,* July 6, 1991, 1, 22. Army report quoted in article.

235 "makes the Iran-Contra": Ibid.

235 "We have a record": Ibid.

235 "seeing eye dog": "Ken Jernstedt Interview," January 16, 1999, www .usshawkbill.com/tigers/ken.htm.

235 **see China one last time:** Emma Foster (Hanks) letter, August 30, 2000, Foster Papers, Yale Divinity School.

235 **"wouldn't change that year for anything":** Foster Oral History, GVSU Collection, 32.

235 **"I had the kind of romance":** Keith W. Kohn, "'Tigers' Recall Glory," *Orlando Sentinel,* April 17, 2004.

236 **"I just remember":** Ben Wright, "Area Man Among Flying Tigers Honored at National Infantry Museum and Soldier Center," *Ledger-Enquirer* (Georgia), October 9, 2012.

236 **"starting all over again":** "96-Year-Old Flying Tiger Crew Chief Returns to the Sky," CNN, September 23, 2016.

Index

Accra, 174

Action Comics, 80

Adventure Comics, 80

Africa, 174, 190

Albuquerque Journal, 161

Aldworth, Richard, 82–84

Alley, Norm, 38

Allison, Ernest, 12

Alsop, Joseph, 62–63, 69, 81–82, 99, 105

    capture of, 105–7

American Volunteer Group (AVG;

    "Flying Tigers"), 2–4, 235

    aerial guerilla warfare and, 151

    Army Air Forces induction, 150, 152,

        169, 175, 176, 197, 200, 202–3, 208

    assessment of accomplishments, 193,

        204, 235

    CAT and, 230

    Chennault's mission to Washington to

        obtain air unit for China, 59–60,

        61–69

    at Chiang Mai, 161–69, 220

    Chinese ceremonies honoring,

        119–20, 152–53, 200, 202

    Chinese warning net and, 112–13

    Christmas and, 120, 125–27

    Christmas raid of, 126–29, 157, 174,

        183, 211

    as covert operation, 3, 67, 235

    discipline in, 94, 95, 179

    drinking and, 94

    end of, 175, 193, 200–205, 228

    fame of, 120–21, 140, 169, 186,

        204, 213

    fatal accidents in, 92–93, 98, 136, 199

    as first American heroes of World

        War II, 140

    First Squadron (Adam and Eve

        squadron) of, 97–98, 109, 110,

        113–16, 118, 131, 148, 161, 186

    first successful offensive mission of,

        132–34

    Flying Tigers Association, 236

    "Flying Tigers" name of, 121

    formation of and recruiting for,

        69–87, 231, 235

    at Hanoi, 197–99

    homecomings of, 208–12

    and Japanese attacks on Pacific

        islands, 104–5

    Japanese buildup assessed by, 107–8

    at Kunming, 109–11, 112–21, 122,

        131, 145, 146, 149, 169, 175,

        183, 185

    Loiwing Revolt in, 179–81

    at Magwe, 157, 159, 160, 162, 170,

        171, 185

    medals awarded to, 235

    medical team for, 75–76

    on morale missions, 178

    movie about, 3, 212–13

    movies watched by, 93–94

    P-40 aircraft of, *see* P-40s

    at Paoshan, 186, 188–89

    parades for, 210–11

    Pearl Harbor attack and, 102–3,

        107–9, 121, 204, 212–13

    photographed for *Life,* 140–41, 170

American Volunteer Group (*cont.*)
  POWs, 220, 221
  purpose of, 105, 108, 150
  at Rangoon, 107, 109, 122–30,
    131–50, 157, 183
  retreat into China, 170
  returned from enemy territory,
    220–22
  returns to China, 216–17
  reunions of, 228–29, 235–36
  Roosevelt and, 3, 64–65, 67–70, 99,
    105, 192–93
  Royal Air Force and, 81, 107, 109,
    122, 135, 138–39, 148, 157, 162,
    163, 165, 172, 180
  Salween River missions of, 190–92,
    195, 198, 199
  Second Squadron (Panda Bears) of,
    98, 109, 110, 113–14, 116, 117, 131,
    138, 161
  Thailand missions of, 136–40
  Third Squadron (Hell's Angels) of, 98,
    109, 129–30, 131
  at Toungoo, 81, 85–86, 88–99,
    102–4, 107–10, 122
  training of, 88–98, 126
  and U.S. entry into World War II, 3,
    101, 105
Anlee House, 41
Arizona, U.S.S., 2, 100, 101
Armstrong, John, 92–93
Army Air Corps (Army Air Forces),
    U.S., 16–17, 56–57, 69, 74, 90, 123,
    124, 193, 194, 224
  AVG induction into, 150, 152, 169,
    175, 176, 197, 200, 202–3, 208
  China Air Task Force,
    205, 216
  Fourteenth Air Force, 215–16, 222
  Tactical School, 13, 16
  Tenth Air Force, 194–95, 205
  23rd Fighter Group, 205
Army Air Service, U.S., 12
Arnold, Hap, 17, 69, 70, 207, 222
Associated Press, 30, 36, 79, 134, 141,
    142, 160, 168, 204
Athens School, 8
Atkinson, Pete, 93, 94
Ayling, Keith, 11

B-17s, 194, 217
B-25s, 194, 203, 205, 206
B-29s, 224
Baisden, Chuck, 127
Baldwin, Stanley, 16–17
balloons, observation, 10
Bangkok, 107
Bartling, William, 164
Battle of Britain, 140
Baumler, Ajax, 206
Bingham, Hiram, 10
Bishop, Lewis, 198, 199, 220, 221
Bissell, Clayton, 176, 197, 208
Black Christmas, 106
Black Sheep Squadron, 218, 226
Bloemfontein, 79, 80
blood chit, 120
Bloody Saturday, 30
Bombay, 208
bombers, 16–17, 151
  B-17, 194, 217
  B-25, 194, 203, 205, 206
  B-29, 224
  with maggot bombs, 189
Bond, Charlie, 108–11, 112, 115, 116,
    120, 145, 146, 162–65, 167–68,
    185–89, 197, 199–205, 207
Boothe, Clare, 3, 185, 194
Boschfontein, 85, 95
Boston Globe, 129, 140, 190
Boxer Rebellion, 27
Boyington, Gloria, 220
Boyington, Greg, 82–86, 95–96, 118,
    143–44, 153–56, 162, 165, 171,
    195–96, 217–20
  Black Sheep Squadron of, 218, 226
  Chennault and, 196, 218
  imprisonment and liberation of,
    225–26
  Marine Corps commission of, 82–84,
    217–18
  missing in action, 220, 224
  at Rabaul, 219
Bradford, Barbara, 209–10
Brazil, S.S., 196
Brereton, Lewis, 194
Bright, Gil, 92
Britain, 62, 64, 67, 97, 109
  Battle of, 140

Japanese war with, 104
Royal Air Force, 81, 97, 107, 109,
    122, 135, 138–39, 148, 157, 162,
    163, 165, 172, 180
U.S. alliance with, 138
Brooklyn Dodgers, 1, 88
Brooklyn Eagle, 1
Brooks, Roelif, 168
Brouk, Robert, 75, 181–82
Buck, Pearl, 76
buck fever, 116, 132, 134
Burma, 3, 52, 71, 81, 82, 85, 97, 104–6,
    109, 110, 122, 149–50, 162, 164,
    165, 169, 170, 177, 181–84,
    185–87, 195
    Magwe, 157, 159, 160, 162, 170,
        171, 185
    Rangoon, *see* Rangoon
    Toungoo, 81, 85–86, 88–99, 102–4,
        107–10, 122, 158, 170
Burma Road, 65, 66, 83, 99, 108, 184,
    188, 190, 192
"Buy a Bomber for Chennault"
    campaign, 193–94
Byrd, Martha, 57, 70, 229, 231

Calcutta, 185–86, 208
Camel, 232
Canton, 205
CAT (Civil Air Transport), 230–31
Central Aircraft Manufacturing
    Company (CAMCO), 52, 69, 70,
    81, 161, 162, 167, 169, 170, 176,
    184, 203, 204
Central Aviation School, 52–53
Central Intelligence Agency (CIA), 220,
    230, 231, 233
Chang, Iris, 32, 39
Chanyi, 153
Chennault, Anna Chen, 223–24, 230,
    231, 233, 234
    Claire's marriage to, 228
Chennault, Claire Lee, 2, 5–21, 121,
    127, 129–30, 144, 148–53, 155,
    159, 161, 169, 175, 176–78, 183,
    184, 186, 190, 193–95, 199, 202–4,
    210, 212, 226
    acrobatic flying of, 12–15, 17, 114
    in advertisements, 232, 233

aerial guerilla warfare tactics of, 151
    as Air Corps Tactical School
        instructor, 13, 16
    Army Air Service commission of, 12
    as army infantry officer, 10–11
    army resignation of, 21, 222–23
    arrival in China, 22–24, 150
    AVG discipline and, 94, 95, 179
    AVG divided into squadrons by,
        97–98
    AVG recruiting and, 70–71, 75,
        80–81
    at AVG reunions, 228–29
    AVG training and, 89–92, 94, 97,
        98, 126
    Boyington and, 196, 218
    cancer of, 233–34
    as Central Aviation School instructor,
        52–53
    Chiang Mai raid and, 164, 168
    childhood of, 5–6
    children of, 9, 12, 16, 20, 37, 55, 57,
        130, 226, 231–33
    China Air Task Force of, 205, 216
    and Chinese ceremonies honoring
        pilots, 120
    China invitations of, 16, 19
    Chinese Air Force and, 19–20, 25–30,
        32–37, 50, 52–53
    Chinese warning net and, 112–13
    Civil Air Transport organized by, 230
    Curie and, 151–52
    death of, 234
    education of, 6, 7, 10
    fame and status of, 194–95, 213, 214,
        226, 232
    family background of, 6
    flight combat views of, 16–17, 20, 28,
        33, 151
    flight training of, 11, 12
    "Flying Tigers" name and, 121
    Fourteenth Air Force of, 215–16, 222
    funeral for, 234
    Goodyear job of, 9–10
    Hawk 75 of, 35–36, 38–39, 42
    health problems of, 11–12, 17, 21, 40,
        130, 150, 231–34
    Ho and, 222
    homecoming of, 226–27

Chennault (*cont.*)
International Squadron of, 41–42, 43–51, 69
International Volunteer Group proposal of, 231
Japanese buildup assessed by, 107–8
Kittyhawks and, 173–75
in Kunming, 49–50, 52–54, 58, 129–30, 150, 173
Kunming defense and, 113–14, 116, 175
letter to Roosevelt on defeating Japan, 215
Loiwing Revolt and, 179–81
Madame Chiang's first meeting with, 24–26
marriages of, *see* Chennault, Anna Chen; Chennault, Nell
on mission to Washington to obtain air unit for China, 59–60, 61–69
in Nanking, 31–40
19th Fighter Squadron commanded by, 13
Pearl Harbor attack and, 102, 103
physical appearance of, 71–72
and pilots' return to China, 216–17
promotion of, 175–76, 179, 197
retirement of, 222–24, 226, 227, 229, 231–32
and return of pilots from enemy territory, 220–22
return to China after World War II, 230
Salween River operations and, 190–92
and shark faces on aircraft, 97
smoking of, 17, 232, 233
Spanish flu contracted by, 11–12
and spare parts for planes, 98–99
Stilwell and, 169, 175, 179, 180, 186, 215, 222
teaching job of, 8–9
and U.S. entry into war, 108–9
on vacation to U.S. from China, 54–57
Willkie and, 215
YMCA work of, 9
Chennault, Clare Lee, II, 92
Chennault, David, 12

Chennault, John, 5–7
Chennault, John Stephen, 9, 56
Chennault, Max, 9
Chennault, Nell, 9, 12, 16, 37, 55, 57, 58, 92, 130, 213, 226
Claire's divorce from, 228
Claire's marriage to, 9, 20, 55, 57, 58
Chennault, Peggy, 12, 17, 20
Chennault, Rosemary, 55
Chiang, Madame (Soong Mei-ling), 19, 24, 25, 28–30, 49, 50, 54, 57, 58, 81, 150, 152–53, 181, 194, 203, 223, 229–30, 233
background of, 24
Chennault's death and, 234
Chennault's first meeting with, 24–26
Chinese Air Force and, 25–26, 28, 29, 35
Salween River operations and, 190–91
Willkie and, 214–15
Chiang Kai-shek, 19, 24, 25, 28–29, 37–38, 40, 50, 51, 54, 119, 151, 152, 153, 169, 203, 214–15, 223, 229–30, 233
Chennault sent on mission to U.S. by, 59–60, 61, 62, 64
Chiang Mai, 161–69, 178, 220
Chicago Tribune, 194–95, 223
Chin, Arthur, 33–34
China:
air force of, *see* Chinese Air Force
army of, 37–38
Boxer Rebellion in, 27
Chennault's arrival in, 22–24, 150
Chennault's invitations to go to, 16, 19
Chennault's mission to Washington to obtain air unit for, 59–60, 61–69
Chungking, 50, 53–54, 59, 153, 175, 201
factions and civil war in, 25, 229–30, 233
Hankow, 40–41, 43–51, 146
Japanese invasion of, 20
Kunming, *see* Kunming
Loiwing, 161, 162, 164, 165, 170, 175, 182–84, 185, 186, 189, 195
Marco Polo Bridge Incident in, 27–28
Nanking, 31–40, 52, 53, 190
Nationalist government in, 25

Shanghai, 18, 23–24, 29–30, 37, 42, 52
  warning net in, 112–13
China Air Task Force (CATF), 205, 216
China-Burma-India Theater, 150, 176,
  194, 215
China Clipper, 55, 57, 60, 80
China Defense Supplies, 70, 98
China National Aviation Corporation
  (CNAC), 37, 58, 109, 174, 175, 201
China Press, 34
China Weekly Review, 45
Chinese Air Force, 15–19, 25–30, 52,
  59–60, 68, 152, 183
  Bloody Saturday and, 30
  Central Aviation School and, 52–53
  Chennault and, 19–20, 25–30, 32–37,
    50, 52–53
  International Squadron and, 41–42,
    43–51, 69
  Madame Chiang and, 25–26, 28,
    29, 35
  Nanking and, 32–35
  Soviet Union and, 41, 53
  warning net and, 112–13
Chinese Expeditionary Force, 169–70
cholera, 189
Christman, Bert, 79–80, 98, 107, 132,
  134–35, 141–42, 188
  death of, 142
Chungking, 50, 53–54, 59, 153,
  175, 201
Churchill, Winston, 140, 215
CIA, 220, 230, 231, 233
Civil Air Transport (CAT), 230–31
CNAC (China National Aviation
  Corporation), 37, 58, 109, 174,
  175, 201
Cole, Tom, 141
Commemorative Air Force, 236
Communists, 25, 221–22, 229–30, 233
Congress, U.S., 3, 67, 70
Corcoran, Thomas, 69–70, 121, 232
Cowles, Gardner, Jr., 214–15
Cronkite, Walter, 217
Cuba, 231
Cuban Air Force, 16
Cuff, Ward, 1
Curie, Ève, 151–52
Currie, Lauchlin, 150, 174

Curtiss-Wright, 7, 15, 19, 30, 56, 66, 67
  Hawk 75, 35–36, 38–39, 42, 56
P-40, see P-40s

Davidson, Marion, 171
Davies, John, 175
Delano, Frederic, 70
De Luce, Daniel, 141–42
Depression, Great, 14, 73, 88
Des Moines Register, 160, 217
Dien Bien Phu, 230, 231
DiMaggio, Joe, 88
Dixie Girls, 23
Donovan, John, 85, 88, 99, 173, 176–77,
  198–200
Doolittle, Jimmy, 194
Doolittle raid, 194
Dulles, Allen, 231
Dulles, John Foster, 231
Dupouy, Parker, 123
Durdin, Tillman, 39, 40

Egypt, 174
Eisenhower administration, 230–31
Enola Gay, 223
"Epitaph on an Army of Mercenaries"
  (Housman), 69

Falkenhausen, Alexander von, 41, 49
Fauth, John, 161
fighter planes, 13, 17
Flying High, 94
Flying Tigers, see American Volunteer
  Group
Flying Tigers, 3, 212–13
Flying Tigers Association, 236
Flying Trapeze, 14–18, 114
Fogleman, Ronald, 235
Ford, Henry, 9–10, 170
Fordlandia, 170
Formosa, 32, 230
Fort Benjamin Harrison, 10–11
Foshee, Ben, 189
Foss, Joe, 218
Foster, Emma Jane, see Petach, Emma
  Jane Foster
Fourteenth Air Force, 215–16, 222
France, 16
Frankfurter, Felix, 61

Free Thai forces, 220, 221
French Indochina, 97, 197, 199, 200, 222
Frillmann, Paul, 49, 50, 91–93, 112, 144, 146–49, 195, 198, 211, 212, 232–33

Gamble, Bruce, 153, 219
Gandhi, Mahatma, 151
Gauss, Clarence, 36–38
Gentry, Thomas, 75, 77
Germany, 54, 217
    Japan and, 39–41, 49
    Luftwaffe, 2, 33, 62, 217
    in Tripartite Pact, 59, 67
    U-boats of, 10, 64, 209
Geselbracht, Hank, 167
Ghost Breakers, The, 94
Gibbon, Elwyn, 42, 43–49
    arrest of, 47–48
Gibbon, Toni, 42, 45–49
Gilbert, Henry, 125, 128
Goddard, Paulette, 94
Goodyear Tire & Rubber Co., 9–10
Great Britain, see Britain
Great Depression, 14, 73, 88
Greene, Paul, 125
Greenlaw, Harvey, 81, 92, 95–96, 154, 156
Greenlaw, Olga, 81, 92, 96, 104, 109, 153, 171, 196
Grew, Joseph, 48
Grover, Preston, 194–95
Guam, 104
Guatemala, 231
Gulf of Martaban, 124, 127, 128, 158

Hammer, Maax, 93
Hancock, U.S.S., 224
Hangchow, 170
Hankow, 40–41, 43–51, 146
Hanoi, 197–99
Hansell, Haywood, 14
Harrington, J. J., 98
Hartford Courant, 107
Hawaii, 13, 22
    Honolulu, 22, 78, 100, 104
    see also Pearl Harbor
Hawk 75, 35–36, 38–39, 42, 56

Hedman, Duke, 172
Heho, 166
Hengyang, 203
Hill, David "Tex," 2–3, 79, 80, 98, 103, 110, 131, 132–35, 141, 161, 175, 178, 180, 183–84, 189, 191, 192, 203–7, 226, 234, 235
Hirohito, 51, 183
Hiroshima, 223
Hirota, Koki, 36
Hitler, Adolf, 40, 49
Ho Chi Minh, 222
Hodges, Fred, 171
Hoffman, Louis "Cokey," 143–44
Holbrook, Roy, 24
Hong Kong, 57, 104–6
Honolulu, 22, 78, 100, 104
Honolulu Advertiser, 168, 170
Hope, Bob, 94
Hopkins, Harry, 101
Housman, A. E., 69
Howard, Jim, 76, 87, 113, 116, 118, 132–34, 192, 193, 217
Hughes, Howard, 98
Hull, Cordell, 36

Ickes, Harold, 101
Illustrated Weekly of India, 96
India, 185–86, 190, 194, 195, 205, 216
Indochina, 97, 197, 199, 200, 222
International Squadron, 41–42, 43–51, 69
Iran-Contra affair, 235
Italy, 16, 54
    in Tripartite Pact, 59, 67
Izumo, 29–30

Jackson, Robert, 70
Jagersfontein, 71, 73, 75, 78, 79
Japan:
    and American pilots going to China, 22–23, 47–48
    American POWs and, 220, 221, 224–25
    Boxer Rebellion and, 27
    British war with, 104
    Burma and, see Burma
    Chennault's assessment of forces of, 107–8

Chennault's letter to Roosevelt on, 215
China invaded by, 20
Chungking and, 50, 53–54
civilian areas bombed by, 118–19
Doolittle raid and, 194
Germany and, 39–41, 49
Indochina and, 97, 197
Ki-48 "Lily" bombers of, 114, 115
Kunming and, 2, 81, 99, 109–11, 113–21
Marco Polo Bridge Incident and, 27–28
Mitsubishi A6M Zero planes of, 69, 219
Nanking and, 31–40
nuclear bombing of, 223
Pacific islands attacked by, 104–5
Pearl Harbor attacked by, 1–3, 100–103, 107–9, 121, 195, 204, 212–13
Rangoon and, 122–30, 145, 147–49
Shanghai and, 24, 29–30
Singapore and, 104, 147
Soviet Union and, 59
surrender of, 224–26
Thailand and, 107, 132, 136–40, 161–65
Toungoo and, 158, 170
in Tripartite Pact, 59, 67
U.S. enters war with, 3, 101, 105, 108
Jernstedt, Ken, 124, 130, 157–61, 235
Johnson, Mr., 147–48
Johnson, Nelson, 59
Jones, Tom, 192, 198, 199
Jouett, John, 16

Karachi, 185
Keeton, Robert, 166
Kelly Field, 11, 12
Kinard, Bruiser, 1
King Neptune ceremony, 78
Kintner, Robert, 62
Klein, Alice, 96
Klein, Chester, 96
Knox, Frank, 65
Korean War, 230
Kościuszko Squadron, 16

Kreuzberg, Frederick, 45
Kuling, 28
Kunming, 2, 49–50, 52–54, 58, 81, 99, 152, 153, 155, 156, 162, 173, 174, 186, 189, 190, 192, 195, 197, 200
AVG at, 109–11, 112–21, 122, 130, 131, 145, 146, 149, 169, 175, 183, 185
Kuykendall, Matthew, 141
Kweilin, 201–3, 205

Lafayette Escadrille, 16, 82
Lamphun, 162
Lashio, 184
Laughlin, C. H., 174, 192
Lawlor, Frank, 166, 189
Lee, Robert E., 6, 234
Leiser, Edward, 41
Lend-Lease, 64
Leonard, Royal, 33
Libya, 16
Life, 3, 61, 140–41, 170, 185, 194, 226, 227
Linchuan, 206
Lin Sen, 203
Lippmann, Walter, 50–51
Little, Robert, 199–200
Longmen Grottoes, 27
Los Angeles Times, 228–29, 234
Losonsky, Frank, 73–75, 78, 94, 98, 103, 155, 156, 236
Losonsky, Nancy Trefry, 74, 75, 236
Louisiana, 4, 5, 37, 57, 58, 89, 176, 177, 193–94, 213, 226, 231
New Orleans, 9, 226–27
Waterproof, 20, 55, 57
Louisiana State Fair, 7–8, 11
Louisiana State Normal School, 8
Louisiana State University, 6
Loiwing, 161, 162, 164, 165, 170, 175, 182–84, 185, 186, 189, 195
Loiwing Revolt, 179–81
Loyang, 27
Luce, Clare Boothe, 3, 185, 194
Luce, Henry, 185
Luftwaffe, 2, 33, 62, 217
Lungling, 190, 191

MacArthur, Douglas, 99, 105
maggot bombs, 189
Magwe, 157, 159, 160, 162, 170, 171, 185
Malaya, 104
Manchuria, 20
Mann, George, 210
Mansfield, Mike, 217
Mao Zedong, 25
Marco Polo Bridge Incident, 27–28
Marion, Iowa, 210
Marion Sentinel, 210, 211
Mariposa, S.S., 208–9
Marshall, George, 65–66
Martin, Neil, 125, 126, 128, 130
Maxwell Field, 13, 16
McCarthy, Joseph, 233
McDonald, William "Billy," 14, 16–18, 22–23, 26, 27, 30, 33–35, 41, 53, 54, 58
McGarry, William, 164–65, 167–68, 220–21
McMillan, George, 80, 93, 99, 102, 127–29, 174, 197, 211–12, 216
Merritt, Ken, 135, 136
Mesoht aerodrome, 136–38
Mexico, 42
Miami Air Races, 14–15
Miami News, 14
Midway Island, 104
Mingaladon aerodrome, 109, 122, 124, 132, 133, 135, 138–41
missionaries, 80, 85, 94
Missouri, U.S.S., 226
Mitsubishi A6M Zero, 69
Montgomery Advertiser, 37
Morgenthau, Henry, Jr., 61, 63–66, 68, 69
Morris, John, 30
Moss, Robert, 137
Mott, Charlie, 136–38, 220, 221
Moulmein aerodrome, 158, 159
Mow, P. T., 15–16, 22, 28–29, 68

Namsang, 162, 164, 165
Nanking, 31–40, 52, 53, 190
Navy, U.S., 10
Nazi Party, 39–41, 49, 190

Neale, Bob, 148, 155, 161, 162, 163, 165, 187, 207
Neutrality Acts, 70
Newkirk, Jane, 72, 73, 93, 108, 161–62, 168–69
Newkirk, John "Scarsdale Jack," 3, 72–73, 92, 93, 98, 108, 113, 114, 116, 131–36, 138–42, 144, 161–63, 165–66
    death of, 166–69, 178
Newkirk, Louis, 168
New Orleans, La., 9, 226–27
New Orleans *Times-Democrat*, 7
New York City, 209–10, 232
New York Giants, 1
New York Herald Tribune, 67–68, 130, 209
New York Times, 15, 39, 40, 45, 47, 48, 53, 81, 129
New York Yankees, 88
nuclear bomb, 223

Older, Chuck, 180
OSS, 220–22, 232–33
Overend, Ed, 127, 129

P-40s, 2, 3, 66, 69, 70, 74, 81, 89–93, 95–97, 103, 107–9, 112–18, 122–27, 132, 134–36, 138, 143, 154, 155, 158, 164–65, 168, 172–73, 178, 186, 194, 201, 236
    and Japanese capture of Loiwing, 184
    Kittyhawk (P-40E), 173–76, 183, 185, 189, 191, 205
    spare parts for, 98–99, 104–5
    shark faces on, 3, 96–97, 121, 140, 228, 236
    Tomahawk, 3, 173, 174, 183
Pakula, Hannah, 29
Pan Am, 174
Pan Am Clipper, 104–5
Panay, U.S.S., 38, 40
Paoshan, 186, 188–89
parades, 210–11, 226–27
Pawley, William, 15, 52, 57, 69–71, 81, 170, 231
Pawleyville, 52, 170
Paxton, George, 135
Pearl Harbor, 13, 102

Japanese attack on, 1–3, 100–103, 107–9, 121, 195, 204, 212–13
Peking, 27
*Penang Trader,*80
Persico, Joseph, 67
Petach, Emma Jane Foster, 75–78, 94–95, 98, 131–32, 137, 139–40, 144, 175, 178, 180, 186, 201, 205–7, 229, 235
    marriage of, 144–45
Petach, Joan Claire, 229
Petach, John, 77–78, 92, 94–95, 98, 131–32, 137–40, 144, 175, 176, 178, 180, 186, 201, 205–6, 229, 235
    death of, 206–7
    marriage of, 144–45
Philippine Islands, 104
physical culture movement, 9
Poland, 16
Pomfret, John, 183
Popular Aviation, 14
POWs, 220, 221, 224–25
President Garfield, S.S., 22, 23
Pyle, Ernie, 2

Rabaul, 219
Rabe, John, 39–40
radar, 113
Raheng aerodrome, 132, 138
Ramsey, Logan, 101
Rangoon, 65, 69, 78, 80, 81, 85, 94
    AVG at, 107, 109, 122–30, 131–50, 157, 183
    Christmas battle in, 126–29, 157, 174, 183, 211
    evacuation of, 145–49
    Silver Grill in, 94, 123, 131–32, 144
Rector, Ed, 79, 80, 103, 107, 108, 117–18, 164, 165, 178, 221
Reed, Bill, 123–27, 129, 130, 157–60, 170–73, 180, 186, 195, 199, 208–11, 216
    death of, 216–17
Republic Pictures, 3, 212
Richards, Lewis, 188
Rickenbacker, Eddie, 218
Rodger, George, 140–41, 170
Rooney, Andy, 217

Roosevelt, Eleanor, 101
Roosevelt, Franklin D., 40, 61–65, 67–70, 101–2, 104, 215–17
    AVG and, 3, 64–65, 67–70, 99, 105, 192–93
    Chennault's letter to, 215
    Pearl Harbor attack and, 101
    war declared by, 3, 108
    Willkie and, 214
Rosbert, Joe, 90–91
Royal Air Force (RAF), 81, 97, 107, 109, 122, 135, 138–40, 148, 157, 162, 163, 165, 172, 180

St. John's Ambulance Corps, 105
St. Paul's Lutheran Church, 212
Salween River, 163, 165, 190–92, 195, 198, 199
Samson, Jack, 57, 58
San Carlos Hotel, 82, 83
Sandell, Sandy, 113, 116
Sanders, Homer, 202–3
Sandman, The, 80
Scaroni, Silvio, 27
Schmidt, Vincent, 42, 46
Schultz, Duane, 193
Scorchy Smith, 79, 134–35, 142
Seagrave, Gordon, 182
Seiple, Bill, 161
Shamblin, Arnold, 206
Shanghai, 18, 23–24, 29–30, 37, 42, 52
Shilling, Erik, 91, 107–8, 230
Shreveport State Fair, 7–8, 11
Shreveport Times, 7, 8, 21
Shu, P. Y., 26
Shwedagon Pagoda, 85, 144
Silver Grill, 94, 123, 131–32, 144
Singapore, 104, 147
Smith, Barbara Bradford, 209–10
Smith, Nicol, 220
Smith, R. T., 71, 80, 88, 91, 102–3, 122–25, 171, 172, 174, 177–81, 184, 192, 197, 199, 200, 208–10
Smith, Sebie, 18, 23, 26, 31–33, 35, 38, 41, 46–47
Soong, Charlie, 24
Soong, T. V., 24, 61–70, 234
Soong Mei-ling, *see* Chiang, Madame
South America, 16, 211

South China Morning Post, 42
Soviet Union, 16
  Chinese Air Force and, 41, 53
  Japan and, 59
Spain, 41, 42
Stanley Internment Camp, 106
State Department, 36, 48, 175
Stewart, Jo, 75
Stilwell, Joseph, 169–70, 175, 177, 179, 180, 186, 197, 215, 222
Stimson, Henry L., 65–66
Stowe, Leland, 129, 139, 140
Stratemeyer, George, 222
Sun Yat-sen, 25
Superman, 80
Sutter, Harry, 58
Sutter, Kasey, 58
Swartz, Frank, 161, 185

target fixation, 117
Temple, Shirley, 141
Tenth Air Force, 194–95, 205
Thailand, 97, 107, 127, 128, 132, 136–40, 161–65, 220
  Chiang Mai, 161–69, 178, 220
Three Aces, The, 80
Three Men on the Flying Trapeze, 14–18, 114
Tiger Rag, 228
Time, 2, 3, 61, 71, 72, 121, 139, 160, 170, 185, 213, 227
Tokyo, 51, 64, 65
  Doolittle raid and, 194
Toungoo, 81, 85–86, 88–99, 102–4, 107–10, 122, 158, 159, 170, 178
Travis, Robert, 217
Trefry (Losonsky), Nancy, 74, 75, 236
Tripartite Pact, 59, 67
Tuchman, Barbara, 169–70, 215
Tulsa, 125
23rd Fighter Group, 205
Tyson, Geoffrey, 195

U-boats, 10, 64, 209
United Press, 1, 30, 48, 50, 203
United States:
  British alliance with, 138
  Congress of, 3, 67, 70
  entry into World War II, 3, 101, 105, 108
  Lend-Lease policy of, 64
  neutrality of, 3, 36, 37, 63, 68, 70, 105
  Pearl Harbor attack, 1–3, 100–103, 107–9, 121, 195, 204, 212–13
  State Department of, 36, 48, 175
Universal Trading Corporation, 67

Vaughn, Stanley, 7, 8
Vautrin, Minnie, 39
Vietnam, 197, 230–31

Wake Island, 104–5
Washington Post, 42, 192, 234
Waterproof, La., 20, 55, 57
Wayne, John, 3, 212–13
Welles, Orson, 211
Wenshan, 154
Williams, Ted, 88
Williamson, John "Luke," 14, 16–18, 37
Willkie, Wendell, 214–15
Wilson, George, 210
Wolf, Fritz, 172–73
World War I, 10–12, 16, 27, 41, 42, 56, 69, 89, 142, 218
World War II, 88, 218, 234, 236
  AVG pilots as first American heroes of, 140
  Japanese surrender, 224–26
  Pearl Harbor attack, 1–3, 100–103, 107–9, 121, 195, 204, 212–13
  U.S. entry into, 3, 101, 105, 108
Wright, Burdette, 56, 66
Wright, Pete, 135–36
Wright Brothers, 7
Wrigley Company, 14

Yee, John, 119
Yellow River, 50
YMCA, 9

Zamperini, Louis, 226